THE FOCUS CLASSICAL LIBRARY

Aristophanes: Acharnians • Jeffrey Henderson
Aristophanes: The Birds • Jeffrey Henderson
Aristophanes: Clouds • Jeffrey Henderson
Aristophanes: Frogs • Jeffrey Henderson
Aristophanes: Lysistrata • Jeffrey Henderson
Aristophanes: Three Comedies: Acharnians, Lysistrata, Clouds • Jeffrey Henderson
Euripides: The Bacchae • Stephen Esposito
Euripides: Four Plays: Medea, Hippolytus, Heracles, Bacchae • Stephen Esposito
Euripides: Hecuba • Robin Mitchell-Boyask
Euripides: Heracles • Michael R. Halleran
Euripides: Hippolytus • Michael R. Halleran
Euripides: Medea • Anthony Podlecki
Euripides: The Trojan Women • Diskin Clay
Golden Verses: Poetry of the Augustan Age • Paul T. Alessi
Golden Prose in the Age of Augustus • Paul T. Alessi
Hesiod: Theogony • Richard Caldwell
Hesiod: Theogony & Works and Days • Stephanie Nelson
The Homeric Hymns • Susan Shelmerdine
Ovid: Metamorphoses • Z. Philip Ambrose
Plautus: Captivi, Amphitryon, Casina, Pseudolus • David Christenson
Roman Comedy: Five Plays by Plautus and Terence • David Christenson
Roman Lives • Brian K. Harvey
Sophocles: Antigone • Ruby Blondell
Sophocles: Electra • Hanna M. Roisman
Sophocles: King Oidipous • Ruby Blondell
Sophocles: Oidipous at Colonus • Ruby Blondell
Sophocles: Philoktetes • Seth Schein
Sophocles: The Theban Plays • Ruby Blondell
Terence: Brothers (Adelphoe) • Charles Mercier
Vergil: The Aeneid • Richard Caldwell

ODYSSEUS AT TROY

Sophocles' *Ajax* and Euripides' *Hecuba* and *Trojan Women*

Translations with Introductions, Notes, and Essays

Stephen Esposito, Editor
Boston University

For the students of Boston University's Core Curriculum
and their quest to understand other times and places.

© 2010 Stephen Esposito, Robin Mitchell-Boyask, Diskin Clay, and Focus Publishing.

Cover photo: Trojan Horse from the movie *Troy* (2004), located in Canakkale Square, Turkey.
© istockphoto / Sadık Güleç

ISBN 10: 1-58510-396-9
ISBN 13: 978-1-58510-396-6

Printed in the United States of America

11 10 9 8 7 6 5 4 3 2

0811TS

Preface

There are many friends to whom I am very grateful for assisting me in the editing of this anthology. First and foremost I thank my dear friend and colleague Stephen Scully who was instrumental in the conception of this volume. He also shared in composing the first part of the introduction and offered many improvements along the way, especially with regard to my *Ajax*. I thank, too, my collaborators Diskin Clay, old friend and former teacher at Johns Hopkins, and Robin Mitchell-Boyask, for answering my various questions about their previously published Focus Publishing translations (2005 and 2006 respectively). Numerous colleagues in the Boston University Core Curriculum have also offered helpful suggestions: I single out David Eckel, David Roochnik, Katherine O'Connor, and Loren Jay Samons. I also wish to thank Ron Pullins, the publisher of Focus Publishing, for his interest in this volume, for his immense patience, and for the great work he continues to do in behalf of the Classics. And special thanks as well to Linda Diering, Ron's production manager at Focus, for her thoroughness and her kindness.

Finally I give thanks to the two shining lights of my life, my wife Madeline and our young daughter Rhiannon. They have been very patient with my burning of the midnight oil. I am especially grateful to Madeline for her unwavering encouragement and love.

With respect to the contents of the book I am responsible for the first part of the introduction and all of the *Ajax* material. I also wrote the brief structural outlines that precede each play. The idea here is to give the reader a quick synoptic view of the entire tragedy because it is sometimes easy to lose sight of the forest for the trees; in the case of *Hecuba* I have used as a template the longer outline found in Robin Mitchell-Boyask's original Focus edition. For purposes of uniformity and clarity I have also revised slightly the "Lists of Characters" as they appeared in the original Focus editions of *Hecuba* and *Trojan Women*; and for purposes of comparison I have added in this section the number of lines spoken by each actor.

I am responsible, too, for five of the six Appendices; Diskin Clay did Appendix 4, which presents a superb translation of *In Praise of Helen* by Gorgias of Leontini, Sicily (c. 485-380 B.C.E.), the highly influential Greek sophist and rhetorician after whom Plato named his renowned dialogue. Appendix 5, the bibliography, is extensive; its purpose is to give students and teachers a sense of the tremendous range of interesting work done on Greek theater generally and these three plays in particular. Furthermore it is hoped that the wide variety of topics covered in the various categories of the bibliography will suggest to students exciting ideas for their essays.

Any errors that remain in the volume are, of course, my responsibility.

Table of Contents

Introduction

Part I: Odysseus on Stage

Stephen Esposito and Stephen Scully

Of all the Homeric heroes, the most frequently depicted on the fifth-century Athenian stage were Agamemnon and Odysseus. Of the two, Agamemnon was never rendered in a sympathetic light. This is not difficult to understand given that he 'sacrificed' his teenage daughter, Iphigeneia, so that the Greek ships could sail to Troy, and once at Troy, he did not distinguish himself as a leader. After the Trojan War his wife, Clytemnestra, and her lover, Aegisthus, murdered him the very day he returned home. Depictions of Odysseus, on the other hand, show greater variety; sometimes he is a 'good guy', sometimes quite the contrary. To understand the reasons for these different portrayals of Odysseus at Troy a brief review of certain key aspects of Athenian history and culture will be helpful.

Athenian democracy was founded in 508/7 B.C.E. as a revolutionary new form of government. Its staying power soon became manifest in the Persian wars. In the battle of Marathon (490) the vastly out-numbered Athenians, along with some allies, defeated the Persian invaders. Subsequently the Greeks, usually with Athens at the forefront, won unexpected victories at Salamis (480) and Plataea (479). These impressive achievements on land and sea served to solidify Athens' reputation as a major force in the Greek world. Confidence in its fledgling democracy and increasing military power led, rather quickly, to excess. From as early as the 460s Athens began to subject, by means of military compulsion, many of the 150 ally cities of the Delian League which had been formed in 478 to prevent another Persian invasion. Over the next fifty years Athens became the most powerful city in the ancient world, turning the *pan-Hellenic* Delian League of so-called 'equals' into a domineering *Athenian* empire. In 432 Athens' popular leader Pericles persuaded his city to go to war with her much smaller arch-rival, Sparta, 130 miles to the southwest on the Peloponnesian peninsula. A comic poet of the time, Eupolis, said of Pericles that "… a certain *persuasion* sat upon his lips. Such was his spell and alone of the orators he left his sting in his listeners." And so the naval power of democratic Athens and the land power of oligarchic Sparta fought an asymmetrical twenty-seven year war that ended with Athens' surprising defeat in 404. This 'Peloponnesian' War, the greatest in Greek history, was brilliantly chronicled for most of its duration by the Athenian Thucydides (c. 460-395), who held the rank of naval captain before he was exiled for twenty years because he allowed the Spartans to capture a strategic city in northern Greece in 424 (Thuc. 5.26).

Moving from military history to political history, we now look briefly at several prominent features of Athenian democracy which are relevant to the city's most influential and enduring literary genre, tragedy. The Athenians themselves attributed the unlikely victories against Persia to their political freedom, which stood in stark contrast to their opponents' servitude to a 'barbarian' king. As time passed the democracy become ever more 'radical', placing unprecedented power in 'the hands of the people.' There were four primary political mechanisms by which this 'radical' democracy gradually took root: the lottery system (by which they selected randomly, rather than elected, most key public officials), the very low property qualification for citizenship (restricted to males), pay for public service (e.g. jury or military duty), and the high degree of 'free speech' (*parrhêsia*).

It was in this last feature, the citizen's right 'to speak out openly and frankly,' that the Athenians took special pride, particularly in the context of speaking before the Assembly, the city's most powerful political body. 'Free speech' (*parrhêsia*), which gained currency as a political catchword in the late fifth century, is the feature of democracy that marks out the genre of drama as a specifically Athenian institution. All Greek cities had assemblies, but the one in Athens was distinguished by its enormous size and intensive nature. It was in the Assembly that Athenians learned the art of competitive rhetoric. Over forty times a year some 6,000 citizens gathered on the Pynx Hill near the Acropolis and participated *directly* in determining their city's destiny. Given their penchant for 'interventionism' (*poly-pragmosynê*) in the affairs of other cities—a *modus operandi* marked by imposing coinage decrees, tribute-lists, tax-collectors, and an enormous fleet of triremes (warships) —Athenians had much to deliberate. Their Assembly was a theater for competing political ideas, emphatically contemporary and particular. The dramatic performances at the Theater of Dionysus were, on the other hand, more remote in time and more generic in their concerns, dealing with the larger-than-life heroes of an ancient mythical past. But the Theater of Dionysus could also be deeply political, not only in theme but in fact. Thucydides (8.93) informs us that the small Theater of Dionysus in the Athenian harbor town of Piraeus, and even the huge Theater of Dionysus in the city, were used for political assemblies at the time of the oligarchic coup in 411.

So in the context of this overview of military and political history what does Athenian democracy have to do with drama? Is there any *substantial* connection? In this sense there is: the Athenian empire was so ever-expanding and aggressive in nature that it forced the citizen body, in a qualitatively different way than in other cities, to deliberate constantly on difficult issues such as the just use of power. The rostrum of the Assembly was one primary place for that debate to occur; the stage of the theater was another. It showed not only the heat of the debate, but the aftermath as well, an aftermath that often involved great suffering. Or, to put it a bit differently, the theater, being "far from the madding crowd's ignoble strife," was a place of pity, a place that gave voice to the silenced and marginalized people: women, commoners, slaves, war-captives, the young, the old, the sick. These characters, in particular, were favorites of Euripides. He took Athens to the other side, to the under side. His plays taught them how to 'read' the sad faces of victims of war, revenge, political 'necessity,' and passion. Athenian democracy, flush with imperial wealth and warships, gave the two dramatists represented in this volume, Sophocles (c. 496-406) and Euripides (c. 480-406), a stage, a big stage on which to hold high their mirrors and reflect what they saw. Often the face in the mirror was not handsome, though by raising the mirror these two men tried to show the city how it could make itself so.[1]

The three tragedies translated herein, Sophocles' *Ajax* and Eurpides' *Hecuba* and *Trojan Women*, fall on either side of the long Peloponnesian War (431-404). *Ajax* was probably performed in the decade of 450-440, in the middle of Sophocles' sixty-year career. In *Ajax*, which may well be the earliest of his seven surviving plays, Odysseus makes his first appearance in the surviving corpus of thirty-two Athenian tragedies. Here we see all the nobility, compassion, and wisdom of Homer's hero. Over thirty years later Sophocles presents a very different version of the same character. In *Philoctetes* (409) we see an Odysseus who attempts to persuade Achilles' upstanding teenage son, Neoptolemus ('Mr. New at War'), to conspire in stealing the magical bow of the crippled hero Philoctetes. Early in the play, as he tries to conscript Neoptolemus into his deceit, he addresses Achilles' son thus: "I know well, my child, that by nature you were not born to contrive such things or utter such evils. Since, however, the possession of victory is something sweet to gain, bring yourself to it; we'll appear to be just on another occasion. Give yourself to me now for a brief portion of a day for something shameful, and then for the rest of time be called the most pious of all mortals." (79-85).[2] An ancient scholar commented on these words of Odysseus as follows: "The poet is accusing the party politicians (*rhetores*) of his own era." We are reminded by this observation that Athens' dramatists, with their annual audience of some 15,000 strong in the Theater of Dionysus, were considered the city's most influential teachers.

Euripides' *Hecuba* and *Trojan Women* were staged in 424 and 415 respectively. In *Hecuba* Odysseus is the advocate and agent of the murder of Polyxena, the teenage daughter of Priam and Hecuba, the former king and queen of Troy. Although Odysseus does not appear as a character in *Trojan Women*, we include the play to show how, even in his physical absence, his malevolent political presence is deeply felt: it was 'his forked tongue' (284) that urged the 'sacrifice' of the Astyanax to Achilles' ghost; and that death of Astyanax, the young son of Priam and Hecuba, inevitably meant the death of Troy. It seems fair to say that the Odysseus of these two 'Trojan War' plays represents the archetype of the fifth-century Athenian demagogue who was a slave of the mob he ruled.

There are, to be sure, numerous and complex explanations for the contrasting 'good guy / bad guy' portraits of Odysseus in these three dramas. We briefly highlight three of those explanations that are most germane to this anthology; each weaves together strands of Athenian political, ethical, and intellectual history.[3]

The first point involves Athenian deliberations about the just use of power, i.e. how to treat the people of cities which resisted Athens' expansionist policies. In 428/7, several years before Euripides presented *Hecuba*, when the city of Mytilene on the island of Lesbos, near Troy, revolted, the Athenians initially voted to kill the island's entire adult

1   Parts of the preceding two paragraphs have been adapted from Esposito's introductory essay 'What is Greek Tragedy?' in *Euripides: Four Plays: Medea, Hippolytus, Heracles, Bacchae* ed. Stephen Esposito (Focus Publishing, 2002) 7-9.

2   Translation by Seth Schein from *Sophokles' Philoktetes* (Focus Press, 2003).

3   Some of the information in the following paragraphs has been gleaned from W. B. Stanford *The Ulysses Theme* [2] (Univ. of Michigan Press, 1963) 90-117.

male population and to enslave its women and children. In a fit of conscience, however, the Athenians reconvened their Assembly on the next morning and, after further debate, rescinded their original decree. As a result of their 'second thoughts' the Athenians killed only 'rather more' than a thousand Mytilenians, demolished the city's walls, took possession of her large navy, divided the whole island into 3,000 allotments, and rented it out to the islanders themselves (Thuc. 3.49-50).

Eleven years later in 416, several months before Euripides presented *Trojan Women*, the tiny and strategically unimportant island of Melos, in the southwest Aegean Sea, refused to submit to Athenian warships. In response, the Athenians, led by Philocrates, son of Demeas ('Mr. Lover of Power, son of the People'), starved the Melians, besieged their city, killed all the grown men, sold the women and children for slaves, and colonized the island, virtually erasing the island's civic identity (Thuc. 5.116). There were no second thoughts this time. It would be imprudent to posit any strict one-to-one correspondence between the events at Mytilene and Melos and Euripides' *Hecuba* and *Trojan Women* respectively, but many scholars have seen a connection between the ethos of political expediency presented in these two historical events and the argument of political 'necessity' that pervades these two 'Trojan War' tragedies.

The second point: In the year 427, the famed orator Gorgias (c. 485-380) from the city of Leontini in Sicily came to Athens and dazzled its citizens with the bewitching power of his words and his ability "to make the weaker argument appear the stronger." Gorgias' rhetorical skills exemplified a new type of itinerant teacher known as a 'sophist' (literally 'a man of wisdom') who traveled from city to city giving lectures and private instruction in the art of persuasion and how to succeed in politics; he made no pretense about teaching civic excellence or virtue. These 'sophists', who monopolized general education in Greece for nearly a century, were often sophisticated word-merchants with radical views on moral and political issues; they specialized in training young men who could afford their high fees. The two plays of Euripides in this volume show the clear influence of these 'sophists.' Special notice can be given in this regard to Helen's self-defense in *Trojan Women* (916-65) where she argues to her (first) husband Menelaus that it is Aphrodite (winner of the Judgment of Paris), not Helen herself, who should be blamed for starting the Trojan War. Helen's marvelous speech shows the clear influence of Gorgias' famous pamphlet entitled *In Praise of Helen*, a translation of which can be found in Appendix Four.

Final point: In the last third of the fifth-century there was a more stringent attitude to truth and morality as the radical democrats and the Athenian mob became ever more suspicious of the numerous intellectual types that were populating the political terrain. Hence slippery figures like Socrates (460-399) did not fare well. For example in Aristophanes' comedy *Clouds* (423) Socrates is presented as a sophistic buffoon; twenty-five years later he is sentenced to death, at the age of 70, by a jury of 500 Athenians. The late fifth century was a time that saw the rise of the *new* politicians, *new* modes of music, and *new* ways of thinking. These innovations were certainly related to the brutal atrocities of the Peloponnesian War that were tearing apart the social fabric of Greece. In this brave new world the figure of Odysseus came under new pressure. In Homer's epic he had been celebrated as the *poly-tropos* hero (literally, "the man of many turns"), which meant that he was both 'a man of many travels' as well as 'a man of many tricks.' In all the upheaval of the late fifth century it was perhaps inevitable that the more deceitful trickster side of

Odysseus should come to the fore. One telling example of this gradual degradation of Odysseus' storied career is that Alcibiades, a student of Socrates, a powerful politician, and Athens' most famous traitor, was called, on account of his devious Odyssean ways with the Persian royalty, *poly-tropos* (Plutarch, *Life of Alcibiades*, 24.4; cf. 2.1).

The three plays of this volume dramatize mythological stories (i.e. the Trojan cycle), not current history, but both playwrights cast these ancient Homeric tales in terms of the issues and anxieties of their own times. We see this particularly in the way characters use, and often abuse, power, how the strong relate to the weak, how men relate to women, and, of especial note, how characters argue, use language, and seek to persuade. Sometimes characters deliver long set speeches to make their case, reminiscent of the type of formal set speech (*rhêsis*) that Athenians often heard in the Assembly and law courts. At other times characters speak in rapid-fire line-by-line exchange (*stichomythia*) in their effort to persuade. Both these modes of speech can be potent forms of persuasion and are often juxtaposed, with set speeches suddenly giving way to the thrust-and-cut intensity of single line dueling. While reading these plays, it is well worth looking at how each tragedian uses these two forms of persuasion to see whether one or the other tends to enflame or to soothe the passions of the moment.

Part II: Drama in Athens

Robin Mitchell-Boyask

Through accidents of history there are far more extant dramas by Euripides than by the other two great Athenian tragedians of the fifth century B. C. E., Aeschylus and Sophocles.[4] This relative abundance has, strangely, at times worked against his reputation in modernity, as critics simply have had a greater ranger of unselected material to pick apart at leisure and have thus restricted the sort of unstinting praise reserved for Sophocles to the "Big Three" of Euripides: the *Medea*, *Hippolytus*, and *Bacchae*. While few serious students of Euripidean drama would fault any praise for this trio, still, in the modern world, it has only been recently acknowledged that more of the Euripidean corpus might warrant praise if we adopt aesthetic criteria beyond the Sophocles-based model espoused in the *Poetics* of Aristotle, written a full century after dramas such as the *Oedipus Tyrannus*, *Medea*, and, indeed, *Hecuba*.[5] The *Hecuba*, which during the Byzantine and the Renaissance eras was particularly popular, is certainly one tragic drama which benefits from a more open mind about what constitutes an effective exploration of the genre, for few other tragedies leave their audiences with such a sense of utter devastation as does Euripides' enactment of the sufferings of the former queen of Troy and her reaction to them. After all, Aristotle himself acknowledged (*Poetics*, Ch 13), "although Euripides manages badly in other respects, he is obviously the most tragic of poets."[6] Aristotle there further stresses that the impact of the unhappy endings is particularly felt "on stage and in performance,"

---

4   On the survival of manuscripts of Greek drama after their initial performances and through the Renaissance, see Csapo and Slater (1995) 1-38.

5   Michelini (1987) discusses the problems of viewing Euripides through a purely Sophoclean perspective.

6   The translation is by Richard Janko (Hackett. Indianapolis, 1987)

and thus it is perhaps no accident that the *Hecuba* has been held in higher esteem during eras when performance has been more central to the understanding of drama, eras such as the Renaissance and our own time.[7]

The Performance of Drama in Athens

The original performances of tragic dramas occurred in Athens every spring in the Theater of Dionysus, during a festival held in honor of the same god, before an audience of 15,000-18,000, composed of Athenians and visitors from throughout the Greek world. This was one of the highlights of the Athenian calendar and the city itself virtually ceased normal activities during its duration. The audience was notionally, if not actually, all male, so that, even if women were present, the intended audience was still the men of Athens. While women were generally restricted from public activities, they did have prominent roles in the religious life of the city, and drama was part of a religious festival, so it is possible that women did attend the theater. The Theater of Dionysus itself was a large, open-air venue on the south slope of the Acropolis, overlooked by the Parthenon, occupying a semi-circular bowl. The stone theater visible today is a Roman reconstruction from the first century C.E., itself a reworking of the theater as extensively renovated by Lycourgos around 325 B.C.E.[8] The fifth-century audience sat on stone benches closer to the stage, and on wooden benches higher up, with the crowd perhaps spilling on to the bare slope higher still; the audience was divided into wedges, possibly according to the tribal affiliation that had organized Athens politically earlier in the fifth century, with one tribe per wedge in the semi-circle and the more prominent citizens seated in front.[9] This arrangement mirrored the seating plan of the Athenian Assembly (more on this below). Actors generally stood on a slightly raised stage in front of a wooden building (*skênê*), which was painted as the drama's setting required.[10] Actors could enter the acting area through a door in the *skênê*, or through two long entrance ramps (*eisodoi*); such entrances would thus be visible to the audience before the characters in the acting area. In between the seats and the *skênê* lay the *orchestra*, the circular (or, possibly, square or trapezoidal) area in which the chorus sang and danced, so the chorus formed a literally mediating body in between the audience and the characters. While the actors and chorus had their distinct spaces, no impenetrable barrier separated them, and the actors frequently moved into the orchestra as the action

7   On the popularity of *Hecuba* during the Byzantine and Renaissance eras, see Mossman (1999) 222-43 and Malcolm Heath, "'*Iure Principen Locum Tenet*: Euripides' *Hecuba*," 218-60 in Mossman 2003.

8   On the nature of the Athenian theater, including the evidence in original sources, see Csapo and Slater (1995), especially 79-80, and Wiles (1997).

9   There is some question whether the theater audience was divided into wedges according to tribal affiliation; see Rhodes (2003) 10. In support of the political mapping of the Athenian audience, see several articles in Winkler and Zeitlin (1990): Simon Goldhill's "The Great Dionysia and Civic Ideology" (97-129), on display, dramatic festival, and the ideology of the *polis*; Josiah Ober and Barry Strauss' "Drama, Political Rhetoric and the Discourse of Athenian Democracy" (237-270) on the relationship between the audiences at the Theater of Dionysus and the Pnyx, the meeting place of the Assembly; and John Winkler's "The Ephebe's Song: *Tragoidia* and Polis" (20-62), pages 39-40 specifically on the seating plan, with bibliography.

10   On the *skênê* see Csapo and Slater (1995) 79-80. Wiles, (1997) Chapter 7 discusses the symbolic uses of the *skênê*.

required; it is generally thought now that the area immediately in front of the *skênê* was only slightly, if at all, raised, thus facilitating such movement by the actors.

Every year three poets were granted a chorus by Athens and each presented three tragedies and a satyr play, a comic drama in which the chorus were dressed as satyrs (mythological creatures whose lower halves were goats and upper humans) and which seemed to have poked fun at the more sorrowful events that had preceded it. These three tragic dramas were not, after Aeschylus, normally trilogic, with a single larger myth enacted across all three, but were independently conceived, though one might imagine thematic links intended among them. The three playwrights engaged, so typically Greek, in a competition with one another for prizes awarded by the city of Athens. We do not know on what basis the judges decided the prizes, but one imagines that their decisions could be controversial (one is tempted to compare the annual uproars over our Academy Awards). Euripides, while achieving enough notoriety to be regularly ridiculed by the comic dramas of Aristophanes, only won first prize five times (and one of those posthumously). His *Medea*, so popular in our time, finished third out of three. His relative lack of success, especially compared with Sophocles, might have contributed to his departure from Athens late in his life for the court of the king of Macedon, a traditional story about Euripides that has recently been called into serious question.[11] But even Sophocles' *Oedipus Tyrannus*, considered the greatest Greek tragedy since Aristotle wrote his *Poetics* in the century after its first production, failed to win and instead took second!

A tragic poet worked inside certain broad, but fixed, parameters. The chorus, during Sophocles' and Euripides' careers, had fifteen members, whose official leader typically engaged the principal actors more directly than the rest of the collective. The chorus members, who, while amateurs, still had to be highly trained at both singing and dancing and capable of representing slave women, old men and warriors (and sometimes all on the same day), were likely young men, possibly otherwise engaged in their military training; the late John Winkler argued, controversially, that the choral dances resembled the precise corporate movements that typified the maneuvers of hoplite soldiers, who moved in exact conformity with shields linked to form a moving wall.[12] Following the prologue spoken by one or two of the actors, the chorus entered the *orchestra*, the central circle in front of the *skênê* through either of two side entrances (*eisodoi*) at the front of the audience (see diagram). There they remained, with extraordinarily rare exceptions (e.g. Sophocles' *Ajax* and the *Eumenides* of Aeschylus) until the end of the drama, when they typically, but not universally, were the last to leave the acting area; in the *Hecuba* I believe Hecuba herself is left by the chorus alone in the orchestra at the end. The chorus did not serve as the voice of the poet, expressing what "he really thought," but served as a sounding board for the main characters or a filter through which the audience could digest the actions and sentiments expressed by the characters. Above all, in many dramas, the chorus itself served as a character, participating in or rejecting the plans of the protagonists. The chorus thus formed the community against which the actions of the heroic figures behind them

---

11   See Scullion (2003).

12   John Winkler, "The Ephebe's Song: *Tragoidia* and Polis," 20-62 in Winkler and Zeitlin (1990). In support of Winkler see Wilson (2000) and Nagy (1995).

were played out. I shall have more to say about the chorus of Euripides' *Hecuba* in the Interpretive Essay.

In addition to the chorus, each playwright received two or three speaking actors, all of them men, and any number of mute extras. These actors were professionals, and, from the middle of the fifth century, had their own competition and prizes. Greek tragedy likely grew out of choral songs in honor of Dionysus, known as *dithyrambs*, and, at some point in the sixth century, a single chorister, perhaps the legendary Thespis, stepped out to sing the words of the hero whose story formed the content of the song. As we see in Aeschylean drama, early tragedy, despite the availability then of two actors, was dominated by the chorus, with individual actors engaging in dialogue or debate with it; the only extended direct conversation between two actors in Aeschylus' *Agamemnon* is the great debate between Clytemnestra and her husband about whether he should walk on the scarlet cloths she has strewn in his path. The two earliest extant dramas by Euripides, the *Alcestis* (438 B.C.E.) and the *Medea* (431) both can work with only two actors, even though Sophocles had introduced the third actor roughly two decades earlier; even Aeschylus' *Agamemnon* (458) requires three actors. The *Medea* is the last extant tragic drama that can be performed with only two, and the final drama we have from the fifth century, Sophocles' *Oedipus at Colonus*, requires some extremely fancy footwork, not to mention lightning-fast costume changes, to be performed with only three actors. But whether two or three were available, actors still had to be capable of embodying multiple parts in each production, across four different works in a single day, an achievement of as much physical endurance as artistic prowess; indeed, the sheer physical demands on the principal actors must have severely limited the available pool. They managed multiple roles, of course, through the use of costumes and simple, though realistic, masks, which likely represented types of characters who could be readily identifiable to audiences (e.g. the Old Pedagogue, the Adolescent Hero, the Virtuous Wife and Mother, the Nurse), many of whom only saw the masks at a great distance. Audiences could quickly identify the characters through a combination of these types and the habit of dramatists to signal immediately their identity through words ("I am Polydorus." "Look, here comes Odysseus.") The actors would also have already appeared, unmasked, alongside the poets at a ceremony called the *Proagon* (literally, the "before the contest") on the day before the three days of tragic performances.

While standing with his actors there in the Odeon of Pericles, next to the Theater of Dionysus itself, the dramatist would also announce the subjects of his dramas, which seem to have been invariably drawn from the traditional, heroic world of Greek myth. While we lack evidence that Athens consciously limited plot materials to myth, we do know that an early tragedian, Phrynichus, so upset the Athenians with a drama, *The Capture of Miletus,* depicting the destruction in 494 of a close ally at the hands of the Persians, that he was required to pay a large fine (Herodotus 6.21). Aeschylus managed to get away with a historical tragedy in *The Persians* because, first, he depicted the seminal victorious moment in Athenian history, their defeat of King Xerxes and his armies at Salamis, but also because he drew those events into recognizably mythic patterns and types. Every other tragic drama that we know relies on myth, but not on myth as a rigid, unchanging set of prescriptions, for the tragedians had enormous freedom to adapt myth to their needs. Aspects of myth that modern audiences tend to regard as canonical, such as the self-blinding of the Sophoclean Oedipus or the infanticidal Medea of Euripides, likely were innovations (and shocking ones at that!) by their authors. So long as the basic idea of the myth held, and Oedipus still kills his father and marries his mother, and the children of Medea die after Jason leaves his family, then the dramatists had a fairly free hand. They could even invent secondary characters, such as Polymestor in the *Hecuba*, and sometimes even major ones, as Sophocles seems to have done with Antigone. But the use of stories drawn from the legendary past does not necessarily mean that Athenian tragic drama was an escapist turn away from the problems of its present, and to the relation of tragedy to Athens we now turn.

Drama and the City of Athens

While the City Dionysia and the institution of tragic drama was likely conceived, if not launched, under the reign of the tyrant Peisistratus during the sixth century B.C.E., the growth and final form of the dramatic festival seems to have been inextricably linked with the development of democratic *polis* of Athens in 508 B. C. E., for the City Dionysia became a quintessential instrument and expression of the democratic Athenian *polis*.[13] The first great Athenian dramatist, Aeschylus, fought at both Marathon and Salamis, the two great victories over Persia that launched the "golden age" of Athens, and he commemorated the latter defeat of foreign imperial tyranny in his *Persians*, in which the young Pericles served as the *choregos*, the wealthy citizen who underwrote the cost of training and outfitting the chorus for a whole year. Sophocles served the Athenian government in several capacities and staged the tensions of Athenian *polis* life through a number of his tragedies. Euripides played no known role in formal public life, and had the reputation of being something of a recluse, yet his dramas are full of the spirit and language of the Athenian Assembly and law courts, the other two great institutions of Athenian democracy.

The City Dionysia was a fundamentally civic institution, radically unlike anything in modern America. The festival as a whole was operated and funded by the state with the clear supervision of one of the nine *archontes*, the principal administrative officials of Athens; immediately following the festival's close there would be a public discussion in the Theater itself of its management at which the appropriate officials would be held accountable for any problems. The Dionysia, however, also provided rich citizens one of their few opportunities to display their wealth publicly in a required "contribution" (*leitourgia*) that gave them the choice of underwriting either the entire expense of the chorus for a playwright or a warship and its crew; this option shows the centrality of drama to Athens and the enormous cost of these single productions (and one might productively compare the cost of a modern aircraft carrier with the budget for the American National Endowment for the Arts!). The festival thus enabled participation by the wealthy and display of their wealth, while also recognizing those who had served Athens well in the previous year and would serve it in the future. During the City Dionysia, the glory of Athens and its citizens was on full display. Before the tragedies, the ten generals of the Athenian army poured out libations to the gods in view of the audience, as part of a series of pre-performance spectacles. Member states of the Delian League, an alliance of city-

---

13   On tragic drama and Athenian democracy see Goldhill (2000), Seaford (1994), and Connor (1989) and (1996). The cautions by Rhodes (2003) against the overemphasis on democracy, as opposed to the ideology of the *polis*, in studies of Athenian drama, are salutary.

states formed to punish Persia and guard against its renewed aggression but which quickly became a *de facto* empire for Athens, would annually pay financial "tribute" to Athens to fund the expenses of the alliance. Before the performance of the tragedies, in the Theater of Dionysus, Athenian officials would bring out the "talents" of silver (one talent=57 lbs. of silver coins) for the full crowd to see, a display of wealth and power that doubtless pleased many citizens in the audience but rankled visitors. At the same time, Athens paraded the sons of soldiers who had lost their lives in war and who had been raised at public expense. Athens then awarded, in the Theater, these youths with their own armor. Moreover, this same audience would witness the recognition of service to Athens with the award of golden crowns. The glory of Athens and its ideology were thus foregrounded and proclaimed in an event whose primary function was to produce theater.

In such a context, one would expect the dramas themselves to express unequivocally the value system or ideology of the Athenian *polis*, and yet nothing could be further from what one finds in the texts of the dramas, that, among other things, problematize, if not undermine, the subordination of familial concerns to the needs of the state; present admirable heroes whose competitive egoism clashes with the cooperative spirit of the democracy; and, especially during the last quarter of the fifth century when Athens engaged in its long conflict with Sparta, seem to question the reasons for and the conduct of war. Tragic drama was part of the public debate about the nature of Athenian society and government. Myth enabled playwrights to address social problems obliquely and in multifaceted ways. The form of drama, where issues are debated and no single voice has authority over the others, mirrors the very structure of the two foundations of Athenian democracy: freedom of speech (*parrhesia*) and equality (*isonomia*). The agents in these dramas often embody values that are contrary to these two ideals, and yet their language is steeped in the concepts and terminology of the audience. Were many Greek tragedies one-sided polemics on particular events of the day, such as, say, many of the films of Oliver Stone, they would not still be living works of art today, with the power both to move and to provoke.[14]

Time and again, the Theater of Dionysus bears witness to debates over the fundamental questions of Athenian society (indeed, perhaps of any society)—the nature of justice, the place of women, the rights of suppliants, the nature of human freedom, the reasons for war—that seem equally or more appropriate for the Athenian Assembly and the law courts, and that suggest linkages between the three as forums for public speech. All three venues engaged in the mediating of conflicting social values through language. The Theater of Dionysus and the Pnyx (where the Assembly met) were the two settings for large-scale meetings of the Athenian people, and their physical natures were quite similar: semi-circular amphitheaters, at the bottom of which speakers would try

---

14   As I completed work on this essay, the Royal Shakespeare Company produced Euripides' *Hecuba* in a new translation by Tony Harrison and starring the great actress Vanessa Redgrave. Both production and translation were criticized for their heavy-handed allusions to the invasion of Iraq by the United States in 2003. Such critics implied the work could speak to such concerns by itself, without the overemphasis on our contemporary world.

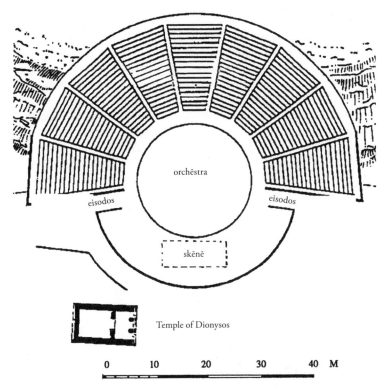

A reconstruction of the theater of Dionysus in Athens during the second half of the fifth century BC. (Based on the sketch by J. Travlos, *Pictorial Dictionary of Ancient Athens* [London 1971] 540.)

to convince their auditors of the rightness of their case.[15] Some scenes in tragedy, such as the final one in Euripides' *Hecuba*, are self-consciously styled as legal trials, with set speeches for both prosecution and defense before a judge. Other tragic debates seem at first more personal and private, but only until one remembers the mass scale of the original audience and the requirements of acting in masks. Let us take two Sophoclean debates for examples, the confrontation between Oedipus and Creon early in the *Oedipus Tyrannus* and the argument over Ajax's burial between Teucer and Menelaus in the *Ajax*. If one were to hand the scripts to two modern actors working in a contemporary theater, they would stand nose-to-nose, yelling directly at each other, confident they could be heard by the 350 people in the darkened, indoor theater. Such an approach would not work with masks in an outdoor theater of 16,000 spectators. For the mask to engage its character and the character the audience, it must face forward. For the actor to be heard in a large outdoor space he must face the audience. Any significant turn to the side undermines

---

15   On the resemblance of the Pnyx and the Theater of Dionysus, see Josiah Ober and Barry Strauss' "Drama, Political Rhetoric and the Discourse of Athenian Democracy, " 237-270 in Winkler and Zeitlin (1990).

the engagement of the mask and makes the actor substantially less audible. The actors must face forward and address the audience, and this position changes the debates from personal confrontations between two people to a set of speeches before an assembly or jury that argue the merits of the characters' positions. The actors address each other through the audience. The argument between Menelaus and Teucer is thus a public debate over the treatment of the bodies of warriors, and, during the trial scene of Euripides' *Hecuba*, Polymestor and Hecuba justify their actions not just to Agamemnon but to the audience as well, which thus becomes, in effect, a jury. The audience was part of the theatrical process. Drama was an integral part of the *polis* life of Athens.

Athenian Drama and the Peloponnesian War

Of the surviving tragedies of Euripides, only the *Alcestis* (438 B. C. E.) was produced outside of the shadow of the Peloponnesian War, which stretched from 431 to 404, ending with the defeat of Athens at the hands of its bitter enemy Sparta. The great danger for the modern reader here is in oversimplifying the relationship of ancient Greek drama to this conflict; one could leap to the conclusion on the basis of the depiction of suffering in Euripides' *Trojan Women* that Euripides must have been vehemently opposed to the war, or, one could look at the extended denunciations of Sparta in the earlier *Andromache* and leap in the opposite direction, ripping the speech out of its immediate context. Ancient Athenian playwrights, unlike, for example, modern film directors, are unknown to have ever held press conferences in which they hold court on their political views and the relationship of those views to their art. As discussed previously in this Introduction, ancient dramatists generally eschewed overtly political dramas with a contemporary basis for their plots. And yet, the sheer frequency of the themes of war, its causes and its effects in the Athenian Theater of Dionysus during the time of the Peloponnesian War indicates that the real war experienced by the members of the audience was energizing the presentation of myths of ancient wars by the actors in front of them. It is thus impossible to figure out definitively Sophocles' political position on the basis of the *Philoctetes*, produced late in the war (409 B. C. E.), but it is also, I think, impossible to overlook the similarity of the desperation of the Greek leaders (and of Philoctetes himself) late in the Trojan War with the growing desperation of Athens in its conflict with Sparta. In general, we can see Athenian drama, especially in Euripides' hands, reflecting the increasing levels of savagery throughout the Greek world during the war, as well as participating in the debate over certain issues raised by the war, through the prism of myth.

Euripides' *Trojan Women* (415), produced roughly a decade after the *Hecuba*, has been the traditional touchstone for scholarly considerations about Euripides and the Peloponnesian War. With its depiction of the suffering female victims who survive the destruction of Troy, the virtuoso display of sophistic rhetoric of Helen, who defends her conduct and the war itself as actually beneficial to Greece, and the climactic announce-ment of the brutal death of Hector's son Astyanax, this tragic drama clearly evokes, if not responds to the events of the Peloponnesian War. But which events? Scholars have suggested the events at Melos the year before or the looming invasion of Sicily. In 416

Athens "invited" the independent, neutral island of Melos to join its empire. Thucydides (5.84-113) presents a version of a dialogue that likely took place between the representatives of Athens and Melos that marks the former as advocating a particularly bleak and amoral version of "power politics" that had increasingly characterized the world of the Peloponesian War.[16] Following the refusal of the Melians to capitulate, Athens immediately commenced a siege, and in the winter before the production of Euripides' *Trojan Women,* "the Melians surrendered unconditionally to the Athenians, who put to death all the men of military age whom they took, and sold the women and children as slaves" (Thucydides 5.116). At around the same time, the Athenian assembly voted, after over fifteen years of war with Sparta, to invade, without a compelling cause, the larger island of Sicily, located six hundred miles away, with the largest armada they had ever assembled (Thucydides 6). Like the expedition against Melos, the attack on Sicily was unprovoked, but this incursion ended in total ruin and Athens never really recovered from it. The prologue of Euripides' tragedy forecasts the destruction of the great Greek armada as it leaves Troy, and thus it also perhaps prophesies that of the great Athenian fleet soon to sail for Sicily. So was *The Trojan Women* a protest against Athenian policy on Melos, an anticipation of the effects of Sicily? Both? Neither? While we lack evidence about the personal political position of Euripides during these years, it is difficult, for me at least, to believe Euripides could have written such an emotionally shattering drama as *The Trojan Women* without some kind of urgent impetus such as a reaction to the sufferings of the Melians.

Such was the situation a decade after Euripides' *Hecuba,* yet already in the mid 420s chaos was growing in the Greek world and Athens was grappling with unforeseen consequences to its military policy, both of which seem reflected in the contemporaneous *Hecuba.* Among the atrocities committed by both sides during those years, Thucydides seems to have found the civil war (*stasis*) in Corcyra most disturbing and most exemplary. Corcyra, an Athenian ally, had fallen into internal upheaval that was exacerbated by interventions by both Sparta and Athens. Oligarchs and democrats fought in the streets and from the rooftops. Corcyra gradually slipped into anarchy. As Thucydides reports (3.81-2):[17]

> There was death in every shape and form. And, as usually happens in such situations, people went to every extreme and beyond it. There were fathers who killed their sons; men were dragged from the temples or butchered on the very altars; some were actually walled up in the temple of Dionysus and died there. So savage was the progress of this revolution, and it seemed all the more so because it was one of the first which had broken out. Later, of course, practically the whole of the Hellenic world was convulsed... [W]ar is a stern teacher; in depriving them of the power of easily satisfying their daily wants, it brings most people's minds down to the level of their actual circumstances... To fit in with the change of events, words, too, had to change their usual meanings. What used to be thought of as a thoughtless act of aggression was now regarded as the courage one would expect to find in a party member; to think of the future and

---

16 On the relationship between Euripidean tragedy and Thucydides' depiction of the Peloponnesian War see the discussions of Hogan (1972) and J. Finley (1938).
17 Translation by Rex Warner (Penguin. New York. 1954).

wait was merely another way of saying one was a coward; any idea of moderation was just an attempt to disguise one's unmanly character; ability to understand a question from all sides meant that one was totally unfitted for action.

Thucydides continues along these lines for some time, but the reader of the *Hecuba* should find them already familiar, because Thucydides is describing the moral universe of Euripidean drama during these years. The phrase, "war is a stern teacher," is rendered more literally in two possible ways from the original Greek. The Greek words about the pedagogic effectiveness of war, *biaios didaskalos*, can mean "violent teacher" and "teacher of violence." The concern here, and elsewhere in Thucydides, is articulated also throughout Euripides' *Hecuba*. Hecuba herself, after hearing the depiction of the courage of her daughter Polyxena in the face of death, speculates how the growth of children in the face of adversity is like and unlike the development of plants; how can her Polyxena be so noble in death when she has suffered so much? But Hecuba herself has had a *biaios didaskalos* and reacts to her children's deaths in way evocative of what Thucydides describes of the citizens of Corcyra, where women took part in the violence by hurling roof tiles down on members of the opposition (Thucydides 3.74). Moreover, Thucydides' account of the abuse of language, the self-serving shifts in rhetoric, resonates in Odysseus' justifications of human sacrifice and Polymestor's account of his "pre-emptive" murder of Polydorus.

The most exact and direct correlation between an episode in the Peloponnesian War and Euripides' *Hecuba* can be found in the events surrounding the city of Mytilene in 428-27, just before the Corcyrean civil war, and which occupies the first fifty chapters of Book 3 of Thucydides' *History*. The city of Mytilene on the island of Lesbos had allied itself with Sparta and had begun to force the rest of the island under their control, thus endangering the role of Athens there. But the revolt failed and thus Athens suddenly found itself, as does the Greek army in the scenario of Euripides' *Hecuba*, with a substantial number of prisoners of war, from which the furious Athenian Assembly voted to kill the entire male population and enslave the women and children (3.36). And yet, overnight, enough Assembly members had second thoughts about the rashness of their decision to kill the innocent along with the guilty, and there was thus a second debate about the prisoners, recorded by Thucydides, which featured the demagogue Cleon, one of Aristophanes' favorite targets, whom Thucydides notes was "remarkable among the Athenians for the violence of his character, and at this time he exercised far the greatest influence among the people." The twisted logic of Cleon's rhetoric, full of such hyperbolic claims as "no single city has ever done you the harm that Mytiline has done" (3.39), resonates in the Euripidean speeches of Odysseus and Polymestor. However, the more measured, merciful speech of Diodotus carried, barely, enough force so that only those guilty of the revolt were executed. A second boat was sent, which overtook its predecessor because the latter was rowing slowly due to the unpleasant nature of its mission.

As Justina Gregory has observed,[18] Euripides' *Hecuba* strongly echoes such debates, for the language of the drama's early scenes is steeped in the discourse of the Athenian Assembly, and the specious appeals to necessity in Odysseus' speech seem almost modeled directly on the similar claims Cleon makes in the debate over Mytiline.

---

18   Gregory (1999, 2002).

Euripides anachronistically has the Achaean army vote on human sacrifice in response to the reported demands of the ghost of Achilles. Hecuba's appeal for a reconsideration of the verdict (287-90) is based more on the parliamentary maneuver over Mytiline than anything in Greek myth. In those same lines, Hecuba herself questions the appropriate treatment of war prisoners, precisely the problem raised by the Mytilenian revolt. More importantly, such words raise the larger issue of the abuse of power by the victorious, an issue that continued for the Athenians well past the end of the war, into the attempts to deal with the treatment of Athenian aristocrats who had played roles in the coup of 411 and the oligarchic government that followed the defeat of Athens by Sparta in 404. Few lines in Greek tragedy are as salient to the decades of their immediate production and to our time as Hecuba's warnings to Odysseus on the need for the powerful to treat the conquered well because fortune will at some point turn (282-3), a maxim the drama itself supports with the later prophecies of Agamemnon's death, and the winds whipping up at the drama's close that both release the Greek ships and send them to their doom as the winds ripen into a maritime storm. Power must be related to justice. As Leonard Bernstein once said of the fruitlessness of Beethoven's hopes for universal brotherhood as expressed in his Ninth Symphony, "When, Lord, oh when?"

Outline of the structure of Sophocles' *Ajax* (circa 440s B.C.E)

Prologue   **(1-133)**
    a) **Search scene #1**: Odysseus looks for Ajax who was driven to delusion by Athena and mistakenly slaughtered livestock instead of the top Greek commanders (1-90)
    b) **Enter Ajax with his bloodied whip**, summoned by Athena, boasting of his night-time murders; Athena toys with Ajax as he mocks his 'prisoner' Odysseus (91-117)
    c) Odysseus' compassion for Ajax despite Athena's invitation to mock his foe (118-133)

Song 1   **(134-200) Enter chorus**: 15 sailors from Salamis ask which god caused their captain's attack on the Greek leaders. They beg Ajax to refute the evil rumors

Act I   **(201-595)**
    a) Tecmessa explains to chorus that Ajax's fury / delusion has now subsided (201-283)
    b) **Monologue #1 of Tecmessa** (284-330): Verifies Ajax's madness and slaughter
    c) **Enter Ajax on a 'trolley'**, sitting blood-soaked amidst the slain beasts. He realizes Athena has caused his ruin and begs chorus to help him die (348-429)
    d) **Debate #1**: Ajax vs. Tecmessa (430-544): What is the nature of true 'nobility'?
        Monologue #1 of Ajax (430-480): To live with honor or to die with honor?
        Monologue #2 of Tecmessa (485-524): Don't commit suicide! We need you!
        Monologue #2 of Ajax (545-582): Bids his son farewell then scolds Tecmessa

Song 2   **(596-645)** Yearning for home, lament for Ajax's 'divine madness' and for his parents

Act II   **Monologue #3 of Ajax** (646-692): **Deception Speech** = play's philosophical climax.
    Ajax reveals a new understanding of the world and its iron law of mutability while fooling Tecmessa / chorus into thinking he's decided not to commit suicide

Song 3   **(693-718)** Joy-before-catastrophe: celebration of Ajax's apparent change of mind

Act III   **(719-865)**
    a) Messenger reports the reasons for Athena's wrath and Calchas' prophecy: "Confine Ajax to his hut just for today and he will live." (719-814)
    b) **Chorus exits**: search parties leave the orchestra searching for Ajax (814)
    c) **Scene change**: from Ajax's hut to a solitary place on Troy's seashore (814)
    d) **Monologue #4 of Ajax**: Suicide Soliloquy (815-865)
    e) **Suicide**: Ajax leaps on his sword (probably) in full view of the audience (865)

Search scene #2   **(866-973)**
    a) **Chorus re-enters**: search parties return to orchestra looking for Ajax
    b) Tecmessa finds Ajax's impaled corpse, facing upwards and covers it with her mantle

Act IV   **(974-1184)**
    a) Teucer uncovers the corpse, extracts the sword, laments poignantly (974-1046)
    b) **Debate #2**: Teucer vs. Menelaus: contest over Ajax's burial (1047-1162)
    c) **Burial ritual**: Hair-cutting over corpse by Teucer, Tecmessa, and Eurysaces (1163-84)

Song 4   **(1185-1222)** Yearning to escape dangers at Troy and return to the joys of home

Exodos   **(1223-1420)**
    a) **Debate #3**: Teucer vs. Agamemnon: a doublet of Debate #2 (1223-1315)
    b) **Debate #4**: Odysseus vs. Agamemnon: an interruption of Debate #3 (1316-75)
    c) Teucer's praise of Odysseus. Burial preparations. Funeral procession (1376-1420)

The *Ajax* of Sophocles

Setting

The first part of the play (1-814) takes place in front of Ajax's large wooden hut (represented by the *skênê* or stage building) at the far eastern end of the Greek naval camp on the north coast of Troy between the mouths of Troy's two rivers (Scamander and Simoeis). *Ajax* commences in the dim light of dawn sometime during the tenth year of the Trojan War (between the end of the *Iliad* and the sack of Troy), soon after Achilles' death and the contest between Ajax and Odysseus for his armor. The long side-passage (*eis-odos*) to the right of the long low stage leads to and from the Greek camp, the *eisodos* to the left of the stage leads to and from the open country of Troy. There are some 26 entrances and exits in *Ajax*, the most of any surviving Sophoclean play.

Cast of characters in order of appearance [1]

Athena	goddess of war, wisdom, and craftiness; daughter of Zeus and Metis
Odysseus	Greek commander at Troy; king of Ithaca; son of Laertes
Ajax	Greek commander at Troy; son of Telamon and Eriboea; from Salamis
Chorus	15 sailors, dependents of Ajax from the island of Salamis near Athens
Tecmessa	war-captive bride of Ajax; daughter of King Teleutas of Phrygia
Eurysaces	young son of Ajax and Tecmessa, 3-5 years old
Messenger	soldier from the Greek camp
Teucer	half-brother of Ajax; bastard son of Telamon and Hesione; noted archer
Menelaus	Greek commander at Troy; king of Sparta; younger son of Atreus
Agamemnon	commander-in-chief of the Greek army at Troy; elder son of Atreus

---

1   In the seven surviving plays of Sophocles the number of speaking parts varies from five to eight. But in a Greek tragedy there were only *three* speaking actors (all of whom were played by male Athenian citizens). The most likely distribution of the eight speaking roles in *Ajax* (with their respective number of lines put in parentheses) is as follows: **Actor #1** (protagonist) = Ajax (287) and Teucer (214); **Actor #2** (deuteragonist) = Odysseus (83) and Tecmessa (209); **Actor #3** (tritagonist) = Athena (75), Messenger (67), Menelaus (63), and Agamemnon (61). The chorus has 361 lines. *Silent characters* include Eurysaces, his attendant, Teucer's attendant, the one or two heralds who accompany Menelaus, the body-guards of Menelaus and Agamemnon as well as the attendants involved in Ajax's burial preparations and the fetching of his armor at 1403-17. Tecmessa, in her fifth and final appearance (1168-1420), is silent.

Prologue[2]

Enter Odysseus, followed by Athena[3] (at some distance) via a side ramp. The goddess stands at the edge of the stage. Odysseus circles around the hut, cautiously peering inside, searching for Ajax.

Athena[4]

Always, son of Laertes, my keen eyes watch you on the prowl,[5]
stalking your enemies, eager to put them to the test;[6]
so now I see you at the seaward huts[7] by Ajax's ships
where he holds his station at the far-off end of the fleet.[8]
All this time you hound him, taking the measure of his tracks,   5
foot-prints freshly stamped in the sand, to see if he's inside or out.
Some keen-nosed coursing, like the sniffing of a Spartan bitch,[9]
guides your steps straight to their goal. For indeed just now
the man happens to be inside, sweat streaming from his head,
and blood from his sword-slaying hands.[10]   10
So there is no longer any need to peer inside this gate.[11]
But explain exactly why you've set yourself this eager quest

---

2   The prologue can be defined as *everything up to the chorus' entry*. Sophocles likes to start his plays with *dialogues*; Euripides begins all 18 of his extant plays with long *monologues* (five of which are by gods).

3   Athena is the only Olympian god to appear in extant Sophocles but gods probably appeared in at least five of his 'lost' plays. *Ajax* is also the only Sophoclean play *to begin* with a speech by a god. Does Athena enter at ground level or on the roof of the stage building? This is a matter of great controversy. I prefer the former option for two reasons: a) other 'prologue gods' in tragedy enter at ground level (with the possible but unlikely exception of *Trojan Women*); b) at verse 37 Athena says she took her post 'on the path' (*eis hodos*), meaning the path along which Ajax must travel. I take this as a sort of word-play by Sophocles on the noun *eisodos*, which is the 'technical' name for the 'side entry-ramp' into the theater, to indicate that Athena entered at ground level; similar uses of the word *eisodos* can be seen at Aristophanes *Birds* 296 and *Clouds* 326.

4   The play's first word 'always' (*aei*) introduces the motif of time and its power over man: the gods, unlike human beings, are not subject to time's vicissitudes; see further the notes at 116-17 and 682.

5   Odysseus peers *warily* around Ajax's hut as if it were the Cyclops' cave. The play's first half, like its second half, begins with a 'search scene'; such scenes are common in Sophocles because of his interest in the various modes of *revelation*, i.e. the ways in which human knowledge is 'veiled' and then 'unveiled.'

6   The key word here is the first one in the Greek line, 'test.' The root *peira* is present in English derivatives like 'experiment,' 'empirical,' 'pirate.' Odysseus is looking to 'test' Ajax who will undergo even more severe 'tests' later (289, 470, 1057). This enterprising habit of confronting adversaries in the 'test' was a trait for which the Athenians were proud as Pericles relates in his Funeral Oration (431 B.C.E.): "For Athens alone of existing cities, when put to the test (*peira*), surpasses her reputation." (Thucydides 2.41.3)

7   The word used for 'hut' (*skênê*) is the technical word for 'stage building' and it is this very 'stage building' that is used to represent Ajax's 'hut' (until line 815 when the 'scene' changes).

8   Ajax held the eastern end of the Greek line of ships, Odysseus the midpoint, and Achilles the west. The endpoints, held by the two greatest warriors, were the outposts of danger and, hence, honor (*Iliad* 11.5-10).

9   Odysseus the hunter has morphed into his own hound.

10   This is the first mention of Ajax's famous sword, which was a gift to him from Hector.

11   The hut's door must be partially, if not fully, open.

since you could learn from one who knows where he is.

Odysseus

O voice of Athena, dearest of the gods to me![12]

How easy it is to recognize that sound,   15

invisible though you are![13] Yes, I grasp your words clearly

like blasts from a bronze-mouthed Etruscan trumpet.

You have judged correctly: it is indeed against an adversary

that I set my course and circle round—Ajax the shield-bearer.

Yes, that's the man, no other, I've been tracking for some time.   20

For just last night he did a deed against us hard-to-conceive

and hard-to-explain—if, in fact, he has done it.

Since we know nothing for sure but wander in doubt.

That's why *I* have volunteered, yoked myself to this task.

Destroyed—that's how we found our booty just now,   25

all the cattle slain, butchered by a *human* hand,

and the herdsmen as well, guardians of the flocks!

So every single soldier lays the blame for this *on that man*.

Some eyewitness who saw him bounding across the plain all alone[14]

carrying a blood-stained sword[15], told me   30

and revealed the details. At once I rushed

to track him down. Sometimes I follow the signs,

sometimes I'm thrown off course, unable to learn where he is.

So you've arrived in the nick of time. For in all things

past and yet to come, it is your hand that steers me.[16]   35

Athena

I knew that, Odysseus, and that's why I took my post on this path

some time ago, a guardian zealous for this hunt of yours.

Odysseus

Really, dear mistress, do I toil to any purpose?[17]

---

12   Odysseus' first words recall his intimate relationship to Athena in Homer's *Odyssey*.

13   A clear indication that Odysseus can hear but *not* see Athena (at least for the moment); certainly the audience *can* see her.

14   Typically the Sophoclean hero is isolated from his community. The adjective 'alone' (*monos*) recurs 19 times, a marker of its thematic importance (cf. 47, 294, 467, 1276, 1283).

15   The same phrase occurs, much more sadly, in the same metrical position at 828.

16   The pretext of Athena's invisibility has, by this point, been dropped completely – a reminder that *realism* was not a concern of Athenian dramatists.

17   Rapid *single* (or double) line dialogue (*stichomythia*) is a common convention used at moments of tension, controversy, and confrontation. Here the cut-and-thrust exchange – Odysseus asks seven consecutive questions - serves to dramatize the scene's uncanniness. The play's other passages of *stichomythia* are 74-90, 96-115, 529-43, 1120-1141, 1318-31, 1346-69.

Athena

Yes, know that these deeds *are* his, as you suspected.

Odysseus

But *why* did he thrust his hand out in a way so hard-to-understand?[18]   40

Athena

Anger weighed heavy on him[19] over the decision about Achilles' armor.[20]

Odysseus

Why, then, does he fall so furiously upon the *flocks*?

Athena

He thought he was staining his hand with slaughter of you all.

Odysseus

What? Do you mean his plot was actually aimed at the Greeks?

Athena

He would have succeeded, too, if I hadn't been so careful.   45

Odysseus

Such reckless, daring schemes! How could he be so bold?

Athena

Yes, his assault came at night—by stealth—all alone![21]

Odysseus

Did he really come close to us? Did he reach his goal?

Athena

There he was, actually at the gates of the two generals![22]

Odysseus

And how did he come to hold back his hand eager for slaughter?   50

---

18   One might also translate 'so irrationally.' Odysseus does not yet know of Ajax's madness; hence his foe's daring violence is 'hard-to-understand' (*dys-logistos*). This rare adjective anticipates the 'hard-to-bear' (*dys-phoros*, 51) imaginings' that Athena had cast over Ajax's eyes, which turn out to be the cause of his 'hard-to-understand' attack.

19   This first mention of Ajax's anger recalls the famous scene in Homer's *Odyssey* scene where Odysseus meets Ajax's still angry soul in the underworld. In that passage (11. 538-67), which is translated at the end of my essay, words for Ajax's 'anger' appear four times.

20   After Achilles' death at Troy his armor was awarded, unfairly in the eyes of Ajax (442-46) and Teucer (1135), to Odysseus. The aftermath of this decision is the focus of Sophocles' play.

21   Quite a contrast with the madman bounding across the plain *in broad daylight* at 30. Quite a contrast, too, with the Homer's stalwart Ajax who never resorted to the kind of stealth that Odysseus employed when he attacked Rhesus at night in *Iliad* 10, or captured the Trojan seer Helenos alone by deceit and at night (*Philoctetes* 606-9), or entered Troy disguised as a beggar (*Ody.* 4.246-50), or sacked Troy in his Trojan Horse (*Ody.* 4. 272– 89; 8.502-20). That Ajax must assimilate himself to the his crafty arch-enemy in order to recover his honor is a fine example of one of Sophocles' favorite themes, the mutability of human fortune.

22   The two generals are the sons of Atreus, or the Atreidae. Ajax reached the *gates* of their huts but never got inside.

Athena[23]

It was I who threw hard-to-bear imaginings[24] over his eyes
and kept him from this incurable joy,[25] diverting him to the flocks
of sheep and the mingled oxen, spoil still undivided and guarded
by herdsmen. There he attacked the many-horned beasts,
mowing them down in a circle, splitting their spines in the slaughter.   55
He thought at one moment that he was slaying Atreus' two sons,
holding them in his very own hands. At another moment
he fancied he was attacking now this commander, now that.
As he roamed to and fro in his fevered and frenzied fits of madness,
I urged the man on, driving him into the hunting-nets of doom.[26]   60
Then, when he took a respite from this slaughter,
having roped and bound the still surviving oxen
along with all the sheep, he drove them to his dwelling
as if he had *men* as his prey, not high-horned heifers.
And now he's in his hut torturing the tied-together beasts.   65
Here—to you as well I'll show his sheer lunacy in full view,[27]
so you can report what you've seen to all the Greeks.

  Odysseus retreats from the door.
Take courage! Wait for him! Don't expect disaster!
I shall turn away the beams of his eyes
and keep him from seeing your face.[28]   70

  Athena turns towards Ajax's hut and raises her voice.

---

23   The goddess proudly explains that it was *she* who prevented calamity for the Greek commanders.

24   Athena puts a spell on Ajax's eyes in order to convert his original murderous 'intention' (*gnômê*, 448) into the 'imaginings' (*gnômai*) here at 52 so that he sees his human enemies in the animals he attacks. When he comes to understand what he has done, Ajax pursues an even more sinister 'intention' (*gnome*, 743). The present illusions are 'hard-to-bear' (*dys-phoros*) because they are a) misleading; b) overpowering / irresistible; and c) oppressive in their result, namely 'a hard-to-bear ruin' (*dys-phoros atê*, 643). The word for 'imaginings' (*gnomai*) refers to *knowledge*-based beliefs or opinions (hence it might be translated 'thoughts'). So here the word carries a bitter <u>irony</u>: Ajax's beliefs are based *not* on true knowledge but rather the misleading illusions of madness. He imagines that he sees clearly when, in fact, he has been blinded.

25   An ominous oxymoron: the (seemingly) happy illusions of Ajax's imaginary triumph are really the symptoms of a fatal disease, i.e. one beyond remedy, as both Ajax (581-2) and the chorus (363, 609) will soon realize.

26   The ferocity of Athena's wrath (*mênis*: 656, 757) is unsettling; Sophocles doesn't reveal why she is so angry until much later.

27   Athena's intent is not only <u>to reveal</u> Ajax's madness but, as the emphatic 'in full view' suggests, *to humiliate* him too. From his own <u>private</u> viewing, Odysseus will, by his subsequent report to the army, make the viewing <u>public</u> as well.

28   This is the same verb, in the same metrical position, which began Athena's speech at 51. This stylistic device of 'ring composition,' by metaphorically entrapping Ajax within its far-flung rhetorical net – <u>*keeping him from*</u> the incurable joy of murder (51) and <u>*keeping his eyes from*</u> seeing Odysseus (69) – reveals the immense gap between human and divine power.

Hey, you there,[29] the one bending back your prisoners' arms
and roping them tight, I'm calling you. Come on out!
Ho, Ajax! Come out in front of your hut.

Odysseus

What are you doing, Athena? Don't keep calling him out!

Athena

Shhh! Keep quiet and don't win a reputation for cowardice!   75

Odysseus

By the gods, don't call him out! Let him be content to stay within.

Athena

For fear of what? Is he now for the first time a *man*?[30]

Odysseus

An enemy of this man, to be sure, and even more so now.

Athena

Well, isn't it the sweetest pleasure to laugh in the face of one's foes?[31]

Odysseus

I am quite content if he stays in his hut.[32]   80

Athena

Do you shrink from seeing a madman in full view?[33]

Odysseus

Yes, though if he had been sane, I wouldn't have shrunk in fear.

Athena

But not even now will he see you, though you're present and near.

Odysseus

How can that be, if indeed he still sees with the same eyes?

---

29   Athena's mocking summons finds a close parallel in the mockery of the mad King Pentheus ('Mr. Agony') by the disguised Dionysus in Euripides' *Bacchae* (912 ff.).

30   The word 'man' (*anêr*) here means 'a true man', i.e. a hero. Athena's implication is this: if Ajax was a real man *before* his madness (and Odysseus didn't fear him then), he is no more fearsome now that he is mad. *Anêr* is the famous first word of Homer's *Odyssey*: "Sing, goddess, of the man". It appears over 80 times in *Ajax* (more than 20 times any other play of Sophocles), underscoring one of the play's key questions: What is a 'real' man?

31   The intensely competitive nature of Greek society dictated that one person's victory came at another's expense. Losing the 'contest' (*agôn*) meant 'losing face.' Such loss of honor before one's peers was to be avoided at all costs.

32   Odysseus' refusal to accept Athena's offer to mock his enemy is astonishing; he is the first character in extant Greek literature to claim that it is *impious* to exult over fallen foes; cf. 121-26.

33   Again, as in 66, Athena's intent is not just revelation but *conspicuous* humiliation of Ajax.

Athena

I will darken his eyes even though they are keen-sighted.[34]   85

Odysseus

Well, after all, anything can happen if a god contrives it.

Athena

Shhh! Just stand right there, stay where you are at this very moment.

Odysseus

I will stay then. Would that I were far away from this peril!

Odysseus withdraws sheepishly to the end of the stage (magically invisible to Ajax).

Athena

Ho there, Ajax! A second time I summon you!
Why do you have so little respect for your ally-in-arms?[35]   90

Enter Ajax from his hut, covered in blood and carrying a huge blood-stained whip.[36] He stands at the doorway, wildly exultant.

Ajax

Hail to you, Athena![37] All hail, Zeus-born child!
How well you have stood beside me! Yes, I shall crown you
with spoils of splendid gold in gratitude for this hunting.[38]

Athena

You have spoken *nobly*! But tell me this other thing—
did you dip your dagger deep in the Argive army's blood?   95

---

34   Has Odysseus already forgotten Athena's promise that she would avert Ajax's eyes (69-70)? Perhaps he doesn't trust her? She reiterates and intensifies her promise by asserting that she will make Ajax *virtually* blind with respect to Odysseus.

35   Athena's seemingly benevolent address to Ajax as 'ally-in-arms' (*sym-machos*) will recur in Ajax's prologue exit-line (117), where he will call her his 'ally-in-armies.' *Sym-machos* thus forms a perfect 'ring composition' around his first appearance. In both cases (90, 117) the description 'ally-in-arms' is false, but whereas Ajax has been deluded into thinking that she is the comrade who 'stands by his side,' Athena is lying, as the prologue thus far has made very clear.

36   Ajax enters (probably) carrying the whip with which he has been torturing the cattle (110, 241-2, 299-300); certainly its presence would give physical witness to Athena's report of his mad rampage. Although there are now three actors now on stage, never is there a three-way conversation; while two actors converse the third stands silent. This is true also of Sophocles' other two early plays (*Antigone* and *Maidens of Trachis*). In the last act of *Ajax* (1223-1420), when Teucer, Agamemnon, and Odysseus are all on stage, this is also the case.

37   Ajax, as his familiar address indicates, can see the goddess; he cannot, however, see Odysseus, who will remain *invisible* to him through the rest of the prologue.

38   A fine example of the tragic irony for which Sophocles was so famous (e.g. *Oedipus Rex*): Ajax's metaphorical hunt for *humans* has become a literal hunt for *animals*. At this point he is no longer mad but his delusion (of having killed the Greek leaders) remains; hence his *gratitude* to Athena, his elation, and his proud boasting over a mission accomplished.

Ajax

I could boast that and I don't deny that I dipped it deep.

Athena

Did you really launch an armed attack against Atreus' sons?

Ajax

So that never again will those two strip Ajax of honor![39]

Athena

The men are dead, as I understand from your account.

Ajax

Dead indeed! *Now* let them take away the weapons that belong to me![40]   100

Athena

Well, and what of Laertes' son?

In what plight have you placed him? Or has he eluded you?

Ajax

That damned fox![41] Did you ask me where he is?

Athena

I did indeed. I mean Odysseus, the one who stood in your way.

Ajax

My sweetest pleasure[42], lady, is the prisoner   105

who sits inside.[43] I don't want him to die just yet.

Athena

Until you've done what or gained what further profit?

Ajax   (*howling with mocking laughter*)[44]

Until he's been bound to a pillar beneath my courtyard roof—

Athena

What evil will you work, then, on the poor wretch?

---

39   Ajax's emphatic use of *his own* name underscores his pride; cf. 864. 'Honor' (*timê*, as in <u>Tim</u>othy, 'honor to God') is a major theme in *Ajax*; without it the hero is nothing (cf. 427, 440).

40   Ajax has no doubt that he was cheated in the contest for Achilles' armor (cf. 442-6; 1135)

41   Another irony since the fox turns out to be Ajax (e.g his *night-time* raid), not the 'trickster' Odysseus. This is the first time in western literature that Odysseus is called by his frequently recurring title 'fox.'

42   Another irony: Ajax is more like Athena than Odysseus is. The superlative adjective here (*hêdistos*) here repeats one that Athena used in 79 where she asked Odysseus if mocking one's enemies wasn't 'the sweetest pleasure.' Whereas Odysseus stunningly declined her offer, Ajax doesn't; or rather he doesn't even need to be asked since for him (saturated in the traditional heroic code) it is obvious that mocking one's foe is 'the sweetest pleasure.'

43   Another irony marking the huge gap (as Sophoclean irony usually does) between appearance and reality: Odysseus is the (unobserved) hunter on the outside, not the hunted on the inside (cf. 7).

44   For an explanation of this stage direction, see note to 301-4.

Ajax

—and first had his back beaten blood-red with the whip.[45] Then he can die.   110

Athena

No, don't torture the poor wretch so cruelly![46]

Ajax

In all else, Athena, I charge you to have your pleasure[47]
but this, and no other, is the just penalty that *he* shall pay!

Athena

Very well then, since doing such is your pleasure,
vent your violence, spare none of the things you plan!   115

Ajax

I'm off to work! But I charge you *this*, to stand by my side
always as just the kind of ally-in-arms you have been today.[48]

Ajax exits through the large central double-door, back into his hut.

Athena

Do you see, Odysseus, the strength of the gods, how great it is?
Whom could you have found with greater forethought[49]
than this man or more accomplished in timely action?   120

Odysseus

I know no one. But nevertheless I pity the poor wretch,[50]
even though he is my enemy, because he has been yoked
harshly to the harness of a dreadful delusion.

---

45   Yet another irony: It is not Odysseus who will be 'blood-red' from being whipped by Ajax, but Ajax who is 'blood-red' from the whipping he himself has given the animals whom he erroneously imagined were men.

46   More mockery by Athena (cf. 71), again analogous to Dionysus mocking Pentheus whom he has driven mad (cf. *Bacchae* 951-2).

47   Ajax giving *orders* to Athena introduces a dangerous note of arrogance; he repeats the same phrase in 116.

48   The adverb 'always' (*aei*) here (117) in Ajax's last line in the prologue appears just one other time in this scene, i.e. as the first word of the play where Athena applied it (truly) to her strong and enduring military alliance with Odysseus. Here Ajax applies it (falsely) to what he thinks is a strong and enduring military alliance with Athena. So, although he has the last word in his long exchange with Athena, it is a fully delusional last word. Over the course of the play Ajax will learn that one cannot say 'always' about human affairs; see note at 682.

49   Homer's Ajax is not a man easily tricked (*Iliad* 7. 198) and has good common sense (7. 288). Here Athena, making a show of her own divine power, credits him with a high degree of *forethought* (the same quality for which he praises Tecmessa at 536), thus making his delusion here all the more horrific and simultaneously preparing us for the clear-sightedness with which he understands his situation after the madness has dissipated.

50   It is probably fair to say that nothing in Greek literature matches Odysseus' compassion at lines 121-6 and nothing so upends the Greek moral code of 'helping friends, harming foes.' Even though we will not see Odysseus for another 1,200 lines after he exits at 133, these verses at 121-6 begin the process of preparing for his reappearance.

Yes, I ponder that man's lot no less than my own.
For I see that we are nothing more than ghosts–   125
all we that live– or vacuous insubstantial shadows.[51]

Athena

So then, looking upon such sights as this, don't *you*
ever speak a scornful word against the gods or take upon *yourself*
any self-important swagger if you happen to surpass someone
in might or in the depth of your profuse prosperity.   130
No, since a single day can sink the scales on all human fortunes[52]
and raise them up again. It is moderate and sound-minded men
whom the gods love, while they hate the wicked.[53]

> *Exit Odysseus and Athena by opposite side-ramps.[54] Enter, then, the chorus of
> fifteen sailors into the orchestra from one side-ramp.*

Choral Entrance Song (*Parodos*)[55]

> *Chorus, _reciting_ in anapests.*

Son of Telamon,[56]

---

51   Mortals are as unreal as 'phantoms' (*eidolon*) and as empty as 'shadows' (*skia*). The word 'shadow' recurs
      twice: at 302 when Ajax, in his madness, talks to some 'shadow' as if it were a real person; and at 1257,
      when Teucer tells Agamemnon not to mock Ajax because he is no longer alive but already 'a shadow.'

52   One of Sophocles' great interests was the mutability of life, of which Ajax's fall (in the play's first half)
      and his rise (in the second half) is a paradigmatic example.

53   The prologue closes with an ending whose proverbial wisdom seems simple enough (although its full
      relevance to Ajax is unclear until 756-77). Yet it raises troubling questions coming from Athena (cf. 79)
      and we should resist the temptation to take the goddess's seeming 'words of wisdom' at the end of the
      prologue as the moral of the whole story. This is the only example in Sophocles where the verb 'love'
      (*philein*) is used of the gods, who are not generally known for their 'love.'

54   The prologue ends with Athena and Odysseus exiting (probably) in opposite directions, symbolic of
      their opposite reactions to Ajax's plight. Athena will not appear again and Odysseus not until the end
      (1317-1401).

55   The chorus of 15 sailors are Ajax's loyal crew from Salamis. They are coming from their quarters at the far
      eastern end of the camp. As they march into the enormous orchestra by way of the side entry-ramp (eiso-
      dos), they recite, to the rhythm of marching anapests, a long first section (134-71). Then, from 172-200,
      they dance the more formal movements of 'turn' (strophe) and 'counter-turn' (antistrophe), linguistically
      complex stanzas that 'respond' to one another metrically and choreographically. The chorus, when they
      danced, did so to the music of an oboe-like reed-pipe (aulos). The final three stanzas here (172-200) are
      sung to complex lyric meters and mark the climax of the chorus' agitation. This entrance-song's two-part
      structure (i.e. a section of recited marching anapests followed sung lyrics) is the oldest form of *parodos*
      in tragedy, similar to Agamemnon (458 BCE) and is not found in Sophocles' other six surviving plays.
          Between prologue and *parodos* enough time has passed for Odysseus to return to the Greek camp and
      report his findings; and enough time, too, for the chorus to react to the rumors. Here they summon Ajax
      from his tent to find out if, in fact, he did attack the army's flocks, as Odysseus has reported. The song
      gives a vivid portrayal of the conflict from their point of view. On the one hand, they see the report of
      Ajax's crime as outrageous slander. On the other, Odysseus has implanted some serious doubt. Overall,
      in contrast to the prologue's harsh presentation of facts, here we get a sympathetic, though sometimes
      unrealistic re-appraisal of Ajax.

56   This phrase recurs at 183, thus forming something of a ring around the ode; despite his physical absence,
      Ajax's father provides a menacing emotional presence (cf. 1010-18).

lord of wave-washed Salamis, firm pillar on the sea,   135
when you prosper, I rejoice in your joy.
But whenever a stroke from Zeus[57] or a furious word
from the Greeks assaults you slanderously,
mighty fear shrinks me and I shudder
like the eye of a fluttering dove.   140
So even now, during the night just spent,
mighty uproar assails us,
threatening infamy[58]—clamorings that you
assaulted the meadow where horses run with mad delight[59]
and butchered the beasts—the Greek booty,   145
spoil still undivided, captive of the spear—
slaughtering them with your sword's flashing iron.
Such are the whispering words
Odysseus insinuates into everyone's ears
impetuously persuading them. Yes, he presently asserts   150
persuasive allegations against you. And everyone
who hears them rejoices more than he who spoke,
insolently mocking your sorrows.[60]
For whoever shoots his arrows at mighty-souled men[61]
could not miss his mark. But if someone leveled   155
such charges against *me*, he could not persuade.[62]

---

57 i.e. a sudden and (thunder-bolt like) divine intervention.

58 The chorus fear for their reputation. 'Infamy' translates a form of the Greek word *kleos* (= glory / fame); more than anything else in life, this is what the Greeks sought. In this play *kleos* is associated with Ajax (216, 769), Telamon (436), Salamis (596) and Athens (861). The root can be seen in many Greek names, e.g. *Kleo*-patra, Patro-*klos*, Peri-*kles*, Sopho-*kles*.

59 These are the lush pastures of the well-watered Trojan plain (cf. *Iliad* 20.221-5) where for nine years the Greek leaders grazed their horses. The translation 'where horses run with mad delight' represents the adjective *hippo-manês* (literally = 'horse-mad' or 'raving with horses') which is usually rendered innocuously as 'swarming with horses.' But given the play's focus on madness, it is possible that this very rare and unusual epithet relates to Ajax; that is to say, the reason that furious Greek slander 'assaults' (*epi-bainein*, 138) Ajax is that he, in his madness, 'assaulted' (*epi-bainein*, 145) the 'horse-mad' meadow to carry out his murderous plan.

60 This phrase translates the Greek word *hybris*; it appears again near the end of the *parodos* (196), thus framing that section of the ode which describes the violence of the Greek reaction to Ajax's deed. *Hybris* means, literally, 'a going beyond.' It is the wanton disregard of decency, violence in word or deed, or insolent transgression. Acts of *hybris* involve the deliberate or self-indulgent abuse of power (especially by strong, over-proud *males*) at the expense of another's honor. *Hybris* appears 14 times in *Ajax*, more often than any other tragedy except Euripides' *Bacchae* (also with 14). In *Ajax* it usually refers to the words or actions of Ajax's foes; it appears at 153, 196, 304, 367, 560, 955, 971, 1061, 1081, 1088, 1092, 1151, 1258, 1385 (the four underlined instances refer directly or indirectly to Ajax's *hybris*).

61 The adjective 'mighty' (*megas*) occurs 36 times (far more than any other Sophoclean play) and 9 times in the *parodos*; five of these nine refer to Ajax, who is, of course, heroic in the chorus' eyes.

62 This is the third time the word 'persuade' (*peithô*) has appeared in seven lines; all three emphasize the rhetorical power of Odysseus' allegations against Ajax.

It is against the man who has wealth that envy and spite creep.
And yet lowly men without the mighty constitute
a feeble tower of defense.[63] For just as the lowly man*
could best be kept upright when allied with the mighty,   160
so could the mighty when served by lesser men.
But, before the event, it is impossible to teach fools
sensible maxims concerning these matters.
Such are the men whose uproar is raised against you.[64]
And we have not the strength to defend ourselves   165
against such charges without your aid, king.
But the truth is that when they have escaped from your eye
they cackle and flap like flocks of fluttering birds;
and before the mighty eagle they would soon shrink[65]
in terror if *you* should suddenly show yourself.   170
Yes, in silence they would cower, speechless![66]

> *The chorus starts <u>singing</u> now.*[67]

Strophe

O mighty Rumor, mother of my shame—[68]
was it, then, Artemis Tauropolos,[69]
bull-tending daughter of Zeus, who launched you
against all the army's herds of cattle in order to pay back,   175
perhaps, some victory that bestowed her no fruits—

---

63 Homer describes Ajax as a 'tower' (*Odyssey* 11.556) and 'wall of defense" (*Iliad* 3.229; so Achilles, 1.284)

64 The word 'uproar' (*thorubos*) occurred also at 142; taken together the two form a 'ring' around this ana-pestic section (134-71) and succinctly express its theme, the vociferous rising of the Greek army against Ajax.

65 This is the longest of the play's six similes. Ironically it recalls a simile comparing Odysseus and his men slaying suitors on Ithaca to eagles swooping down from mountains to attack some birds (*Odyssey* 22.302-8). Possibly the chorus is making an oblique etymological pun on the hero's name (*Aias*) from 'eagle' (*aiguptos*).

66 Fittingly the song's first (anapestic) section ends with the silencing of Ajax's enemies.

67 Lines 172-200 are composed of three sung and danced stanzas: <u>Strophe</u> (172-81) = What god caused Ajax's attack? Artemis or Ares? <u>Antistrophe</u> (182-91) = Can the rumor be true? If not, Ajax, don't stay hidden in your hut. <u>Epode</u> (192-200) = Rise up and refute the rumor and ease my pain!

68 The word 'rumor' (*phatis* = literally 'what people <u>say</u>') recurs at 186 and 190, thus forming a ring around the first two stanzas and again succinctly expressing its theme. The Athenians had an altar to Rumor; in a 'shame culture' *what people say* is the main way of assessing conduct.

69 Artemis is considered a possible agent of Ajax's misfortune for several reasons: she was famed as the 'Mistress of Animals'; often associated with madness; easily-angered; and pro-Trojan. Since Ajax has killed bulls (296) and given her no offerings, he might well have aroused her wrath. As a protectress of the bull (*tauros*) she was worshipped with a festival (the *Tauro*-polia) on the southeast coast of Attica where there was a community of Salaminians.

either cheated of her splendid war-spoils or angered
because of a deer-hunt that bestowed her no gifts?
Or did Enyalios, War Lord of the bronze breast-plate,[70]
blame you for not acknowledging his alliance in battle   180
and, by scheming against you in the night, avenge the insult?

Antistrophe

Never, certainly, was it by the prompting
of your mind alone, son of Telamon, that you went
so far astray as to fall upon the flocks.
No, it might be a sickness sent by the gods![71] May both Zeus   185
and Phoibos Apollo ward off the ignoble rumor of the Greeks!
If those two mighty magistrates spew out
scurrilous lies and craft cunning stories and the king
of the profligate stock of Sisyphus' sons[72] does the same,
do not, my lord, do not any longer keep your eyes thus hidden   190
in your hut by the sea nor take upon yourself this ignoble rumor.

Epode

Come now, rise up from the seat
where you have been firmly fixed for too long
in this leisurely contest of inactivity,[73]

---

70   In Homer this god is the equivalent to Ares, who was, like Artemis, associated with madness, esp. in
     military contexts (cf. Sophocles, *Maidens of Trachis* 653-4).

71   Is the cause of Ajax's misery the gods or his enemies? The chorus vacillates. The present 'sickness sent
     by the gods' (*theia nosos*) will later become 'a madness sent by the gods' (*theia mania*, 611); at this point,
     however, the sailors don't know about their captain's madness.

72   Sisyphus was the sinister king of Corinth who was alleged to have gotten Anticleia pregnant before she
     married Laertes; hence Odysseus' enemies often called him 'son of Sisyphus' (cf. *Philoctetes* 417, 1311).
     In 415 B.C.E. Euripides wrote *Sisyphus*, a (now lost) satyr play that concluded the tetralogy of which
     Trojan Women was the third play.

73   A stunning oxymoron with an important purpose. The 'contest' (*agôn*), a concept central to the Greeks'
     highly competitive *modus operandi*, cannot, by definition, be *leisurely* and *inactive*. Hence, for example,
     the play's first *agôn* pits Ajax as prot-*agon*-ist against Odysseus as ant-*agon*-ist, with the result being
     agony for Ajax, which is indeed the very meaning of his name (see 430-32). Here the chorus speaks of
     this contest as being 'leisurely' (*scholê*) in reference to the several days that have passed since the award
     of Achilles' arms to Odysseus, during which time the brooding Ajax has refused to participate in the
     fighting. Sophocles uses this ominous oxymoron at the climatic conclusion of the Entrance Song to
     introduce the theme of the 'contest' since it provides the driving force behind the rest of the play; to wit,
     the *agôn* for Achilles' armor (935, 1240) leads to Ajax's '*agôn* of inactivity' which will lead to the *agôn*
     over the burial of Ajax's corpse (1163) which he insists must not lead to an *agôn* over his armor (572).
     At this point Ajax has the 'leisure' (*scholê*) to brood in his hut; later his 'leisure' (816) for such reflection
     will be much briefer.

igniting a fiery disaster that blazes up to heaven![74]   195
The insolent mockery of your enemies, in your absence,
races fearlessly through the wind-swept ravines.[75]
All their taunting tongues
mock you, bringing heavy pain.
So I stand stuck in the depths of sorrow.   200

Act One[76]

Enter Tecmessa from Ajax's hut.[77]

First Lyric Dialogue (Tecmessa and chorus-leader)[78]

Tecmessa

Defenders of the ships of Ajax,
descendants of the race of Erechtheus' earth-born sons,[79]
lamentations have come over us,
we who care for Telamon's house so far away.
The dreaded, mighty, raw-powered Ajax[80]   205

---

74 A stunning image that assimilates Ajax's crisis to that of a raging forest fire. The phrase could just as well
    be translated 'blazing with *heaven-sent* ruin.' So is the cause of Ajax's ruin himself (i.e. his 'contentious
    inactivity' of refraining from battle) or the gods (i.e. their wrath at him)?

75 The magnificent metaphor of 195 continues: the insulting rumors of Ajax's foes are like the flames of a
    burning forest feed by wind-gusts and Ajax, by sitting in his hut, adds yet more fuel to the conflagra-
    tion.

76 This long complex first episode is divided into two parts by the (second) entrance of Ajax at 348. **The
    first half (201-347),** which clarifies Ajax's plight, is divided into four parts: 201-62 = an emotional *lyric
    dialogue* between Tecmessa and the chorus-leader; 263-83 = a less emotional iambic dialogue between
    the same two parties; 284-332 = a long (messenger-type) speech by Tecmessa explaining what happened
    the previous night and what is happening now in Ajax's hut; 333-47 = an emotional dialogue between
    Tecmessa, the chorus-leader, and Ajax (who is shouting from offstage). The much longer **second half
    (348-595),** which foreshadows his resolve to die, is divided into five parts: 348-429 = a lyric dialogue
    with Ajax singing as Tecmessa and the chorus-leader speak; 430-524 = a long speech of Ajax (430-80),
    answered by a long speech of Tecmessa (485-524); 525-44 = a rapid exchange (*stichomythia*) between Ajax
    and Tecmessa; 545-82 = a long second speech of Ajax; 585-95 = another rapid exchange (*stichomythia*)
    between husband and wife.

77 She is Ajax's war-captive concubine. For more on her see section II of my essay under *Ajax's family*.

78 The chorus, at the conclusion of the Entrance Song, had urged Ajax to come out of his hut and refute
    the slanderous rumors of the Greeks. This is followed immediately and unusually by an emotional lyric
    dialogue between Tecmessa and the chorus-leader (201-62); she *speaks* while they *sing* (221-62).

79 The sailors of the chorus from Salamis link themselves closely to the Athenians as descendants of the
    earth-born king of Athens, Erechtheus, who was the ancestor of all Athenians and a cult figure who
    represented their claim to auto-chthony, i.e. birth from the *earth* (cf. *Iliad* 2.546-9, *Ody.* 7.80-81). This is
    the earliest surviving text that indicates a chthonic origin for the Athenian people. Erechtheus' residence,
    the Erechtheum, with its famous caryatids, was built on the Acropolis c. 421-407 B.C.E. Euripides wrote
    a (now lost) play about him (c. 422).

80 Tecmessa's string of three epithets sums up well the fierce nature of Ajax. The first adjective, 'dreaded'
    (*deinos*) connotes his grim fearsomeness; the second, 'mighty' (*megas*), recalls the heroic descriptions in the
    Entrance Song where it appeared 9 times. The 'raw' (*ōmos*) in 'raw-powered' connotes untamed strength
    and spirit; 'raw' occurs three other times, always with reference to Ajax (548, 885, 930; cf. 927).

now lies low, stricken sick by a turbulent storm
that has muddled his mind.[81]

Chorus-leader

What heavy woe has this past night received in exchange
for the already grave affliction of the bygone day?
Speak to us, daughter of Teleutas from Phrygia,[82]   210
since impetuous Ajax is constant in his affection for you,[83]
the bedmate captured by his spear;
certainly you know and could suggest some explanation.

Tecmessa

How, then, shall I tell a tale too terrifying to be told?
For you will learn of a suffering equal to death.   215
It was *madness* that seized him, our famed
night-time Ajax,[84] so that he has fallen into disgrace!
Such a sight you could see inside the hut—[85]
slaughtered victims, slain by hand,
that man's sacrificial offerings, dipped in blood.[86]   220

Strophe

Chorus-leader   *(singing)*

What report about the fiery,
hot-tempered warrior have you disclosed,
one not to be endured
yet not to be escaped!
It's a tale told   225

---

81   The sailors liken Ajax's lack of clarity to a tempest-tossed mariner caught in muddy waters.

82   Phrygia was a large, ill-defined region in west central Asia Minor. *Phrygian* is synonymous with *Trojan* and sometimes carries a pejorative connotation (as at 1292).

83   The juxtaposition of 'impetuosity' and 'affection' seems almost like a contradiction in terms. 'Impetuous', connoting 'furiously rushing,' is a frequent Homeric epithet of the War-god Ares. It is used later of Ajax acting like Ares (613) and of Ajax when he is dead and no longer 'impetuous' (1213); these three instances of the word, all applied to Ajax by the chorus, appear nowhere else in extant Sophocles.

84   The jarring juxtaposition expresses Tecmessa's pain; Ajax gets infamy (*dys-kleia*, 143), not fame (*kleos*, 216) by his night-time raid.

85   By theatrical convention the chorus and the spectators (i.e. the play's internal and external audiences respectively) *cannot* see 'the sight' inside Ajax's hut, that spectacle must be brought out to us and soon it will be (at 348).

86   Tragic irony and pathos combine here as Tecmessa describes her husband's *perverted sacrifice*. Ironic, because the word she uses for 'sacrificial offerings' normally refers to animals slaughtered and offered to the gods before consulting an oracle. But this is no offering to, or consulting of, the gods here. Pathetic, because we know that Tecmessa's word 'dipped in blood' refers to the Greek soldiers into whom Ajax 'dipped his dagger' (95); and all too soon that same sword will do its bloody work again to this man who has become 'like to iron hardened by dipping' (650).

by the mighty men of the Greeks[87]
which the mighty power
of their story-telling magnifies.
Oimoi, I fear what is approaching! In full view[88]   230
the man will die because he has slaughtered willy-nilly,
with his frenzy-stricken hands and dark sword,
the grazing beasts and their horse-mounted herdsmen.

Tecmessa   *(speaking)*[89]

Oimoi! So it was from there, from those pastures,
that he came to us leading the fettered flock.
Some of these prisoners he butchered on the ground in his hut,   235
others he struck in the sides and ripped apart.
And lifting up two white-footed rams
he hacked off one's head, then the tip of its tongue
and hurled it down; the other he bound upright
to a pillar. Then he grabbed a mighty strap   240
from a horse's harness and flogged the ram
with a whistling double-wrapped whip
abusing the beast with bitter insults
which some god, not a mortal, taught him.

Antistrophe

Chorus-leader   *(singing)*

It is time, in truth, for each one of us now,   245
having cloaked his head in a hood,[90]
to steal away on foot
or yoke himself to the rower's swift seat
and let the sea-faring ship
sail on her way. Such threats   250
do the joint commanders, Atreus' powerful sons,[91]
launch against us. I am petrified to share the pain
of a violent death by stoning
smitten alongside this man

---

87   The chorus is referring sarcastically, as in 187-9, to Agamemnon, Menelaus, and Odysseus.

88   Excellent irony. This is the first ominous foreshadowing of what lies ahead – and not only *what*, but *in what manner* (i.e. 'in full view'; cf. 66, 81). That said, it is clear that, as of yet, Ajax's suicide is the farthest thing from their minds. Rather they fear being *publicly* stoned to death alongside their captain for treason (see 250-56); he will, on the contrary, die very *privately*.

89   Tecmessa reports the havoc she has witnessed inside the hut but still has no idea of why Ajax did it.

90   The sailors want to veil themselves to conceal their shame.

91   Menelaus and Agamemnon, the joint commanders of the Greek army; both appear later, at 1047-1162 and 1226-1373 respectively.

whom a monstrous doom   255
holds fast in its grips.

Tecmessa *(speaking)*
No longer is it so. For his fury subsides like a southern gale
after a sharp outburst when its bright lightning ceases.
And now, though sane again, he has fresh grief.
For to observe one's self-inflicted sufferings   260
when nobody else has assisted in the deed
intensifies the mighty pangs of agony.

Chorus-leader
Well, if he has stopped his raging, I reckon he is very fortunate.
For now that the trouble has vanished, there will be less talk.

Tecmessa
And if someone were to allot you a choice, would you prefer   265
to distress your friends, while feeling pleasure yourself,
or to be a partner among partners, sharing your grief with theirs?

Chorus-leader
Certainly, lady, the trouble that's double is greater.

Tecmessa
Then it is *now*, when he's no longer sick, that we're in deep trouble.

Chorus-leader
What did you mean by this? I don't understand what you mean.   270

Tecmessa
That man, when *he* was in the grip of his sickness,
took delight in the evils by which he was possessed
and by his presence he distressed us when *we* were sane.
But now, when his sickness has subsided and he breathes again,
his whole being is plagued by piercing pain   275
and we, likewise, suffer no less than before.
Have we not, then, sorrows twice as great as before?

Chorus-leader
We do indeed. So I fear that some blow has come from a god.
For how can it be otherwise if, after he has stopped his raging,
he's no more cheerful than when he was sick?   280

Tecmessa
That's how matters stand: you must recognize it.

Chorus-leader
And whence began this evil that swooped down upon him so suddenly?
Disclose his misfortunes to us since *we* share your sorrow.

Tecmessa[92]

Every detail of the deed you shall learn as partners in my pain.
In the dead of night, when the camp's evening watch-fires   285
no longer burned bright, he seized his double-edged sword,
eager to steal out on some senseless mission. And I rebuked him:
"What on earth are you doing, Ajax?
Why are you setting out on this enterprise?
No herald has summoned you, no trumpet sounded.   290
Indeed the entire army is sound asleep now!"
But he shot back this trite and tired tune:
"Woman, women should be seen, not heard."[93]
And I, so schooled, ceased, while he rushed off alone.
As to what happened yonder I cannot say.   295
But he came back inside, hauling hobbled bulls,
herdsmen's dogs, and wooly prey. Some of them he beheaded.
Others he turned upside down, slitting their throats,
splicing their spines. Still others he tortured while tied up,
falling on the flocks as if they were human creatures.   300
At last *bursting out the doors*, he dragged up wild words,[94]
ranting at some shadow[95]—first against Atreus' sons,
then at Odysseus—howling with laughter at how much humiliation,
how much vengeance he had inflicted on them during his raid.
Then *bursting back into the house* again, with difficulty, somehow,[96]   305
slowly he comes back to his senses. And when he surveyed the shelter,
heaped high with the havoc and ruin caused by his delusion,
he beat his head and bellowed. Amidst the wreckage

---

92   **Tecmessa's first major speech:** In this response to the chorus-leader she explains the events of the previ-
     ous night (when Ajax raided the Greek command post) and his present activity in the hut. So, besides
     giving us our first in-depth 'look' at Tecmessa, this speech serves to impart basic information about
     Ajax's situation; in this it functions like a traditional messenger-speech. Tecmessa's only other speech is
     485-524.

93   I have used an English proverb to render the Greek one (literally: "Woman, to women silence brings
     adornment."). At times Ajax is reported to have treated Tecmessa affectionately (211-12, 639, 808); this
     is certainly not one of them. His surly dismissal foreshadows things to come.

94   301-4: These lines are quite unusual in that Tecmessa is reporting her private experience (from inside
     the hut) of what was said between Athena and Ajax on stage at 91-117, a dialogue which the spectators
     have *already* seen (from outside the hut). Her description of him 'howling with laughter' (303) suggests
     that he did just that somewhere between lines 104-8.

95   From her vantage point inside the hut Tecmessa could neither see nor hear Athena so it seemed to her
     as if Ajax was 'ranting at some shadow.'

96   Ajax's recovery comes in gradual, inexplicable stages, a foreshadowing of Agave's recovery from madness
     in the much more elaborate 'psychotherapy scene' of Euripides' *Bacchae* (1263-1300).

of the corpses of slaughtered sheep he sat, wrecked,[97]
his clenched nails clutching and clawing his hair in his hands.   310
And for a long, long time he just sat, speechless.
Then he unleashed those terrible threats that still haunt me
if I didn't reveal every detail of the mischance that had befallen him;
He asked about the sorry situation in which he found himself.
And I, friends,[98] being overcome by fear, rehearsed it all,   315
every detail of what he did, as much as I knew for sure.
But straightaway he exploded in long sighs of sorrow,[99]
sighs such as I'd never heard from him before.
For he always insisted that such plaintive lamentations
were the mark of a cowardly and heavy-hearted man.   320
In the past, whenever he had cause to grieve, he groaned deep,
like a lowing bull[100], without any sound of shrill wailing.
But now, laid low by such a pathetic plight,
without food, without drink[101], amidst cattle slain by his sword,
quietly the man sits, fallen down.[102]   325
And clearly he wants to do some dreadful deed;[103]
for his words and lamentations somehow suggest as much.
That's why I've come out here to find you, friends.
Go in and support him, if somehow you can.[104]

---

97 **wreckage…wrecked.** The word play reflects the Greek: the hunter has become the hunted, the victor the victim. The articulation of this kind of complete reversal of fortunes, expressing the mutability and instability of the human condition, is a speciality of Sophocles (cf. Oedipus).

98 Tecmessa needs all the help she can get; hence her repeated invocation 'friends' (*philoi*) here and at 328.

99 For the first time Ajax understands what he has done.

100 The cattle-slayer is now himself like a bull, bellowing as they did in the throes of death. Tecmessa will describe these groans again at 929-32. Homer uses the verb 'lowing' of the painful groans of wounded and dying warriors (e.g. Sarpedon, *Iliad* 16.486). One might say this is the beginning of Ajax's dying. The bull symbolizes virility but Ajax is hardly feeling very manly. Sophocles uses the same 'bellowing bull' image of Oedipus (*Oed. Rex* 1265) and Heracles (*Maidens of Trachis* 805) after their respective 'recognition' scenes. In his last entrance the broken-hearted King Lear, carrying the corpse of angelic Cordelia, bellows out: "*Howl! Howl! Howl!* O you men of stones!…She's gone forever." (V.iii.258).

101 Since Ajax's re-entry into the hut after his rampage, Tecmessa has offered him sustenance but he has refused it. The fasting reflects inner turmoil and inconsolability; similarly Achilles in the *Iliad* (books 18-24), Penelope worrying over Telemachus (*Ody.* 4.788), Medea surrendering to grief (*Medea* 24).

102 A foreshadowing of Ajax's appearance at his next entrance (348). The silence of 315 and the quietude here recall his earlier 'long-drawn-out contest of inactivity' (194) when he quit battle in anger over Achilles' armor; that earlier anger has now turned to something more broodingly sinister.

103 The first ominous, if indefinite, foreshadowing that Ajax *himself* will do something terrible (cf. 361).

104 Tecmessa's request that the chorus actually enter Ajax's hut (i.e. the stage building) does not come to pass. Only once in extant tragedy does the chorus actually leave the orchestra and enter the stage building (Euripides' *Helen*, line 385). It is a *general* rule that what is inside must come outside.

For men like him are won over by the words of friends.[105]   330

Chorus-leader

O Tecmessa, daughter of Teleutas, it's a bitter tale you tell us,
how his misfortune drove the man into a wild and fatal frenzy.

Ajax's cries are heard from offstage.

Io, moi moi.[106]

Tecmessa[107]

Soon, it seems, you'll learn more. Or didn't you hear Ajax wailing?
Didn't you hear how he bellows?   335

Ajax

Io, moi moi.

Chorus-leader

The man seems either to be sick or else to be grieved by the remnants
of his former sickness, which are still with him where he is.

Ajax

Io pai, pai. O my son, my son!

Tecmessa

Oimoi, wretched me! Eurysaces, he is shouting about you.[108]   340
What ever is he so eager for? Where ever are you, son? Oimoi!

Ajax

I am calling Teucer. Where is Teucer?
Will he forever be plundering for booty while I perish?[109]

Chorus-leader

The man seems to be coming to his senses. Hurry up! Open the door![110]

---

105 Tecmessa's faith in the powers of persuasion seriously underestimate the intransigence of the heroic temper.

106 This is the first time Ajax has been heard since he exited so proudly and confidently at 117. How things have changed. His first sounds are inarticulate monosyllabic screams which cannot be easily translated. It is common to render these cries by expressions like 'Alas, alas' but this fails to capture the feeling of the Greek. So here, and throughout, I have usually *transliterated* these cries from the Greek to give a sense of the original sound with the hope that the *sound* will carry a sense of the agony.

107 333-47: This emotional dialogue between Tecmessa, the chorus-leader, and Ajax (who is shouting from offstage, i.e. inside his hut) serves as a bridge passage between the first and second halves of the Act One, i.e. between 201-332 and 348-595 respectively.

108 Ajax's young son (first mentioned here) is, naturally, the *first* person he calls upon. Sophocles is preparing us for the boy's appearance at 545-95.

109 Teucer (Ajax's half-brother) is his *second* thought – for it will be Teucer to whom Ajax entrusts his son (562). But at the moment he is off on a predatory raid in enemy country (cf. 564, 720). Teucer's absence is necessary for the plot since his presence might have prevented his brother's suicide. He will not arrive until it's too late (974).

110 This bidding of the chorus is answered by Tecmessa in 345: *Behold, I am opening the door!* The repetition of *Open the door!* generates anticipation and underscores the gravity of the forthcoming revelation.

Perhaps, when he sees us, his sense of shame might sober him.[111]   345

Tecmessa

Behold, I am opening the door. You can look at the deed
he has done and see how it is with the man himself.[112]

> *Enter Ajax, wheeled out on a trolley[113], sitting motionless amidst slaughtered
> animals.*

Lyric Dialogue #2 *(Ajax, Tecmessa, and the Chorus-leader)[114]*

Strophe #1

Ajax *(singing)*

O beloved sailors,
you alone of my friends,
alone abiding in the right way,   350
look at me![115] What a wave,
lashed by a storm-surge of blood,
races round and round just now, encircling me!

Chorus-leader *(speaking to Tecmessa)*

Oimoi! How you seem to bear witness too truly!

---

111   This is the first time the issue of Ajax's shame (*aidôs*) has been raised (cf. 473, 505-7). *Aidôs* occupies a central place in Greek 'shame culture'; it can be defined as a sense of respect for the feelings of *others* that inhibits hurtful / offensive behavior; as such it serves to promote social conformity via fear of being disgraced in public. Homeric heroes cared much less about what was objectively right or wrong than they did about their standing *in the eyes of other people*. The chorus-leader hopes Ajax will be ashamed of being seen in a rage or in a state of inconsolable grief.

112   Tecmessa must be referring to Ajax's wild and disheveled appearance amidst the slaughtered cattle.

113   The theatrical mechanism used for revealing interior scenes was a large moveable platform called the ec-cycl-êma ('the thing wheeled out'). This device, which was pushed out of the central doorway, is used two other times in Sophocles (*Antigone* 1294, *Electra* 1464), both times to reveal (female) corpses. How are we to imagine this stunning revelation of Ajax? Was the great man actually sitting amidst slaughtered beasts on the eccyclêma? Or might there have been some kind of scene-painting on the stage building wall (a convention Sophocles is said to have introduced)? In whatever way we imagine the physical setting, the horror of the spectacle vividly evokes Ajax's psychic turmoil (cf. 205-7). Fittingly he will remain sitting, rather than standing (cf. 426-7, 545), for the next 250 lines, during which time he will decide to commit suicide.

114   Here begins the second half of the Act I (201-595); it has five parts (see note at 201 for full analysis of Act I). This intense lyric dialogue is the first of those five parts. The first lyric dialogue (201-62) at the beginning of Act I was a two-way interaction between Tecmessa speaking and the chorus-leader singing. This second lyric dialogue (348-429) is a more complex three-way interaction with Ajax singing (three strophic pairs) while the chorus-leader and Tecmessa speak (although only intermittently). Ajax dominates this scene.

115   Anyone who is against Ajax has gone astray from 'the right way' (of loyal friendship).

The deed before us shows how completely he is out of his mind.[116]   355

Antistrophe #1

Ajax   *(singing)*
O comrades of my crew,
you who helped me navigate our ships skillfully,
you who embarked with me, plying the oar through the ocean,
I see that you, alone of my shepherds,
will assist me.   360
Well, come, slay me![117]

Chorus-leader
Hush! Don't speak so blasphemously! Don't treat evil
with an evil cure[118] and keep adding to the anguish of your doom!

Strophe #2

Ajax   *(singing)*
Don't you see me—the bold, the brave-hearted,
the fearless fighter of his foe! Yes, me, so awesome   365
in the might of my hands amidst harmless beasts!
Alas the howling laughter! Alas the utter humiliation![119]

Tecmessa
I beseech you, lord Ajax, do not keep saying such things.

   Tecmessa approaches Ajax near the door of his hut.

Ajax
Won't you get out of here?[120] Be gone to other pastures!
Aiai, aiai!   370

---

116 The sight of Ajax sitting amidst a heap of slain sheep leads the chorus to think Ajax is 'out of his mind' (a-phrontistôs, similar to our 'schizo-phrenia'). Earlier Tecmessa told the chorus that Ajax had returned to 'sanity' (phronimos, 259) and the chorus-leader had begun to think the same thing (phronein, 344) but soon Tecmessa will urge Ajax to 'come to his senses' (phronêson, 371). Clearly the boundary line between sanity and insanity is not clear.

117 An abrupt, emphatic, and shocking request. This is the first time Ajax openly expresses his wish to die (cf. 326), although the exact meaning of this line in Greek is unclear (either "Slay me!" or "Slay me together with the cattle!" or "Help me slay myself!").

118 The choral concern about Ajax applying 'an evil cure' (akos) to his evil disease reminds us that not long ago his seemingly happy illusions of imaginary triumph constituted an 'incurable' joy (an-akestos, 51).

119 At 303-4 Ajax was the one subjecting his enemies to laughter (gelôs) and humiliation (hybris); now those same two potent words are reused here, but this time Ajax is on the receiving end. Ironically Odysseus, the man whom Ajax most fears mocking him with laughter (gelôs, 79), has already steadfastly refused Athena's offer to do so.

120 Why is Ajax so rude to Tecmessa? Because he failed to follow her prudent advice at 288-91?

Tecmessa

By the gods, yield and come to your senses!

Ajax

Ah me, my unhappy fate! I've let those god-damned fiends
slip from my hands!
Instead I assaulted cattle with crooked horns
and those *famous* flocks of goats,   375
spilling their black blood.

Chorus-leader

But why go on grieving after a deed that's been done?[121]
For these things could not be other than they are.

Antistrophe #2

Ajax   *(singing)*

O you who see everything, who hear everything,
instrument of evil, son of Laertes,   380
filthiest trickster in all the army,
how loudly you must be laughing in your delight!

Chorus-leader

Everyone laughs and weeps by the whim of the gods.

Ajax

Would that I, though shattered by disaster, could see him!
Io moi moi!   385

Chorus-leader

Say nothing too proud! Don't you *see* what ruin you're in?

Ajax

O Zeus, father of my ancestors,[122]
if only I could kill that treacherous trickster,
that repugnant rogue,
and those twin-sceptered kings   390
before I finally die myself![123]

Tecmessa

When you pray for this, pray as well for me to die
together with you. For why should I live once you're dead?

---

121 So Macbeth: "Things without all remedy should be without regard: what's done is done." (III.2.11-12). And the sleep-walking Lady Macbeth, holding a candle to dispel the memory of murder: "What's done cannot be undone. To bed, to bed, to bed." (V.i.59)

122 Aeacus, Ajax's grandfather, was the son of Zeus and Aegina (Iliad 21.189); for a full genealogy chart see Appendix Two.

123 Suicide is perhaps on Ajax's mind.

Strophe #3

Ajax   *(singing)*

Io, darkness, my light!
O gloom of the underworld, to eyes like mine most bright![124]   395
Take me, both of you,
take me to live in your house,
take me! For I am no longer worthy
to look upon the race of gods for any help
or upon the race of men, creatures of a day.   400
It is Zeus' daughter, valiant goddess,
who tortures me to my destruction.[125]
So where is one to flee?
Where shall I go? Where shall I stay?
[If every conceivable way of escape has disappeared   405
and revenge is close at hand to repay my devotion
to such a foolish hunt][126]
and all the army, with swords brandished
in both hands, would slay me?

Tecmessa

Alas, I am indeed a wretched woman—that so sound a soldier   410
should speak such words which he would never before have dared.

Antistrophe #3

Ajax   *(singing)*

Ah, you rushing rivers that surge to the sea,
you caves along the coast and wooded pastures on the shore,
for a long time, much too long,
you have detained me at Troy.   415
But no longer will you keep me here,
no longer will I draw up the breath of life.
Let the man of sense understand this.
O neighboring streams of the Scamander[127]
so well-disposed to all the other Greeks,   420
no, no longer shall *you* look upon *me*

---

124 In this striking double oxymoron, the normal symbolism of light = life / joy is reversed (cf. *Iliad* 17.645-6). Similarly Oedipus, ashamed of his patricide and incest, chooses the blackness of blindness.

125 For the first time Ajax understands Athena to be the agent of his destruction. How he learns this is never made clear (cf. 450-53).

126 The brackets here (and elsewhere) indicate textual difficulty in the Greek original.

127 Chief river of the Trojan plain and hence a frequent landmark in the *Iliad*. Hector called his son Scamander though all others called the boy Asty-anax, 'lord of the city' (*Iliad* 6.402).

—I shall speak a mighty word—
a soldier such as Troy never saw
in all the armada that sailed
from the Greek land.   425
But now I lie here thus, in the dust,
stripped of honor.[128]

Chorus-leader

In truth I don't have the power to restrain you but I don't know how
I am to let you speak on, so grave are the evils into which you have fallen.

Ajax[129]

Aiai! Who ever would have dreamt that this name of mine,   430
Aias, would echo so exactly these agonies of mine?[130]
Twice now I have cause to cry out *ai ai*—
even thrice—with such calamity have I collided!
For I am a man whose *father*, after having won by his battle-prowess
the first prize of all the army, and the most beautiful one,[131]   435
returned home from this land of Mt. Ida[132], crowned with glory.
But I, the *son* of that man—after sailing with no less strength
to the very same Troy and having defended the Greeks
no less by the deeds of my hand—
I die in such disgrace, stripped of honor by the Greeks.   440
And yet this much, at least, I think I know:
if Achilles had still been alive and was to award to anyone

---

128 This is the essence of Ajax's problem; without 'honor / worth' (*timê*) he is nothing (cf. 440). In the prologue he had proudly boasted to Athena (98): "So that never again will those two dishonor Ajax!"

129 **Ajax's first major speech:** After his outpouring of emotion in the preceding lyric dialogue (348-429), Ajax suddenly becomes calmer and analyzes his situation rationally. This crucial speech reveals the constitution of his world view and what he considers important. The speech's two sections move from his deep feeling of shame at dishonoring his father and being mocked by his enemies (430-56) to his possible responses to that public disgrace (457-80). Ajax's subsequent speeches (545-82, 646-92, 815-65) might be said to be fuller articulations of the main points set forth here.

130 The first major speech of Ajax (Greek *Aias*) begins explosively with a cry of pain as he realizes that the painful sound of the repeated syllables of *aiai* (which he had first cried out at 370) echoes his own name; in other words he realizes that his Greek name *Aias* means 'he who is destined to cry aiai, woe, woe' (cf. 904, 914). Although in Sophocles' play Ajax's name carries his tragic destiny, in Athenian history it did not; as one of the city's ten mythical heroes Ajax gave his name to the *Aiantis*, one of the ten tribes of Athens.

131 Ajax's father, Telamon, won first prize for his 'battle-prowess' (*aristeia*: 434, 1300) in the first Trojan War; that prize was 'the very beautiful' princess, Hesione, daughter of Laomedon, King of Troy.

132 This was large mountain range southeast of Troy, along the coast, which dominated the geography of the Troad; from Mt. Ida's heights flowed the Scamander River and its tributary, the Simoeis.

his armor[133] as the first prize for prowess, no one else
would have snatched them before me. But, as it turned out,
the sons of Atreus procured them for a man who is a scheming   445
stop-at-nothing scoundrel, and they have thrust aside *my* triumphs.
If my distorted eyes and warped wits hadn't swerved perversely
from my intention, never would they have put a matter of justice
to the vote in this way against another man.
But, as it turned out, just when I raised my hand to slay them,   450
Zeus's daughter, the invincible goddess with grim Gorgon eyes,[134]
tripped me up, casting upon me a fit of lunatic frenzy
so that I steeped my hands in the blood of these dumb beasts.
Now those men exult, laughing at me because they have escaped,
though certainly without *my* consent.[135] But if someone of the gods 455
should strike, truly even the coward could elude the braver man.
So now what must I do?[136] Since clearly I am hated
by the gods, detested by the Greek army,
and abhorred by all of Troy and these her plains!
Shall I sail homeward across the Aegean, abandoning my station   460
by the anchored ships and leaving the sons of Atreus all alone?
And what face shall I show[137] when I appear before my father,
Telamon? How will he ever bear to look upon me
when I appear naked, stripped of the prize for prowess,
a prize which *he* won as a great crown of glory?   465
No, doing *that* is intolerable.[138] Well, shall I charge the ramparts
of the Trojans, dueling alone against them alone, performing
some useful deed and then, at the end of it all, perishing?
Such action would, no doubt, delight the sons of Atreus.

---

133 This is the first mention of the famous contest for the arms of Achilles. Ajax believes that Achilles, had he been alive, would have awarded his panoply to Ajax. And he believes that Odysseus stole them. But those are just his opinions; nothing in *Ajax* establishes them as facts.

134 Athena's regular Homeric epithet is 'with gleaming eyes' (*glauk-ôpis*); Ajax sarcastically substitutes 'with grim Gorgon eyes' (*gorg-ôpis*). Medusa was a Gorgon (an underworld female monster; *Odyssey* 11.633) whose head was cut off (by Perseus) and put on the shield of Athena. Athenians would have been very familiar with Ajax's visualization here because the famous forty foot statue in the Parthenon of Athena held a large Gorgeion (Medusa's head) on her shield. Its (apotropaic) purpose was to ward off evil (and the evil eye).

135 Parts of Ajax might be crushed by the slings and arrows of outrageous fortune, but his *will* is not one of those parts.

136 This is the fundamental question of all Greek tragedies and marks the radicalization of human responsibility: a character faces a crisis and must make an existential decision that only he or she can make.

137 The important motif of 'face/eyes' runs throughout the play and reflects importantly on the theme of shame; see note at 1004.

138 Ajax rejects possibility #1 (457-66), i.e. going home / desertion.

No, *that* cannot be.[139] Some test must be sought[140]   470
such that from it I'll show my aged father that in my real nature,
at least, the son who was born from him is no gutless coward.
Shameful it is for the man who experiences
no change in his miseries to desire a long life.[141]
For what joy abides in tomorrow, and tomorrow, and tomorrow,   475
now pushing the pieces towards death's door, now pulling them back?
I count as worthless the kind of man
who warms himself with vain and vacuous hopes.
To live with honor or die with honor—that is the choice
the man of nobility[142] must make.[143] You have heard the whole story.[144]   480

Chorus-leader

No one will ever say, Ajax, that you've given a bastard speech.
No, it is a child of your own heart. Yet all the same,
stop and permit your friends to overrule your purpose
so that you dismiss these anxious thoughts.[145]

---

139   Ajax rejects possibility #2 (466-70), i.e. rushing the ramparts alone.

140   The play began with Odysseus putting Ajax to the 'test' (*peira*, 2) after Ajax's 'enterprise / test' (289) had put Odysseus to the test; so, despite all their differences, these two Homeric heroes think alike in a fundamental way. Given Athena's upending of Ajax's 'enterprise / test' (1057) against Odysseus, the desperate man must find now some final 'test' to prove to his father that he is a man of nobility.

141   Having indicated his intention, Ajax now explains his reasons for choosing suicide (473-80).

142   The word for 'nobility' is *eu-genês* (as in *Eugene* or *eugenics*); this is its first appearance in the play (cf. 524, 1095, 1229). *Eu-geneia* means both 'nobility of birth' and 'nobility of character.' Ajax focuses heavily on the former, i.e. on living up to the reputation of his 'father' (*patêr*: 434, 462, 471; cf. 437, 463, 472). The play raises, in a fundamental way, what it means to be a 'man (or woman) of nobility.' Hamlet's "to be or not to be" raises a similar question.

143   Ajax must choose possibility #3 (470-480), because it is better to be a dead lion than a living dog. That is *the heroic code*, which was first and most famously expressed in the *Iliad* when Achilles spoke about having to choose between a short life with glory or a long one without it (9. 410-16; cf. Ajax at 15.511-13). It is not accidental that Ajax mentions Achilles by name at 442.

144   Not quite the 'whole' story: stunningly there is not one mention of Tecmessa in Ajax's 51 line speech – as if, in his solitude (and solipsism) he had not even felt her presence. And only in this last sentence does Ajax curtly acknowledge the presence of the chorus-leader.

145   These four verses by the chorus-leader bridge Ajax's and Tecmessa's long speeches and anticipate her attempt to persuade Ajax to overrule his present purpose.

Tecmessa[146]

O master Ajax, the crushing misfortune imposed by necessity[147]   485
is certainly the gravest evil that grips mortals.
I was born the daughter of a father who was *free*—
prosperous and powerful if any Phrygian was.[148]
But now I'm a *slave*. For so it was decreed by the gods, I suppose,
and above all by your strong hand. That's why, since the time   490
I came to share your bed, I consider only *your* best interests.
So I beseech you, by Zeus who has watched over our hearth
and by the bed wherein you were joined with me,
don't deem me worthy to suffer the stinging rumor of your foes,
letting me fall into some stranger's hands!   495
For on the day you die and by your death desert me,
be sure that on that selfsame day I shall be seized
and man-handled by the Greeks and, together with your son,
shall eat the nurturing bread of bondage.
Then some master of mine will greet me scornfully,   500
shooting from his bow some insult such as this:
    "Behold this lady, the bed-mate of Ajax,
    once the army's mightiest warrior!
    The nurturing mother's enviable life
    now exchanged for a slave's lowly subsistence!"   505
Such will be some master's insult. Thus it is that destiny will harass me;
but for you *and* your family these words will bring shame.
So respect and honor your father—feel shame before him.
Don't abandon him in grim old age. Feel shame, too,

---

146 **Tecmessa's second major speech:** Because of its high emotional charge this beautiful speech is not so
easily broken down into sections but there seems to be something like a three-part movement: 485-504 =
a reckoning of her fate as a slave to the Greeks if Ajax dies; 505-513 = an emphatic appeal to his sense of
shame / pity for his family; 514-24 = a reckoning of her hard life, both past and future if Ajax dies, with
an emphatic final appeal for him to remember her domestic kindnesses to him. Sophocles has modeled
Tecmessa's speech on the poignant appeal of Andro-mache ('She who fights for her man') to her husband
Hector ('Holder of the city') begging him not to go outside Troy's gates to fight Achilles. If he does, and
dies, his son Astyanax ('Lord of the city') will be left an orphan and his wife a widow. Andromache concludes by famously calling Hector her "father, mother, brother and husband" (*Iliad* 6.407-39). Echoing
this Tecmessa beseeches Ajax to show respect for his family— father, mother, son, and wife (506-13).

147 Tecmessa's potent expression *anankaia tychê* is not easily rendered: literally it means 'a (mis)chance imposed
by necessity', hence 'a fateful chance' or 'a doom imposed by fate' or 'the crushing calamity that leaves
its victim no chance of escape.' Here she means her imminent fate as a *slave*. In a similar context Hector
uses the phrase 'strong necessity' of the imminent *slavery* facing Andromache if he should die (*Iliad* 6.
458; cf. 16.835). Later, after Tecmessa has heard the ominous messenger's report about Ajax's fate, she
will repeat the exact same phrase (*anankaia tychê*, 803). And later still, after she has discovered Ajax's
corpse, she will speak of the imminent 'yoke of slavery' (944).

148 The word Phrygian is a synonym for Trojan (cf. 1054); sometimes it is meant pejoratively (as at 1292);
cf. note at 210.

before your mother,[149] shareholder of many long years.   510
Often she prays to the gods that you return home alive.
And pity your son, my lord, who, if robbed of the nurture
of youth, will pass his life alone, bereaved of you,
under the eye of orphan-masters who are neither kin nor kind.
Consider how great will be the evil you bequeath that boy and me   515
when you die. For me there is no longer anything to which I can look
except you. You annihilated my fatherland with your spear
and another destiny struck down my mother and father.[150]
So now they dwell, dead, in dark halls of Hades.
What fatherland, then, could there be for me except you?   520
What prosperity could I have? *All* my safety depends on you.
So hold fast the memory of me, too. Surely for a true man
it is right to cherish memory, if perhaps he has enjoyed some pleasure.
Of kindness kindness is the mother always.[151]
From whomsoever such memory fades,[152] after he has been   525
treated well, he could nevermore be reckoned a man of nobility.[153]

Chorus-leader

Ajax, I could wish you had pity in your heart even as I have;[154]
for then you would praise this woman's words.

Ajax

Yes, she will most certainly obtain praise from me
if only she will undertake to do exactly what is commanded.

---

149 Here, at the exact center of her speech, Tecmessa appeals emphatically to Ajax's strong sense of 'shame' (*aidôs / aischros*), using the word three times in three lines (505-7); for the importance of this theme, see the note at 345. Ajax's mother was Eriboea, daughter of Alcathoüs, king of Megara (cf. 569).

150 Sophocles does not say how Tecmessa's parents died but he goes out of his way to make clear that Ajax did not kill them.

151 Tecmessa's word for 'kindness' (*charis*) has a wide range of meanings – 'grace', 'gratitude,' 'good will,' 'favor', even 'sexual favor' (as Tecmessa implies at 521). Something of the semantic range of *charis* is captured in our words 'eu-*charist*' and '*charis*-ma.' Tecmessa is stressing here the reciprocal nature of *charis*; indeed my translation, at the risk of being clumsy, imitates Tecmessa's emphatic juxtaposition *charis charin*; she has shown 'kindness' to Ajax and deserves 'kindness' in return. The metaphor and *personification* of 'kindness as *mother*' is itself the rhetoric of a mother who 'always' (that is Tecmessa's emphatic last word) tries to start from a place of good 'grace.' But insinuating this ethos into the blood-drenched killer sitting in front of her is a tall order; indeed later she will say that she has been 'deceived' about him and 'thrown out of his former *kindness*' (807-8).

152 Tecmessa repeats words for 'memory' (*mnêmê*) three times in four lines; she is urging Ajax to bear *authentic* witness to the 'good will' she has lavished on him.

153 Tecmessa ends her 40 line speech with the same word 'nobility' (*eu-genês*, literally = 'good / noble birth') that ended Ajax's 51 line speech (at 480). Her use of the word and its careful placement is a clear (if gentle) rebuttal of his: Ajax thinks of nobility in *martial* terms (war), she thinks of it in *marital* terms (family).

154 Will Ajax be moved by Tecmessa's pleas? Sophocles holds the answer in suspense during this transitional passage of *stichomythia* (rapid single-line exchange) at 525-44.

Tecmessa

Of course, my beloved Ajax, I will obey your every word.

Ajax

Then bring me my son so that I may see him.   530

Tecmessa

Oh, but in my terror I released him from my keeping.

Ajax

During these troubles of mine, or what exactly do you mean?

Tecmessa

Yes, afraid that somehow in his misfortune he might meet you and die.

Ajax

That would truly have been in character with my destiny.

Tecmessa

Well anyhow, I guarded him so as to prevent that happening.   535

Ajax

I applaud your deed and the forethought you showed.

Tecmessa

Then how, under these circumstances, can I help you?

Ajax

Allow me to speak to him and see him face to face.

Tecmessa

Certainly. He is being guarded by servants nearby.

Ajax

Then what's the delay in his arrival?   540

Tecmessa

Son, your father is calling you. Bring him here, servant,
whichever one of you is just now guiding him with your hands.

Ajax

Is he coming, the man you're calling, or hasn't he heard your word?

Tecmessa

Here comes one of the servants right now bringing the boy near.

Enter Eurysaces down a side-ramp, led by a servant holding his hand.

Ajax[155]

Lift him up, lift him up here![156] For he won't be frightened   545
to look on this newly-slaughtered blood, if he is truly mine,
truly his father's son. But straightaway he must be broken in,
like a young colt, to the rugged and raw customs of his father[157]
and moulded to the likeness of his nature.

The servant lifts Eurysaces over the animal carcasses and into Ajax's arms.

O son, may you prove luckier than your father[158], but like him   550
in all other ways; then you would prove yourself no coward!
Yet even now I have cause to envy you for this at least,
that you have no inkling of these ills. Yes, the sweetest life
consists of ignorance, understanding nothing—that is,
till time teaches you joy and sorrow. But when you come to this,   555
you must show your father's foes your birth and breeding[159]—
what sort of son you are and by what sort of father you were reared.
Meanwhile be nourished by light breezes and cherish
your boyhood days, a joy to your mother here.[160]
Of one thing I am certain: *none* of the Greeks will insult you   560
with hateful scorn even though you are separated from me.
So staunch a gate-keeper is Teucer whom I shall leave him behind
as the resolute and unhesitating guardian of your nurture[161]
even if at the moment he is gone far off, hunting down enemies.

To the Chorus

Shield-bearers and seamen,   565
to you, as to him, I charge this common kindness;

---

155   **Ajax's second major speech**: This final farewell to his son is modeled on Hector's to Astyanax (*Iliad* 6. 466-84). It can be broken down into three parts: 545-57 = the training of Eurysaces in his father's rugged ways; 558-64 = Teucer's role as guardian in Ajax's absence; 565-82 = instructions to Teucer (via the chorus): to bring the boy to Telamon; to bury Ajax's weapons with Ajax; and to give his shield to Eurysaces.

156   Ajax's impatient command to the servant leading Eurysaces suggests that Ajax is at higher than ground level, i.e. that he is still on the trolley (*eccyclēma*) which rolled him in at 348.

157   A lovely oxymoron in Greek (*ōmos nomos*), summing up succinctly the paradox that is Ajax. The word for 'custom' (*nomos*) represents the norms of *civilized* life, while the adjective 'raw' (*ōmos*) represents the *savagery* of the animal world. Normally one 'breaks in' a colt for the purpose of *taming*; this father is not interested in taming his son. On Ajax's 'rawness' see note at 205.

158   Ajax imagines that his calamity has come about by bad *luck*! (The word 'luckier' might also be translated 'happier'.)

159   'Nobility' for Ajax is consistently related to birth, i.e. to one's father.

160   Are these words (three in Greek) signs of tenderness towards Tecmessa? It hardly seems so. This is the only mention of her in the entire speech (which is his farewell to his son, not Tecmessa) and her pleas for 'kindness' (*charis*) have been totally rejected, as she will later emphasize (808).

161   Sophocles keeps us waiting, as he did at 342-3, for the appearance of Teucer, but he is giving us a good idea of what we will see.

and tell Teucer my bidding,
namely to bring this boy to my home and show him
to Telamon and to my mother, I mean Eriboea,[162]
so that he may always support and nourish their old age   570
[until they reach the innermost chambers of the god below].
As for *my* armor, there shall be no contest of setting them up
as a prize[163]—no, no judges, certainly not the man who wrecked me!

To Eurysaces

But you, son, take the very thing that begets your name Eurysaces[164]—
'Broad-shield'—wielding it by the strong-sewn arm-strap,[165]   575
my seven-fold leather-laden spear-proof shield![166]
The rest of the arms will have been buried in my grave with me.[167]

To Tecmessa (crying)

Quickly now, receive this child here and shut the house up tight!
And don't keep up this weeping and wailing in front of the hut!
Truly she's prone to pity and wont to wail, a woman.[168]   580
Shut the door double-quick! It's not the mark of a skilled surgeon

---

162 Ajax stresses that he doesn't mean Teucer's mother, Hesione, a Trojan princess captured in war (1301-3). Ajax says very little about his mother and she is named only here (cf. 508); Telamon is named 7 times and referred to often.

163 Ajax has two concerns: first, his son (570) and second, his armor. He insists that after his death there will be no 'contest' nor 'judges' (*agôn-archai*) over his armor as there was over the (misappropriated) armor of Achilles. But the entire second 'half' of the play (866-1420) will be an *agôn* over Ajax's corpse (and, by extension, his armor) and the man at the center of rescuing that corpse and those arms will be, ironically, Odysseus, 'the man who wrecked me.' On the 'contest' as a theme, see note at 194.

164 Ajax is playing on the etymology of his son's name: *Eury* = 'broad' and *sakos* = 'shield'. Ajax makes the pun clear by beginning 574 with the Greek name *Eury-sakes* and ending 575 with *sakos* ('shield') so that the couplet is neatly framed.

165 Are we to imagine that the shield is actually onstage and that the boy puts his hand in the arm-strap? Probably not. First, there is little evidence for it; this is the only passage that has any suggestion of the on-stage presence of the shield. Virtually all important stage action in Greek tragedy is given clear signaling by the text. Second, Ajax states emphatically that his armor, with the exception of the shield, *will have been buried with me* (577); he is clearly looking towards the future in response to Tecmessa's charge of being abandoned. The shield *will* be his protection of them *after* he has committed suicide. Third, it would have been a huge stage-prop on an already crowded 'trolley' (if indeed the animal carcasses were represented somehow realistically).

166 The four Greek words that make up this line express the extraordinary nature of Ajax's shield; Teucer's shield had only four layers of ox-hide (*Iliad* 15.479).

167 Ajax's emphatic and unusual verb form 'will have been buried' (a future perfect passive!) underscores his confidence that he will be buried as a hero. Teucer will exhibit the same confidence when, referring to Ajax's corpse, he repeats the very same verb form at 1141.

168 Ajax's gruffness suggests that Tecmessa has started to weep. In Greek the words 'pity' and 'wailing / lamenting' are the same (*oiktos*). Earlier she had begged for 'pity' (*oiktos*, 510; cf. 525) but all she will get is 'wailing' (*oiktos*, 895).

to chant somber incantations over a pain that calls for cutting.[169]

Chorus-leader

I become afraid when I hear such vehement zeal
and your tongue with its sharpened edge[170] gives me no pleasure.

Tecmessa

My lord Ajax, what ever do you desire to do in your heart?[171]   585

Ajax

Stop the questions and cross-examination! Restraint is a splendid thing![172]

Tecmessa

O how my spirit sinks! As a suppliant I beg you
by your very own son and by the gods, do not betray us!

Ajax

You vex me much too much. *The gods*! Don't you understand
that in no way am I still a debtor under bond to them!   590

Tecmessa

Hush! Don't speak so blasphemously!

Ajax

                                        And you, speak to those who listen.[173]

Tecmessa

But won't you be persuaded?

Ajax

                        You already speak far too much.

Tecmessa

Yes, because I am frightened, my lord.[174]

Ajax

                                        Servants, won't you shut the doors right now!

---

169   Ajax mocks Tecmessa for her belief in the healing power of incantations but Homer tells the story of a young Odysseus being wounded in a boar hunt and of the men who "stayed the black blood by singing an incantation." (*Ody.* 19.457-8). In referring to a pain that calls for the 'cutting' (*tomos*) of the surgeon's knife Ajax foreshadows the 'very sharp cutting' (*tomô-tatos*) that he will describe at 815 and enact at 865.

170   The chorus-leader picks up on Ajax's last image of the pain that calls for 'cutting.'

171   585-95: Another bridge passage of rapid *single*-line exchange (*stichomythia*) between Ajax and Tecmessa that culminates in the tense *half*-line exchange (*antilabe*) at 591-5 (cf. 981-3).

172   Ajax's words are doubly ironic. First, he is hardly a man who has shown 'restraint / sound-mindedness' (*sophrôsyne*). Secondly, it was his arch-enemy, Athena, who first gave this advice (132-3) and when she did, her target was Ajax's lack of restraint.

173   A major part of Tecmessa's problem is that Ajax just does not listen to her (cf. 287-94).

174   This line, with its emphasis on Tecmessa's 'being frightened' (*tarbein*) forms a ring composition with the same verb at 545 when Eurysaces came on stage and Ajax asserted that he would not 'be frightened' (*tarbein*) by the blood-shed around him. Thus the entire scene from the boy's entrance to his exit (all the time being cradled in Ajax's blood-soaked arms) is surrounded by words of 'fear.'

Tecmessa

In the name of the gods, be softened.[175]

Ajax

You seem to me to think like a fool
if you suppose that even now you can school my character.[176]   595

Exit Ajax (on the trolley) into the hut, followed by Tecmessa and Eurysaces

Second Choral Song (= First Stasimon)[177]

Strophe 1

O island of glory, Salamis,
you dwell, if I recall,
happily amidst the sea that strikes your shores,
conspicuous and in full view to all eyes always.
But for me in my misery *ancient is the time*   600
[when I wait in Troy's grassy meadows
beneath Mt. Ida][178] *and immeasurable are the months*
when I make my bed,
always worn away by time,[179]
holding the evil expectation that one day soon   605
I shall complete the journey
to the abhorred Hades,
invisible annihilator[180] who cannot be turned away.

---

175 These are Tecmessa's final words to Ajax.

176 These are Ajax's final words to Tecmessa. After 395 lines Act I comes to a heart-breaking and ominous end. Four of the last five verses (591-4) are divided between the two speakers to create maximum tension. This technique of *half*-line exchange, called *antilabê*, is used very sparingly (cf. 981-3).

177 This is the first *stasimon* or choral song 'proper' (to be distinguished from the two preceding 'lyric *dialogues*'). The word *stasimon* refers to any choral ode after the Entrance Song (*parodos*) that is sung by the chorus alone, i.e. without the participation of actors. There are no actors on stage during the singing and dancing of this ode which has 4 stanzas: Strophe #1 (596-608) = a yearning for the homely pleasures of Salamis after 9 wearying and dangerous years at Troy; Antistrophe #1 (609-21) = a lamenting of Ajax's *god-sent madness* and loss of heroic stature (*aretê*); Strophe #2 (622-34) = an imagining of the sorrow of Ajax's aged mother (Eriboea) when she hears his fate; and Antistrophe #2 (635-45) = an imagining of Ajax as better off dead than alive and an imagining, too, of the sorrow of Ajax's father (Telamon).

178 The brackets here (as throughout) indicate textual problems in the Greek.

179 The piling up of seven 'time' words in five verses underscores how, for the chorus, the wearying years at Troy seem like an eternity. This is a perfect set-up for Ajax's forthcoming speech in which he focuses on 'time' using similar words (e.g. 'immeasurable time') but from his long perspective the entire Trojan War will seem like just a fleeting moment.

180 Sophocles puns on the ambiguity of Hades' name which means *both* 'he who is unseen' (i.e. invisible) because mortals cannot see death coming *and* 'he who makes (one) unseen' (i.e. the annihilator). The word-play underscores the finality of death.

Antistrophe 1

And now Ajax sits beside me, hard-to-heal,
a new competitor whom I must wrestle in the contest—   610
oimoi, moi—who shares his home with a madness sent by the gods.[181]
In some bygone day, Salamis, you launched him forth
full of power, full of Ares' impetuous war-spirit.
But now, a lonely shepherd of his mind's thoughts,
he's been found to be a mighty sorrow to his friends.[182]   615
And the former deeds of his hands,
deeds of mightiest valor,
have fallen, fallen to ruin,
hateful deeds in the eyes of those hateful men,
the loathsome sons of Atreus.   ·   620

Strophe 2

Surely his mother,
nursed by ancient days,
white and wizened from old age,
upon hearing of the sickness
that eats at his heart   625
—cry woe, cry woe—
the ill-fated woman won't refrain
from the nightingale's dirge, that piteous bird.[183]
No, she'll shriek shrill songs of sorrow
while the thuds   630
of thumping hands
will fall
on her breasts,
and a tearing of grizzled hair.

Antistrophe 2

Yes, better hidden in Hades would be the man   635

---

181 Earlier the chorus had wondered if Ajax's ailment might not be 'a god-sent _sickness_' (_theia nosos_, 185); now they identify it more accurately as 'a god-sent _madness_' (_theia mania_).

182 Ajax has become a _mega penthos_, 'mighty sorrow,' to those who love him. Something similar happened to Menelaus, king of Sparta. After Helen was abducted to Troy with Paris, Menelaus fathered a son (by a slave) whom he named _Mega-penthes_, 'Mighty Sorrow,' in honor of his much-missed Helen (_Ody._ 4. 11).

183 This bird personifies a mother's perpetual plaintive lamenting at the loss of a son. The story goes that wicked King Tereus of Thrace married the Athenian princess Procne, then raped her sister Philomela. To avenge this barbaric act Procne murdered their son Itys, cooked his flesh, and served it to Tereus. He, in turn, chased Procne (and her sister Philomela) but the gods turned Procne into a nightingale (and Philomela into a swallow). Sophocles told this story in a (lost) tragedy entitled _Tereus_.

who suffers from sick senses straying idly,[184]
he who came from his father's lineage
to the noblest station of all the war-worn Achaeans,
yet is no longer steadfast in his nurturing passion;[185]
no, now he stands estranged from that disposition.   640
What misery awaits you, forlorn father,
soon to learn the hard-to-bear ruin of your son,
a doom such as no lifetime of any of the descendants
of Aeacus[186] has ever yet nurtured
apart from this man right here![187]   645

Act Two[188]

> *Enter Ajax from his hut, sword in hand, followed by Tecmessa.*

Ajax

All things, in his long and immeasurable march, Time[189]
begets[190] from darkness into the light and then once again hides.[191]

---

184   The chorus emphatically begins their final stanza with a way of thinking that is new for them: Ajax is
      going to die from his madness and, indeed, would be better off dead than alive; similarly the chorus in
      Oedipus Rex (1367-8) after seeing that their king has blinded himself.

185   Ajax was once a man of nurturing passion (*trophê*) but all that has changed; the chorus foreshadows the
      theme of change in Ajax's 'deception' speech (646-92).

186   He was Ajax's grandfather, i.e. father of Telamon and Peleus (Achilles' father); such illustrious descendants
      made the Aeacidae a renowned clan; see the genealogy chart in Appendix Two.

187   The sailors presumably point toward Ajax in his hut, as if to cue his entrance.

188   Ajax's so-called 'deception' or 'dissembling' speech; on the reason that it is called such, see the note to
      line 807. This is certainly one of the most beautiful and complex of all monologues in Greek drama.
      It is highly unusual for one speech to comprise an entire Act. Ajax enters carrying his sword, followed
      by Tecmessa; at the end they depart by *opposite* side-ramps. The speech has four parts: 646-49 = brief
      introduction on the power of Time; 650-66 = Ajax's pity for Tecmessa and Eurysaces; 667-83 = his
      recognition that, because of the iron law of mutability, one must learn to *yield*; and 684-92 = direct
      addresses / instructions to Tecmessa and chorus.

189   Ajax bookends his memorable opening verse with the speech's key thematic words.

190   Ajax opens with a radically new perspective, as if a philosopher were speaking. This is unexpected
      because his brusque dismissal of Tecmessa had made clear that his character (*êthos*, 595) was not subject
      to being schooled (i.e. changed). In Ajax's absence during the previous choral ode (596-645) his sailors
      had reflected on their miserable ten year sojourn at Troy, speaking of 'ancient time…immeasurable…over
      time' (*palaios…chronos…an-ârithmos chronôi*, 600-4). Now Ajax similarly speaks of 'long and immeasur-
      able time' (*macros…an-arithmêtos chronos*, 646), unwittingly reflecting the choral language but thinking
      from a much broader perspective. His emphatic first word *apanta*, 'all things,' reveals immediately that
      he now sees himself as just one part of a much vaster cosmos *and* as subject to its vicissitudes.

191   Ajax pronounces his central theme boldly and beautifully in this line's chiastic (a-b-b-a) word-order: verb
      ('begets') – noun ('darkness') – noun ('light') – verb ('hides'). 'Everything' (*apanta*, 646) is circumscribed
      by the long march of 'Time' (*Chronos*) who begets all life from obscurity and then conceals it again. Ajax
      has come to understand, at least on an intellectual level (cf. 677-8), that the very *being* of human beings
      is framed by the horizon of *time*, which is to say, framed by inevitable *change*. This old-school warrior
      has come face to face with an unsettling paradox: one of life's *unchanging* truths is that it is constantly
      changing.

There is nothing not-to-be-expected[192] but even the fierce oath
is taken prisoner by time and proven weak; so, too, stubborn wills.
For even I—who was lately so fierce and firm, like iron hardened   650
by dipping[193]—yes, my speech has become womanish and weak
and my sharp edge smoothed by this lady here.[194]
I feel pity at leaving—leaving behind, among my enemies,
a widow and her orphaned son.[195] Well, I shall go to the bathing-place
and meadows by the shore to wash away my defilement[196]   655
and escape the heavy wrath of the goddess.[197]
And going to where I can find some solitary spot, untrodden,
I shall hide this sword of mine[198], most hateful of my weapons,
after digging a deep pit in the earth where none shall see it.
But let night and Hades keep it safe down below.   660
For not since the moment that this hand received this sword
as a gift from Hector, my most hostile foe,[199]

---

192   Ajax's wastes no time beginning his 'deception.' At 716 the chorus repeats his adjective 'not-to-be-expected' (*a-elptos*) thinking he has decided *not* to commit suicide.

193   This is the only time Ajax uses a simile. As he holds his lethal sword, he likens his previous hardness of heart to iron hardened by dipping. Despite the suggestion of an imminent (and happy) change of mind, the image projects an ominous overtone.

194   Ajax insinuates that Tecmessa's persistent attempts at persuasion (*peithein*, 592) have, after all, softened him. But, alas, his 'keen edge' (*stoma*) is double-edged in that it can allude not only to the sharpness of his earlier 'speech' (*stoma*) but also to the sharpness of the sword in his hand.

195   Ajax's 'leaving – leaving behind' is ambiguous: does he feel pity, as she had hoped earlier (510; 525-6), at 'leaving' his wife and son, i.e. at abandoning them to the enemy, with the result that he will *not* 'leave'? Or does he feel pity because he actually *is* going to 'leave' (via suicide) and feels remorse at that choice? If that is a case of conscious ambiguity, is his 'I feel pity' (*oiktirô*) also meant to deceive or does he, in fact, really 'feel pity' for Tecmessa in the way Odysseus had earlier 'felt pity' for him (*ep-oiktirô*, 121)? His pity is not, I think, part of the deception. If, as seems clear, Ajax's *primary* ambiguity is about 'leaving,' and if Tecmessa is going to fall for that deception (as Ajax can safely assume she will), what would be the point of being deceptive about his 'pity'? Not only does that seem redundant but it also takes away from the growing complexity of Ajax's character.

196   Tecmessa understands Ajax to mean cleansing (by ritual sea-bathing) his blood-stained hands and the religious pollution of slaughtering herdsmen. He actually means to wash off *the shame of his failed expedition* (symbolized by Athena's heavy wrath) by killing himself. The seashore is traditionally associated with the solitude of heroes; Achilles went to the seashore after Agamemnon took his girlfriend Briseis and also after Hector killed his best friend Patroclus (*Iliad* 1.350; 24.12).

197   Earlier Ajax had recognized Athena as his destroyer (401-2). His word for 'wrath' (*mênis*), which recurs at 757, connotes a fierce and enduring anger desirous of revenge. *Mênis* is the first word of the *Iliad* and of Western literature: 'Wrath, sing, goddess, Achilles' wrath…'. Achilles is the only human in the *Iliad* whose wrath is indicated by *mênis* (four times); otherwise it is reserved for gods. Homer applies it once to Athena when she becomes furious with the 'Lesser' Ajax, son of Oileus, for assaulting Cassandra at her shrine in Troy: *Odyssey* 3.135; cf. 4.499.

198   Does Ajax mean he will 'hide' (*kruptein*, 658) his sword in the earth, burying it innocuously, as day 'hides' night (*kruptein*, 647), or does he mean that he will 'hide' the sword in the earth (i.e. fix it upright in a pit) so he can 'hide' it in his body (cf. 899)?

199   Ajax and Hector had a duel that was called off because of nightfall, at which time they exchanged gifts; Hector gave Ajax his fatal sword (cf. 817; *Iliad* 7.303-5).

have I yet gotten anything good from the Greeks.
Yes, it's true, the proverb that men pronounce:
"Enemies' gifts are no gifts at all and bring no benefit."[200]   665
Well then, we will know *henceforth* how to yield to the gods
and in turn we will learn how to pay homage to the sons of Atreus.[201]
They are the rulers and one must yield. Why not?[202]
For even fiercest and most powerful forces yield to the honor
and authority of office. Thus winter's snow-strewn streets give way   670
to summer's fruit-laden harvest; and the endless rotations
of night, circling round, stand aside for the white steeds
of dawn to set ablaze their radiant lamp. And the breath
of gusting gales sets the groaning sea soundly asleep.[203]
Likewise all-powerful Sleep releases those he has bound   675
but those he has captured he does not hold fast *always*.[204]
So how shall *we* not learn moderation and good sense?[205]

---

200 How can a 'gift' (*dôron*) be 'no gift' (*a-dôron*)? In a famous scene of Virgil's *Aeneid* (2.49), the Greeks wheel the Trojan Horse before the city gates as a 'gift' (i.e. religious offering) to Minerva, goddess of Troy, whereupon the prescient Trojan priest Laocoon warns his people thus: "I fear the Greeks, even when they bring gifts." (*timeo Danaos et dona ferentes*).

201 Ajax's listeners will infer from his emphatic *future* emphasis ('will…henceforth') that he has renounced suicide in favor of a 'future' life with his family. But Ajax knows that he has no such 'future.' So what does he mean by 'henceforth' and why does he use, for the first time in any of his *speeches* (cf. 407), the first person *plural* ('we'), not just once but twice? Who are the 'we' (cf. 677)?

202 Earlier Tecmessa had begged Ajax to 'yield' (371). Now he seems to agree, using 'yield' three times in four verses (667-70). But 'yielding' is the last thing one expects from the Sophoclean hero. Are we really to imagine Ajax 'yielding' and 'paying homage / reverence' (667) to the detested sons of Atreus? This seems pretty close to a lie.

203 An elliptical expression: the winds, of course, *first* stir up the sea and *then* give it rest; i.e. calm follows the storm.

204 In explaining *why* he will yield to the gods and the rulers Ajax has given three straightforward examples from the great forces of nature: winter / summer; night / day; storm / calm. But Ajax's final example (sleeping / waking) is ambiguous. Here is a literal (if clumsy) translation of 676 to help unravel the ambiguity: [All-powerful Sleep] / "loosens, having bound, and having captured, not always holds." Like verse 647 this one has a chiastic (a-b-b-a) word-order: verb ('releases') – past participle ('having bound') – past participle ('having captured') – verb ('holds'). On one level, then, Ajax's elegant syntactical chiasmus imitates the cycle of waking - sleeping / sleeping - waking. But there's a catch. We know Ajax is only going to complete the *first* half of that cycle. So how does his chiasmus communicate that? Ajax has *personified* Sleep here (contrast 674) as 'all-powerful' (*pan-cratês*), calling to mind that 'Sleep' (*Hypnos*) was the well-known *twin* brother of Death (*Iliad* 14.231). So he is thinking of Sleep as *permanent* sleep (cf. 832). Because he is 'all-powerful,' Hypnos can 'unbind' Ajax by 'binding' him (i.e. with death). Paradoxically, then, Ajax, by being 'bound' is 'released,' set free and indeed 'saved' (which is his very last word in the speech, 692). The intricacy of this ambiguity is, of course, beyond his auditors and, ironically, partially beyond Ajax himself; later this metaphor of 'loosening / binding' will reappear at a crucial juncture (1317) and 'all-powerful Sleep' will be replaced by a new and most unexpected 'loosener.'

205 The (misleading) implication is that 'we' can indeed learn 'moderation' (*sôphrosynê*). But it is one thing to *learn* it and another to *live* it, especially for Sophoclean heroes.

Well I, at least, shall. For *only now* do I understand[206]
that our enemy is to be hated only so far, knowing that
he will, in turn, become a friend hereafter; while as regards a friend
I shall want to serve and help only so far,[207] knowing that
he will not remain so *always*.[208] For to most men
the harbor of fellowship is treacherous and untrustworthy.[209]
So, as regards my intentions, all will turn out well.

[handwritten margin note, near 680]: we will be friends ... they are silent

Addressing Tecmessa directly

But you, woman,[210]
go inside and keep praying to the gods that what my heart desires   685
so passionately[211] will be completed through to the end, the very end.

Addressing the chorus of sailors

And you, comrades-in-arms, honor these wishes of mine
in the same way as this lady here. Also instruct Teucer, if he comes,
to take care of us[212] and remain loyal to you at the same time.
For I am going to the place where I must journey.[213]   690
So do what I bid you and soon, perhaps, you all might learn that

---

206 Ajax concludes here the 'self-knowledge' section (which began with '*we will know* henceforth,' 666) wherein he has explained *how* he has come to learn to yield and be moderate.

207 Ajax applies to relationships the principle of alternation that he has learned from nature: sometimes enemies become friends and friends enemies. Ajax wants his listeners to focus on the first half of the equation; he is focused on the second half. The Greeks whom he served so nobly (437-40, 616-20) have become his enemies and for him an enemy is always an enemy (665; contrast 1359).

208 Ajax has come to understand that one cannot say 'always' (*aei*) about human affairs, any more than one can say 'always' (*aei*, 676) about Sleep, or the forces of nature (670-74). On the theme of 'always' (the play's first word) see the note at 116-17.

209 The traditional moral code of 'helping your friend (*philos*) and hurting your enemy (*echthros*)' entailed a clear distinction like that between winter / summer, night / day, storm / calm, and waking / sleeping. But that distinction has now disintegrated for Ajax (as 679-84 makes evident): his friends in the supposed harbor of fellowship have become his enemies. From his own experience he extrapolates what seems to 'most men' (*hoi polloi*), the proverbial wisdom of lines 682-3. But Ajax despises the *hoi polloi* (who reappear as the 'democratic' majority vote in the judgment of Achilles' arms at 1243) and their prudential truths. If this is the brave new world he wants none of it.

210 Finally Ajax addresses Tecmessa, though not by name; he never uses her name, only the chorus-leader does (331, 784, 895). This does not mean that Ajax is unaware of her presence throughout; his preceding ambiguities must have an on-stage audience or they would be pointless.

211 More ambiguity. The verb *eraô* which Ajax uses here is the strongest Greek verb for 'sexual passion'; its noun form is *erôs* (cf. 693, 1205), whence our 'erotic.' The same verb occurs again later when Tecmessa speaks of Ajax's passionate desire for death (967). One might say, then, that Ajax, in his deep shame, had an *erôs* for *thanatos* (death), although soon (693) the chorus will misinterpret what he has said here.

212 Ajax's mention of Teucer foreshadows his forthcoming role. The plural 'us' will mislead Tecmessa to believe that Ajax is thinking of her and their son; he is really thinking of his own burial (cf. 826-30).

213 His listeners will think that Ajax is referring to the beach (654-6); he means the underworld. His expression 'I *must* journey' is striking, almost as if he has no choice; in a sense he is right, since to the road to the underworld (i.e. death) is a road we all *must* travel.

even though I am unhappy now I have been saved.[214]

Ajax exits by the side. Tecmessa re-enters Ajax's hut.

Third Choral Song[215]

Strophe

I shudder with the passion of love,[216] I soar aloft on wings of joy.
Io joy! Io joy! Pan, Pan!
Hail Pan, Pan, sea-roaming god, appear to me![217]   695
Leave behind the snow-smitten ridges of Mt. Cyllene,[218]
O lord who leads the gods in dance,
so you can join us and strike up
the dances of Mt. Nysa and of Cretan Cnossos,[219]
spontaneous self-taught dances![220]   700
Yes, now I want to dance [...]!

---

214   This is the final and most misleading of Ajax's ambiguities. Tecmessa had insisted that her being 'saved'
      (*sôizein*, 519) depended totally on him. Now that *he* has been 'saved' (*sôizein*, 692), she can believe that
      she has too. But Ajax means that he has been 'saved' because no evil can affect a dead man (cf. 394-7).
      Sophocles often ends a scene with a significant word; here the verb "I have been saved" bypasses not only
      Tecmessa but Ajax himself, the unexpected master of ambiguity; for soon, in the burial contest (*agôn*),
      Ajax, despite all his foresight (119), will be 'saved' in a way he could never have expected (cf. 648).

215   Ajax's sailors, now alone in the orchestra, explode into an ecstatic, almost erotic, Bacchic song and dance,
      convinced that Ajax has renounced his suicide plan. The song's intense joy is reflected by its brevity:
      Strophe (693-705) = a rapturous outpouring of joy invoking Pan and Apollo to join their dance; and
      Antistrophe (706-18) = the reason for the joy, Ajax's surprising change of mind. This is the one of four
      'joy-before-catastrophe' songs in the Sophocles. It may well be that he invented this technique of making
      'the fall' ever more tragic by preceding it with the chorus' delusional joy (cf. *Antigone* 1115-64; *Oedipus
      Rex* 1086-1109; *Maidens of Trachis* 633-62).

216   To express their excitement the sailors speak of shuddering with *erôs*, picking up on Ajax's earlier expres-
      sion of *erôs* ('what my heart *desires so passionately*') in the 'deception' speech (686). The noun *erôs* occurs
      in only one other passage, namely the next choral song (1204-5), when the rapturous *erôs* of the present
      moment will be emphatically extinguished.

217   Pan was the god of sudden ecstatic pleasure or fear (*pan*-ic). His name means 'guardian of flocks' so
      he was a mountain spirit. Here, however, the chorus invites him, in his role as protector of their native
      shores, to inspire their celebration on the shore of Troy. Pan's association with both dancing and Salamis
      appears already in Aeschylus' *Persians* (472 B.C.E.) where the god gained glory for guiding the Athenians
      and Salaminians in their great naval victory of 480: "There is a certain island [Psyttaleia] in front of
      Salamis...where *dance-loving Pan haunts the sea-shore*" (448-9).

218   This isolated 7,800 foot peak in northeast Arcadia (in the central Peloponnese) was the birthplace and
      home of Pan and his father Hermes.

219   The point is to strike up *lively Dionysiac dances* such as were performed in the Bacchic processions of
      satyrs and nymphs at Mt. Nysa, birthplace of Dionysus, and such as were performed on the great Cretan
      city of Cnossos, in honor of Ariadne, bride of Dionysus (cf. *Iliad* 18.590-605). Nysa was the name of
      numerous mountains, all fictional and all associated with Dionysus. It was a sacred, mystical mountain
      that traveled wherever the god's cult did and perhaps is to be linked with the second half of Dio-*nysus*.

220   The sailors need no training for their impromptu stomping and whirling.

And may Apollo, lord of Delos,[221]
traverse the Icarian Sea[222] to be with me
in presence manifest
and in spirit ever gracious.   705

Antistrophe

Ares has dispelled the dreadful sorrow from my eyes![223]
Io joy! Io joy! Now, O Zeus, now again
the shining white light of the bright day
can approach our swift sea-speeding ships
since Ajax again forgets his toils and troubles   710
and once more has fulfilled the ordinances of the gods
with all the appointed sacrifices,[224] showing due reverence
and the greatest loyalty to their divine law.
<u>All things does mighty time extinguish and then set ablaze.</u>[225]
So I would say that there is nothing that can be declared impossible   715
since Ajax, in a way not-to-be-expected, has had his mind
changed back again from his fits of anger[226]
against the sons of Atreus and from his mighty feuds!

---

221 This island was Apollo's birthplace and sacred home in the middle of the Cycladic Islands. He is invoked
     because of his association with music and dancing (and Dionysus) as well as with pollution, purification,
     and healing, all three of which Ajax needs. Delos was well-known to Sophocles' audience since it served
     as the treasury of the Delian League, an alliance formed in 478/7 against the Persians. In 454 BCE
     the Athenians, after their disastrous Egypt expedition, moved the treasury to their Acropolis for better
     security.

222 Its name is given by the island of Icaros, between Delos and Asia Minor, where Icarus, son of Daedalus,
     drowned after his wax wings melted.

223 The chorus has felt 'sorrow' (*achos*) for the last 500 lines, ever since the first choral ode when they 'stood
     stuck in sorrow' (200). As the god of war, violence, and bloodshed Ares is the daimonic power behind
     Ajax's rampage; they remarked earlier that Salamis launched forth Ajax 'full of <u>Ares</u>' impetuous war
     spirit' (613). Since Ares brings violence he can also take it away.

224 The chorus hopes that by now Ajax has gone to the seashore and performed the purification rituals that
     he promised earlier (654-6, 666-7).

225 The chorus restate Ajax's newly-learned lesson about time and mutability (646-7) because they consider
     that to be the cause of his happy change of mind.

226 Ajax had begun his 'deception' speech by claiming that there is nothing 'not-to-be-expected' (*a-elptos*,
     648). The chorus repeat his adjective, having been totally deceived by his ambiguity.

Act Three[227]

Enter Messenger by side ramp.[228]

Messenger

Dear friends, first of all, I want to make an announcement:
Teucer is here, having just returned from the steep cliffs of Mysia.[229]   720
When he reached the general's headquarters in the middle of camp
immediately he was abused by all the Greeks. For having learned
that he was coming from afar they surrounded him
and from all sides of their circle pummeled him
with a volley of abuse. There was no one who stayed out of it,   725
contemptuously calling him "the blood-brother of the madman
who plotted against the army," adding that he wouldn't succeed
in escaping the traitor's death, torn to shreds by stones.
They reached such a fever pitch that swords suddenly
stood ready in their hands, fully drawn from the sheaths.   730
But the strife, after running to its furthest bounds, ceased
when elders interceded with calmer words of conciliation.[230]
But where is our Ajax, so that I can tell him this?
For to my master I must disclose the entire tale!

Chorus-leader

He isn't in his hut but has just departed,   735
having yoked a new resolve to a new mood.[231]

Messenger

Iou! Iou![232]
Then he who sent me on this mission sent me too slow

---

227 This episode has two main parts: <u>719-814</u> = the messenger from Teucer reports that Calchas, seer of
the Greek army, has prophesized that if Ajax stays in his hut just for today, he will live hereafter free of
Athena's wrath; and <u>815-65</u> = Ajax's soliloquy and suicide. These two parts are divided at 814 by a (highly
unusual) 'scene change' from Ajax's hut to the seashore and by the (highly unusual) departure of the
chorus to search for Ajax. In sum, the first part of Act 3 creates a crisis atmosphere and the second part
justifies that sense of crisis.

228 In Sophocles and Euripides the entry of messengers is usually unannounced. Messengers are conduits of
information; they rarely have much personality. This messenger is Teucer's forerunner (781) and a sup-
porter of Ajax. Given the ominous ending of the 'deception' speech (648-92) we expect that he is coming
to announce Ajax's suicide. Sophocles will 'frustrate' this expectation and draw out the catastrophe.

229 Teucer was on a raiding expedition there (321). Mysians were allies of the Trojans from the south side
of Mt. Ida.

230 Teucer's quarrel with Agamemnon and Menelaus looks back to the quarrel (and sword-drawing) of
Achilles vs. Agamemnon in *Iliad* 1.190 ff. and the intercession of the elderly Nestor.

231 The chorus thinks that Ajax, having learned the wisdom of yielding and obedience, has gone to the
seashore to cleanse himself, but the repetition of 'new' has an ominous ring.

232 This is the same cry of horror that Jocasta and Oedipus shout out upon recognizing the tragic truth (*Oed.
Rex*, 1071, 1182). The messenger apparently senses that Ajax's fate is sealed.

or else I myself am shown to have been too slow.

Chorus-leader

Why, what has been neglected in this urgent matter?   740

Messenger

Teucer forbade us to allow this man who is now inside his hut
to go outside until he himself happened to be present.

Chorus-leader

Well, let me tell you, Ajax is departed, having turned
from his intention towards one more profitable. In this way
he could be reconciled with the gods with whom he had been angry.

Messenger

These are words full of folly and more folly   745
if indeed Calchas prophesizes with any intelligence.[233]

Chorus-leader

What prophecy? With what knowledge of this matter do you come?

Messenger

This much I know since I happened to be present.
Calchas, on his own, moved away from the circle of chiefs
seated in council, separating himself from the sons of Atreus.   750
With all kind intent he grasped Teucer's right hand and spoke,
urging him by every possible device to confine Ajax to his hut
during the day that has now appeared, this, the present one[234]
and not to release and leave him to himself
if he ever again wished to see Ajax alive.   755
For, as Calchas went on to say, it is *for this day alone*
that Athena's wrath still drives him. Yes, declared the seer,
it is bodies grown too strong and stupid
that are the sort to fall into grievous afflictions
sent by the gods, whenever a man is born a mere mortal   760
but then doesn't think in accord with the limits of human nature.
For Ajax, from the very moment he set forth from home,
was found to be foolish despite his father's sound counsel.
For Telamon addressed him thus:
  "Son, seek to prevail with the spear,
  yet always seek to prevail with the help of the gods."   765

---

233 Calchas ('He who ponders dark thoughts'), son of Thestor, was "by far the best of the bird-interpreters,
     who knew the things that are, the things to come, and the things past, and guided the ships of the Greeks
     to Troy by his seer's art which Phoebus Apollo gave to him." (*Iliad* 1.69-72).

234 This entire line is taken up with Calchas' solemn description of this momentous and potentially 'tragic
     day' (cf. 778, 801-2).

But Ajax answered boastfully and thoughtlessly:[235]
    "Father, backed by the gods even a mere nobody
    could achieve such conquests. But *I* am confident
    that even without them I shall win this fame."[236]
Such was his arrogant boast. Then, on a second occasion,[237]   770
when divine Athena, spurring him on, enjoined him
to turn a murderous hand against his enemy,
he shot back a reckless retort, too blasphemous to be repeated:
    "Queen, stand beside the rest of the Greeks
    but the tide of battle will never burst forth through *my* line."   775
With such bravado he incurred the full fury of Athena's wrath
because he didn't think in accord with human nature.
Yet if indeed he is still alive on this very day,[238]
perhaps we might, with the help of the gods, be his saviors.
Such was the story the seer told.[239] Straightaway, rising from his seat,   780
Teucer sends me with this mandate for you to observe.[240]
But if our purpose has been frustrated and foiled,
then that man no longer lives, at least if Calchas is a wise seer.[241]

Chorus-leader

O cruelly vexed Tecmessa, offspring of an ill-fated family,
come and see this man and what words he speaks.   785
For his story shaves so close to the skin that one cannot rejoice.

    Enter Tecmessa alone from Ajax's hut.

Tecmessa

Why rouse me anew from my resting place,[242] a forlorn woman
who has only just now found a respite from unremitting griefs?

---

235 Ajax's folly is repeatedly stressed in this passage: stupid (758), foolish (763), thoughtless (766).

236 Just about the only thing that the Homeric hero cared about was attaining 'fame' (*kleos*); cf. note at 143.

237 The messenger reports two incidents that preceded the play. They are presented in ascending order of importance and both naturally relate to Ajax's military prowess (762-70 = his father; 770-77 = Athena).

238 Again the reappearance of the 'tragic day' motif which carefully frames the messenger's 35-line speech (748-82), occurring respectfully in his sixth line from the beginning and end.

239 Calchas' prophecy (751-80) has three purposes: to motivate the vacating of the stage and orchestra for Ajax's suicide; to emphasize that Ajax's death is not caused by Athena; and to put a definite limit on her wrath.

240 Teucer stayed behind in the assembly of Greek leaders to look after Ajax's interests; he has no reason to suspect that his brother is contemplating suicide.

241 No prophet in Greek tragedy is ever wrong; even less so do we expect Calchas to be mistaken since he has been presented as an independent and fair-minded prophet (which is not always the case in tragedy).

242 Tecmessa, at Ajax's instruction (684), had gone into the hut and has been sitting quietly there since 692.

Chorus-leader
Hear from this man, since he comes bringing a report
about Ajax's plight which has caused me grief.   790

Tecmessa
Alas, what are you saying, fellow? Surely *we're* not doomed?

Chorus-leader
I don't know about *your* plight but as for Ajax I do know that
I have no confidence about him if he is indeed outside.

Tecmessa
Well actually he is outside so I feel anguish at what you're saying.

Chorus-leader
He is the very man Teucer expressly orders us to confine   795
under the shelter of his hut and not to let out alone.

Tecmessa
But where is Teucer and for what reason does he say this?

Messenger
That man has just now arrived. And he expects
that this going forth of Ajax will bring his destruction.[243]

Tecmessa
Oimoi, wretched me! From whom ever did he learn this?   800

Messenger
From Thestor's son, the prophet Calchas.[244]
Death or life—that's what he said this very day brings for Ajax.

Tecmessa   *Turning to the chorus*
Alas, friends, protect me from the crushing misfortune
imposed by necessity.[245] *You there*, urge Teucer to come quickly!
And you, hasten to the western coves! *And you*, get on   805
to the eastern coves![246] Search out my husband's ill-fated departure!

---

243 Calchas had not said *how* Ajax would die, just that he would unless he stayed inside the hut.
244 Thestor ('The one who prays') was the son of Idmon the Argonaut, who was a son of Apollo. On Calchas, see note at 746.
245 Tecmessa means slavery; she is repeating a powerful expression she used earlier; see note on 485.
246 Tecmessa, once submissive, now takes charge; she divides the 15 sailors (apparently) into three groups (five apiece?), one group (along with the messenger) to fetch Teucer, the other two to search for Ajax.

For I realize that about this man I have been deceived[247]
and that from his former kindness I have been cast out.[248]
Oimoi, what shall I do, child?[249] I must not sit still.
No, I, too, shall go, as far as I have strength to do so.   810
Let us away, let us run—it's no time for sitting still
if we want to save a man who's speeding to his death.

Chorus-leader

I'm ready to go[250] and I'll show readiness in more than words alone.
For speed of action and speed of foot shall follow them at once.

> *Exit Tecmessa, messenger, and chorus (in three separate groups) hastily down
> the side ramps. During the commotion of this massive and highly unusual exit
> —the stage and orchestra are emptied—the (small) stage crew brings onstage
> a simple screen and places it over the central stage door so that Ajax's hut is no
> longer the backdrop. The stage now represents the 'untrodden' stretch of the
> Trojan seashore described by Ajax at 654-7.[251]*

---

247 This is the only appearance of any form of *apatê* which virtually always in Sophocles (12 of its 13 occurrences) means 'trick' or 'deceit' (rather than 'mistake'). So Tecmessa is saying that she was 'deceived' about Ajax. She does not say that she was deceived *by* him but rather *about* him. She is not, in short, claiming that she knows for sure that he *intended* to deceive her. But, especially in combination with the next line, there is the sense (at least in my reading) that she feels like he did deceive her. Tecmessa's single word here, *apatê-menê* ('having been deceived'), is the main reason that verses 642-92 have come to be known as Ajax's 'deception' speech.

248 Tecmessa had earlier (522) urged Ajax to remember that "Kindness (*charis*) is always the mother of kindness (*charis*)." That message did not get through, as her repetition of *charis* here makes clear. Furthermore she ends this verse, as she ended 807, with an emphatic (five-syllable) perfect past participle (*ek-beblê-menê*) whose final two syllables rhyme with the final two syllables of the participle in 807 (*apatê-menê*). Word rhyming and assonance at the end of a line is as uncommon in Greek as it is common in English, so Tecmessa is making a clear point by her careful choice and placement of words: she has been 'deceived' and 'cast out.' Later Menelaus, using the same participle that Tecmessa uses here, says that Ajax's body will be 'cast out' to the seagulls (*ek-beblê-menos*, 1064; cf. 1388, 1392).

249 This is the same question Ajax asked at 457; Tecmessa will repeat it at 920. In her *distraught* state she speaks as if her child were on stage, although he almost certainly is not (cf. 944). Likewise the *distraught* Hecuba calls upon her absent child Cassandra (Euripides, *Trojan Women*, 500).

250 This is the cue for Tecmessa, the chorus, and the messenger (having apparently split into three groups; see 804-5), to begin their exit. In the 32 surviving tragedies the chorus exits from the orchestra only five times.

251 No other tragedy has a 'scene change' except Aeschylus' *Eumenides* (458 B.C.E.) which moves from Apollo's temple at Delphi to the Temple of Athena in Athens (line 231).

*Enter Ajax alone by a side ramp carrying his sword. He walks slowly forward
and plants his sword in the ground, blade facing upwards.*[252]

Ajax[253]

The slayer stands steadfast where it should cut most sharply[254]   815
if a man has leisure even to indulge in such reflections.[255]
First of all, it was a gift from Hector, of all my foeman-friends[256]
the one most detested in my heart and most hateful to my eyes.
Yes, it is fixed firm in this enemy soil of Troy,
sharpened anew on an iron-eating whetstone.   820
And I have fixed the blade myself, packing the earth around it
so as to be most kind in killing this man quickly.[257]
So *we* are well-equipped.[258] Under these circumstances

---

252 The staging of Ajax's suicide is the most controversial of all scenes in tragedy. In no other play does violent death take place before the spectators and so it is not certain that it does here either. But less than 5% of the Greek tragic corpus survives so this consideration cannot be decisive. Some have suggested that Ajax is rolled out on the trolley (*eccyclêma*), gives his speech, and then is rolled back in to commit suicide. But the trolley always presents an *indoor scene* within a *specific* building; this scene is clearly outdoors on the seashore. The text offers its own more economical and powerful staging. Repeated emphasis is given to seeing the sick man 'in full view' (*peri-phanê*, 66), the mad man 'in full view' (*peri-phanôs*, 81), the man about to die 'in full view' (*peri-phantos*, 229). This repetition suggests that the suicide does take place in view of the audience; presumably a retractable blade could have been used. But what happens to the actor after the suicide? It is not practicable for him to remain on stage for the next 555 lines. Somehow the Ajax actor must exit and a 'dummy' replace him so he can reappear as Teucer. My stage directions follow what I consider the most practical solutions to the various problems (A.F. Garvie, 1998, pp. 203-4).

253 **Ajax's fourth major speech:** This soliloquy, delivered in complete solitude by the sea, has three parts: 815-23 = three reasons for his suicide; 824-858 = five invocations to various gods; and 859-65 = a farewell to Salamis and Athens.

254 Ajax *personifies* his executioner, i.e. sees the fatal sword as an *agent* of Hector (cf. 658, 662). Earlier he had said that some diseases called for the 'cutting' (*tomôs*) of the surgeon's knife (582). Now he has that surgeon's knife and it will 'cut most sharply ' (*tôm-atatos*).

255 After his 'hard-to-account-for' (*dys-logistos*, 40) attack on the Greek leaders, the angry Ajax withdrew, in the fashion of Achilles, for several days of solitary brooding which the chorus described as his 'leisurely contest of inactivity.' That long 'leisure' (*scholê*, 194) has passed; now he has only the brief 'leisure' (*scholê*, 816) of the next six lines (817-22) wherein he 'reflects upon / gives an accounting of' (*logos*) the sword and why it will 'cut most sharply'; he allots two lines for each of his three reasons.

256 Earlier Ajax had said that "the gifts of enemies are no gifts at all" (*a-dôra dôra*, 665; cf. 662, 1029). Now we see why. Hector is Ajax's 'foeman-friend' (*xenos*, as in our 'xenophobia') because, after their duel in the *Iliad*, they had exchanged tokens of friendship as was sometimes done by enemy warriors. Hector gave Ajax "a sword, whose handle was studded with silver nails, a sheath, and a well-cut (leather) sword belt" (*telamôn*, which is also the name of Ajax's father); Ajax gave to Hector "a shining purple war-belt" (7.303-5). Now those offerings of fellowship turn out to be 'gifts that are no gifts' because they are *fatal* to each man. Hector was tied to Achilles' chariot by Ajax's war-belt and dragged to death by it (1029-31). Likewise Hector's sword is now the unexpected agent of Ajax's death; so the dead kill the living. Virgil, clearly impressed by the pathos here, has Dido stab herself with the 'gift' of her guest-friend Aeneas (*Aeneid* 4. 647).

257 Ajax gives the three reasons for why the sword will 'cut most sharply': a) it is the gift of an *enemy* (Hector) and bears his *hatred*; b) it has been newly *sharpened* and planted in *enemy* territory; c) it has been fixed by Ajax himself so as to kill kindly by killing *quickly*.

258 Ajax speaks of the sword as his friend in this last of their many dangerous missions together.

it is you, Zeus, who must assist me first, as is but fitting.
I will ask you for no large gift of honor to take.   825
Send some messenger, I pray, to carry the bad news to Teucer
so that he may be the first to lift up my corpse
after I have fallen upon this blood-stained sword.
Let me not be spied first by one of my foes
and thrown out, exposed to the dogs and birds as booty![259]   830
Such is my supplication to you, O Zeus. At the same time I call on
Hermes, conductor of souls to the underworld, to set me asleep soundly
with one swift leap that brings no convulsions, no struggle,
when I have ripped through my ribs with this sword here.
Yes, and I summon as advocates those who are forever virgins,   835
who always see all sufferings among mortals—
the holy, far-striding Furies! Let them mark my misery—
how I have been ruined by the sons of Atreus.[260]
[May they seize those wicked men and destroy them wickedly
even as they see me fallen, slain by my own hand.   840
So may they, too, perish, slain by their dearest offspring.]
Go to it, you swift avenging Furies,
drink deep,[261] suck the blood of every soldier
in the army! Spare none of them!
And you, who steer your chariot up through the steep sky,   845
O Sun-God Helios, whenever you see the land of my father,
check your gold-studded reins and announce the desperate acts
I have done and the fate that has befallen me! Yes, announce them
to the old man, my father, and the hapless woman who nursed me.
Poor mother! Surely when she hears this news   850
her wailing will resound throughout the entire city.[262]
But it's no part of the business at hand to lament vainly like this.

---

259 Mutilation of the corpse was one of the biggest fears of the Homeric warrior because it carried so much
shame. With lines 829-30 Ajax succinctly motivates the entire second half of the play.

260 Here and in his third speech (667-8), Ajax emphatically blames Agamemnon and Menelaus without
making any mention of Odysseus (contrast 445-6). Sophocles is setting up the surprise ending.

261 Ajax's curse on the Greek leaders invokes the Furies (*Erinyes*) as blood-sucking vampires! The monstrous
female Furies have long, accurate memories and often work as the agents and enforcers of the three Fates
(*Moirai*), punishing or correcting those who disturb the natural order of things. If the sun were to stray
from its course, the Furies would put it back (Heraclitus B 89 DK). Teucer will similarly invoke a Fury
at 1390.

262 Eriboea's 'wailing' (*kôkutos*; cf 322) will echo throughout Salamis as did the 'wailing' of Priam and
Cassandra throughout Troy when they learned of Hector's death (*Iliad* 22.408-9, 24. 703). One of the
five rivers of the Underworld was called *Kokutos* (*Cocytus*), River of Wailing.

No, the deed must be begun and with some quickness.[263]
O Thanatos, Thanatos, come, witness and watch me![264]
[But in that other world, too, I shall speak to you when I'm with you.   855
And I address you, bright light which I still see
in this shining day, and you too, Sun the charioteer,
I address you for the very last time and never again hereafter.]
O radiant light of day, O sacred soil of Salamis, my native land,
O firm pillar of my father's hearth, farewell![265]   860
O glorious Athens and you, her race, with whom I was nurtured,[266]
and you springs and rivers of this land
and you plains of Troy, I call on you who nurtured me![267]
This is the very last word Ajax says to you;[268]
henceforth only to the dead in Hades shall I tell my story.[269]   865

> *Ajax leaps on his sword in full view of the audience. Silence for a time.*
>
> *Enter the two half-choruses by opposite ramps.*

---

263 Ajax's word 'quickness' (*tachos*: 822, 853) fittingly surrounds and marks off his petition to the five invoked gods.

264 Thanatos, god of Death, twin brother of Sleep (*Hypnos*), is fittingly and emphatically the last of the deities Ajax invokes.

265 Up to this point Ajax has been focused on the gods: Zeus to apprise Teucer (824-31), Hermes to conduct him to Hades (832-4), the Furies to exact revenge on Atreus' sons (835-44), Helios to apprise his parents (845-54), and Thanatos to bring the end (854). After all that, he can rest, so to speak, and remember the two places (Athens / Salamis and Troy) he loved because they 'nurtured' him. Salamis began the play as his 'firm pillar' (135) and so it remains to the very end.

266 One of the ten tribes of Athens was named after Ajax; he was a 'national' hero. Sophocles celebrates here the powerful and enduring connection between the man and the city that adopted him; certainly this must have been a poignant moment for the Athenian audience, all the more so just before the suicide leap.

267 In his ten years at Troy Ajax gained both glory *and* infamy; but in the long view of things it is the place he will be buried and where 'men will always remember' his fame (1165-6).

268 Ajax had begun by saying he would give us 'an accounting of words' (*logos*, 816); now he has done so and, as Hamlet said in his last words, "The rest is silence" (V.ii.362). Ajax has invoked sacred Salamis, glorious Athens, and Troy's springs, rivers, and plains. Now for the last time, using his own name – fraught with all its glory and tragedy – and a *third* person verb, he bids these nurturing places of the natural world a dignified farewell. They are his friends and his final audience and he knows they are sad to see him go.

269 Ajax's proud last word, in the *first* person singular, is "shall I tell my story" (or "shall I speak": *myth-êsomai*, as in our '*myth*-ology'). In the land of ghosts Ajax will tell his story to Aeacus, his grandfather (cf. 387), and dear old deceased friends such as Achilles and Patroclus. But when he meets Odysseus, who sings his praises at some length, there is no need to tell his story; he just turns and walks away. His arresting silence tells his story; the anger still remains. This famous scene from *Odyssey* 11.538-67 is translated at the end of my essay.

EPI-PARODOS (= second entry of the chorus)[270]

Chorus #1

Double, double, toil and trouble![271]
Where, where, oh where have I not gone?
And still no place draws me to share
the secret of his whereabouts.
Look! Look!   870
Again I hear some sound.

Chorus # 2

Yes, you hear us, your comrades, fellow-sailors of your ship.

Chorus # 1

What news, then?

Chorus # 2

The entire shore west of the fleet has been searched for tracks.

Chorus # 1

Well, have you discovered anything?   875

Chorus # 2

Yes, an abundance of toil but nothing more to see.

Chorus # 1

Well, as a matter of fact, neither does the man reveal his presence
anywhere along the path to the east where the sun rises.

---

270   The *parodos* (134-200) was the chorus' first *entrance* song; the *epi-parodos* is their second. It is very unusual
      to see a chorus *re*-entering the orchestra, a place they rarely leave. The sailors had left in three groups
      (cf. 804-5; 813-14) just before the suicide speech at 815-65. Now they return by opposite ramps in two
      groups. This is a 'mirror scene' (in reverse) of the play's opening where Odysseus warily hunted for Ajax
      in front of his hut and the spectator did not know the outcome. Here the sailors frantically search for
      him along the seashore and the spectator does know the outcome.
      The frenzied hunt is reflected in the scene's complex seven-part structure. Although it is difficult to
      comprehend this intricate structure as one reads the text, it is worth analyzing briefly in order to appre-
      ciate how carefully Sophocles has worked to create formal order out of considerable on-stage chaos. The
      overall movement, after the introduction, is a-b-c-a-b-c. 866-78 = introduction (a-strophic exchange
      between the two half-choruses). *STROPHE* (879-914) = a] 879-90 = lyrics by chorus alone. *ENTER
      TECMESSA*. b] 891-914 = lyric dialogue (spoken iambic trimeters mixed with emotional lyrics between
      Tecmessa and the chorus); c] 915-24 = speech by Tecmessa. *ANTISTROPHE* (925-60) = a] 925-36 =
      lyrics by chorus alone; b] 937-60 = lyric dialogue (spoken iambic trimeters mixed with emotional lyrics
      between Tecmessa and the chorus); c] 961-73 = speech by Tecmessa (her last words in the play). This
      complex design can be seen in its fuller context in the diagram of the play in Appendix One.

271   In Shakespeare the three witches tried to brew toil and trouble for Macbeth with their demonic incanta-
      tion (IV.1.10-11). Here the Greek has a similar feel: *ponos ponôi ponon pherei*, 'toil brings toil upon toil.'
      The noun *ponos* is repeated consecutively in three *different* cases so as to announce emphatically the main
      theme of the second half – the toil of finding Ajax, the toil of extricating the sword, the toil of warding
      off those who would forbid burial.

The Entire Chorus
Strophe

Who, I pray, who of the toiling sons of the sea
engaged in sleepless hunting,[272]   880
or who of the goddesses of Mt. Olympus,[273]
or of the rivers
flowing into the Bosphorus,[274]
who might tell me if he sees
the raw-hearted man   885
roaming somewhere?
For it is a grievous thing that my ship,
after all the weary wandering and long laboring,
cannot speed to him on a favoring wind,
cannot see where he is, the feeble lifeless man.[275]   890

Enter Tecmessa by a side ramp, unseen by the chorus.[276]

Tecmessa

Io moi moi!

Chorus-leader

Whose cry was that? From the thicket there, a cry like a forlorn flute!

Tecmessa

Io, ill-fated woman!

Chorus-leader

There she is! The young bride, captive of his spear, I see her,[277]
Tecmessa, steeped in the anguish of her wailing.   895

Tecmessa

Destroyed, devastated, demolished! O friends!

---

272 In ancient times, as now, fishing was a tough line of work and the only one that required a night shift.

273 The reference here is not to the pantheon of gods of Mt. Olympus on mainland Greece but to minor local nymphs of the Mt. Olympus (7,600 feet) in Mysia, visible in the distance to the east of Troy (cf. 720).

274 The chorus mean not the 'traditional' Bosphorus near Istanbul but rather the Hellespont (modern Dardanelles) which is the narrow strait, 200 miles northeast of Troy, that connects the Aegean Sea to the Sea of Marmara.

275 The chorus, of course, does not know that Ajax is dead but their adjective, which means both 'feeble' and 'lifeless' (cf. 1411), seems almost like a stage direction for the *corpse* to be discovered. No sooner do they say 'lifeless' and Tecmessa explodes with a blood-curdling scream, *io moi moi* (891).

276 Her entry *within* the strophe (at the intersection of the choral lyrics and the lyric dialogue) rather than *between* the strophe and antistrophe (at 925) is very unusual. Clearly it is designed to surprise. Her unannounced entry announces the moment of great revelation. From this point forward the body of a dead man will be *the* visual centerpiece of the play.

277 The exact status of Tecmessa (slave? bride? wife? concubine?) is hard to pin down. There is real tenderness here in the chorus' description of her as 'young bride' (*nymphē*). And sadness, too, in their adjective 'captive of his spear,' (*dori-lēptos*), which is same word they used to describe the beasts of burden Ajax seized and murdered in his mad rampage (146).

Chorus-leader

What is it?

Tecmessa

Ajax—here lies our Ajax, newly slaughtered,[278]
folded *around* his hidden sword.[279]

Chorus-leader

Oimoi, my hopes of homecoming! Vanished, gone!   900
Oimoi, my lord,
you have slain me, your shipmate!
Miserable man! Broken-hearted woman!

Tecmessa

So it is with him. We can only cry out *aiai, Aias!*[280]

Chorus-leader

Ill-fated man—by whose hand, then, did he do this deed?   905

Tecmessa   *(looking under Ajax's garment at the mangled form beneath it.)*

He himself by himself![281] That's clear. This sword accuses him!
He fixed it fast in the ground—then fell on it.

Chorus-leader

Alas, my blind folly!
It was all alone, then,
that your blood was shed,   910
shielded from your friends.
Alas, so deaf, so dumb—I wasn't careful![282]
Where, where does he lie, the intractable man
named for his agony, Aias![283]

---

278   Earlier Ajax had commanded Tecmessa to lift Eurysaces up into his arms insisting that the boy wouldn't be frightened to see the heap of bloody *animals* 'newly-slaughtered' (*neo-sphagês*); now she must look on both the *sword* which he called 'the slayer / slaughterer' (*sphageus*, 815) and the *body* it has 'newly-slaughtered' (*neo-sphagês*, 898).

279   Tecmessa says Ajax is 'folded' around the sword because the blade has raised his garment to an apex from which the folds descend. In his 'deception' speech Ajax said he was going to 'hide' (*kruptô*, 658) his hateful sword and so indeed now it is 'hidden' (*kruphaios*, 899).

280   Tecmessa seems to be punning on Ajax's name by using the verb *aiazein*, which usually means 'to cry out *aiai*,' but could, in this context (cf. 914), mean 'to lament for Ajax.'

281   Sophocles uses this phrase five times in his surviving seven plays, always of suicide.

282   Ajax failed to carry out his homicide against the Greeks because Athena had been so 'careful' (45); he succeeded in his suicide because his sailors were not 'careful.' Or so it seems to them.

283   Early on Ajax realized that his failed murder attempt showed the 'aptness of his name' (*ep-ônumos*, 430; cf. 574). Now the chorus not only confirms the 'difficulty in his name' (*dys-ônumos*, 914) but implies that it arose from his 'difficulty in tractability' (*dys-trapelos* = 'hard to turn': 913). Ajax is, by nature, the opposite of Odysseus, 'the man of many turns.'

Tecmessa begins to cover the sword-pierced corpse with her cloak, in full view of the audience.

Tecmessa

Mark me! He must not be looked at![284]   915

No, I will cover him with this all-enfolding cloak.[285]

For no one who is a true friend could bear to see him

as he blows up through his nostrils and out from his murderous wound

the blackened blood of his self-inflicted slaughter.

After Tecmessa has shrouded the corpse (915-19), the stage crew carries the screen forward (from the front of the stage building where it has been con-cealing the central door) to center stage so that it now also conceals Tecmessa, the 'dead' Ajax actor, and the stage door, thus allowing the Ajax actor to exit unseen and a 'dummy' to be placed on the ground as the new corpse. From 920 to 975 (when Teucer arrives) Tecmessa speaks from behind the screen.[286]

Tecmessa   *(from behind the screen, where she remains, with the corpse, until 975)*

Oimoi, what shall I do?[287] Which of your friends will lift you up?   920

Where is Teucer? If he should come, how timely his arrival would be!

Then he could join in the burial rites of this fallen brother.[288]

O ill-fated Ajax, in what a state you are for the man you are!

How worthy you are, even in your enemies' eyes, to receive lamentations!

Chorus

Antistrophe

So, then, hapless man, you were fated,   925

you were fated over time to fulfill

by your stiff-hearted resolve

a dire destiny of boundless toils and troubles.

Such, I see, were the groans you bellowed out

raw-minded man,[289] all night and through the shining day,   930

---

284 These are the first words of the first speech of this complex scene and they are heart-breaking. The main word here is *theatos*, as in our 'theater' (= the place for looking). Tecmessa wants no spectators to see this sword-pierced, blood-drenched body, once so proud and beautiful.

285 Tecmessa was wearing a *pharos*, an 'outer cloak'; the word also has the connotation of 'death-shroud.'

286 This staging would require Tecmessa to speak her 16 lines (in this 55 line duration) from behind the center-stage screen (which conceals her and Ajax's corpse). This is the most awkward part of the staging scenario that I have adopted (following A. F. Garvie, 1998).

287 Tecmessa had asked the same question to the chorus earlier (809), *before* Ajax's death.

288 The end of the strophe, which marks the midpoint of the *epi-parodos*, introduces the theme that will dominate the rest of the play, namely the burial of the body.

289 This epithet 'raw-minded' (*ômo-phrôn*) in the fifth line of the antistrophe responds to 'raw-hearted' (*ômo-thumos*, 885) in the fifth verse of the strophe. Such close and emphatic verbal correspondence (possibly reflected in the choreography) not only links the two halves of the scene in a formal way, but it underscores the chorus' growing awareness of just how raw, fierce, and uncompromising Ajax has been.

groans full of hatred at Atreus' sons,
groans fraught with fatal passion.[290]
So clearly that time was the great beginning
and mighty magistrate of sorrows
when the contest for Achilles' [golden] arms   935
was set up to decide the most valiant warrior.

Tecmessa

Io moi moi!

Chorus-leader

Genuine sorrow, I know, goes to the heart.

Tecmessa

Io moi moi!

Chorus-leader

In no way do I disbelieve you, lady, even as you twice cry out *Oimoi*!   940
Oimoi! Since just now you have been violently robbed of one so beloved.

Tecmessa

You can *opine* about these sorrows but I *know* their pain all too well.

Chorus-leader

Yes, I agree.

Tecmessa

Alas, my son, to what a yoke of slavery we are going,
what taskmasters now stand over the two of us!   945

Chorus-leader

Alas, you have given voice to the unspeakable deeds
of Atreus' two ruthless sons
by this cry of sorrow.
But may the god keep it away!

Tecmessa

These things would not have reached this state but for the gods.   950

Chorus-leader

Far too heavy is the heartache they have brought to pass.

Tecmessa

Yet such is the affliction and sorrow that Pallas Athena,
dread goddess, daughter of Zeus, creates so as to oblige Odysseus.

---

290 The groans to which Tecmessa refers at 929-32 are those she described at 321-2 where Ajax bellowed like
a bull.

Chorus-leader

Surely, then, that much-enduring hero[291]   955
exalts maliciously in his black-faced heart,
yes, and laughs his loud laugh
at these miseries caused by this madness. Pheu! Pheu!
Alas, the twin kings, those fine sons of Atreus,
will laugh with him when they hear the news.   960

Tecmessa

Well, *let* them laugh, *let* them rejoice over this man's misfortunes!
Even if they didn't feel the need for him when he was alive,
perhaps they'll lament his death in the straits of war.
For men whose judgment is evil don't know the good
they hold in their hands until they throw it away.   965
To me his death is as bitter as it is sweet *to them*
and pleasant *for him*.[292] For everything he desired
so passionately he has got *for himself*—the very death he wanted.
Why, then, should they laugh scornfully over him?[293]
His death is a matter for the gods, not for them—no, not for them!   970
So let Odysseus revel in his insolence—it is to no purpose!
For them, you see, Ajax lives no longer, but *for me* he is gone,
completely gone, leaving only misery and mourning.[294]

---

291 The chorus-leader sarcastically uses one of Homer's favorite epithets of Odysseus (cf. 445-6); he cannot, of course, understand the irony behind his sarcasm.

292 Ironically both Ajax and his adversaries delight in his death; Tecmessa emphatically does not, reminding us how self-centered Ajax's suicide is.

293 This is the fourth occurrence of the word 'laughter' (*gelôs*) in 13 lines, twice by the chorus (957-8) and twice by Tecmessa (961, 970). It is an emphatic note on which to end the antistrophe and indeed the entire *epi-parados*. It also serves to link a crucial theme of the *parodos* (search scene #1) to a crucial theme of the *epi-parados* (search scene #2), namely the interest in mocking one's enemy by Athena and the sons of Atreus respectively (cf. 989). For more on the important role of 'laughter' see the note on line 79.

294 These lines are Tecmessa's last in the play.

Act Four[295]

Enter Teucer, with an attendant, by a side ramp.

Teucer

Io moi moi![296]

Chorus-leader

Hush! I think I hear Teucer's voice shouting out   975
a song of sorrow that hits the mark of this disaster.

Teucer

O dearest Ajax! O bright face of brotherly joy, have you
indeed done your business as the prevailing rumor reports?

Chorus-leader

He is dead, Teucer. You must know this.

Teucer

Alas, then, what a heavy misfortune!   980

Chorus-leader

In such circumstances…

Teucer

Aye me! All the suffering![297]

Chorus-leader

…you have every reason to lament.

Teucer

Alas, over-passionate haste!

Chorus-leader

Yes, too rash indeed, Teucer.

Teucer

Aye me! But tell me of his son!
Where is he! Where in this land of Troy will I find him?

---

295   There are three main parts: 974-1046 (72 lines) = the (long-awaited) arrival of Teucer, his lament over
Ajax (and uncovering of the corpse at 1003-5), and the extrication of the sword from the corpse (at
1024-7); 1047-1167 (121 lines) = the arrival of the Spartan king, Menelaus (the first of Ajax's enemies)
who comes to forbid the burial of Ajax; and 1168-84 (17 lines) = the short but poignant climax, namely
the ritual commemoration over the corpse by Teucer, Tecmessa, and Eurysaces (as a suppliant).

296   Teucer's first words on stage, even though he does not yet see the corpse, echo Tecmessa's cry of anguish
when she discovers Ajax (891, 937). Although he shares her grief, he also shares his brother's attitude
towards women: Teucer does not talk to Tecmessa first but to the chorus-leader and when he does address
Tecmessa at 985-89 he does not use her name but curtly commands her to fetch Eurysaces.

297   This kind of tense *half*-line exchange is called *antilabe*; it was used once previously in a frigid exchange
between Ajax and Tecmessa (591-4) that concluded Act I. Here it serves to highlight the timeliness of
Teucer's arrival and raises a nervous question: where is Ajax's son?

Chorus-leader

Alone beside the huts.[298]

Teucer   (*to Tecmessa*)

                        Well quickly, quickly,   985
won't you bring him here before one of our enemies steals him
like the cub of a lioness made desolate by the death of her mate?[299]
Go on, get moving, share the labor! Mark me—
everyone loves to laugh over the dead when they lie helpless.

    Exit Tecmessa by a side ramp.[300]

Chorus-leader

Well, in fact, while he was alive, Teucer, he commanded you   990
to care for this boy as indeed you now do care for him.

Teucer   (*seeing the corpse for the first time*)[301]

Alas, of all the sights that these eyes have ever seen[302]
this is the most painful! Of all the journeys
that have grieved my heart
the one I just traveled is the most gut-wrenching!   995
O most beloved Ajax, when I learned of your doom,
I pressed hard on your path and tracked you down.[303]
A swift rumor, as if sent by some god, sped through
all the Greek army—that you were dead and gone!
And as I heard this, helpless and still some distance away,   1000
I groaned deep in sorrow. But now the sight of you shatters me.
Oimoi!

---

298 This is where Tecmessa had left Eurysaces when she exited (814) to search for Ajax.

299 Homer describes Ajax, more than any other Greek warrior, as a lion; now his brother must take on that role and protect Eurysaces, the lion-cub.

300 The *character* Tecmessa will return at 1168 in a non-speaking role (played by an 'extra' wearing her costume and mask). But the *actor* playing Tecmessa will soon return playing the role of Odysseus (1317).

301 **Teucer's first major speech:** In Tecmessa's absence Teucer laments over Ajax's corpse in a three-part funeral oration: 992-1001 = an emotional account of Teucer's sad journey from the Greek camp to the seashore, knowing what he would find; 1002-23 = the uncovering of Ajax's face (by an attendant) and Teucer's lament at the sad sight, and at his failure to help his brother, and especially at his fear of the inevitable accusations of bastard, coward, and traitor from his father Telamon; 1024-39 = the extraction of the sword (by Teucer, 1024-7) and his recounting (to the chorus) of the significance of the fatal exchange of gifts between Hector and Ajax, and the role that the Fury of revenge and Hades played in this exchange.

302 Until this point neither Ajax's corpse nor Tecmessa have been visible to Teucer because they have been concealed behind the screen that was put into place at 920. His cry here is a cue for the screen to be removed. Now the corpse becomes visible to him but only at 1004 is the shroud removed so that he can see his brother's face. The repetition of visual words underscores the horror of the revelation.

303 Teucer's language recalls not only the recent search for Ajax by Tecmessa and the chorus but also by Odysseus at the beginning of the play. Now it is a brother, not an enemy, who has hunted Ajax down, although ironically it will take the best efforts of both brother and enemy to 'save' Ajax.

Come, you, lift off the covering so I may *see* the whole horror.

Teucer's attendant pulls back Tecmessa's cloak covering Ajax's face.
O face hard-to-look-at and full of bitter daring,[304]
how many sorrows you have sown for me by dying!   1005
For where—tell me—where can I go now, among what sorts
of people, me, who supported you nowhere in your toils
and troubles? No doubt Telamon, your father and mine,
would greet me gladly and graciously when he sees me
returning without you! How could he not—being the kind of man   1010
who can't laugh for pleasure even in good fortune! What thought
will such a man keep concealed? What insult won't he hurl
against the bastard born from an enemy's spear and a captive concubine,
against one who betrayed you, most beloved Ajax,
by cowardice, by unmanliness, or by treachery—all to gain control   1015
of *your* royal powers and *your* palace after *you* had perished!
Such taunts will he hurl—an ill-tempered man, ornery in his old age,
who flies into a fury at nothing, all for the pleasure of provoking strife!
And in the end, banished from my fatherland, I'll become a castaway,
branded by his arguments a slave instead of a free man.   1020
So much for home![305] But here at Troy my enemies are many,
my advantages few, and even those few that I've found
have vanished now that you're dead. Oimoi! What am I to do?
How shall I extract you, sad man, from the spike of this sword—
so sharp and spiteful in its shimmering shine—the slayer which,   1025
after all, made you breathe out your last breath! Do you see how Hector,
though dead, was destined finally to kill you?

*Addressing the chorus, and holding the sword which he has just extracted
from Ajax.*
By the gods, consider the fate of these two men.

---

304 Two points here. **a)** Earlier Tecmessa had told the chorus, 'He must *not* be looked at' (*ou...theatos*, 915)
and so she *covered* Ajax's face; now Teucer, as the attendant *uncovers* Ajax, cries 'O face hard-to-look-at'
(*dys-theatos*, 1003). This would mean that Ajax jumped backwards onto the blade at 865. Sophocles'
rendering of this scene might well have been influenced by a red-vase depiction by the Brygos painter,
c. 470 B.C.E., which shows Tecmessa covering a face-up Ajax, with the sword projecting up through
his back. **b)** The symbolic motif of 'eyes / face' (*omma*) runs throughout and culminates here. Earlier
Ajax's enemies were afraid to see his 'eyes' (167) but then Athena ('with her grim Gorgon eyes', 451)
distorted them with grievous illusions to prevent murder (52, 447) and averted them so they couldn't see
Odysseus in the prologue (69). As a result of Ajax's deeds the eyes of his sailors shuddered like a dove's
(140), although Ajax's 'deception' speech momentarily set their eyes free (706). In his shame Ajax hid
his 'eyes / face' from the Greek army (191) and from his father (462). Now, at last, his brother must look
at that 'face' of bitter daring and cruel courage (1004).

305 In lines 1008-21 Teucer focuses on his fear of being disgraced by his father, Telamon; this was exactly
what his brother Ajax feared in his very first speech (at 434-40 and 462-66).

Hector, lashed fast, was dragged from the rail of Achilles' chariot[306]
by the war-belt which this man had given him, his flesh frayed   1030
and mangled all that time till he gasped out his life.
And this man, who possessed it as gift from that man,
has been killed by the sword in a fatal fall. Was it not a vengeful Fury
that forged this sword[307] and did not savage Hades fashion this war-belt,
yes, the God of Death, grim reaper and fine craftsman!   1035
So I, for my part, would say that it is the gods who have contrived
these things[308] just as they always contrive all things for mortals.
But whoever finds these views unacceptable in his judgment
let that man be content with his opinion as I am with mine.

Chorus-leader

Cut short your speech! Consider this man's burial,   1040
how you'll hide him in a grave, and what you'll presently reply.
For I see an enemy and he'll likely be laughing when he arrives,
mocking our misfortunes, as is the wont of scoundrels.

Teucer

But who, indeed, is the man you see coming from the army?

Chorus-Leader

It's Menelaus, for whose sake we set forth on this sailing.   1045

Teucer

I see him. Now that he's near, he's not difficult to know.

*Enter Menelaus (accompanied by one or two heralds) at the very moment
when Teucer is in the process of raising Ajax's corpse from the ground.*

---

306   In the *Iliad* Achilles killed Hector in a fight, pierced his ankles, and *then*, when he was dead, dragged
      him to the Greek ships and around Patroclus' tomb (22.395-404, 464-5; 24.15-16). Sophocles revises
      the story so that Ajax's gift is the (indirect) *cause* of Hector's death; cf. the note at 817.

307   In his suicide speech Ajax invoked the Furies for help (835-44); Teucer sees them as agents of his
      death.

308   After Teucer has extracted Hector's sword from Ajax's body he addresses the sailors (1028-37) and these
      lines (1036-7) bring that address to a climax with an appreciation of role which the gods have played
      in the sword's storied history. This climax is a good reminder that the Greeks saw virtually all human
      activity as *doubly motivated* by human and divine will. And there is something else to be noted about
      Teucer's poignant lament (992-1039). For all its sorrow there is a sense that this speech allows the play
      to turn a corner and begin to rise back after the great fall. The unveiling of the face (1004-7) and the
      pulling of the sword from Ajax's body by his brother (1024-7) – the two acts which divide this speech
      into thirds – these serve to unite the brothers for the first time and also they provide a cathartic release
      for the play itself. The Trojan past of Hector and his sword will now fade away as themes. The more recent
      past must be reckoned with and worked through so that the corpse which now dominates the stage can
      receive its proper due.

Menelaus

Hey there, yes you!³⁰⁹ I forbid you to join in the bearing or burial
of this body in any last rites. Let it lie just where it is!

Teucer

To what purpose have you spewed and spent such ugly words?

Menelaus

It's what seems most fitting to me and to the commander-in-chief.   1050

Teucer

Could you kindly, then, tell me why you put forward your charge?

Menelaus³¹⁰

Because we had hoped that we were bringing him from home
to be an ally-in-arms and friend of the Greeks; but we've discovered
in our dealings with him that he's more hateful than the Phrygians.³¹¹
He plotted the bloody slaughter of the whole army   1055
and marched out under the cover of night to slay us with his spear!
And if one of the gods hadn't extinguished his enterprise
we would have suffered the same fate that befell him,
being most foully slain and left lying in shame while *he* was still alive!
But now a god has exchanged one victim for another,   1060
diverting his violent outrage so that it fell on sheep and cattle.
So there is no man possessed of so much power
as to entomb his body in a grave.
No, he will be thrown out on the yellow sand³¹²
and become food for birds that haunt the shore.   1065
So don't stir up some storm of menacing strength!
Although we couldn't master him while he was alive,
we shall rule him when he's dead, even if you don't wish it,
keeping him in line by force of hand. For on no occasion,
while he lived, was he ever willing to listen to any words of mine.   1070
Now, in truth, it's the mark of a vile man that he claims the right
to disobey his superiors, even though he is only a commoner.

---

309 Menelaus' discourteous 'greeting' of Teucer, already foreshadowed by the chorus-leader, signals his rude
     and arrogant harshness, a trait that typifies this contemptible Spartan king throughout Greek tragedy.

310 **Menelaus' only major speech**: It can be divided into four parts: 1052-62 = an account of Ajax's attempt
     to murder Menelaus and his comrades; 1063-70 = his refusal to allow Ajax's burial; 1071-83 = the reason
     for his refusal (which becomes a lesson in Spartan civics and the consequences of disobedience and
     intemperance); and 1084-90 = a return to his refusal to allow Ajax's burial.

311 These people were neighbors of the Trojans and so synonymous with them (cf. 210, 488, 1292)

312 The same perfect passive participle 'thrown out' (*ek-beblê-menos*) was used by Tecmessa to describe her
     own fate (808).

For a city's laws could never carry it on a prosperous course[313]
if fear doesn't find a firm and principled place there,
nor could an army any longer be ruled with discipline   1075
if fear and a sense of shame don't serve as safeguards.
But a man, even if he has built a burly body,[314]
must expect that he may fall even from a small misfortune.
Be certain of this: the man who enjoys safety and security
is the man in whom fear and a sense of shame abide.   1080
But wherever he's allowed to run riot and do whatever he wants,
expect that this city, though at first sped by steady winds,[315]
sooner or later sinks deep down into the depths.
So for me, too, let a certain timely fear be fixed firmly[316]
and let's not expect that after doing whatever we please,   1085
we won't pay a price which will cause us pain. These things go
round and round by turns. Once he was a man full of fiery insults
and violent outrage;[317] but now it's my turn to think big thoughts!
So, in front of everyone, I forbid you to bury him[318]
lest, in burying him, you sink into your own grave!   1090

Chorus-leader

Menelaus, after laying down a foundation of wise judgments,
don't be a man full of insults and outrage against the dead.[319]

---

313   At lines 1073-6 Menelaus sounds very much like the demagogue Cleon, the most violent and powerful politician in Athens in 427 B.C.E., who, in his frustration at the disobedient assembly during the
Mytilenian debate, lectured them about civics: "Ignorance combined with restraint (*sôphrosynê*) is more
beneficial than cleverness combined with lack of discipline." (Thucydides 3.37.3). In contrast to the
innovative and hyper-aggressive Athenians, the old-fashioned Spartans were famed for their restraint
(cf. Thuc. 1.70-71).

314   Menelaus implies that Ajax's main virtue was his huge body.

315   The 'Ship of State' metaphor was natural for a sea-faring people like the Greeks.

316   For the fourth time since 1074 Menelaus emphasizes the place of 'fear' in his version of the well-run city.
There was a shrine to 'Fear' (*Phobos*) near the dining hall of the Spartan *ephors* ('over-seers'); the Athenians
had shrines to 'Shame' (*Aidôs*) and 'Pity' (*Eleos*), both of which befit the Odysseus of this play.

317   Menelaus coins a lovely phrase in describing Ajax as an *aithôn hybristês* (literally, 'a man of flaming
hybris'), all the more striking given the drabness of Menelaus himself. It is worth noting that he is the
first and only adversary to accuse Ajax of *hybris* (cf. 304). On the importance of this theme see the note
to 153.

318   Menelaus ends where he began 50 lines earlier: "I forbid you to join in the burial..." (1047).

319   The chorus-leader boldly and unexpectedly throws back at Menelaus the insulting noun *hybristês* which
he used of Ajax at 1088; these are its only two occurrences in the play.

Teucer[320]

Never again, gentlemen,[321] would I be amazed at a man who,
being a low-born *nothing*, later misses the mark for that reason,
when men who are reputed to be high–born nobility   1095
miss the mark so widely in their oratory. Come, sir, please,
repeat that preface. Are you really claiming that *you took* Ajax
and *brought* him here as an ally for these Achaians? *You* did this?
Didn't he, in fact, sail of his own volition, as his own master?
On what grounds are *you* this man's captain? On what grounds   1100
do *you* possess the authority to lord it over the troops *he brought*
from home? You came as king of Sparta, not as our master.[322]
Nowhere was there set down any protocol of command
whereby your right to govern him exceeds his to govern you.
[You sailed here as a *subordinate* to others, not as general   1105
of the whole force such that you could *ever* be in charge of Ajax!]
No! Go on commanding those you command and chastise *them*
with your high and holy words! But as for this man, whether it's you
who order us not to bury him, or whether it's that other general,[323]
I will lay him out for burial as justice and duty demand,   1110
not fearing that big mouth of yours. For he certainly didn't undertake
this expedition for the sake of *your* wife,[324] like those toil-worn lackeys,
but on account of oaths to which he was sworn and bound.[325]
No, it certainly wasn't for *you*! He isn't in the habit of bestowing esteem
on those he regards as *nobodies*![326] So go fetch some more heralds 1115
and your generalissimo, then come back! Know that for all your bluster
and bravado I wouldn't twist and turn in fear so long as you what you are.

Chorus-leader

As I said before, I dislike such taunting in a time of trouble.
For stern statements sting, even if they're more than just.

---

320 **Teucer's second major speech:** This reply to Menelaus has three parts: <u>1093-96</u> = the folly of Menelaus'
     pompous and errant speech; <u>1096-1108</u> = consternation at Menelaus' claim that *he* brought Ajax to Troy;
     <u>1109-1118</u> = insistence that Ajax *will* be buried despite Menelaus' bluster.

321 Teucer, in his contempt for Menelaus, addresses Ajax's sailors first and never mentions his antagonist by
     name, just as Menelaus never mentioned him by name.

322 Sophocles is tapping into his audience's long-standing antipathy to Sparta.

323 Sophocles is preparing us here (and at 1116) for the entrance of the Greek commander-in-chief,
     Agamemnon, at 1226.

324 Menelaus' (first) wife was Helen.

325 Helen's suitors swore an oath to her father Tyndareus that they would support the successful suitor if his
     wife should ever be stolen; Helen was stolen (by Paris) and all the suitors had to go to Troy (cf. Thucydides
     1.9; Euripides, *Iphigeneia at Aulis* 61).

326 Teucer began by insinuating that Menelaus was a 'nothing' (1094) and so he ends, though even more
     vehemently.

Menelaus

Our archer-man seems to have no shortage of puffed-up pride.[327]   1120

Teucer

Proud, indeed, for it's no sordid skill I've acquired.

Menelaus

You'd really boast something big if you'd gotten a shield!

Teucer

Even lightly armed I'd be a match for you in all your hoplite gear.[328]

Menelaus

How fiercely does your tongue feed your ferocity!

Teucer

Yes, in a just cause, it's proper to think big thoughts.   1125

Menelaus

What? Is it just for this man, who has slain me, to prosper?

Teucer

Slain? Surely a strange word, if, though dead, you're actually alive!

Menelaus

Only because a god saved me, but in that man's eyes I am dead.

Teucer

Don't dishonor the gods if you've been saved by the gods![329]

Menelaus

Are you insinuating that *I* would disparage the gods' laws?   1130

Teucer

You do just that if you intervene to prevent the burial of the dead.

Menelaus

Well, I do forbid the burial of my enemies; it is not honorable.

Teucer

What? Did Ajax ever confront *you* as an enemy?

Menelaus

He hated me, I hated him, and you knew it.

---

327 Homer describes Teucer as the Greeks' best archer (*Iliad* 13.313-14; cf. 8.266-334; 23.859-69). The Greeks, both in literature and life, often showed a certain contempt for archers because they fought from a distance. The slaves who served as Athens' police force were *archers* from Scythia.

328 Hoplites were heavily-armed infantrymen (breast-plate, spear, shield) who fought the enemy at close quarters.

329 Teucer means that Menelaus would be dishonoring the gods if he prevented Ajax's burial; this brings to mind Antigone's famous claim in her play, probably produced within a few years of *Ajax* (c. 450-440 B.C.E.), that burial of the dead represents one of the 'unwritten and unshakeable laws of the gods' (453).

Teucer

Of course he hated you—you crooked vote-tampering thief![330]   1135

Menelaus

He was tripped up by the judges' joint decision, not mine.

Teucer

You could certainly put a fair face on the art of clandestine conniving!

Menelaus

Someone whom I know shall suffer sorely for saying such things!

Teucer

No more grief, I believe, than what we'll inflict on you.

Menelaus

One thing only shall I say: you *must* not bury this man!   1140

Teucer

And one thing only shall you hear in reply: he *will* be buried forthwith![331]

Menelaus

Once upon a time I saw a bold-tongued braggart
urging his crew to set sail in the winter.
In him you would have found no voice when he was caught
in the eye of a raging storm. No, he cowered under his cloak   1145
and suffered all the sailors to stomp on him at will.
Just so for both you and your brawling mouth—
some huge storm, blowing out of a tiny cloud,
might soon extinguish that blazing bluster.

Teucer

So, too, have I seen a fellow full of folly[332]   1150
who mercilessly mocked his neighbors' misfortunes.
And then someone resembling me and similar in disposition
looked at him and said something like this:
   "Sir, do the dead no wrong! If you do,
   know for sure that you shall suffer!"   1155
Face to face, with such advice, he admonished the reckless fellow.
And now I see that man, and he is, so it seems,
none other than you! I haven't spoken in riddles, have I?

Menelaus

I am leaving since it would be a *disgrace*, indeed, if one who could

---

330 Teucer, even more strongly than Ajax, thinks the vote for Achilles' arms was fraudulent (cf. 442-6, 1336-41).

331 Teucer's strong rebuttal brings to an end this rapid *single*-line exchange (*stichomythia*), a technique used to mark moments of high tension (see the note at 38-50).

332 Teucer *counters* and parodies Menelaus' moralizing and contemptuous parable with one of his own.

use compulsion should be caught merely chastising with words.   1160

Teucer

Be gone then! It is indeed *more than a disgrace* for me, too,
to hear a profane man chirping his petty chatter.

Exit Menelaus by a side-ramp.

The Entire Chorus

There will be some contest of great struggle and strife![333]
But quick as you can, Teucer, make haste
to search out somewhere a hollow trench for this man   1165
where he can rest—a gloomy tomb of mold and mildew,
yet one which men will remember always.[334]

Enter Tecmessa and Eurysaces.[335]

Teucer

Look! Here come those near and dear to this man,
in the nick of time, both child and wife,
to tend to the burial rites of this corpse of sorrow.   1170
Come, child, stand close and as a suppliant
cling to your father,[336] who begot you.

Teucer gently and slowly leads the boy towards Ajax's body.
Now kneel, as one who turns for help, holding in your hands

---

333   The 'contest' (*agôn*) over Ajax's burial has, of course, already begun but there chorus announces that
there is more to come; on the importance of this theme, see the note at 193-4. Thematically the chorus'
five lines of anapests (1163-7) serve to introduce the next brief funereal scene; structurally they mark
the transition from Menelaus' (final) exit to the entrance of Tecmessa and Eurysaces.

334   This is the play's most specific reference to Ajax's (implied) future hero-cult. His tomb will serve a
double function: to prevent mutilation of the corpse by enemies and to provide a place for perpetuating
his memory that counter-balances death's dankness. With the phrase 'hollow trench' Sophocles recalls
Hector's resting place at *Iliad* 24.797.

335   She had exited (989) at Teucer's request to fetch her son. Here the two enter (probably) through the
central door (since the distinction between the two different stage settings, hut vs. seashore, has probably
been blurred by now). It is very unusual for an actor to enter without speaking; also unusual to make a
completely silent appearance. But Tecmessa does both because of the 'three actor rule'; the other actors
are needed to play the roles of Teucer, Menelaus / Agamemnon, and Odysseus. Although Tecmessa and
her young son will be silent 'extras' for the final 250 lines, they will still be important visual and ritual
presences.

336   Teucer, who must leave the scene to find a burial place for his brother, bids Eurysaces to cling to Ajax's
body; in that posture he will be protected by Zeus in his role as 'protector of suppliants.' The choreography of the stage tableau suggests a suppliant clinging to an altar or an inviolable place of asylum; Ajax's
body is becoming, in death, somehow as sacred as it once was polluted. In contrast to the solemnity and
beauty of this poignant scenario with the little boy ('Broad-shield') safe-guarding his father, we recall
Ajax, blood-stained on the trolley amidst cattle carcasses, cradling Eurysaces in his arms (545 ff.).

these locks of hair—mine, hers, and yours as the third[337]—
precious treasures to supplicate the spirit of the dead.[338]

Teucer cuts a lock of his own and one from Tecmessa. Then, as he pronounces his curse, he gives the hair to the boy.

But if any from the army 1175
should wrest you violently from this body, may he be banished,[339]
cast from his country dead and unburied, a wicked reward
for a wicked man! And may his entire family—stem and stock—
be severed at the root in the same way as I have shorn this strand of hair![340]

Teucer cuts a lock of Eurysaces' hair and hands it to the boy.

Hold him, son, and guard him,[341] and don't let anyone   1180
move you! Fall to your kneels, and hold him fast!

As the child kneels and clasps the corpse, Teucer turns to the chorus.

And you, sailors, don't just stand near like women in waiting!
No, be real men and rally around until I've returned,
having prepared his grave, though all the world forbids me!

Exit Teucer by a side ramp to make burial preparations.

Tecmessa remains on stage as does the boy clinging to his father.

---

337 Similarly Patroclus' comrades laid locks of hair on his corpse (*Iliad* 23.135). That hair represents a sense of solidarity and a recognition of shared mortality, and allows a part of the living suppliant to escort the dead spirit to the underworld. Here the three closest relatives make an offering with the child's being 'the third' because three was a lucky and sacred number.

338 The boy's offerings of hair represent a sort of store-house of ritual strength that link him as a suppliant closely to his father's spirit and create contact with the chthonic gods, enticing them to protect the corpse and in the (reciprocity of the) process, to protect the suppliants as well.

339 After the supplication and offering of hair comes the third ritual element of this scene, Teucer's curse on any wicked violator of this supplication's sanctity; Ajax's curse on his wicked foes at 839-44 was less conditional but had the same intense energy.

340 Teucer's curse is a speech act of homeopathic magic.

341 Earlier Eurysaces was the one 'guarded' (by his mother from his father: 535, 539); now, in the imminent absence of Teucer, whom Ajax appointed as the boy's future 'guardian' (562), Eurysaces himself will temporarily serve as the symbolic / ritual 'guardian' of his father and, by extension, of his mother. Some scholars prefer to take the lock of hair rather than Ajax himself as the direct object of the two verbs here ('hold' and 'guard'); I prefer the latter because it underscores a significant role reversal: Eurysaces, once the 'protected,' is now the 'protector,' having had activated (by Teucer) the etymological meaning of the name his father gave him, 'Broad Shield' (574-6).

Fourth Choral Song (= Third Stasimon)[342]

Strophe 1

Which, I wonder, will be the last one?   1185
When will the long number of years,
which in their restless wanderings beget our vagrant days,
when will they cease, years that forever bring on
the unrelenting ruin of the toils of the warrior,
the toils of swords slicing through Troy's sweeping plains,   1190
the toils that reward the Greeks with sorrow and shame?

Antistrophe 1

Would that *he* had first vanished
into the vast sky or plunged down into Hades
—whose dark house all mortals must share—
that man who first showed the sons of Greece the hateful weapons   1195
of Ares—whose suffering all mortals must share.
Alas, those toils of his that have begotten so many more toils!
Yes, *that man* it was who wrought ruin on the human race.

Strophe 2

That man dispensed for me
neither the pleasure of garlands   1200
nor of well-filled wine-cups for comradeship
nor the sweet noise of the pipes—to my sorrow—
nor the pleasure of sleep at night
No, from the passions of love,
alas, from the passions of love,   1205
he has cut me off.
And now I lie neglected in this way,
my hair always soaked
with thick dew,
constant reminders of ruinous Troy.   1210

Antistrophe 2

Once indeed he was my fortress

---

342 The four stanzas of this third stasimon have a chiastic arrangement: the first and last express, respectively, yearnings to leave Troy and return home; the two middle stanzas express the sorrows that the inventor of war has brought to mankind. It is a fitting moment of sorrowful reflection between the previous angry quarrel scene and the forthcoming one. Strophe #1 (1185-91) = Let us leave Troy's miseries; Antistrophe #1 (1192-98) = A curse on the inventor of war; Strophe #2 (1199-1210) = For that man put an end to life's simple joys; Antistrophe #2 (1211-22) = Since impetuous Ajax is no more, let us return home to holy Athens.

against the terrors of night
and the enemy's arrows—yes, he was impetuous Ajax.[343]
But now this man has been given up to a hateful destiny.
What pleasure, then, what pleasure shall still attend upon me?   1215
Would that I might be
where the wooded headland
washed by the waves
watches over the sea
beneath the flat summit   1220
of Cape Sunium[344]
where we might greet holy Athens.[345]

Exodos (Last Act)[346]

Re-enter Teucer, in haste, by a side-ramp.

Teucer

On guard! I've scurried back since I saw the general,
Agamemnon, hastening here to trouble us. It's evident that he is
about to unlock his mouth and unleash that foul, foolish tongue.   1225

*Enter Agamemnon in a hurry (along the same ramp), attired in the full rega-
lia of commander-in-chief; he is probably accompanied by several soldiers.*

Agamemnon[347]

You there! So it's you, they say, who's dared to bark out
those terrible threats of yours and not yet paid the price!

---

343 The furious Iliadic hero is no more; on this striking adjective see the note at 211.

344 This steep, rugged, and spectacular promontory at the southernmost tip of the Attic peninsula still today has perched on its plateau, some 200 feet above the sea, 18 of the original 42 Doric columns (20 feet high) of the once glorious temple of Poseidon built c. 440. There was also an early fifth-century Ionic temple to Athena there. For Athenian sailors Sunium was a sign that they were almost home; their city was only 45 miles up the coast. In 413 the Athenians fortified the promontory as a naval outpost (Thucydides 8.4).

345 The final words of the final antistrophe (and indeed of the final choral ode) are 'holy Athens' which *respond* to the final words of the corresponding strophe, 'ruinous Troy'; for Ajax's sailors the two dominant landscapes of his life stand in sharp contrast although they did not for Ajax himself (cf. 859-63).

346 This last act has three main components: **1223-1316** = the arrival of Ajax's second (and, accordingly, more serious) opponent, Agamemnon, who, like his brother, forbids Ajax's burial; **1317-72** = the unexpected arrival of Odysseus who breaks the impasse by persuading Agamemnon to yield; and **1373-1420** = Teucer's praise of Odysseus and the preparation for the funeral procession.

347 **Agamemnon's first major speech:** In the *Iliad* Agamemnon, leader of the Greek expedition against Troy, king of Mycenae, and older brother of Menelaus, was notoriously arrogant, ill-mannered, and sanctimonious. Not surprisingly he acts the same here (as often in Greek tragedy). His speech can be divided into four parts of roughly equal length, arranged in chiastic order; the first and last sections focus on various insults of Teucer while the two middle ones focus on insults of Ajax: 1226-35 = Teucer and his birth from a *slave*-mother; 1236-45 = Ajax as not such an great warrior and a sore loser in the contest for Achilles' armor; 1246-54 = Ajax as a burly and disobedient ox who needs to be whipped into line; 1255-63 = Teucer and his low 'barbarian' birth and speech.

Yes, I mean *you*, the son of that spear-captured slave woman!
No doubt if you'd been born and bred by a noble mother[348]
you'd be spouting lofty words and prancing on your tip-toes,   1230
seeing that you, being a *nothing*, in behalf of this *nothing*
have stood against us, swearing so solemnly that
we didn't come as generals and admirals of the Greeks
or of you, but that Ajax set sail as his own boss. So you claim!
Are these not impudent insults to hear from slaves?   1235
In defense of what sort of man are you croaking so insolently?
Where did he go or where did he stand, where I did not?
Are there, then, no true men among the Greeks except him?
To our sorrow, it seems, we proclaimed for them at that time
the bitter contest for Achilles' armor, if, by Teucer's showing,   1240
we're going to be vilified always and everywhere as scoundrels.
Nor will it ever satisfy you people, even when defeated so soundly,
to yield to the verdict that satisfied the majority of judges.
Instead, no doubt, you'll always be slinging stinging insults
or stabbing us stealthily in the dark, you who came short of the prize!   1245
Yet surely from such behavior there could never arise
any fixed and firm establishment of law,
no, not if we're going to expel the just victors
and bring up to the front ranks those laggards from behind.
No! This *must* be stopped! For it isn't men with big burly bodies   1250
or broad backs who stand most steadily; no, it's those
of sound mind who triumph always and everywhere.
Huge as the ribs of the ox may be, yet it's a small whip[349]
that keeps him going straight on the road.
I see the same medicine coming soon to remedy you   1255
if you don't acquire some measure of good sense.
That man's no longer alive but already a shadow,[350] yet your boldness
struts ever more outrageously and your mouth runs ever more freely!
Won't you learn moderation! Recognizing what you are by birth,
and by nature, won't you bring along some one else, a free-born man,   1260

---

348   Teucer's mother, Hesione, was a beautiful princess and daughter of the slain king of Troy, Laomedon; she
      was also a *war-captive* taken by Telamon in the first expedition against Troy led by Heracles (cf. 434-6,
      1301-3).

349   If Agamemnon had his way, Ajax, the whipper of oxen would become the ox who is whipped.

350   Odysseus had earlier (126) used the word 'shadow' in a deeply moving and compassionate way to describe
      the finality of the human condition. His sensitivity and insight, which we will soon witness again, is
      completely absent from Agamemnon's self-righteousness.

who can come before us and plead your case for you?[351]
Since when you're the speaker, I could no longer learn anything;
for your *barbarian* tongue talks babble that I don't understand.

Chorus-leader

Would that both of you had the good sense to learn moderation!
I can offer to you both no better advice than this.   1265

Teucer[352]

Alas! How very quickly gratitude for the dead
fades away from men's minds and is found to turn traitor
if this man no longer remembers you, Ajax,
not even in brief words, this man whom so often
you protected, exposing your own life to the spear!   1270
But now all your efforts are dead and gone, flung off with contempt.

    Turning to Agamemnon

And you who just now have spoken so many mindless words,
have you no memory at all, none at all, of the day[353]
when once you all were hemmed inside your own ramparts,
already all but gone, reduced to *nothings*, routed by the spear,   1275
and Ajax alone came to the rescue? Don't you remember
when the blazing fire was already raging around the tall masts
and the decks of ships' sterns, and Hector was leaping high
across the trenches and onto the hulls of your ships?
Who warded off that disaster? Didn't *he* do these deeds,   1280
this man here who, you claim, never set foot where you did not?
In your eyes didn't Ajax do as justice and duty demanded? And again
when he, all alone, fought against Hector alone, man against man?[354]
He was chosen by chance, not conscripted by command!
No, he cast down among the rest not some runaway ballot,   1285

---

351 Agamemnon's arrogance is a perfect set-up for the arrival of his best 'friend' Odysseus, who, ironically, *will* plead Ajax's case.

352 **Teucer's third major speech:** This reply to Agamemnon can be divided into five parts: 1266-71 = an introductory address to the dead Ajax about Agamemnon's ingratitude for good deeds done; 1272-88 = Agamemnon's failure to remember Ajax's valor against Hector on two important occasions; 1288-98 = Agamemnon's base birth from 'barbarian' parents; 1299-1307 = Teucer's noble birth from Telamon and Hesione; 1308-15 = Teucer's threat that only over his dead body will Ajax be forbidden burial.

353 Teucer recalls, in 1273-80, Ajax's finest hour in the *Iliad*, when he led the defense against Hector's attack on the Greek ships (15. 415 ff.). Teucer emphasizes twice Agamemon's failure to 'remember' (cf. 1276) Ajax's glory days; it is precisely such *memories* that distinguish Odysseus later on.

354 Teucer recalls, in 1283-7, Ajax's duel with Hector to decide the war (*Iliad* 7. 38-312). In Achilles' absence, nine Greek heroes (including Agamemnon and Odysseus), put their lots in Agamemnon's helmet to see who would fight Hector. Selection could be avoided by dampening one's clod of earth so that it did not leap out of the helmet. When Nestor shook the helmet, "a lot leap out, the one they had all wished for, Ajax's." (*Iliad* 7.182-3).

a clod of crumbling damp dirt, but the lot that was sure to leap out
lightly from the hollow of the crested helmet, before all the rest!
It was this man here who did this deed and I stood beside him,
me—the slave, the one born from the *barbarian* mother. You skunk!
How can you, speaking such nonsense, dare to look anyone   1290
in the eye? Don't you know that the father who begot your father
was Pelops, *a barbarian*, a Phrygian by birth![355] And that Atreus,
who in turn begot you, set forth before his brother Thyestes
a most impious feast, the flesh of his own children![356] You yourself
were begotten from a Cretan mother[357] whose very own father,   1295
catching her in the embraces of some interloping adulterer from abroad,
doomed her to destruction, to be devoured by the dumb fishes!
Born of such base breeding, have you the nerve to mock mine?
I am born from Telamon, my father, one who won
by his prowess the army's prize for pre-eminence   1300
and so takes as his bedmate my mother, a princess by birth,
daughter of Laomedon, whom Alcmene's son gave to that man[358]
as a special gift, selected for her beauty from the spoils of war.
As the noble son of such noble parents on both sides
should I bring shame upon my blood-kin   1305
whom now, laid low amidst such toils and troubles,
you cast out unburied and are not ashamed of saying so?
Know this for sure, that if you all throw this man out anywhere,
you'll also be throwing out our three corpses to lie beside him![359]
Yes, since it is honorable for me to die conspicuously in public   1310
toiling for this man, rather than to die in battle on your wife's behalf,
or should I say on behalf of your *and* your brother's wife![360]
So look not to my interests only, but to yours as well. Since,
if you bring me any more grief, you'll wish some day that you
had played the coward rather than the bold bully at my expense.   1315

---

355 A rising crescendo of triple insult by Teucer to counter Agamemnon's insult of his ancestry (1263). Pelops
     (father of Atreus, who was father of Agamemnon) was the son of Tantalus, king of Lydia, which was
     part of Phrygia, where Troy was located (cf. 487, 1054). Teucer's point is that Agamemnon is related to
     the barbarian allies of the Trojans.

356 Atreus, to avenge the adultery of his brother Thyestes, set before him as a feast at Mycenae three of his
     (butchered) sons (cf. Aeschylus, *Agamemnon* 1590–1602).

357 Aerope, Agamemnon's mother, was the daughter of Catreus, king of Crete; as Teucer tells the story,
     Catreus caught his wife in the act of adultery.

358 Alcmene's son was Heracles, who led the first expedition against Troy.

359 Teucer means Tecmessa, Eurysaces, and himself; the boy is still clinging as a suppliant to Ajax's corpse
     at center-stage (cf. 1180), with his mother beside him.

360 With lovely sarcasm Teucer speaks as if he forgot whose husband Helen really was. His point is that this
     is *their* war which they are fighting for the sake of a woman, and an unfaithful one at that.

Chorus-leader

Lord Odysseus, know that you have arrived just in time if you're here
not to share in the binding but rather in the loosening of the quarrel.[361]

Enter Odysseus suddenly and unexpectedly.

Odysseus

What is it, men? For from afar I heard Atreus' sons
shouting loudly over this valiant corpse.[362]

Agamemnon

Why of course we shouted. King Odysseus, have we not just now   1320
been called the most shameful names by this fellow?

Odysseus

What sorts of names? For I can pardon a man who,
when assaulted by abuse, counter-attacks with insults.

Agamemnon

He heard shameful words because he did shameful deeds to me.

Odysseus

Well, what did he do such that you've actually been injured?   1325

Agamemnon

He says that he won't allow this corpse to go without its proper
portion of burial rites, but will bury the body in spite of me.

Odysseus

Well, in the circumstance, may a friend speak the truth
and remain your ally no less than before?

Agamemnon

Speak. For otherwise I would surely be a fool   1330
since I consider you my greatest friend among the Greeks.

Odysseus[363]

Then hear me. By the gods, don't harden your heart

---

361 With these words the chorus-leader announces the movement of the rest of the play. For the last 270
     lines, since Menelaus' arrival at 1047, the plot has been tied up in the knots of the angry past. Clearly it
     will take a significant change of perspective to find a way out of this labyrinth of hate. With regard to
     Sophocles' diction here it is worth noting that his words 'binding' and 'loosening' anticipate Aristotle's
     use of similar words to describe the 'complication' and 'resolution' of a dramatic plot; see his *Poetics* 1455
     b 25 (written c. 330).

362 The transition (out of loud quarreling and name-calling) to the second stage of the Exodos is made by
     14 lines of rapid exchange (*stichomythia*; cf. the note at 38-50) between Odysseus and Agamemnon
     (1318-31). Odysseus' laudatory description of Ajax's body as 'valiant' (cf. 401) already suggests the new
     and different energy he will inject into the proceedings.

363 **Odysseus' reply to Agamemnon:** This brief but important speech has three parts: 1332-35 = Allow Ajax
     to be buried; don't let violence and hatred prevail over justice; 1336-41 = I, too, once hated Ajax but I
     can't deny his battle prowess and the honor he earned thereby; 1342-45 = So it would be unjust not to
     bury him and it would violate the gods' laws.

and so ruthlessly throw this man out unburied.
Nor let the spirit of violence overrule you
with such a pitch of hatred that you trample on justice.   1335
For me, too, he was once the most detested man in the army
ever since I prevailed to gain the armor of Achilles.
And yet, even though he was such to me,
I could not dishonor him by denying that he was,
in my eyes, the best and bravest of all the Argives,   1340
as many of us as came to Troy, apart from Achilles.
So that he would be dishonored by you unjustly. For it is not him
at all that you would be destroying, but rather the laws of the gods.
And as for the man of merit, if he should die,
it is unjust to harm him, even if you happen to hate him.[364]   1345

Agamemnon
Do *you*, Odysseus, champion *his* cause in this way against *me*?[365]

Odysseus
Yes, I do. Though I hated him while to hate was honorable.

Agamemnon
Well, shouldn't you also trample on him when he's dead?

Odysseus
Son of Atreus, don't exult in advantage that brings dishonor.

Agamemnon
But for the king to show piety and reverence is not easy.[366]   1350

Odysseus
It is easy, however, to honor the wise counsel of friends.

Agamemnon
Your 'man of merit' ought to obey those in authority.[367]

Odysseus
Stop! Surely your authority is the victor when you surrender to friends.

---

364 In this 14 line speech (1332-45) Odysseus uses the word 'justice' three times (1335, 1342, 1345; cf. 1363) and 'dishonor' twice (1339, 1342; cf. 1349). Furthermore he began at 1335 by urging Agamemnon to let go of his 'hate' (*mis-ein*, as in our word *miso*-gyny) and now he returns to that crucial point (1345; cf. 1347). For Odysseus, the moral code of 'helping friends and hating foes' does not apply to the dead; by *divine* law they deserve burial (1343; cf. 1129, 1154).

365 Agamemnon's question begins another passage of *stichomythia* (1346-69) which is longer and more tense than the preceding one (1318-31). Odysseus has set forth his position firmly (1332-45) and Agamemnon is struggling to accept it.

366 Certainly not easy for the likes of Agamemnon. A fragment of Sophocles' lost *Ajax the Locrian* reads thus: "Kings (*tyrannoi*) are wise (*sophoi*) because of the company of wise men (*sophoi*)."

367 Agamemnon is referring to Odysseus' use of that phrase at 1345 (cf. 1399).

Agamemnon

Remember the kind of man to whom you grant this favor!

Odysseus

The man was once my enemy, but a noble one.   1355

Agamemnon

Well, what will you do? Have you such respect for an enemy corpse?

Odysseus

Yes, since in my eyes his valor wins out over his enmity.[368]

Agamemnon

I assure you, such men are too unstable and fickle to be trusted.[369]

Odysseus

In truth, many who now are friends become bitter foes later.[370]

Agamemnon

Well, are *these* the sorts of friends that you recommend acquiring?   1360

Odysseus

What I do *not* care to recommend is a stubborn soul!

Agamemnon

You will, with this day's work, show us up as cowards.

) sense of a word that
) has shifted

Odysseus

No! Rather, as all the Greeks will say, men of justice!

Agamemnon

Are you urging me, then, to let them bury the dead?

Odysseus

I am. For I, too, shall myself come to this some day.[371]   1365

Agamemnon

In truth it's always the same. Every man toils for his own profit.

Odysseus

Well, for whom should I toil rather than myself?

Agamemnon

Then this deed shall be known as your doing, not mine.

---

368 This line summarizes everything Odysseus has been saying and it represents the final radical break from
     the pettiness of Menelaus and Agamemnon and from the past. No higher honor could be given Ajax than
     to have his hated arch-enemy, the man whom he thought destroyed him, recognize his 'valor' (*arête*; cf.
     616). The moral authority of this recognition graces the scene on the stage – child and mother huddled
     around the once great warrior – with a certain uncanny and tragic beauty.

369 Agamemnon is referring to Ajax (not Odysseus) and his changing from friend to foe.

370 Odysseus is affirming the law of alternation that Ajax learned earlier (679-82) but was unable, finally,
     to accept as part of his life.

371 Odysseus' wisdom and humanity recall his moving words at 121-6.

Odysseus

If you act in this way, you will at all events be worthy at least.[372]

Agamemnon

Well, anyway, be fully assured that on *you*   1370
I would bestow an even greater favor than this.[373] But *he*,
both there and here, in death and in life, will remain
my most hated enemy. *You* can do whatever you wish.[374]

Exit Agamemnon and his soldiers by a side-ramp.

Chorus-leader

Whoever denies, Odysseus, that you are by nature
wise in judgment, while you act thus, is himself a *fool*!   1375

Odysseus

And now, what's more, to Teucer I declare myself
henceforth as much a friend, as formerly I was a foe.
And I wish to share in burying him who here lies dead
and share in the toil and leave out none of those rites
that mortals should toil over in homage to the most excellent men.   1380

Teucer[375]

Most excellent Odysseus,[376] in every way I commend you
for these words; indeed you have much deceived my expectation.
For although you were the most hateful of Greeks to this man,
you alone stood by him with a helping hand. And in his presence,
though he was dead and you alive, you didn't harden your heart   1385
to exalt maliciously over him like that frantic thunder-struck fool,
the general who came—he and that blood-brother of his—

---

372 Odysseus' compliment wins Agamemnon's final consent and brings the issue (and the *stichomythic* exchange) to an end.

373 Agamemnon agrees to allow the burial not because he has been persuaded that Ajax is worthy of that honor but as a personal 'favor' (*charis*) to his best friend.

374 These four lines bring to an end Agamemnon's appearance and also conclude the second section of the Exodos. It is worth noting briefly the symmetry with which Sophocles has designed this section: a] 1318-31 = 14 lines of *stichomythia* (to introduce the Odyssean change of tone); b] 1332-45 = 14 lines of speech by Odysseus (to state his themes of honor, justice, and refusal to hate the dead); c] 1346-69 = 24 lines of *stichomythia* (to contrast the high road taken by Odysseus with the low road taken by Agamemnon); d] 1370-74 = 4 lines of speech by Agamemnon (to bring his appearance to a close with consent to bury Ajax). Sections A and B as well as C and D each have, respectively, 28 lines (although in different proportions to suit their different purposes).

375 **Teucer's response to Odysseus' intervention:** This speech has three parts:1381-85 = high praise of Odysseus for his words and deeds; 1386-92 = harsh blame of the hybris of Menelaus and Agamemnon and a curse on them; 1393-99 = instructions to Odysseus on the ways in which he can, and cannot, participate in the burial rites of Ajax.

376 In the previous line Odysseus had called Ajax 'most excellent' (*aristos*); now Teucer returns the compliment.

eager to throw Ajax out, disgraced and robbed of burial.
So may the father who presides over this Olympian sky above[377]
and the Fury of unfading memory and all-accomplishing Justice   1390
destroy those knaves, returning evil for evil,
just as they wanted to throw out this man in undeserved disgrace.
But as for you, O seed of venerable father Laertes,
I am loathe to let you touch his body or take part in the burial
lest I vex the dead by doing so. For all the rest, however,   1395
do indeed join in and if you wish to bring along
any soldier from the army, we shall hold no grievance.
I will arrange for all the rest. But be assured
that in our judgment you are a 'man of merit.'[378]

Odysseus
Well, such was my wish. But if it doesn't please you   1400
for me to participate, I shall depart, accepting your decision.

> *Exit Odysseus by a side-ramp.*

Teucer (*addressing his attendants, the chorus, and Eurysaces*)
Enough. Already the time has been much protracted.[379]
Quickly, some of you prepare a hollow trench with your hands.[380]

> *Exit a first group of attendants by one side ramp.*

And you others, set up the water cauldron
on its tall tripod over the surrounding fire   1405
to ready the ritual and holy washing.

> *Exit a second group of attendants by the other side ramp.*[381]

Let one troop of men fetch from the hut
the fine armor which he wore under his shield.[382]

> *Exit a third group of attendants into Ajax's hut.*

> *Teucer then turns to Eurysaces.*

And you, son, with such strength as you have,

---

377 Teucer's curse here at 1389-92 recalls Ajax's earlier curse against the sons of Atreus where he invoked the Furies as blood-sucking vampires (835-44).

378 At 1345 Odysseus had called Ajax a 'man of merit' (*esthlos*), although Agamemnon rejected that term (1352). Now Teucer returns the compliment to Odysseus.

379 The delay was caused by the arrivals of Menelaus (147-1162) and Agamemnon (1226-1373).

380 Earlier the chorus had directed Teucer to find a 'hollow trench' (1165) in which to bury Ajax. He has, in the interim, chosen that spot and now it must be prepared.

381 The staging (and even the text) of the ending is controversial. What seems most important is that there be some sort of *unified* funeral procession (with the chorus involved); this would contrast nicely with the disorderly exiting of three groups at line 815.

382 Ajax had give instructions at 572-77 that all his armor except his shield be buried with his body; the shield, of course, will be given to Eurysaces.

lovingly lay your hands on your father and together with me   1410
lift his body;[383] for still the black life-force
blows upwards from the warm veins and vessels.[384]

> *Eurysaces puts his hands on his father's corpse; after some moments he helps*
> *Teucer raise Ajax's body.*

Come one and all, whoever claims
to be here as a friend, let him hurry, come quickly
to toil for this man who was good in every respect.   1415
[For there was no one of mortals ever better
than Ajax when he was alive: this is what I say.]

> *The third group of attendants returns with Ajax's body armor; the funeral*
> *procession now begins to form into a unified group.*

Chorus-leader

In truth men can understand many things
once they've seen them. But before it comes into sight,
no one is a prophet of the future and how he will fare.[385]   1420

> *Exit by a side ramp, Teucer carrying Ajax's corpse over his shoulders; there*
> *follows, in solemn procession, the chorus, Eurysaces, and Tecmessa.*

---

383 At 545 Ajax had asked the attendant to lift Eurysaces into his bloody arms. Now the boy must help his uncle raise his father, presumably onto Teucer's shoulders.

384 As the play ends, Ajax, who has been dead for about an hour (i.e. the 555 lines since verse 865), is still bleeding from the sword wound; but it is less the loss of blood that Sophocles focuses on than the loss of the heroic life-force. The description is so vivid that we almost forget that the corpse of Ajax is now just a stuffed 'dummy' of some sort.

385 The authenticity of lines 1418-20 is uncertain, as is the case with many closing lines in tragedy. Their most important function probably has less to do with their proverbial (and somewhat banal) wisdom about life's uncertainties than it does with their signaling the end of the play.

Outline of the structure of Euripides' *Hecuba* (circa 423 B.C.E.)

Prologue and lyric laments   (1-215)

> a) Ghost of Polydorus, youngest son and last heir of Hecuba and King Priam, announces his own murder and foretells his sister Polyxena's death (1-58)
>
> b) Hecuba sings of a nightmare that foreshadowed her son's murder (59-97)
>
> c) Entry song of chorus of enslaved Trojan women about the vote of the Greek army (urged on by wily Odysseus) to sacrifice Hecuba's youngest daughter, Polyxena, in order to placate Achilles' ghost (98-153)
>
> d) Hecuba and Polyxena sing matching monodies of despair (154-176 =197-215) that surround an agonizing lyric dialogue (177-196)

Act I   (216-443)

> a) Odysseus vs. Hecuba: debate over the sacrifice of Polyxena (216-333)
>
> b) Polyxena decides to accept her death willingly and to die 'free'; she bids farewell to Hecuba as Odysseus takes her away (334-443)

Song 2   **(444-483)** Somber reflection of the widows on their pitiful destiny as slaves

Act II   (484-628)

> a) Talthybius (old Greek herald) narrates Polyxena's death to Hecuba (484-582)
>
> b) Chorus and a defiant Hecuba react to his report (583-628)

Song 3   **(629-656)** Lamentation about the power of Necessity and Troy's fall

Act III   (657-904)

> a) Maid delivers a covered corpse to Hecuba, who vows revenge (657-725)
>
> b) Hecuba begs Agamemnon for help; he agrees not to intervene (726-904)

Song 4   **(905-952)** Lamentation about Troy's fall, with a curse on Paris and Helen

Act IV   (953-1022)

> Hecuba lures Polymestor (and sons) into Agam.'s tent with the promise of money

Song 5   **(1023-1034)** Act-dividing lyrics predicting the fate of the unsuspecting victims

Exodos   (1035-1295)

> a) Hecuba relates the blinding of Polymestor and murder of his two sons (1035-55)
>
> b) Polymestor enters, screaming in agony, crawling on all fours (1056-1108)
>
> c) 'Trial': Polymestor vs. Hecuba. Agamemnon, acting as 'judge', convicts Polymestor; Hecuba is vindicated but must go into slavery. Polymestor utters dire prophecies about Hecuba and Agamemnon (1109-1295)

The *Hecuba* of Euripides

Setting

The scene is the Greek encampment on the shore of Chersonese in Thrace, shortly after the fall of Troy. Dawn is about to break. The *skênê* (stage building) is a simple tent, which serves as the living quarters of the slaves of Agamemnon. Of the two side entrance-ways (*eisodoi*) on each side of the long low stage the right one leads to the soldiers' camps, the left to Thrace and the sea.

Cast of characters in order of appearance [1]

Ghost of Polydorus	murdered son of Hecuba and Priam, queen and king of Troy
Hecuba	queen of Troy, old widow of Priam, now a slave of Agamemnon
Captive Trojan women	mute actors
Chorus	captive Trojan women
Polyxena	youngest daughter of Hecuba and Priam, still a virgin
Odysseus	greatest surviving Greek, famed for his intelligence and speech
Talthybius	minor Greek warrior, who serves as a herald for Agamemnon
Serving maid of Hecuba	
Agamemnon	king of Argos and commander-in-chief of the Greek army
Attendants of Agamemnon	mute actors
Polymestor	King of Thracian Chersonese (the Dardanelles), ally of Priam
Sons of Polymestor	mute actors

---

1   We have no records for which of the three actors were assigned to which characters, so we construct the assignments by which characters do not appear at the same time. While thematic and structural parallels make assigning the deuteragonist to Odysseus and Polymestor very tempting, the lengthy songs sung by Polyxena and Polymestor suggest those two extremely different characters were performed by a deuteragonist who specialized in such emotional monodies; likely, though by no means certain.

The most likely division of the eight speaking roles in *Hecuba* (with their respective number of lines put in parentheses) is as follows: **Actor #1** (protagonist) = Hecuba (483); **Actor #2** (deuteragonist) = Polyxena (94), serving maid of Hecuba (16), and Polymestor (170); **Actor #3** (tritagonist) = ghost of Polydorus (58), Odysseus (57), Agamemnon (99) and Talthybius (85). The chorus has some 233 lines.

The ghost of Polydorus appears above the skênê.[2]

Ghost of Polydorus

I am here after leaving the hiding places of corpses and the gates of shadow
where Hades dwells apart from the gods,[3]
I, Polydorus, was the child of Cisseus' daughter, Hecuba,
and Priam was my father,[4] who, when there was danger that
the Phrygians'[5] city fall by Greek spears,   5
terrified, in secret he sent me from the Trojan land
towards the house of Polymestor, our Trojan guest-friend,[6]
who cultivates this most fertile Chersonian land which you see here,[7]
ruling his horse-loving people by the spear.
My father secretly sent much gold with me,   10
so that, if ever Ilium's[8] walls should fall,
then his living sons would not lack livelihood.
Since I was the youngest of Priam's sons, he also sent me
furtively from the land; for I was able to bear neither armor
nor a spear with my young arm.   15
So while the country's walls remained upright,
and the towers of the Trojan land were intact,
and Hector[9] my brother was fortunate with his spear,
I grew quite well with the Thracian man, my father's guest-friend,
with upbringing like some sapling—a wretch;   20
but when Troy and Hector's life are

---

2   He makes reference to being "above" his mother at line 29, and his needs for a tomb seem to parallel
     and comment upon the desire of Achilles for honor to be given to his tomb, and Achilles is said to have
     appeared above it. The area above the *skênê* is generally reserved for gods. Among the surviving Greek
     dramas, the *Hecuba* uniquely begins with a speech by a ghost. Sophocles' lost *Polyxena*, the likely model
     for this drama, almost certainly commenced with a solo speech by the ghost of Achilles. The ghost here
     suggests the work of mysterious powers otherwise unvoiced throughout the *Hecuba*, establishes a certainty
     that highlights the ignorance of the living characters, and symbolizes a problematic past, remembered,
     and then effaced.

3   Technically one of the Olympian generation of gods, Hades, a name which designates both the lord of
     the Underworld and the place itself, is kept apart from his peers who inhabit the sky.

4   Priam, as King of Troy, was one of the most powerful and wealthy rulers in Greek myth, who, in the
     Iliad, sees all of his sons save Paris cut down by Achilles.

5   Phrygia was a large, fairly undefined geographical area that encompassed much of west-central Anatolia
     in Asia Minor. In the *Hecuba* "Phrygian" is used interchangeably with "Trojan."

6   *Xenos*. See Introduction and Interpretive Essay on the importance of the guest-host relationship in Greek
     ethics. Euripides here immediately stresses that Polymestor violates the fundamental morals of Greek
     society.

7   The Chersonese is a peninsula of Thrace that runs along the Hellespont, making it a natural stop-over
     for ships sailing from Troy towards the Greek mainland.

8   Ilium is another name for Troy.

9   Hector was the greatest of the Trojan warriors. His death at the hands of Achilles, after his parents Priam
     and Hecuba beg him to enter the city walls for safety, is the climax of Homer's *Iliad*.

lost,[10] and the hearth of my fathers was razed,
and Priam himself before the god-founded altar falls
slaughtered[11] by Achilles' son,[12] desecrated with blood,
my father's guest-friend then slays me,
long-suffering, for the sake of gold,   25
and, after the slaying, to the salty swell
he released me, so that he himself could keep the gold in his house.[13]
And I lie upon the shore, sometimes in the sea's tossing,
borne along by the many cycles of the waves,
unlamented, unburied. But now above my mother,   30
Hecuba, I float, having abandoned my body,
suspended now already for a third day,[14]
for as long as in this Chersonesian land
my ill-starred mother from Troy has been present.
And all the Achaean ships at rest   35
lie thick on the shores of the Thracian land here;
for the son of Peleus[15] appeared above his tomb
and Achilles checked the entire Greek army,
although they were directing their sea voyage homewards.
He demands to take my sister Polyxena   40
as a blood-victim for his own tomb and a prize.
And he will obtain this, and from his men friends[16]
he will not lack gifts; the assigned destiny drives

---

10   Greek usage frequently retains for vividness a present tense when narrating a past action. I attempt to
     retain this practice here and in other sections of this drama.

11   The verb denotes sacrificial killing. Seaford (1994) 340 observes, "murder in tragedy is generally envisaged
     as sacrifice."

12   Neoptolemus was summoned by Odysseus from his home in Skyros after the death of his father. At
     the fall of Troy, Neoptolemus murdered Priam at an altar in his own house, in front of his family, an
     episode the Roman poet Vergil later depicts at *Aeneid* 2.506-58. Neoptolemus thus moves from literally
     sacrificing Polyxena to a gross perversion of the sacrificial act when he murders her father.

13   Virgil presents a slightly different version of the murder of Polydorus (*Aeneid* 3.22-67) in which his
     corpse, covered in protruding wooden spears, is transformed into a bush, and when Aeneas arrives and
     tugs at a branch he finds blood oozing from the plant and the plaintive voice of Polydorus begging for
     burial.

14   Greek time-counting is inclusive, so Polydorus has been aloft for two days since his murder, with the
     time of the play being the dawning of the third day. Collard notes, "the number three implies ritual or
     mysterious significance." For example, in the *Iliad* Patroclus makes three attempts at the walls of Troy
     before Apollo intervenes, and Achilles chases Hector around Troy three times before their duel.

15   Achilles. Homer had located Achilles' tomb at Sigrum on the coast of Troy (*Odyssey* 24.82). On the
     conflicting accounts of the location of the tomb see Pantelis (2002) 68-69.

16   "Men friends" warrants explanation. *Andrôn philôn* is much more highly gendered than merely *philôn*,
     which would have sufficed in itself to designate the reciprocal bonds of heroic society. The addition of
     andrôn ("men," dictionary form is *anêr*) speaks to the codes of heroic masculinity that are brutally indif-
     ferent to the needs of Hecuba and Polyxena.

my sister to die on this day.
Two corpses of two children,   45
my mother will behold, my own and her ill-starred daughter,
because I will appear in the surf at the feet of a slave-woman,
so that, wretch that I am, I can get a grave;
for I demanded the powers below that I
acquire a grave and fall to my mother's hands.   50
So this will be mine, as much as I wished it to happen.
But I'll now withdraw[17] away from aged
Hecuba, for she here passes from behind the tent of
Agamemnon, fearing my phantom.

   (Hecuba enters from inside the tent through the skênê *door, supported by two*
   women, who serve as slaves alongside their former queen.)
Oh—
Oh you, mother who, though born from ruling households,
saw slavery's day, how your current misery
matches your previous success; and some one of the gods
ruins you in repayment for your earlier prosperity.

Hecuba[18]
Lead the old woman from the house, children.
Lead your fellow slave lifting her up,   60
once your queen, you women of Troy.
[Take, bear, send, lift me]
grasping my aged hand.
And I, leaning on the twisted staff with my hand,   65
I will speed the slow-footed step
of my joints, placing it out in front of me.

Oh blinding light of Zeus, Oh shadowy night,[19]
why ever am I carried away at night thus
by fears, by phantoms? Oh mistress Earth,   70
mother of black-winged dreams,
I send back the nocturnal vision,
[which, through dreams, I saw, learned and understood

---

17   Polydorus possibly exits through a trapdoor on the roof of the *skênê*; see Mastronarde (1990) 259-60 for
     the ways he could leave that area.

18   Hecuba here sings a monody. Gregory (1999) notes this song resembles "a pattern also found in the
     Ion, the opening monologue spoken by a supernatural character is followed by a solo aria sung by the
     protagonist." This solo replaces the more typical choral entry song, which is thus transformed into a
     lyrical exchange with Hecuba concerning the sacrifice of Polyxena.

19   A number of tragedies, most famously the *Agamemnon* and *Antigone* begin their actions just as the day
     breaks. Such settings suggest that these dramas, including the *Hecuba*, were performed first in their
     trilogic group. Each day's performances at the City Dionysia began at dawn.

as a fearful vision concerning my child kept safe at Thrace,   75
and about my dear daughter Polyxena.]

Oh gods of the earth, save my boy,
who, the sole remaining anchor of my house,
inhabits snowy Thrace   80
under protection of his father's guest-friend.

Something new will happen;
some mournful song will come to mourning women.
Not ever has my spirit so incessantly
shuddered, feared.   85
When ever could I see the god-like mind of Helenus
and Cassandra,[20] Trojan women,
so they might discern these dreams for me?

For I saw a dappled deer by the wolf's bloody claw   90
slaughtered, rent from my knees without pity.
And this is my fear now: Achilles' phantom
came above the high crest of the tomb.
He was demanding as a prize
some one of the many-troubled Trojan women.   95
So from my, from my girl,
send this thing away, you gods, I beg you.[21]

Chorus   *(entering from right; the rhythm of their words is a recitative)*[22]
Hecuba, quickly to you I drew away,
leaving our master's tents,
where I have been alotted and assigned as   100
slave, driven away from the city
of Ilium, at the lance's point,
spear-hunted by the Achaeans,[23]
relieving nothing of your sufferings,
but bearing a heavy burden of   105

---

20   Helenus and Cassandra were children of Priam and Hecuba who were also prophets. Cassandra was made a prophet by Apollo in exchange for sexual favors. When she refused him, he spat in her mouth and made her prophecies unbelievable to all who heard them. Helenus is praised in the *Iliad* (6.77) as "the best of the seers."

21   Most editors reject lines 90-7 as inauthentic. I follow Gregory's arguments in retaining them.

22   By "recitative" I mean a type of song that is more chanted than sung, here in the anapestic meter which was originally for marching and often thus used to accompany arrivals and departures (although 59-67 of Hecuba's preceding monody was also in anapests). In general, this is the choral song called a *parodos*, which the chorus sings "along the way" as it enters the orchestra.

23   The term Achaeans designates the people we call Greek who fought at Troy. It is interchangeable here with Danaans below.

news to you, lady, a herald of pains.
For in the full assembly of the Achaeans
it is resolved[24] that your daughter will be a sacrifice to
Achilles; you know when he mounted his tomb,
and appeared with golden weapons,   110
and he checked the sea-faring flotilla
whose sails strained at their ropes,
shouting out this:
"Where, then, Danaans, do you think you're going,
leaving my tomb without a prize?"[25]   115
A wave of great strife crashed down together,
rumor ran asunder through the Greeks'
army of spearmen; to some it seemed best to give
blood-sacrifice to the tomb, while to others it didn't.
But there was one looking after your welfare,   120
the one keeping the god-visited Bacchant's[26]
bed, Agamemnon.
And the two sons of Theseus, the budding shoots of Athens,
were orators of double speeches;[27]
but they agreed in one sentiment,   125
to garland Achilles' tomb
with fresh greenery of blood, but they said they'd never
prefer the bed of Cassandra
to the spear of Achilles.
The efforts of the contested speeches   130
were somehow equal, until the shifty-minded
sweet-talking, crowd-pleasing liar,
the son of Laertes,[28] persuades the army
not to reject the best of all the Danaans

24   This is a legislative formula from the Athenian assembly, applied here anachronistically. On the role of contemporary political terms from the Assembly see Michelini (1987) 143-44 and Hogan (1972) 250-51. Gregory (1999) 58 and (2002) discusses how the language of the contemporary Athenian assembly draws connections between the mythical past of the story and the political present of the audience.

25   The Homeric Achilles had been obsessed with honor and its visible tangible signs, such as war booty. His desire for more, even from beyond the grave, marks him as avaricious, characterized by the same greed that characterizes Polymestor's lust for gold.

26   Cassandra is technically not a female follower of the god Dionysus, as the designation "Bacchant" suggests, yet the wildness of her prophetic ravings would have made her resemble one.

27   Acamas and Demophon, the sons of Theseus by Phaedra. The mention of Athens and its greatest hero further links the action to contemporary Athens; see Michelini (1987) 142-43.

28   Odysseus. Although the hero of one of the two great Homeric epics, in the fifth century Odysseus' persuasive abilities lent him easily to being characterized in a manner that would suggest a Sophist or a demagogic Athenian politician.

because of a slave's sacrifice,   135
nor that anyone of the dead
standing by Persephone[29] should say
how from Troy's plains
Danaans departed ungrateful to Danaans
who came on behalf of Greeks.[30]   140
Odysseus will come quite soon
to drag your foal from your breasts
and launch her from your aged hand.
But go to temples, go to altars,
[sit suppliant at Agamemnon's knees,]   145
call on the gods in heaven and
those below the earth!
For either prayers will prevent you
from being bereft of your unhappy child,
or you must behold her cast down on the tomb,   150
a virgin blood-reddened
by a black-gleaming stream
from her gold-bearing neck.

Hecuba (*singing in lyric meters*)   (*strophe*)[31]
How unhappy I am! what ever should I shout?
What kind of cry? what lament?   155
Wretched woman of wretched old age,
of slavery not endurable,
not bearable? *oimoi moi.*
Who protects me? What family?
What city? Gone is my old man,   160
gone my sons.
What path do I take, this way or that?
Where is there some one of the gods
or spirits to help me?
Oh, you've brought suffering   165
Trojan women, you've brought suffering and
pains, you have destroyed and destroyed me utterly;
no longer is my life

---

29   The Queen of the Underworld and wife of Hades.

30   The *Iliad* betrays no sense of such nationalism among the Achaean warriors, who see themselves more
     as a loose confederation under Agamemnon's authority.

31   Lyrical passages in tragedy are typically structured through organized, balanced pairs of strophe and
     antistrophe. There is no antistrophe in Hecuba's song; rather, Polyxena's subsequent lament (197-215)
     provides the response, matching her mother's song in form.

admirable in the light.
Oh wretched foot, lead, 170
lead me, aged, to this hall here; Oh child, Oh daughter
of a most grievous mother—come out, come out
of the house—hear your mother's voice.
[Oh child, come out so that you may know
what, what sort of report I hear 175
about your life.]

> *Polyxena enters from the* skênê. *She must be carrying or wearing some kind*
> *of special clothing, as she instructs Odysseus to help her with her robes just*
> *before she departs. This exchange occurs in irregular lyrical dialogue.*

Polyxena

Ah.
Mother, mother, why do you cry? Heralding
what news have you flushed me from the house
like a bird with this terror?

Hecuba

Oh my child! 180

Polyxena

Why do you mourn me? The prelude seems bad for me.

Hecuba

Aaiai your life!

Polyxena

Out with it! Don't hide it any longer.
I fear, I fear, mother,
why ever do you raise your lament... 185

Hecuba

Oh child, child of an unhappy mother...

Polyxena

But what is this thing you will announce?

Hecuba

Your slaughter—the collective wisdom of the Argives
assigns you to the tomb
for the son of Peleus. 190

Polyxena

Oh no, mother! What do you mean?
Explain those sad troubles to me,
mother, explain them![32]

32　There are punctuation difficulties in the Greek here.

Hecuba

I proclaim, daughter, ill-spoken rumors;
they announce to me the judgment of the Argives'   195
vote about your life.

Polyxena   *(antistrophe)*

Oh terribly suffering one, Oh all-enduring,
Oh mother of a wretched existence!
Such, such an outrage
despised and unspeakable   200
has some god sent you.
No longer here by you, no longer
a wretched child by a wretched old woman
shall I share slavery.
For you will see me like a mountain-bred calf,   205
you wretched will see me a wretched sapling
.... [33]

torn from your hand and
cut at the throat, sent down under earth
to the gloom in Hades, where with corpses
I wretchedly shall lie. [34]   210

[And miserable you, mother,
I mourn you with tear-drenched dirges,
but for my life, its outrage and mutilation,
my lament takes no part, but a stronger fortune has fallen
to me to die]   215

Chorus

And now look: Odysseus comes hurriedly by foot,
Hecuba, to signal some new story to you.

Odysseus   *(entering from the right. Odysseus then stands between Polyxena
and Hecuba, almost as a judge who hears both sides of a debate)*

Lady! I think you know the army's decision
and that the vote is final; but still I shall speak
It seemed best to the Achaeans to sacrifice   220
your daughter Polyxena at the high mound of Achilles' tomb.
They assign us to be the escort and collector of the maiden.
The administrator and priest of the sacrifice
will be the son of Achilles.

33   There is a gap in the manuscript here.

34   Note how Polyxena here, remarkably, worries more about her mother's suffering than her own death,
but this magnanimity prepares her noble behavior at the sacrifice.

So you know what you must do. Don't be torn away by force   225
and don't come into some scuffle of hands with me;
Consider your defenses and the presence of your
troubles. It's a wise[35] thing to keep your wits even in troubles that compel.

Hecuba

Aiai. A great trial[36] is at hand here, it seems,
full of groans and not empty of tears.   230
And I, at least, did not die when it was necessary that I die,
nor did Zeus destroy me, but he sustains me, so that I see
other troubles greater than troubles—I the wretched one.
But if it is possible for slaves to raise questions to free men,
neither painful nor biting the heart,   235
then it's necessary for you to respond in turn
and for us who ask these things to listen .

Odysseus

It is possible. Ask away. I don't begrudge you the time.

Hecuba

Do you remember, when you came as a spy to Troy,[37]
shapeless in rags, and from your eyes   240
drops of blood dripped down your chin?

Odysseus

I remember; it didn't just touch the edge of my heart.

Hecuba

And Helen recognized you and informed me alone?

Odysseus

We remember that we'd come into great peril.

Hecuba

And as a humble man you touched my knees?[38]   245

---

35   The Greek word *sophos* can mean wise or clever. Many texts from this era, especially Euripides' *Medea*,
     play off this ambiguity.

36   *megas agôn*. The *agôn*, a highly stylized rhetorical debate, is central to many Greek dramas, especially in
     Euripides. The debate here foreshadows the later one between Polymestor and Hecuba, and this mirroring
     would mark Hecuba's reversal from powerless victim to powerful avenger. On Euripides' use of the *agôn*
     see Lloyd (1992).

37   The story of Odysseus' reconnaissance mission to Troy is told in *Odyssey* 4.235-64, though there it is
     Helen alone who recognizes him and Hecuba is not mentioned. Note that Odysseus' disguise as a blind
     man with bloody eyes foreshadows Hecuba's real punishment of Polymestor.

38   The touching of the knees is part of the gesture of supplication, a condition that should guarantee the
     safety of the supplicator. For supplication scenes in Greek literature, see Gould's classic article *Hiketeia*,
     which has been reprinted with an addendum in Gould (2001) 22-77. Gould observes (23) that supplication
     "is essentially an act which seeks a *reciprocal* act on the part of him to whom it is addressed, above and
     beyond the concepts of reciprocity which are built into the structure of Greek social relationships."

Odysseus
So that my hand grew still as death on your robes.

Hecuba
What, indeed, did you say then as my slave?

Odysseus
The inventions of many words, so that I not die.

Hecuba
And then I saved you and sent you out of the land?

Odysseus
So that I see this light of the sun now.   250

Hecuba
Are you not therefore ashamed at these plans,
you who experienced such things at my hands as you claim you experienced,
but you treat us not well, yet as badly as you can?
Ungrateful is your race, you who value the
demagogue's honors; would that you were not known to me,   255
you who, when harming your friends, don't worry,
if you would say something currying favor to the mob.[39]
But yet why, believing this to be a clever thing,
did they set a vote of murder against my daughter?
Was it that necessity compelled them to human sacrifice   260
at a tomb, where it's more normal to kill cattle?
Or was it that the desire to pay back the killers of Achilles
with killing justly aims murder against her?
But this girl did nothing wrong to him.
[Helen is the one he ought to request as sacrifice for his grave.   265
That woman destroyed him and drove him to Troy.][40]
But if it's necessary that some one of the spear-won women die,
and one surpassing in beauty, this shouldn't come from us:
the daughter of Tyndareus[41] is most splendid in form,
and she was found to be committing wrong no less than us.   270
        I set this argument in the competition for justice;
listen now to the things which you must answer back
when I demand. You touched my hand, as you say,
and this grey cheek in supplication;

---

39   These words reflect the growing sense in Athens that the Assembly had, following the death of Pericles, become too much under the sway of skillful speakers who could manipulate the people for their own personal ends without any concern for the greater good.

40   I accept Gregory's arguments here, following Kovacs, against the authenticity of these two lines.

41   Helen, like many male heroes, had two fathers, the divine Zeus and the mortal Tyndareus. Hecuba seems to want to deny Helen's divine lineage here by stressing her mortal father.

(Hecuba reaches out to Odysseus)

In return I lay hold of the same parts of you   275
and I demand back the favor from then and I beg you,
that you don't tear my child from my hands.
Don't kill her! Enough are dead!
In her I have joy and forget my troubles;
this girl is my consolation in place of many: 280
city, nurse, crutch, journey's leader.
There is no need for rulers to rule what they need not,
nor for the lucky to believe they will always succeed;
for I was once also, yet I no longer am,
but a single day removed all blessings from me.   285
Still, oh face of a friend, show some reverence[42] for me,
give pity. Go to the Achaean army
and dissuade them, since there's jealous anger[43] at killing
women whom you didn't kill earlier when
you tore them from their altars, but you pitied then.   290
Among you there is a custom of equality
to free men and slaves concerning blood.[44]
Your status, even if you should speak badly,
will persuade; for a speech coming from the disreputable
is not as strong as the same one coming from the reputable.   295

Chorus

A man's nature is never so rigid
that, hearing your groans and lamentations
of long weepings, it would not shed a tear.

Odysseus

Hecuba, accept my instruction and don't by your anger make
the one who speaks favorably hostile in his thoughts.   300
I am ready to save your bodily life, at whose hands I've been
fortunate, and I don't speak in vain.
And what I said to all I will not deny:

---

42   The verb here is a cognate of the noun *aidôs*, a Greek word that English cannot represent with any single
      term. It communicates a reciprocal sense of honor, shame, respect and what is owed. Context typically
      determines which of those senses are predominant in a particular usage. See Cairns (1993) and the
      discussion in the Interpretive Essay of this volume. Of course, Odysseus is not a "friend," but the adjective
      here, *philos*, connotes the reciprocal bonds that he should feel from their previous relationship.

43   *Phthonos* is the jealous anger of the gods at excessive human success.

44   This is an anachronistic appeal to Greek law in general and fifth-century Athenian law in particular; by
      using the terms *isos* (equal) and *nomos* (law) together Hecuba unknowingly evokes for the audience their
      treasured principle of *isonomia*, a bedrock of Athenian democracy which guaranteed equal protection of
      the laws and equal participation in politics.

since Troy has been sacked we give your daughter
as a sacrifice to the first man of the army as he demands.   305
For in this matter many cities struggle,
whenever some man, though noble and eager,
still takes away nothing more than his inferiors.
But to us Achilles is worthy of honor, lady,
a man having died most nobly on behalf of Greece.[45]   310
Isn't this therefore shameful, if we use him as a friend while he's
looking at the light of day, but, when he's dead, we no longer do?[46]
Well then. What will someone say, if ever there appears again
some mustering of the troops and some struggle with enemies?[47]
Will we fight, or will we be in love with our own lives,   315
seeing that the dead man is not honored?
And certainly, to me at least while I'm alive, if I should
have something small each day, it would be totally enough;
but my tomb I would want thought worthy
to be seen; for gratitude lasts a long time.[48]   320
       But if you claim you suffer pitiful things, listen to me in response:
there are among us old women and men
no less wretched than you,
and young brides bereft of their bridegrooms
whose bodies here the dust of Ida[49] hides.   325
Endure this. But as for us, if we think wrongly in
honoring a noble man, we will accept a charge of stupidity;

45   The Homeric Achilles would be surprised to learn he died *pro patria*. The Achilles reported in this drama seems even more self-centered than his Iliadic predecessor; see Pantelis (2002) on how Achilles changes from the *Iliad* in fifth-century tragedy.

46   The ideas of shame and honor here would be a particularly powerful argument. Traditional Greek ethics were largely based on shame, an externally validated criterion of praise and blame, which is contrasted with guilt, whose source is internalized, though Cairns argues that we overrate this distinction between shame and guilt. Honor also is not a sense of internal self-worth, but the measure of one's standing in the eyes of others. In Homer Achilles withdraws from the Trojan War over a slight to his honor, and in Sophocles' *Ajax* the hero Ajax attempts to kill his commanders and then commits suicide because of the sense of humiliation after they award Achilles' armor to Odysseus. What others would praise or censure played a large role in the decisions of most ancient Greeks. In the fifth century B.C.E., Socrates' concern with absolute standards of morality to which the individual would aspire, regardless of the majority regarded as right, was revolutionary. The *Hecuba* straddles these two worlds.

47   Note the Polymestor later (1136-44) uses this same justification of a general future threat to kill Polydorus.

48   Gratitude is *kharis*. The context of the drama makes this assertion quite ironic, since most of the characters here show no sense of stable *kharis* and Odysseus is, as he speaks, proving himself ungrateful to Hecuba.

49   Mt. Ida, the most prominent feature of the landscape around Troy. Note also that the Chorus later will link the war-time suffering of women on both sides of the conflict, though certainly not to the same end as Odysseus suggests.

You barbarians[50] don't consider your friends friends,
nor do you hold in awe those who died nobly,
so that Greece may prosper,   330
while you receive what matches your designs.

Chorus

Aiai. Slavery is always by nature bad
and it compels unnecessary suffering during violent conquest.[51]

Hecuba

Oh daughter, my words were thrown
to the sky in vain concerning your murder;[52]   335
But you, if you have greater power than your mother,
make haste, hurling all your voices
like the mouth of a nightingale, that you not be deprived of life.
Fall pitifully at the knee of this Odysseus
and persuade him—you have the excuse; for even he has   340
children—that he should pity your lot.

Polyxena

I see you, Odysseus, hiding your right hand
under your cloak and turning your face
back away, lest I reach out and touch your cheek.
Courage. You have escaped my prayer to Suppliant Zeus.[53]   345
Thus shall I submit both for the sake of necessity
and because I desire death.[54] But if I shall not want it,
I shall appear a base and life-loving woman.
Why then must I live? My father was once lord
of all the Phrygians; this was the first part of my life   350
when I was raised with lovely hopes
to be the bride of kings, with no small envy in my marriage,
whosoever's house and hearth I would approach.

---

50 Euripidean drama frequently returns to theme of Greeks vs. barbarians, though often to question who is the real "barbarian." See Edith Hall's *Inventing the Barbarian* (1989) on the "discovery" of the Greek sense of superior "Greekness" after the Persian Wars early in the fifth century and its representation on the Athenian stage.

51 See the Interpretive Essay for my comments on slavery in Euripidean drama.

52 Hecuba is careful to differentiate between true sacrifice to the gods and murder (*phonos*), as here.

53 The physical touching of the body is both an important part of supplication and a powerful gesture in the theater. The actor playing Odysseus clearly must be making a very visible effort to keep away from contact with Polyxena. Compare the importance of the Nurse's physical contact with Phaedra in *Hippolytus.* The cult designation Suppliant Zeus occurs elsewhere in tragedy at Aeschylus' *Suppliant Women* 616 and Sophocles' *Philoctetes* 484.

54 The text here plays off the Greek belief that a successful sacrifice depends upon the victim's consent to death which thus released the sacrificer from the pollution of murderous bloodshed.

And I was an ill-starred mistress to the women of Mt. Ida
and admired by wives and maidens,   355
equal to the gods save for death alone.
But now I am a slave. First, the very name, unaccustomed,
makes me love death;
then, the chance my lot would fall to masters
savage in their hearts, the kind who'd buy me for silver,   360
assigning the sister of Hector, and of many others,
to compulsory cooking in the house, compelling me
to sweep the house and to stand at the loom,
passing the painful day;
and my bed—*my bed!*—a slave bought from some place   365
will touch, a bed once thought worthy of kings.
No! Never! From free eyes I release
this light, to Hades assigning my body.
So lead me, Odysseus, and, leading me, put an end to me.
For I see among us a courage neither from any hope nor expectation   370
that I must ever prosper again.
Mother, you, please don't get in my way,
whether with words or actions; share this desire with me
to die before something shameful or unworthy happens to us.
For whoever is not accustomed to taste troubles,   375
he endures, but aches placing the yoke on his neck.
He would be more fortunate dead
than alive; for a bad life is a great trial.

Chorus

The stamp of noble men is awesome and visible
among mortals, and the name of noble birth   380
goes further for those worthy of it.

Hecuba

You have spoken well, daughter, but pain
goes with the good. But if there must be favor
for the son of Peleus and your side must escape
reproach, Odysseus, don't kill this girl,   385
But take me to the pyre of Achilles and
stab me—don't spare me. For I bore Paris,
who killed the son of Thetis,[55] striking him with his arrows.

---

55   Achilles. Paris, whose seduction of Helen caused the Trojan War, killed Achilles with the help of Apollo
      while Achilles was trying to assault the walls of Troy.

Odysseus

Not your death, old woman, did the phantom of Achilles
demand, but this girl's.   390

Hecuba

So then murder me with my daughter
and twice as much blood will fall
for the earth and the corpse who demanded this!⁵⁶

Odysseus

Your daughter's death is sufficient, and one death
must not be added to another; we don't owe yours.   395

Hecuba (*moves towards Polyxena and lays hold of her*)

There is great necessity for me to die with my daughter.

Odysseus

How so? I didn't know I'd acquired a master. 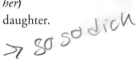 so so dich

Hecuba

Nonetheless, like ivy to oak, so will I cling to her.

Odysseus

No, if at least you'd obey those wiser than you.

Hecuba

So I won't willingly release this child.   400

Odysseus

But neither will I depart, leaving this child here.

Polyxena

Mother, listen to me. And you, son of Laertes,
give some slack to my reasonably enraged parent,
and you, oh wretched woman, don't fight the powerful.
Do you want to be thrown down to the ground and scrape your   405
aged skin, violently shoved off,
torn away in public disgrace by a young man's arm,
the very things you will suffer? Don't let it happen to you. For it is not worthy.
But, oh my mother, give me your hand so sweet
and throw your cheek against mine.   410
Since never again, but just now I shall behold
the sun's final ray and circle.
Welcome the end of my speeches.
Oh mother who bore me, I depart now below.

Hecuba

Pitiful you are, child, but I am a wretched woman.   415

---

56   Blood-offerings to the dead were poured on the ground and believed to be drunk by the dead.

Polyxena

There in Hades I shall lie apart from you.

Hecuba

Oh no. What should I do? Where shall I end my life?

Polyxena

A slave I shall die, born from a free father.

Hecuba

Oh daughter, we will slave in the light.

Polyxena

Unmarried, without wedding songs that were my rightful lot.

Hecuba

And we now have lost our share of fifty children.[57]

Polyxena

What should I say for you to Hector and your aged husband?   420

Hecuba

Announce that I am most wretched of all women.

Polyxena

Oh bosom and breasts that gladly nursed me.

Hecuba

Oh daughter of a fate miserable and out of season.   425

Polyxena

Farewell, mother, farewell from me also, Cassandra—

Hecuba

The others "fare well," but for your mother this isn't possible.[58]

Polyxena

—and my brother Polydorus among the horse-loving Thracians.

Hecuba

If he really still lives; I am skeptical, as I am totally luckless.

Polyxena

He lives and he will close your eyes in death.   430

Hecuba

I am dead before death because of troubles.

---

57   Here, and elsewhere, Hecuba speaks of Cassandra, now a slave and bedmate of Agamemnon, as if she
       were already dead.

58   Hecuba here plays off the two senses of the verb *khairein*, which, like its English equivalent, signifies
       greetings and departures, as well as pleasure in success.

Polyxena

Attend me now, Odysseus, and place my robes about my head[59]
since even before the sacrifice my heart is wasted
by mother's laments and I waste hers with mourning.
Oh light of day: since I can address your name,   435
No time remains with you save for how long I go
between the sword and the pyre of Achilles.

Odysseus leads Polyxena off to the camps at the right

Hecuba   (*collapsing*)

Oh I. I faint. My limbs lie loose.
Oh my daughter. Touch mother, stretch out your hand.
Give. Don't leave me childless. I am lost, friends…   440
[If only I could see the Spartan woman, sister of the Dioscouroi,[60]
Helen. For through her lovely eyes
most shamefully did she bring Hell to Troy's happiness.[61]]

*Hecuba is left lying on the ground—perhaps in the middle of the orchestra—
while the chorus circles around her.*

First Choral Song

Chorus   *strophe a*

Breeze, sea breeze,   445
since you attend the seafaring
swift skiffs against the sea swell,
to where will you send miserable me
on my journey? At whose house as a bought
slave will I arrive?
to the haven in the Dorian land?[62]   450
or in Phthia[63] where they say

---

59   As noted above, Polyxena must have carried some clothing into the acting area, which she now ask Odysseus
      to help her don, or she already wears a garment that allows her to be veiled. Given the importance attached
      during Talthybius' narrative to her more general disrobing, the initial investiture must have occurred
      on stage, in order to load the later narrative with the memory of her garments. Veiling can visually mark
      approaching death or the status of a bride; see Oakley and Sinos (1993). Polyxena is subsequently cast as a
      Bride of Death, on the model of Persephone.

60   The Dioscouroi are Castor and Polydeuces.

61   This alludes to the "Helen ode" in the *Agamemnon* (681-90), continuing its pun on the stem *hel-*, which
      denotes destruction.

62   "Dorian" was a name the Greeks gave to one of their two main linguistic and religious groupings (the
      other being Ionian). Their ancestor was said to be Heracles. Thucydides 1.2 holds that the Dorians were
      relative newcomers who conquered the Achaeans roughly eighty years after the fall of Troy. In the fifth
      century, Ionians were not welcome at the new Spartan colony of Heraclea, so the Athenians re-instituted
      the Ionian Festival of Delian Apollo (Thucydides 3.92), to which the *Hecuba* alludes in the succeeding
      antistrophe.

63   The homeland of Achilles.

the father of the finest waters,
Apidanos, makes fields fertile?
Or in the islands, miserably sent   *antistrophe b*
by the briny oar,   455
keeping a pitiful livelihood in the house,
where both the first-born palm
and the laurel extend their sacred
shoots for Leto,   460
a pleasing talisman for the birthpains from Zeus.[64]
With the Delian maidens
shall I praise the golden headband and bow
of divine Artemis?[65]   465
Or in the city of Pallas   *strophe b*
on the saffron robe
will I yoke the foals of Athena
with their lovely chariots on
cunningly wrought embroidery,[66]   470
bright woven saffron threads, or
the race of Titans[67]
which Zeus son of Kronos
puts into deepest sleep
with fires flaming about?
Oh my children,   *antistrophe b*   475
Oh my fathers and my land,
which falls to ruins in smoke,
smouldering, spear-won
by the Argives; but I in a foreign
land am called   480
slave, having left Asia,

---

64   The goddess Leto bore Artemis and Apollo for Zeus. Leto's difficulty giving birth to them is told in *The Homeric Hymn to Apollo*; in that poem Leto uses the palm and laurel to support herself while in labor (117).

65   The island of Delos is an important center of the worship of Artemis and Apollo. This passage alludes to the Dance of the Maidens at the Delian Festival of Apollo, which may have just recently been restored by the Athenians (Thucydides 3.104).

66   This alludes to the robe woven for Athena at the Panathenaic Festival in Athens, whose climax was a presentation of this robe at the statue of Athena Polias. The chorus members thus imagine themselves as inhabitants of Athens, practicing the same rituals as the members of the audience, but, as slaves and foreigners, they would be excluded from the weaving of the robe. Even their happier possible lives are marked by delusion.

67   This refers to the Titans' younger brothers, the Giants. The battle of the Olympians against the Giants, called the Gigantomachy, was a popular subject in art; on the Gigantomachy, see Apollodorus, *The Library of Greek Mythology* 1.6.1-2.

homes in Europe traded for
bedrooms in Hades.

> *The Chorus perhaps stops moving at a place that conceals Hecuba, who still*
> *lies prostrate on the ground from her collapse at 438-40. Talthybius enters,*
> *unannounced, from the camp at the right. His entrance may have been*
> *visible throughout much of the ode, since he is unlikely to have been moving*
> *with much haste due to the message he is bringing Hecuba.*[68]

Talthybius

Where, you Trojan girls, can I find her who once was
queen of Ilium, Hecuba?   485

Chorus

Here she is lying near you, with her back on the ground,
Talthybius, wrapped up in her robes.[69]

Talthybius

Oh Zeus, what should I say? that you are watching humans
or that you have acquired this reputation in vain,
[and we, falsely, believe there is a race of gods,]   490
and that chance oversees all things among mortals?[70]
Was this not the queen of the Phrygians rich in gold,
was this not the wife of Priam rich in blessings?
And now her entire city is razed by the spear,
and she herself a slave, aged, childless, upon the ground   495
lies, defiling with dirt her wretched head.
Woe, woe! I am an old man, but still may I die
before falling to some shameful chance.
        Get up, unhappy one, and lift further
and raise your side and snow-white head.   500

> *Talthybius has moved to Hecuba's side during his speech and finally crouched*
> *down to help her up.*

Hecuba

Let me be. Who is this who does not let my body
lie? Why do you disturb me in my grief, whoever you are?

---

68 I speculate that the Chorus blocks the view of Talthybius because he needs to ask about Hecuba's
whereabouts. There are other instances, for example, *Heracles* 1189, where a speaker fails to recognize a
veiled character, but Talthybius does not seem to see any character at all.

69 If the Chorus surrounds or simply stands between Talthybius and Hecuba, then it steps back back her
to allow him to see her. Hecuba has mirrored her daughter's veiling by covering her head, but Hecuba's
action signals mourning, not marriage (however ironic). Both gestures mark Polyxena's passage to death
and foreshadow the entrance of the covered corpse of Polydorus.

70 At 491 and again at 498, Talthybius evokes *tuchê*, chance, an important theme in a play where its characters fortunes suffer such violent reversals (which were echoed in the contemporaneous experience of
the audience). See my note on line 786.

Talthybius

I am Talthybius. I have come to do the work of the Danaans.
Agamemnon sent me, lady.

Hecuba

Dearest man! Have you come to announce it seems best
to the Achaeans to add me to the sacrifice at the tomb?   505
How then you would say things friendly to me! Come on,
let's hurry up. Lead me on, old man!

Talthybius

Your girl is gone, lady, and I've come after you so
that you bury her. Both the
two Atreids[71] and the Achaean people send me.   510

Hecuba

Oh no! What will you say? You haven't really come for us
so we can die, but to signal troubles?
Dead you are, Oh child, ripped from your mother!
We are childless after you. Oh wretched me.
How did you make an end of her? Did you show her proper respect?   515
Or did you approach the terrible deed by killing her as an
enemy, old man? Speak, even if you'll say unwelcome things.

Talthybius

Double are the tears you require me to reap, lady,
in pity of your daughter; for both now by speaking her troubles[72]
I will wet this eye and so I did before when she died by the grave.   520
The whole mob[73] from the Achaean army was present
by the tomb for the sacrifice of your girl.
The son of Achilles took Polyxena by the hand
and stood her upon the mound's top. I was nearby.
The young men chosen from the Achaeans were gathered   525

---

71   The two sons of Atreus, Agamemnon and Menelaus.

72   Messenger-speeches in Greek tragedy typically narrate events that cannot be enacted on stage because
     they require a substantial change of scene, a large crowd and bloodshed. Messengers in Euripidean drama
     never report the events they witness in neutral terms; see de Jong (1991), 63-79.

73   Gregory points out here that context should determine whether the Greek word *okhlos* is pejorative in
     the English sense of "mob" (605, 607, 868) or the more neutral "crowd" (521, 533). But I think that we
     need to retain the same English term for both, as the audience would hear the same Greek word in each
     place and consider how a crowd becomes a mob. This drama does offer a telling study of mob psychology
     as it depicts the wildly fluctuating responses of the crowd during the debate over human sacrifice, their
     rapid shifts in response to Polyxena herself, and the conversion of the suffering group of Trojan women
     into a gang willing to kill children. This mutability leads Hecuba to order the *okhlos* to be kept from
     Polyxena's corpse.

to restrain the bucking of your calf[74] and
followed behind. Taking in his hands a full cup
all of gold, the son of Achilles raises with one hand
libations to his dead father. To me he signals
to herald silence to the whole army of the Achaeans.   530
And I posititioned myself in their midst and said:
"Silence, Achaeans, may the whole people be quiet,
Silence, quiet." And I made the mob calm down.
And he said: *"Oh son of Peleus, my father,*
receive from me these libations of appeasement,   535
summoners of corpses. Come, so you may drink the dark
pure blood of a girl, which to you we present as a gift,
the army and I. Become favorable to us
and grant release to the prows and moorings
of our ships and grant us all to   540
happen upon a gentle homecoming to the fatherland."
So many things he spoke, and all the army joined in prayer.
Then he took hold of a gold-crusted knife,[75]
dragging it from its scabbard, and he nodded to the young men
picked from the army of the Argives to grab the virgin.   545
And she, as she considered the situation, made this speech:
"Oh Argives who sacked my city of Troy,
I consent to death. Let nobody touch my skin.
I will offer my neck firm in resolve.
By the gods, let me go and kill me   550
free, so I may die free; for among the dead
I feel shame to be called slave though I am royalty."[76]
The people roared their approval, and lord Agamemnon
said to the youths to release the virgin.
[And they released her, as soon as they heard   555
the last word, from him whose power is greatest.]
And when she heard this command of her masters

---

74   This language reminds all that Polyxena is being substituted for a normal sacrificial animal in an action
     that should produce a communal meal.

75   A gold cup for the wine and a gold knife for the sacrifice contrast sharply with and thus comment on
     the squalid existence Polyxena now escapes. And were these trinkets acquired from the royal house of
     Hecuba in Troy?

76   In Greek sacrificial practice, the staging of the victim's consent to be sacrificed was critical in absolving
     the sacrificers of guilt; see Burkert (1985) 55-58. Euripides here likely wants his audience to remember
     that Agamemnon has already seen a virgin sacrifice before the war, but of his daughter Iphigenia; in
     Aeschylus' *Agamemnon* the Chorus remembers how Agamemnon gagged his daughter before she could
     curse him, let alone make a speech.

she grabbed hold of her robes from her highest shoulder
and tore them down almost to her hips,
and revealed her breasts and bosom,[77]   560
as beautiful as those of a statue, and dropping
her knee to the earth she spoke the boldest speech of all:
"Look right here, young man, if you are eager
to strike my chest, strike here, but if it's under the neck   565
you want, then this throat is here and ready."
And he both willing and unwilling by pity of the girl,
cuts with his blade the pipes of her breath;
her life streamed away. But she even in death still
planned carefully ahead and fell with propriety,
hiding what one must from the eyes of males.[78]   570
And after she let go her breath in fatal slaughter
all of the Argives took up different tasks;
some from their hands threw leaves
on the dead girl,[79] while others were building the pyre by
bringing pine logs. But anyone slacking off   575
heard such abuse from another who wasn't:
"Are you just standing there, you miscreant, holding
in hand neither robe nor adornment for the young lady?
Aren't you going to give something to her who was
so great in resolve and best in spirit?" In saying such things   580
about your dead daughter, I see you are of all women
best in children and worst in luck.

Chorus

Some awesome sorrow is this which boiled over on Priam's daughters
and on my city by the compulsions of the gods.

Hecuba

Oh daughter, I know not what part of troubles I shall look to   585
when there are so many present. For if I should touch one,

---

77 Polyxena clearly has no erotic intent in this action. The baring of breasts by older women can suggest
mourning, as in the case of Hecuba's desperate gesture to Hector while he flees from Achilles (*Iliad* 22.80-
83) or an attempt to appeal to the early maternal bond, as when Clytemnestra tries to stop Orestes from
killing her (Aeschylus, *Libation Bearers* 868-98). Such situations, of course, do not apply to Polyxena.
Scodel (1996) 125 argues that the gesture controls the exposure of her body and thus affirms her freedom.
Thalmann (1993) 146 posits a ritual significance to the action, wherein the signs of her former self are
shed in a rite of passage. However, while her intention is not erotic, her gesture does have an erotic effect
on her audience.

78 The tone of this episode oscillates between the nobility of Polyxena's gesture, and the voyeurism attached
to the description of her nudity. Both here and in Hecuba's later fears there is unmistakable reference to
the effect of her visible sexuality on the army.

79 The showering of leaves was a form of congratulation to victorious athletes in the Olympics.

this one here doesn't let me go, and then some other grief
calls me aside in succession of troubles.
And now I could not wash from my mind
your suffering so as not to mourn you;   590
but now you've really removed the excess in the reports
of your nobility. Isn't it amazing, that if some bad soil
gets some timely luck from the gods it bears corn well,
but good soil, if it misses the things it needs,
then it gives a bad harvest? But among men always   595
the wicked is nothing else than bad,
and the good is always good, and because of disaster
he does not corrupt his nature but is always good?[80]
[Do parents make the difference, or education?
Still, also a good upbringing   600
teaches what is right; if someone should learn this well,
he knows the shameful, having learned it by the yardstick of the good.]
And yet a mind shoots forth these things in vain like arrows;
(to Talthybius) but you go and tell this to the Argives:
let nobody touch her, as far as I'm concerned, but keep the mob away   605
from my girl. In a large army
the mob is insatiable and the anarchy of sailors is
stronger than fire, and the man not doing anything evil is tagged evil himself.
(to serving woman) And you then take an urn, my old handmaid,
dip it in the salty sea and bring it here,   610
so that I may give my child her final bath,
the unmarried bride, the virgin no-virgin,[81]
and I might lay her out—how worthily? from where?
I couldn't! But as I am able (for what would I suffer?)
collecting a gown from the spear-won women,   615
who sitting by me dwell inside these tents,
perhaps one has slipped by her new masters
some theft from her own home.
        Oh image of my house, Oh once blessed homes,
Oh you richest, blessed above all in children,   620
Priam, here am I the aged mother of your children;
thus we have come to nothing, stripped of our
earlier spirit. And then do we puff ourselves up,

---

80   These lines are central to Nussbaum's meditation (1986) 397-421 on the relationship between nature and nurture in this tragedy.

81   Following the pattern of the virgin Persephone who married Hades himself, girls who died before their weddings were thought to have married Death. See Seaford (1987).

one of us because of his wealthy houses,
another because he is called "honored among citizens"?   625
These things are nothing, the vain plans of minds
and boasts of the tongue. That man is most blessed,
to whom each day nothing bad happens.

> *Hecuba and attendants re-enter the* skênê*; Talthybius exits to the right, the*
> *serving woman to left.*[82]

Second Choral Song

Chorus   *strophe*

For me disaster was necessary,
for me pain was necessary,   630
from that moment when first Alexander[83] cut the pine
forest of Mt. Ida, to launch his sea voyage
for the bed of Helen, whom gold-gleaming   635
Helios illuminates
as most beautiful.

Labors and compulsions[84] stronger than   *antistrophe*
labors come circling around,   640
a common trouble from a private
idiocy,[85] deadly upon the land of Simois,
and disaster came to the others.

Strife was judged, on Ida
a shepherd man judges   645
the three daughters of the blessed ones,[86]

leading to the spear and murder and outrage of my chambers;   *epode*
Some Spartan girl, with many tears at home   650
also groans around fair-flowing Eurotas,[87]
and upon her own grey head the mother of

---

82   Euripides has now motivated, in terms of the plot construction, the connection between the deaths of the two children, for as soon as Hecuba dispatches the Serving Maid to the seashore for Polyxena's bath water, Euripides begins to escalate the tension over Hecuba's discovery of the death of her son.

83   Paris. Mt. Ida was where the infant Paris was exposed after it was prophesied that he would destroy Troy. He was suckled by a bear and eventually found by a shepherd, and thus Paris spent his youth on the slopes of Mt. Ida. See Apollodorus, *The Library of Greek Mythology* 3.12.5

84   *Anankê*, here "compulsion" or "necessity" continues the theme of necessity, real and apparent, which circulates throughout the drama. See Interpretive Essay.

85   Literally, "from a private folly." Our word "idiot" is derived from the Greek *idios*, which merely means "private." Simois was one of the two rivers of Troy.

86   Strife (*Eris*) was the goddess who, after not being invited to the wedding of Peleus and Thetis, threw the golden apple among Hera, Athena and Aphrodite, to make them quarrel over who was fairest. Zeus sent them with Hermes to Paris on Mt. Ida. Strife thus caused strife. Apollodorus, *The Library of Greek Mythology* 3.12.3.

87   Eurotas is the main river of Sparta.

dead children
sets her hand, claws her cheek,   655
setting her bloody nails for mangling.[88]

Serving Maid   (*entering from left, accompanied by at least two mute extras carrying a covered body into the orchestra*)[89]
Women, where is all-suffering Hecuba,
who is victorious over every man and woman in a contest
of troubles? None will take her crown prize away.[90]   660

Chorus
What is it, you wretched person, with your cries of bad tidings?
How these painful announcements never seem to rest.

Serving Maid
To Hecuba I bring this pain: amidst troubles
it's not at all easy for mortals to speak auspiciously.

Chorus
She happens now to be passing through the house.   665
Look, she appears at the sound of your words.

   (*Hecuba appears at the* skênê *door and enters the acting area*)

Serving Maid
Oh, all-wretched and still more so than I can speak,
queen, you're dead, you no longer exist, though still you behold the sun's light,
childless, husbandless, stateless, destroyed.

Hecuba
You spoke nothing new, hurling abuse at those already aware,   670
But why have you come to me attending
this corpse of Polyxena , whose burial was announced
as the earnest work of all the Achaeans?[91]

Serving Maid
This woman knows nothing, but, I think, she laments
Polyxena, and doesn't grasp her new woes.   675

---

88   The reference to Sparta here connects the homeland of Menelaus and Helen with the city that is fighting Athens at the time of the *Hecuba*'s production.

89   The audience is likely here in suspense as to which corpse will be brought back first, the son's or the daughter's; since Talthybius has been directed to secure Polyxena's corpse, the greater expectation might be for her. As soon as the cortege becomes visible at the left, it knows that was wrong. Note also the recurring motif of covering, begun by Polyxena and continued by Hecuba.

90   The servant here imagines a contest of suffering in the Olympic Games, to be rewarded, as with other events, with a laurel crown of victory.

91   The audience, having seen the entrances from the left, knows that this corpse cannot be Polyxena's, as she had exited to the right. Hecuba, however, lacks this knowledge because she had been inside.

Hecuba

Not again! Surely you don't bear here
the Bacchic head of the prophet Cassandra?

Serving Maid (*unveiling the corpse as she speaks*)

You lament the living girl, but the dead boy here you don't yet
mourn; so gaze upon the bared body of the corpse,
see if some astonishment appears to you, even beyond expectation.   680

Hecuba

Oimoi. I see a boy, my boy, dead,
Polydorus, whom a Thracian man was keeping safe in his house for me!
I am finished, lost, I no longer exist!

> (*Hecuba breaks into irregular, sung, lyrics, while the others remain in iambic speech*)

Oh child, child,
aiai, I begin my Bacchic song   685
from a god of Vengeance,[92]
in late-learning of my troubles.[93]

Serving Maid

Did you, unhappy woman, recognize your son's disaster?

Hecuba

Unbelievable, unbelievable, new new things I weep!
Troubles after troubles meet troubles.   690
Never will a day without groans and tears
hold me!

Chorus

Terrible, Oh sad one, terrible troubles we suffer.

Hecuba

Oh child child of an unhappy mother
by what lot are you dead? by what fate do you lie there?   695
by the hand of what human being?

Serving Maid

I don't know. I found him at the seashore...

---

92   The text is disputed here. I generally keep Diggle's reading, but move the comma to after *alastoros* (vengeance) because Polydorus' death as an act of vengeance makes little sense. Hecuba here begins to plot revenge, and Bacchic imagery in this drama is associated with vengeance.

93   Late-learning is a common theme in Greek tragedy as characters learn late, usually too late, the truth about themselves and their situation. One thinks here, for example of Theseus and Hippolytus in Euripides' *Hippolytus*, or Deianira and Heracles in Sophocles' *Trachiniae*, two dramas produced within a few years of the *Hecuba*.

Hecuba

    Thrown out, on the smooth sand,

    or felled by a bloody spear?   700

Serving Maid

    An ocean wave bore him from the sea.

Hecuba

    Oh no! *Aiai.* I understand the sleepy vision

    of my eyes, (no dark-winged ghost

    passed by me), the vision I saw about you,   705

    Oh child, that you no longer lived in Zeus' light.

Chorus

    Who killed him then? Can you say by interpreting dreams?

Hecuba

    My, my, guest-friend, the Thracian horseman,   710

    where his old father had placed him in hiding.

Chorus

    Oh no. What will you say? He killed him to get the gold?

Hecuba

    Unspeakable, unnamable, beyond wonders,

    unholy and unbearable. Where is the justice of guest-friends?   715

    Oh most damnable of men, how you butchered his

    flesh, cutting with an iron knife

    his limbs—you did not pity this boy.[94]   720

Chorus

    Oh suffering one, how the divinity that made you

    most-suffering among mortals is heavy on you.

    But I see the shape of the master here,

    Agamemnon, so let's be silent, friends.   725

    (Agamemnon enters from right)

Agamemnon

    Hecuba, why do you delay coming to cover your child

    in a grave, especially since Talthybius gave me your order

    that none of the Argives touch your daughter?

    We let you have your way and didn't touch her;[95]

    but you are dawdling so much that I'm amazed.   730

---

94 The knife marks could suggest some kind of ritual mutilation of the body by Polymestor. In any case, the extent of the trauma to the corpse indicates Polymestor did not simply stab Polydorus and kill him.

95 The Greek could mean "we left her alone", but Agamemnon does seem to be complaining about the lack of follow-through from Hecuba after her specific demands were made.

I have come to fetch you, for matters have been
handled well there, if any of these matters could be "well".
Wait. What man do I see here at the tent,
one of the Trojan dead? For the robes enfolding
his corpse tell me he's not Argive.   735

Hecuba
(*turning aside*) Miserable one!—For I address myself addressing you—[96]
Hecuba, what should I do? Throw myself at the knees
of Agamemnon here or bear my troubles in silence?

Agamemnon
Why, turning your back to my face,
do you weep? Won't you say what's been done? Who is this here?[97]   740

Hecuba   (*still talking to herself*)
But, if, considering me a slave and hostile,
he should shove me from his knees, we'd be put to more pain.

Agamemnon
I am not a prophet by nature, so that, without hearing,
I'd still learn the path of your plans.

Hecuba   (*still talking to herself*)
Do I then calculate his mind to be more hostile   745
when he really isn't hostile?

Agamemnon
If you wish me to know none of this,
you've reached the same place as me. For I also do not wish to hear.

Hecuba
Without this man I would not be able to avenge
my children.[98] Why do I keep turning these things over?   750
Daring is necessary, whether I am lucky or not—

(*She turns to Agamemnon and sinks to her knees in supplication, grabbing his
legs with one hand and reaching up with the other*)
Agamemnon, I beseech you by your knees here
and by your cheek, and your blessed right hand...   *gestures of supplication*

---

96   A very self-conscious phrase, but Euripides needs to signal to his audience that Hecuba is talking to herself, not a terribly common event in the Athenian theater; cf Medea when she deliberates killing her own children.

97   A masked actor performing in a large outdoor theater cannot communicate tears by shedding false ones. The actor who performs Hecuba must be engaging in large gestures to communicate weeping.

98   The family of a murder victim was legally obliged to move against the murderer; see MacDowell (1978) 109-11. Thus, as Mossman (1999) 180 observes, the audience would view retribution as the inevitable consequence of this discovery. The reference to "children" and not just "child" suggests she views her response as directed to Polyxena as well as to Polydorus.

Agamemnon

Seeking what matter? Is it to make your
life free? That's fairly easy.[99]   755

Hecuba

No, not at all. With vengeance exacted on the wicked
I would willingly spend my whole life in slavery.
It's nothing at all you might guess, my lord.—

Agamemnon

And for what assistance, then, do you call us?

Hecuba

Do you see the corpse here over which I weep?   760

Agamemnon

I see. But I can't understand what's coming next.

Hecuba

I brought this one to life once and I carried him inside me.

Agamemnon

But which of your children is this one, you wretched woman?

Hecuba

He's not one of the sons of Priam dead under Ilium.

Agamemnon

Well, did you then give birth to another one than them?   765

Hecuba

Yes, and with little profit, it seems, I bore the one you see here.

Agamemnon

Where did he happen to be when the city was destroyed?

Hecuba

His father sent him away, fearful of his death.

Agamemnon

To where then did he remove him alone from his other sons?

Hecuba

Into this land, the very place where he was discovered dead.   770

Agamemnon

To the man, Polymestor, who rules this land?

Hecuba

Here he was sent as the guardian of that most bitter gold.

---

99   Euripides quickly establishes the moral vapidity of Agamemnon with this trifling comment about slavery,
      which jars so strongly against the hardships of slavery established throughout the earlier parts of the
      drama.

Agamemnon
And at whose hands or by what fate is he dead?

Hecuba
Who else? The Thracian guest-friend killed him.

Agamemnon
Oh wretch.[100] And I suppose he lusted to seize the gold?   775

Hecuba
Exactly, when he recognized the disaster of the Phrygians.

Agamemnon
But where did you find him? Or did someone bring the corpse to you?

Hecuba   *(gesturing to her serving maid)*
This woman did, stumbling upon it at the seashore.

Agamemnon
Was she looking for it, or working at some other task?

Hecuba
She went to bring some bathwater from the sea for Polyxena.   780

Agamemnon
The guest-friend killed him, it seems, and threw him out.

Hecuba
Buffeted by the sea, his flesh hacked through.

Agamemnon
Oh your sadness of unmeasured hardships!

Hecuba
I am lost. No trouble still remains.

Agamemnon
Alas, alas! What woman was born so unfortunate?   785

Hecuba
None. Unless you mean Fortune herself.[101]
　　　But listen why I fall at your knees.
If I seem to you to suffer things lawful to the gods,
then I would accept them. But if the opposite, then may you become
an avenger for me against the man, the most sacrilegious guest-friend   790
who, fearing neither those below the earth, nor those above[102]

100　It is unclear whether the Greek indicates Polydorus, Polymestor or Hecuba.

101　*Tuchê.* This is the personification of luck that Oedipus ironically posits as his parent (*Oedipus Tyrannos* 1080) just before the truth of his birth is revealed. *Tuchê* does not imply good or bad fortune, but rather simply "what happens," or "chance." In order to preserve the repetition from Hecuba's *dustuchês* (unfortunate) to Agamemnon's *Tuchê* (fortune), I had to use an English term with a more positive connotation than the Greek.

102　That is, the chthonic gods and the Olympians.

has done the most sacrilegious act,

[he who often shared my dinner table,

holding the first rank of hospitality[103] among my friends,

and though he received such things as are required, with forethought   795

he committed murder. And if he wanted to kill him, he didn't even deem

him worthy of a grave, but cast him out to the sea.]

While we may be slaves and without strength,

the gods still are strong and their ruler is

Law. We believe the gods exist by reason of law[104]   800

and we live with clear distinctions between unjust and just.

If law, having returned to your hands, will be destroyed,

and if whoever kills their guests does not pay,

or dares to carry off the sacred things of the gods,

fairness is not possible among men.   805

Therefore, counting these things among the shameful, have reverence for me:

Pity me, and having stepped back like a painter,

behold me and examine such troubles as I have.

I once was queen, but now I am your slave,

once lucky in children, now I am at once old and childless,   810

cityless, alone, most wretched of mortals...

(Agamemnon turns away and breaks physical contact. Hecuba thus rises to
her feet in response)

      Ah miserable me, where do you turn your feet away from me?

It seems I'll do nothing now; Oh how miserable I am!

Why then do we mortals labor and pursue   815

other studies as if they're all necessary,

but we do not work to fulfill our understanding of

Persuasion,[105] the sole ruler of mankind,

by giving it money in payment, so that it would then be possible

to persuade and acquire at once whatever one wished?

---

103 "Hospitality" here is *xenia*.

104 The word translated as "law" twice here can mean "law" or "custom." In either case it denotes some
guiding principle. What, exactly, this phrase "reason of law" means is disputed, but its import is crucial,
since the distinction between nature (*physis*) and custom (*nomos*), and the question of whether human
values come from one or the other, is fundamental to the intellectual and moral crises of the second half
of the fifth century. Hecuba could mean "we believe in the gods by convention," as Nussbaum (1986)
400 argues. Gregory 1999 and Kovacs (1987) 101 maintain, on the other hand, that Hecuba would be
foolish to argue that a villain should be punished on the basis of a universe governed by conventions,
not absolutes. Further, Hecuba elsewhere advocates traditional views of the gods. Much of how one
understands the play can come down to these lines.

105 Persuasion, *Peithô*, is personified as a goddess throughout Greek tragedy, and is especially visible as a
problem in Aeschylus' *Oresteia*. Buxton (1982) 32-36 observes that the goddess Peitho was worshipped
in cult in Athens.

How, therefore, could one still hope to succeed?   820
For those who once were my sons no longer exist,
and myself I am driven by the spear to shameful acts,
and I see the smoke here leaping out over the city.
        And yet—perhaps this is a stranger to my argument,
to toss in Aphrodite; but still it will be said:—   825
by your side my daughter lies,
the seer of Phoebus,[106] whom the Phrygians call Cassandra.
Where will you tally your pleasurable nights then, lord,
or for those passionate embraces in the bed
what thanks will my daughter have? and I for her?[107]   830
[both from the shadow and from the love-charms
of night arises the greatest joy to mortals.]
Listen then now: this dead one here—do you see him?
By treating this one well you'll do a favor for your
brother-in-law.[108] My speech still lacks one part.   835
If only voice were in my arms
and hands and hair and the step of my feet,
whether by the arts of Daedalus[109] or some god,
that all together they might grasp your knees,
weeping, bringing all sorts of prosecution speeches.   840
Oh master, Oh greatest light to the Greeks,
be persuaded, extend to an old woman a hand of
vengeance, even if it's nothing, still do it!
For it is the mark of a noble man both to serve justice
and everywhere always to treat badly the bad.   845

Chorus

Remarkable how everything happens to mortals,
and the laws of necessity[110] demarcate them,
placing the most bitter enemies in friendship
and putting in enmity those previously friendly.

Agamemnon

With pity I hold you and your son and your fortunes,   850
Hecuba, and your suppliant hand,

---

106 Apollo.

107 Note the return of appeals to the codes of reciprocity (*kharis*).

108 Polydorus, who is, of course, neither alive nor really a brother-in-law.

109 The legendary Athenian artisan who created, among other things, the device that allowed Pasiphae to
      mate with a bull and the wings with which he and his son Icarus tried to escape from Crete.

110 "The laws of necessity" (*nomoi anankês*) is a remarkable expression since *anankê* was so often personified
      as an absolute force outside of and indifferent to human reason and civilization.

[handwritten: "I would love to realy but I can t beause the army, and Im responsiby to them"]

and, on account of the gods and justice
I wish the unholy guest-friend to pay this price of justice,
if only somehow it might both appear that I am favorable to you
and I would not seem to the army for Cassandra's sake   855
to plan this murder for the lord of Thrace.
For there is a matter where confusion has fallen on me:
this man the army considers an ally,
and the dead one their enemy; but if this one here is kin to me,
then this matter is separate and is none of the army's business.   860
Think these things over; since, on the one hand, you have me willing
to work with you and provide swift help,
but on the other, I'm slow, if suspected by the Achaeans.

Hecuba

(Deeply sighing)[111]
There is nobody among mortals who is free;
for either he is a slave of money or chance,   865
or the city's populace or written law[112]
keep him from using his character according to his judgment.
But since you are in fear and allot more weight to the mob,
I myself shall make you free of this fear.
For understand, first, that, if I should plot some trouble   870
for the murderer of this man here, you would not be an accomplice.
Next, if some uproar or defense appears from the Achaeans
on behalf of a suffering Thracian man, for such things he will suffer,
keep them away, while still not appearing to do me a favor.
But as for the rest, don't worry, I'll take care of it nicely.   875

Agamemnon

But how? What will you do? Will you take a blade in your
old hand and kill the barbarian man,
or do it with poisons or by some other means?
What band of men will you have? Where will you get allies?[113]

Hecuba

These tents here conceal a mob of Trojan women.   880

Agamemnon

You mean the spear-prizes? the prey of the Greeks?

---

111 The Greek text has the single word, *pheu*, the marker of a lament or sigh.
112 This could indicate lawsuits as well as written law. Written law and the rule of the majority were bases of Athenian democracy.
113 Euripides here begins to prepare his audience to expect Hecuba to murder Polymestor, so that her mutilation of his eyes should come as a surprise.

Hecuba

With these women I shall take vengeance on the murderer of mine.

Agamemnon

And just how will women acquire power over men?

Hecuba

Terrible is their number, and, with deceit, hardly beatable.

Agamemnon

Terrible indeed. Yet still I find fault with feminine force.   885

Hecuba

But why? Did not women take down the sons of Aegyptus
and utterly empty Lemnos of men?[114]
But so let it be! Let go this argument,
then send this woman here safely for me through the army.
And you (*turning to the serving maid*), approach the Thracian guest-friend,
and say: "*Hecuba the former queen of Ilium invites you,
on a need no less yours than hers. Your sons too,
since the children also must hear the words from
her.*"—Agamemnon, you hold back on the burial
of freshly slaughtered Polyxena,   895
so that the sibling pair, a double anguish to their mother,
may lie close by in a single flame, and then be covered in the earth.

Agamemnon

These things will be so. And yet if the army could
set sail, I could not grant this favor to you.
But now, since god releases no fair breezes,   900
they must remain watching for calm sailing.[115]
May it turn out well somehow, for this matter is common to all,
both to each private citizen and to the city,
that the bad suffer badly, and the good succeed.

---

114   These stories are the two most common paradigms for group female violence against men. Aegyptus was
      feuding with his brother Danaos over the throne of Egypt. The former had fifty sons and the latter as
      many daughters. Eventually, marriages were arranged among all of the children, but Danaos persuaded
      his daughters to kill their new husbands on their wedding night. Only one, Hypermnestra, spared her
      husband. The women then fled to Argos as suppliants. Aeschylus composed a trilogy on this subject,
      whose last part, *Suppliant Women*, still survives.
          The Lemnian Women were punished with a foul odor for their failure to honor Aphrodite, and so
      their husbands refused to sleep with them. In response, the women murdered their husbands, and they
      lived without men until the Argonauts arrived.

115   This observation complicates the earlier accounts of why the fleet cannot leave. As Gregory notes here,
      Greek usage would not allow for Achilles to be called a god (*theos*), so either the belief in divine agency
      here is a sham, or the gods are working in more mysterious ways. On the winds and the gods, see Gregory
      (1999) xxix-xxxi, Thalmann (1993) 153-54 and Mitchell-Boyask (1993) 116-19.

Agamemnon leaves to right, the servant, to left. Hecuba remains; possibly
collapsing, if keimenê *("lying") in line 969 is to be taken literally*

Third Choral Song

Chorus

You, Oh fatherland Ilium,	*strophe a*	905

will no longer be counted among the unsacked cities;
such a cloud of Greeks conceals you,
sacking you spear by spear,
your crown of towers hacked off,
stained in defilement with the most miserable smoke,   910
wretched city,
no longer will I set foot in you.

At midnight I was lost,   *antistrophe a*
when after feasts sweet sleep upon my eyes   915
was spread, and retiring from the dances and songful
offerings, he lay down,
my husband, in our bedchambers,
his spearshaft in its holder,
no longer watching   920
for a naval brigade
that had trod Ilium's Troy.

I was arranging my hair,   *strophe b*
bound up with nets,
beholding my golden mirrors'   925
limitless gleamings,
so I might fall into bed.
But clamor came through the city;
And this was the order down through
Troy's town: "You
sons of Greeks, when, when
after sacking the summit of Ilium   930
will you come to your own homes?"

Abandoning my bed,   *antistrophe b*
barely clothed, like a Dorian maiden,[116]
clinging to august Artemis,[117]
I, wretch, achieved nothing.   935
But, having seen my bedmate dead,

---

116 Herodotus 5.88.1 indicates that Dorian was a standard term attached to the clothing *peplos* which all
Greek women once wore.

117 Artemis, the virgin goddess of the hunt who was a special figure in cult for unmarried girls. The Chorus
here probably is imagining clinging to a statue of Artemis for protection.

I am led upon the salty sea,
looking away back to the city, when
the ship moved my foot from
homecoming   940
and split me
from the land of Ilium;
miserable, I collapsed in pain.
The sister of the Dioscouroi,[118] Helen,   *epode*
and the herdsman of Ida,
baneful Paris,   945
I curse them both,
since their marriage blasted me
from my ancestral land
and made me homeless—no, not marriage
but some misery from a spirit of vengeance.
May the salt sea not return her home again   950
nor may she reach
her father's house.

> *Polymestor enters from left, accompanied by sons and bodyguards, and
> Hecuba's servant.*

Polymestor

Oh Priam most beloved of men, and you most beloved,
Hecuba, I weep beholding you and your city
and your offspring who died just now.[119]   955
Alas.
Nothing can be trusted, neither good reputation
nor that one who succeeds won't then fail.
And the gods themselves disturb things back and forth,
establishing confusion, so that by ignorance
we worship them.[120] But why must one   960
lament these matters and make no progress before troubles?
Yet you, if you at all would reproach my absence,

---

118   Castor and Polydeuces, whose other sister, Clytemnestra, is mentioned in Polymestor's prophecies at the
      end.

119   This sequence should indicate that the shrouded corpse of Polydorus is still present, and Polymestor,
      like Hecuba earlier, mistakes it for Polyxena. Kovacs, however, argues that the body was removed at the
      close of the previous scene, but, in my view, there are no clear signs of removal, and the corpse' presence
      is vital to the action of this scene.

120   These remarks might clarify the earlier ambiguities in Hecuba's speech whether we believe in the gods by
      convention or the gods rule by law. Polymestor's actions characterize a godless man and his words here
      about the gods more openly advance a skeptical view of divine agency than in Hecuba's speech, which
      thus seems designed to balance Polymestor's here.

please hold off; for I happened to be away in the midst of
the borders of Thrace, when you came here. And then after I'd arrived home,
I barely set foot outside my house when   965
this slavewoman of yours here fell into the same place,
speaking words, which, when I heard, I came.

Hecuba   (*keeping her face turned from Polymestor*)
I am ashamed to look you in the eye,
Polymestor, while lying here in such troubles.
To be seen by someone who knew me when prosperous, shame[121] holds me   970
that I happen to be in this lot where I am now,
and I would not be able to look at you right in the eyes.
Please don't consider it hostility to you,
[Polymestor; besides, custom is somewhat responsible,
that women don't behold men face-to-face.]   975

Polymestor
And it's no wonder at all! But what need do you have of me?
On what matter did you send my foot from my house?

Hecuba
A private matter of my own do I want to speak to you
and your sons; order your attendants (for my sake)
to stand back from this house here.   980

Polymestor
Go away. For this solitude is secure.

    (*attendants exit left*)
A friend you are, but a still greater friend to me is
this army of Achaeans. However, you must explain
why the successful man must provide protection to
his unsuccessful friends. Thus I am prepared.   985

Hecuba
First tell me about my son whom you keep in your house,
Polydorus, from my own hand and from his father's,
whether he still lives. The rest I'll say second.

Polymestor
Sure! Your part in him prospers.[122]

---

121 *Aidôs*. An almost intranslatable word and a concept central to Greek culture. See Cairns (1993), who
     studies in great detail the history of this complex concept, which embraces respect, reverence, a concern
     for proper conduct and status. It is fundamentally related to the other terms of reciprocity such as gratitude
     and honor that drive the ethical dynamics of this tragedy.
122 It is important to keep in mind the appearance of the acting area, for Polydorus' covered corpse is a few
     feet away from Polymestor while the Thracian king proves himself a liar in these lines.

Hecuba

Oh my dearest man, how you speak in a way worthy of yourself!   990

Polymestor

What second matter do you wish to learn from me?

Hecuba

Does he still remember me at all, his dear mother here?

Polymestor

And in fact he was seeking to approach you here in secret.

Hecuba

And the gold's safe which he bought from Troy?

Polymestor

Safe and guarded in my house!   995

Hecuba

Keep it safe now, and don't covet your neighbors' things.

Polymestor

No way! May I benefit from what is here already, lady!

Hecuba

So do you know what I wish to tell you and your sons?

Polymestor

No, I do not. In your speech you will signal this.

Hecuba

There is, you man dear to me then and so dear to me now...   1000

Polymestor

What matter must both I and my children know?

Hecuba

The gold of Priam's sons, its ancient hiding places deep in the earth.

Polymestor

This is what you want to show your son?

Hecuba

Indeed! Through you, of course. For you are a pious man.

Polymestor

Why then do you need presence of my children here?   1005

Hecuba

It's better, in case you should die, that these ones know.

Polymestor

You've spoken well. And it's also wiser thus.

Hecuba

So do you know where are the chambers of Trojan Athena?

Polymestor

The gold is in that place? What sign is there?

Hecuba

A black rock rising above the earth.   1010

Polymestor

So is there anything else of what's there you wish to tell me?

Hecuba

I wish you to keep safe the money with which I came here.

Polymestor

Where is it then? Do you keep it in your robes or have you hidden it?

Hecuba

It is kept safe in a mass of plunder inside these chambers.

Polymestor

But where? You're surrounded like a harbor by Achaeans here.   1015

Hecuba

The chambers of the spear-won women are private.

Polymestor

And it's safe inside and empty of men?[123]

Hecuba

None of the Achaeans are inside, but we women are alone.
But come into our house; for in fact the Argives long
to free their ships' footing from Troy towards home.   1020
Thus having accomplished all you needed you may return
with your sons to where you lodged my child.[124]

> *Polymestor and sons enter the* skênê, *followed by Hecuba. The Chorus is left alone.*

Chorus

Not yet have you paid, but perhaps you *will* pay justice;
as someone having plunged into a harborless sewer[125]   1025
you will fall away from your heart's desire,
your life lost. For where liability
concurs with Justice and gods there is
a deadly deadly trouble.   1030
The hope of this path will trick you and has driven you

---

123 Hecuba is careful to show that Polymestor does not wish to share the gold with Agamemnon, as he tries to claim in the trial scene.

124 Clearly this is language that is ominous for the audience, yet it continues to raise the expectation, begun at 1006, that Hecuba will kill, not blind, Polymestor.

125 Literally, the English word "sewer" here is used as an equivalent for a Greek term for "bilge," a word with little import for us. But the bilge is, essentially, the ship's sewer.

to deadly Hades, you miserable man;
and you'll leave life by a hand unaccustomed to war.[126]

Polymestor   (within)
Omoi, I'm blinded at the light of my eyes, wretch![127]   1035

Chorus Leader[128]
Did you hear the Thracian man's lament, friends?

Polymestor
I cry omoi again even more, children, at your miserable slaughter!

Chorus Leader
Friends! New troubles are accomplished inside the house.

Polymestor
But may you not escape by a nimble foot;
for I'll strike and crash open the heart of this house.   1040
Look, a blow is readied by a heavy hand.

Chorus Leader (shouting in to Hecuba)
Do you want us to attack? How it's high time
for our presence as allies for Hecuba and the Trojan women!

    Hecuba emerges from the skênê.

Hecuba
Go on and smash, spare nothing, break open the gates;
For never will you set bright sight in your eyes,
nor will you see alive your sons whom I killed.   1045

Chorus Leader
So have you laid low the Thracian guest-friend, and do you rule him,
my lady, and have you actually done such things as you claim?

Hecuba
You will see him very soon before the house,
blind, moving by blind feet,   1050
and the bodies of his two boys, whom I killed
with these best Trojan women; to me has he paid

---

126   These lyrics divide the act into two parts and their vicious determination for vengeance, contrasted with Hecuba's mild surface demeanor, leaves little doubt that Polymestor will experience some catastrophe. But note that even the Chorus still expects Polymestor's death, an expectation denied immediately in the following line.
　　　The adjective apolemos ("unaccustomed to war") in 1034 is used elsewhere by Euripides (Ion 217) to describe the hands of the Bacchants which hold the deadly wands of Dionysus (thyrsoi); this might thus connect to the designation of the Chorus as "the Bacchants of Hades" below at 1077.

127   Shouts from within the skênê also occur early in Sophocles' Ajax, Euripides' Medea and Aeschylus' Agamemnon 1343-46, a scene to which this one possibly alludes.

128   At such moments the leader of the Chorus often steps out of the collective and addresses the named characters as an individual.

justice. And here he comes, as you see, from the house.
But I'll get out of the way and stand back from
the roiling, unconquerable, Thracian rage.   1055

Polymestor *(enters crawling from the* skênê. *The actor now wears a mask reddened to represent the blood from his eyes. At his entrance the* eccyclêma *is wheeled out to display the corpses of his sons.*[129])

    Omoi I, where should I go?
where stand, where find harbor?
walking like a four-footed mountain beast
on hand and foot? What sort of path
shall I take, this one or that,   1060
desiring to seize the man-murdering[130] women of Ilium,
the ones who destroyed me?
cruel cruel daughters of the Phrygians,
in what corners do they cower in flight from me?   1065

If only you, Helios,[131] might heal, heal
the blinded bloody sockets of my eyes,
exchanging them for light.
Ah, ah—
Silence! I detect the secret step   1070
here of women.[132] Where could I rush at them,
and sate myself with their flesh and bones,
setting out a feast fit for savage beasts,
reaping outrage in
retribution for my atrocity? Oh wretch,   1075
where, how am I carried, leaving my children alone

---

129 The *eccyclêma* was a wheeled cart (literally it means "the rolled out thing") that was used to display, sometimes, the imagined interior behind the *skênê* or, at other times, the bodies of people killed off-stage. It enables the playwright to expand quickly the visual world of his action.
    Here it would have been impossible for the Athenian audience not to think of the emergence of the newly blinded Oedipus of Sophocles here, for the *Oedipus Tyrannos* likely would have been produced only one to three years before the *Hecuba*. Agamemnon refers to the presence of the corpses at 1118.

130 The audience would likely have been startled to hear one of Hector's main epithets in the *Iliad*, one also used to describe Achilles' hands after they have killed Hector (24.479), designating the Trojan women.

131 The sun god.

132 This signals that the Chorus and Hecuba must be moving around Polymestor at this point, perhaps mocking him.

for the Bacchants of Hades[133] to carve up,
slaughtered, a bloody banquet for dogs,
mercilessly hurled out on the mountainside?
Where can I stand, where sit? where walk?[134]   1080
as a ship with its ropes set at sea,
gathering my saffron-flax robe,[135] driven as a guard
of my children upon this den of death?

Chorus

Oh wretch, you have done such unbearable troubles;   1085
punishments to you who committed acts terrible and shameful
[has some god given who is heavy on you.]

Polymestor

Aiai, come, clan of Thrace, spear-bearing, armed,
on your fine horses, subjects of Ares.   1090
You Achaeans.—you Atreids—help help, I cry, I help!
Oh come, by the gods come!

Does anyone hear, or will none defend me? Why do you delay?

Women destroyed me, the spear-won women; terribly,
terribly we have suffered.   1095

Oh my outrage.
Where should I turn? Where should I journey?
Flying up to heaven's
high vault,   1100
where Orion or Sirius[136] flings burning

---

133   "The Bacchants of Hades" is an extraordinary image. The female followers of Dionysus are imagined as
      living in ecstatic joy with their master (think of the Messenger's description in the *Bacchae* 677-727), but
      also capable of actions of tremendous, frenzied violence (think of the next lines of the *Bacchae* when they
      attack the shepherds and then a cow, and, later, when they tear apart Pentheus with their bare hands);
      hence their connection with death and destruction. Euripides uses this image again in the *Heracles* when
      Amphitryon calls his son a "Bacchant of Hades" (1119) in reference to the state Heracles was in when
      he killed his wife and children. Close by (1086, 1122) there are two other references to his murders as
      done while acting as a Bacchant. Froma Zeitlin studies the Bacchic imagery in the essay on the *Hecuba*
      in her 1996 book.

134   Throughout this monody Polymestor's references to his difficult movement and his rapid-fire, brief,
      repeated series of questions echo and mirror Hecuba's anguished laments about her fears for Polydorus
      in her entrance song (63) and monody after the Chorus informs her of the decision to sacrifice Polyxena
      (154-64). These echoes and Polymestor's position on the ground reinforce the sense that Hecuba has
      fulfilled the structure of revenge that turns its new victim into a copy of the avenger.

135   Like when a ship gathers in its sails while preparing to enter a harbor, so Polymestor pulls in his clothing
      to increase his mobility.

136   See Apollodorus, *Library* I.4.3 Orion was a giant whom Artemis killed. Orion was blinded by his
      prospective father-in-law Oinopion but healed by the rays of the sun god Helios. Dawn (Eos) then fell
      in love with him. Sirius, the Dog Star, was associated with drought and heat during fall.

beams of fire from their eyes, or should wretched I
speed into the dark-skinned ship of Hades?   1105

Chorus

It is understandable, whenever someone suffers troubles stronger than
bearing, to attempt escape from a wretched life.

Agamemnon *(enters from right, with attendants)*

I heard your screams and came; for the child of the mountain rock,
Echo, was not silent, but has clattered through the army,   1110
producing an uproar. If we hadn't known
the towers of the Phrygians had fallen by the Greeks' spear,
this crashing here would have provided fear in no small portion.

Polymestor

Oh best of friends, I heard and recognized, Agamemnon,
your voice. Do you see what we suffer?   1115

Agamemnon

Uh.
Polymestor, you miserable man, who destroyed you?
Who blinded your eyes, bloodied their pupils,
and who killed these boys here? Surely whoever it was
held a great rage at you and your children.

Polymestor

Hecuba, along with spear-won women,   1120
destroyed me—not just destroyed, but worse still.

Agamemnon

What are you saying? (*To Hecuba*) You, *you* did this deed, as he says?
You had the heart, Hecuba, to do this impossible[137] act of daring?

Polymestor

Omoi, what will you say? Is she somewhere nearby, is she?
Give me some sign, say where she is, so that I can grab her with my hands,   1125
tear her apart and cover her skin with blood.

Agamemnon

You there, what is happening to you?

Polymestor

        By the gods I beg you,
let me aim my furious fist against this woman here.[138]

---

137 *Amêchanon* also conveys a sense of "unhealable."

138 Agamemnon's question, and Polymestor's furious interruption of Agamemnon's line, indicates that the
     actor must be moving with great agitation.

Agamemnon

Control yourself. Expel the barbarian from your heart and
speak, so that having heard both you and this woman in turn   1130
I may decide justly in return for what you are suffering so.[139]

Polymestor

I would speak then. There was a certain youngest son of Priam,
Polydorus, a son of Hecuba, whom his father Priam
gave from Troy to me to raise in my house,
since he was suspicious of Troy's fall.   1135
This one I killed; but why I killed him,
listen, how it was done well and with wise forethought.
      I feared lest the boy, left hostile to you,
would raise up Troy and inhabit it again,
and that the Achaeans, having realized one of Priam's sons was still living,   1140
would gather another armada against the land of the Phrygians,[140]
and then ravage this plain of Thrace
in plunder, and there'd be trouble for the neighbors of the
Trojans, the very one in which now, my lord, we were laboring.
Hecuba recognized the fatal lot of her boy   1145
and led me along by this story: how she'd tell me of
the golden treasures of Priam's clan, hidden in Ilium.
She leads me alone with my children into
the tents, so that nobody else might know these things.
I sit on a couch in the middle, having bent my knee;   1150
many daughters of the Trojans, some from the left,
some from the right, took their seats,
as if by a friend, and they were praising the Edonian[141] hand's
weaving, gazing upon these robes under the light;
others were examining my two Thracian spearshafts   1155
and made me naked of my twin-pronged protection.
And as many mothers as there were, full of admiration,
tossing the children in their hands, passing them hand-to-hand

139 This is a trial scene, one that uses the conventions of the Athenian court system, and the outcome of
the debate, given Agamemnon's earlier vacillations to Hecuba, is very much uncertain. As the plaintiff,
Polymestor speaks first.

140 In isolation, this could be an effective argument for Agamemnon, as he had overseen, on similar grounds,
the murder of Astyanax, Hector's very young son, after the fall of Troy. Euripides dramatizes this shattering
event a decade later in *The Trojan Women*.

141 A tribe in western Thrace, connected with Mt Pangaeon which was near the oracle of Dionysus mentioned
by Polymestor later (1267). The Chorus in Sophocles' *Antigone* (955-65) sings of an Edonian king who
angered Dionysus and was thus imprisoned in a cave by the god. There is thus a double connection with
Dionysus, and with Dionysian violence, in this simple adjective.

so the children might be far from their father.
And then from gentle speeches (how do you suppose?)   1160
they immediately take blades from somewhere in their robes and
stab the boys, and others, like octopuses,[142]
all together grab me, holding my arms
and legs. While desiring to defend my boys,
if I could lift up my face,   1165
they seized my hair, and if I stirred my hands
in my misery I achieved nothing because of the mob of women.
Finally, a woe worse than woe,
they completed their terrible deeds; for my eyes—
they grabbed their brooches—they stab the
wretched poor pupils of my eyes and   1170
bloody them; and then throughout the tents they
ran in flight. And I leapt out,
like an animal pursuing the foul murderous bitch dogs,
tracking them along every wall like a hunter,
striking, smashing. I have suffered such things
in pursuit of your favor[143] and in the actual killing of your enemy,   1175
Agamemnon. And so that I may not stretch out my speech too long—
if someone of those who lived before spoke badly of women,
or someone who lives now or someone in the future,
I shall speak having already abridged all these matters: 1180
neither sea or earth nurtures a race
such as this one; and, every time, the one who meets them understands.

Chorus

Don't be so bold, nor blame
the entire female race, lumping them in with your troubles.[144]

---

142 Diggle here had adopted the substitution of *polupodôn* (octopuses) for *polemiôn* (enemies) in the
manuscripts; Gregory finds the comparison of Trojan women to octopuses "bizarre." But this is, I submit,
a bizarre scene. Moreover, a surviving fragment of Sophocles' lost *Iphigenia* (frag. 307) support's Diggle's
reading. Clytemnestra advises her daughter Iphigenia, about to be betrothed to Achilles, though falsely
through the machinations of Agamemnon: "Be mindful to change the color of your true thought to
[match] your man, as the octopus [adapts its color] to a rock." Aside from the comparison based upon
a blur or multiple arms, there seems to be a connection based on the need to disguise one's true self in
order to survive.

143 Again, *kharis*. Polymestor clings to the codes of reciprocity in the implication that he acted in their
mutual interest.

144 The representation of misogyny in Greek tragedy is complex and needs to be handled with care. On the
one hand we see comments like these, which attempt to show men scapegoating females for their own
behavior. Moreover, openly misogynistic characters such as Hippolytus and Creon are shown destroyed
in part because of the consequences of such attitudes, and other plays, such as the *Medea*, seem to go out
of their way to tell the woman's side of the story (even if it is still men who are telling it). On the other
hand, dramas such as the *Medea* also could be seen as reinforcing those misogynistic stereotypes.

[For there many of us, some of whom who are called hateful   1185
while others are naturally among the number of the wicked.]

Hecuba

Agamemnon, for humans it was never necessary
for the tongue to have more power than deeds;
But, if one has done good things, one should have said good words,
but if his deeds were wicked, then his words be rotten,   1190
and never able to speak well about injustice.
So the experts about these things are clever,
but they are not able to be clever forever,
and they die badly. Nobody has ever escaped.
        Your business is part of my preamble;   1195
but I'll go to this man and I'll answer his arguments,
you who claim to have been doubly lightening the Achaeans' load
and acting because of Agamemnon when you killed my boy.
But, you most vile of men, first, never would the barbarian race
ever become friends with the Greeks,   1200
nor could it. Currying what sort of favor[145]
were you so eager? To form some alliance in marriage,
or being a kinsman, or holding what cause?
Or were they intending to sail back here and
hack down your harvest? Whom do you think this will persuade?   1205
The gold, if you want to speak the truth,
killed my boy, and your profit.
        Next explain this: how was it, when Troy
prospered, and the towered wall still surrounded the city,
and Priam lived and Hector's spear flourished,   1210
why then, if you really wanted to do favor for this man,
did you not kill the boy you kept and raised in your house,
or bring him alive to the Argives?
But when our light was put out
and the city signalled by smoke it was under enemies,   1215
you cut down a guest-friend who'd come to your hearth.
        In addition to these arguments now hear how you appear evil.
You should have, if you really were a friend to the Achaeans,
brought the gold which you say was not yours but his to keep
and given it to the men who are needy and   1220
who for a long time have been away from their ancestral land.
But you, not even now, can you bear to release it from

---

145 *Kharis*. Hecuba throws Polymestor's use of reciprocity right back at him throughout her rebuttal.

your hand, and keep it under your control at home.
And by protecting my boy as you should have protected him,
safe and sound, you would have a great glory;   1225
For amidst troubles the good become friends
most clear; good deeds keep friends every time.
And if you needed money while he prospered,
my boy would have been a great treasure for you;
But now you don't have that man for your friend,   1230
and both the benefit of the gold and your own boys are gone,
and you did it yourself. But I say to you,
Agamemnon, if you defend this man, you will appear evil;
you will benefit a guest-friend neither pious
nor trustworthy where he should be, nor just.   1235
We will say you rejoice in evil men,
being such a one yourself—but I don't verbally abuse my masters.

Chorus

Pheu pheu. How good matters always give
to mortals the occasion for good words.

Agamemnon

Burdensome it is for me to judge another's troubles,   1240
but still a necessity. For it also brings shame
if I take this matter into my hands and then shove it away.
To my mind, so that you know, you seem to have done a favor neither to me
nor to the Achaeans by killing a man who was a guest-friend,
but merely so that you could have the gold in your own home.   1245
You say things advantageous to yourself because you're in trouble.
So it was easier among you people to kill a guest-friend quickly;
but for us Greeks this thing is shameful.[146]
How then, having found you innocent, could I escape reproach?
I would not be able. But, since you dared to do   1250
things not noble, submit also to things not of your liking.

Polymestor

Oimoi. By a woman, it seems, I am beaten by a
slave woman, and I will now have to submit and pay justice to my inferiors.

Agamemnon

But is it not justly, since you did evil?

---

146 The irony here is that Agamemnon's own father, Atreus, killed his brother's sons while Thyestes was a guest
     in his house. And this murder motivates Aegisthus' role in death of Agamemnnon, which Polymestor
     prophecies at the end. Who is the barbarian?

Polymestor

Oimoi my children here and my eyes, wretch!   1255

Hecuba

You feel pain. Why? Don't you think I feel pain for my boy?

Polymestor

You rejoice in your outrageous treatment of me, you villain?

Hecuba

Must I not rejoice in my vengeance against you?

> (Here Polymestor must shift in tone, since the content of his attacks shifts markedly.)

Polymestor

But not too fast, whenever the ocean damp—

Hecuba

—won't ferry me to the borders of Greece?   1260

Polymestor

—will cover you when you have fallen from the masthead—

Hecuba

—when I've happened upon a violent fall at whose hands?

Polymestor

You yourself will place your foot on the ship's mast.

Hecuba

With wings on my back, or in what sort of way?

Polymestor

A bitch dog you'll become, possessing fiery eyes.[147]   1265

Hecuba

How is it you know of my metamorphosis?

Polymestor

The prophet to the Thracians, Dionysus, said these things.[148]

Hecuba

And he prophesied nothing of your current troubles?

Polymestor

No, for otherwise you would never have taken me thus with deceit.

---

147 There is no evidence of a tradition of such a transfiguration before Euripides. Scholars are divided in their interpretations of this metamorphosis. Does it signify an externalization of her internal savagery, as argue Michelini (1987) 172, Nussbaum (1986) 398, and Segal (1993) 161-62; or is it a punishment, but more symbolic of the fierce maternal loyalties thought to characterize dogs, as argue Kovacs (1987) 109, Mossman (1992)197, and Gregory (1999) xxxiv?

148 The Greek word *mantis* can designate both the human speaker for the deity as well as the god himself.

Hecuba

Dead, or alive here shall I complete my life?[149]   1270

Polymestor

Dead; your tomb shall acquire the name...

Hecuba

Won't you say it is named after my shape?

Polymestor

The tombstone[150] of a wretched bitch, a signpost for sailors.

Hecuba

Nothing is a concern to me since you, at least, have paid back justice to me.

Polymestor

And necessity is that your daughter Cassandra die.   1275

Hecuba

I spit it back in your face. I give these for you to keep yourself.

Polymestor

The spouse of this man here, a bitter housewife, will kill her—

Hecuba

May the daughter of Tyndareus not yet be so wild with madness![151]

Polymestor

—and this man himself, when she raises up the axe.

Agamemnon

You there, are you mad, and are you in love with falling into troubles?   1280

Polymestor

Kill me then, since bloody baths await you in Argos.[152]

Agamemnon

Will you not haul him off violently, servants?

Polymestor

Do you feel pain, listening?

Agamemnon

        Will you not restrain his mouth?

---

149 This line is hopelessly corrupt in the manuscripts. See Collard (1991).

150 Cynossema ("tomb of the dog") is the name of a promontory sticking out from Thracian Chersonese into the Hellespont. See Gregory (1999) xxxv-xxxvi.

151 This time the daughter of Tyndareus is Clytemnestra, Helen's sister. I think it is important for one to retain the ambiguity of *mêpô* as "not yet" (its more common meaning, instead of "never", as Collard suggests) as it might hint at the desire in Hecuba for violence to Agamemnon.

152 Clytemnestra and his cousin Aegisthus (her lover) kill Agamemnon while he lies defenseless in the bath following his homecoming.

Polymestor

Shut it! For my speech is complete.

Agamemnon *(to attendants)*

      Will you not as quick as you can
expel him somewhere on a deserted island,   1285
since he mouths in this way with too much boldness?

Agamemon's attendants drag Polymestor off to the left. Polymestor likely fights.

Hecuba, you, Oh you miserable woman, come here and
bury the two corpses;[153] and you must draw near
the tents of your masters, women of Troy, because I see
these winds here escorting us homewards.   1290
May we sail well to our fatherland, and may
we see our affairs well at home, freed of these toils here.[154]

(Agamemnon exits right)

Chorus Leader

Go to the harbors and tents, friends,
to try on the hardships of our masters.
For necessity does not bend.   1295

After Agamemnon exits right and the Chorus follows, Hecuba is left alone with the corpses, which are withdrawn with the eccyclêma. *Hecuba follows and enters the tent in order to prepare her children for burial.*

---

153 The two corpses belong to Polydorus, whose body has remained on stage throughout the trial, and to Polyxena, whom Hecuba will finally now go to bury, an action delayed since the discovery of Polydorus' body. Thus will be fulfilled the initial prophecy of Polydorus' ghost that Hecuba would see two corpses of her children on a single day (44-5).

154 Why are the winds suddenly rising? These winds could in fact be the beginnings of the great god-sent storm that will wreck the Achaean fleet (*Odyssey* 4.496-516), killing many of its warriors, forcing Menelaus far to the south, and blowing Agamemnon safely across the Aegean so that his wife can kill him at home.

Outline of the structure of Euripides' *Trojan Women* (415 B.C.E)

Prologue **(1-152)**

    a) Poseidon, builder of Troy's walls, blames its sack on Hera and Athena (1-48)

    b) Athena asks her uncle Poseidon to punish Greek hybris by destroying their home-bound fleet; he agrees. Both gods exit and won't return (49-97)

    c) Solo song by the key protagonist, Hecuba, the city's aged queen, who has been lying prostrate near Agamemnon's tents; she laments Troy's fate (98-152)

Song 1 **(153-234)**

    a) Animated lyric exchange between two half-choruses of young Trojan widows and Hecuba. The choruses lament their impending slavery; Hecuba warns of letting her frenzied daughter Cassandra come outside (153-196)

    b) Half-choruses unite and wonder where they will be sent as slaves (197-234)

Act I **(235-510)** "Cassandra scene"

    Talthybius, the Greek herald, enters to tell Hecuba the captives' fates; Cassandra will be Agamemnon's slave, Polyxena has been sacrificed at Achilles' tomb, Andromache goes to Achilles' son, and Hecuba goes to Odysseus; Hecuba recoils at the thought, calling him odious (235-307)

    b) Cassandra enters with a torch, dancing like a raving maenad, paradoxically claiming that the Trojans are really more fortunate than the Greeks; then she uncannily prophesizes Agamemnon's murder and her own (308-465)

    c) Hecuba, collapsing, laments all her suffering past, present and future (466-510)

Song 2 **(511-567)** Fall of Troy and fatal night of the Trojan Horse—the work of Athena

Act II **(568-798)** "Andromache scene"

    a) Hecuba and Andromache lament their losses and the gods' hostility (568-609)

    b) Andromache recounts the sacrifice of Polyxena and recalls her slain husband Hector; Hecuba still has hope for Astyanax and a new Troy (610-708)

    c) Talthybius brings news of Astyanax's death sentence; Andromache delivers a beautiful farewell to her son, then blasts the Greeks, esp. Helen (709-798)

Song 3 **(799-859)** Sack of sacred Troy; gods' betrayal (stories of Ganymede, Tithonus)

Act III **(860-1059)** "Helen scene"

    a) Menelaus comes to get Helen, claiming he'll kill her back in Greece (860-894)

    b) Hecuba vs. Helen; powerful confrontation and tense debate (895-1059)

Song 4 **(1060-1117)** Zeus accused of betraying Troy; curse on Menelaus' ship and Helen

Exodos **(1118-1332)** "Astyanax scene"

    a) Talthybius arrives with Astyanax's washed corpse on his father's great shield; Hecuba delivers funeral oration and puts robe over his body (1118-1215)

    b) Hecuba blasts the gods for not caring. Funeral procession exits. Soldiers torch Troy. Hecuba bids her city farewell; blasts the gods again. She and chorus kneel and beat the earth, invoking the spirits of their dead (1216-1332)

The *Trojan Women* of Euripides

Setting

An open space outside Troy's walls, which are represented by the stage building (*skênê*) with massive central doors. The time is shortly after the city has been sacked by the Greeks. The Trojan men have been killed or have fled, the women and children captured. In the foreground on stage are tents housing the women who have not been allotted to the Greek army, but are reserved for the Greek commanders. The walls of Troy are already smoldering. At the end of the play flames will engulf the citadel. Of the two side entrance ways on each side of the stage, one leads to the Greek ships, the other to Troy.

The play opens with Poseidon, carrying his trident, on top of the walls. Hecuba is rolling in grief before the gates at center stage. Poseidon does not look down on the scene below him until line 36, when he points to Hecuba ("this poor creature").

Cast of characters in order of appearance[1]

Poseidon	god of the sea, builder of Troy's walls (with Apollo's help)
Athena	goddess of war, daughter of Zeus and Metis, niece of Poseidon
Hecuba	queen of Troy, old widow of Priam, now enslaved
Chorus	captive Trojan widows, young prisoners of war
Talthybios	herald of the Greek army; he is accompanied by armed soldiers
Cassandra	daughter of Priam and Hecuba, a prophetess, priestess to Apollo
Andromache	mother of Astyanax, wife of Hector, daughter-in-law of Hecuba
Menelaos	Greek general, brother of Agamemnon, former husband of Helen
Helen	daughter of Zeus and Leda, wife of Menelaos and then of Paris
Astyanax	young (and only) son of Hector and Andromache (mute actor)

---

1   The most likely division of the eight speaking roles in *Trojan Women* (with their respective number of lines put in parentheses) is as follows: **Actor #1** (protagonist) = Hecuba, who is on stage the entire play (436); **Actor #2** (deuteragonist) = Poseidon (72), Cassandra (125), Andromache (124), and Helen (62); **Actor #3** (tritagonist) = Athena (25), Talthybios (124), and Menelaos (49). The chorus of fifteen Trojan Women has some 315 lines. The play is unusual in that it has no messenger speech.

Poseidon

You see me here before you. I am Poseidon.

I have left the salt depths of the Aegean sea, where sea nymphs trace the fairest
    choral dance[2] with their eddying feet.

From that time when Apollo and I built stone towers[3] to enclose this city

with straight plumb lines, never has affection for this Phrygian city   5

been absent from my heart.

The city now smolders. It has been sacked and destroyed

by the spear of the Argives.

It was Epeios of Phokis[4] under Parnassos who

inspired by the strategem of Athena,   10

fashioned a horse pregnant with armed soldiers

and sent it within these walls with its cargo of death.

[For this reason men of future generations will call it

the "horse of the wooden spear" for it held within hidden spears.][5]

Deserted now are the sacred groves of the gods.[6]   15

Their great temples drip with blood.

King Priam has fallen at the steps of the altar

of Zeus of the Enclosure;[7] he lies there dead.

Great quantities of gold and plunder from Phrygia

are now being carried down to the ships of the Achaeans.   20

who are waiting for a wind from the east to bring them

in the tenth year of sowing to the longed-for sight

of their wives and children. These are the Greeks

who made the expedition against this city.

---

2   The reference to the ring dances of the Nereids is not purely ornamental. It contrasts with the writhing of
       Hecuba on stage (116, 146-52) and her memory of the magnificent dances of the women of Troy during
       the time of its prosperity (333). There is a like contrast in the *Iliad*, when the Nereids emerge onto the
       shore of the Troad to answer Thetis' dirge for Patroklos and Achilles, who is now locked in the events
       that will lead to his death (18.35-51). In Homer the sheer music of the names of the Nereids is antiphonal
       to the grimness of human events on the shore of the Troad.

3   According to a Greek legend, reflected in *Iliad* 21.441 (and in Euripides, *Andromache* 1009 and *Helen*
       1511), Apollo and Poseidon were forced to serve King Laomedon of Troy for a year, during which time
       they built the walls of Troy.

4   The builder of the Trojan horse. The strategem for finally taking Troy is attributed to either Athena or
       Odysseus—which amounts to the same thing.

5   These lines are bracketed by most editors as a later marginal and metrical addition to explain the obvious.
       But stating the obvious is a habit in the prologues of Euripides

6   Poseidon's timely abandonment of Troy, the city whose wells he helped build, is the first expression of the
       grim theology of Euripides' *Trojan Women*. Without the human tribute of prayers, libations, sacrifice,
       and festivals, there can be no "honor" (*time*) for the gods. Even before Troy's destruction, Athena had
       abandoned her, as is clear from Athena's silent gesture of rejection as the women of Troy bring their
       offerings to her temple on the citadel (*Iliad* 6.311).

7   This was the Zeus whose altar stood within the enclosure of a household. In the Epic Cycle, Priam was
       slaughtered by Achilles' son, Pyrrhos, as he took refuge at the altar of Zeus (cf. *Trojan Women* 481-3).

I too am leaving fabled Ilion and my altars.   25
I am defeated by Hera,[8] goddess of Argos, and by Athena,
who together combined to destroy the Phrygians.
When a terrible desolation takes a city,
the world of the gods sickens and will not receive its honors.
The River Scamander echoes the laments of the captured women
who have been assigned by lot[9] to their owners.
Their new masters are an Arcadian, a Thessalian,   30
and the sons of Theseus[10] who are the first family of Athens.
The Trojan women who have not been distributed by lot sit there below.

Poseidon points his trident to their tents below him.

They have been reserved for the great men of the army.
Among them is Helen, daughter of Tyndareos,
a woman from Laconia, now properly a captive bride.   35

*Pointing to Hecuba, who is rolling in dirt before the gates of Troy and look-
ing at the audience*

And this poor creature, if you can bear to look at her,
lies stretched out before the gates.
Her daughter, Polyxena, has been put to death
at the mound of Achilles' grave, a dreadful death she does not know of.   40
The children of Priam and Hecuba are no more.
The daughter Lord Apollo released
in her frenzy, still a virgin,
Agamemnon has "married" by brute force in an adulterous bed,
violating both the god's property and the piety due to him.

Athena now appears on the walls of Troy.

I have said enough. I say farewell to my city,   45

---

8   That is, the two goddesses spurned by Paris, Athena and Hera, have combined to destroy Troy to avenge
     the insult of Paris having preferred Aphrodite in exchange for Aphrodite's bribe of Helen. The reason
     for their hatred of Troy is alluded to but left unexplained in the *Iliad* (24.22-34; cf. 3.39 and 13.769).
     This background is brought explicitly into *The Trojan Women* by Hecuba in 924-33.

9   The principle of the division of the human spoils to be led from Troy is this: most of the women of the
     city, including the women who make up the chorus, are distributed by lot (*kleros*). But the selection of the
     most important of the captive women has been made by the commanders of the army beforehand. Helen,
     "now properly a captive bride" (35), is reserved for Menelaos, although she is from Sparta. Cassandra is
     reserved for Agamemnon; Andromache for the son of Achilles, Pyrrhos (also called Neoptolemos); and
     Hecuba for Odysseus.

10   This is the first conspicious symptom of deliberate anachronism in the play. In the *Iliad*, the Athenians
     play an inconsiderable and easily forgotten role. Menestheus is mentioned in the Catalogue of Ships
     (*Iliad* 2.546-56). In *The Sack of Troy* of the Epic Cycle, Akamas and Demophon play some role (*Homeri
     Opera*, V p. 139 Allen), but the sons of Theseus are important to the conception of victors and vanquished
     articulated in *The Trojan Women*.

once fortunate in its dressed stone towers. You would still be standing
firm on your foundations, if Athena,
daughter of Zeus, had not destroyed you.

Athena approaches Poseidon on cue.

Athena

Can I speak to you, a great divinity and a god honored among the gods,
who in birth is closest to my father? Can I abandon the enmity that has
   separated us?   50

Poseidon

Lady Athena, you can.
Conversation with kin is a powerful drug over the mind.

Athena

I commend your moderate attitude.
I come to you on matters that concern us both, and, my Lord, I will be open
   with you.

Poseidon

You are not bringing some new announcement from the gods–   55
from Zeus or from another god?

Athena

No. I come on account of Troy, the city on whose walls we stand,
to make a claim on your power.

Poseidon

Can this be? Have you cast aside the hatred
you once had for this city? Have you come to pity it   60
now that it is in ashes?

Athena *Moving along the walls to get a view of the Greek camp*

First, come over here. Can we now speak with one another?
Will you agree to do what I want done?

Poseidon

Indeed, I will. But I would like to know what you have in mind.
Have you come here on account of the Achaeans– or the Phrygians?

Athena

I want to cheer the Trojans, who were once my enemies.   65
I want to inflict upon the Achaean army a bitter home-coming.

Poseidon

Tell me: how can you leap from one emotion to its opposite?
How rapidly you shift from extremes of hate to extremes of love!

Athena

Are you unaware that I and my temples have been outraged?

Poseidon

I am aware of the outrage. I knew of it from the moment Ajax
began to drag Cassandra from your altar by force.[11]   70

Athena

And the Achaeans did not lift a finger or utter a word against him!

Poseidon

And yet it was thanks to your power that they sacked Ilion.

Athena

Yes. And with your help I want to do them harm.

Poseidon

I am ready to help you as I can. What do you want me to do?

Athena

I want you to inflict on them a home-coming that will be bitter-sweet.   75

Poseidon

While they are still on land or upon the salt sea?

Athena

When they have left Ilion and have set sail for home.
Zeus will hurtle down upon them rain and hail unceasing
and sable blasts from the height of heaven.
He promises he will give me the fiery bolt of lightning   80
to strike the Achaeans and burn their ships in a blaze of fire.
Now for your part, Poseidon: Make the sea ways of the Aegean
roar with waves and white caps and swirling water;
choke the Hollow of Euboea[12] with corpses.
Teach the Achaeans to respect my palaces in the future   85
and revere the other gods.

Poseidon

This will be accomplished. A favor requires no long argument.

---

11   This is one of the two crimes committed by the Greeks during the sack of Troy that angered Athena
especially and turned her against them. The other was the removal of her sacred image (*palladion*) from
her temple on the acropolis of Troy by Odysseus and Diomedes. Both these outrages are included in
Athena's question to Poseidon: "Are you unaware that I and my temples have been outraged?" (69).
Poseidon, however, seems to be only aware of the case of Cassandra, who had taken refuge at the altar
of Athena and was dragged from its sanctuary by Ajax, son of Oileus, but in this play at least not raped
by him. In Arktinos' *The Sack of Troy* the lesser Ajax was destroyed by Poseidon for his sacrilege, when
he had found safety from shipwreck on the Gryai Rocks (the tradition of *Odyssey* 4.499-510).

12   This stretch of coast is hard to locate precisely, but the run from Troy would take the Greek fleet across
the Aegean to Lemnos and Skyros and the dangerous Kapherean promontory on the southeast tip of
the island of Euboea known as the "hollows." This is the cape where the Persian fleet came to grief in
a sudden squall in the summer of 479 B. C. This storm too was god-sent; cf. Herodotus, *The Persian
Wars* 8.12-14. It might have figured in the *Palamedes* as the coast on which Palamedes' father, Nauplios,
engineered the shipwreck of some of the returning Greek fleet.

I will roil up the salt expanses of the Aegean Sea;
the capes of Mykonos and the reefs of Delos;[13]
Skyros and Lemnos and the Kapherean promontories   90
will all receive the corpses of many dead men.
You, Athena, go up to Olympos, take the lightning bolts
from your father's hands, and bide your time.
Wait until the army of the Achaeans is under full sail.
That mortal is a fool who destroys a city,   95
its temples, its tombs, and the precincts of the dead,
making them a waste. He will be destroyed himself.

> *Exit Poseidon and Athena.*

> *Hecuba has been pitching from side to side in silent grief before the gates of*
> *Troy. She is dressed in black; her gray hair is unbound and covered with dust*
> *and ashes. A group of women also dressed in black emerge from the entrance*
> *to the orchestra (Parodos) and gather around her. This is the chorus of Trojan*
> *women.*

Hecuba[14]

Rise up, ill-fated woman. Raise your head
and neck from the ground.
   Troy is no more.

> *Turning to the breached and smoldering walls.*

This is Troy, and we are the kings of Troy.   100
Hold on as divinity shifts its course.
Our course carries us through the straits.
Some god steers us.
In this disaster I cannot even direct the prow
of my life against the wave.
Aiai! Aiai!   105
Why should I not groan in this inarticulate misery?
Gone are my country, my children, my husband.
O, great billowing glory of my ancestors,
you collapse to this. So you amounted to nothing after all.

---

13   According to the epic of *The Returns* (the *Nostoi* of Agias), these rocks (the Gryai) were located off the
     Cycladic islands of Mykonos (where Ajax's grave was shown), Delos, and Tenos.

14   *Hecuba's Lyric Monologue*: Thematically, Hecuba's language expresses the contrast between her present
     state as she grovels on the ground before the tent of Agamemnon and the vanished prosperity of Troy.
     She conceives of her body as a ship driven over a sea churned up by the storm of her misfortunes. The
     metaphorical language with which she describes her body carries forward the intimation of the disasters
     at sea that await Ajax, son of Oileus, and the Achaeans (demanded by Athena at 77-78) and Odysseus
     (forecast by Cassandra in 431-43).

Hecuba remains silent for a time.

Why should I remain silent? Why should I speak out? 110
Why should I raise the cry of lamentation?
I groan over this body
contorted by the weight of some heavy god. I lie stretched out
on my back on this hard bed.
I feel the pain of my head, my temples, 115
my breast.
How I long to roll and toss
and surrender my back and spine to both walls,
like a ship's keel rocking from side to side,
pursuing strain after strain of lamentation and tears.
For the unfortunate even lamentation is a Muse[15] 120
—to descant misfortunes no chorus can dance to.
You ships' prows
coming to sacred Ilion[16]
propelled by swift oars over the indigo sea
passing the safe harbors of Greece 125
accompanied by the hateful anthem to Apollo, the Paian,
and the voice of melodious pipes,
you ships' sterns fitted by the plaited
and cultured papyrus of Egypt.[17]
You came, *ai! ai!*, to Troy's heartland 130
in pursuit of the loathed wife of Menelaos,
the shame of her brother Kastor,
the infamy of the River Eurotas,
the woman who slaughters Priam,
Priam who sowed the seed of fifty children, 135
who slaughters sorrowing Hecuba.
She had run high aground on the beach of this ruin.
oimoi. I groan as I feel this humbled state,
as I lie stretched out next to the tent of Agamemnon.
In my old age I am dragged from my home as a slave. 140

---

15   With Hecuba's description of her "Muse" and the disasters none can dance to, the chorus of Trojan
      women enter the orchestra. They enter in two groups (half choruses); Hecuba addresses them at line
      142. The chorus is made up of young women who have lost their husbands in war.

16   Like so much of the language of *The Trojan Women*, Hecuba's description of the past and the arrival of the
      Greek fleet on the coast of the Troad seems conventional, formulaic, and "poetic." It is symptomatic of
      the fact that poetry and reality have become severely disjointed. Ilion is "sacred" even as it is abandoned
      by its gods.

17   A line sometimes daggered and thought corrupt because it seems so far-fetched. But much of what Hecuba
      says *is* far-fetched, especially as she describes the vicarious experience of life on board a ship in 686-93.

My head bears all the pitiful marks of mourning.
I am a trophy from the sack of Troy.

> *Turning to the chorus who have formed in two groups around the tent of Agamemnon.*

Enough. You. Pitiful wives of Trojan husbands who were once
armed with bronze swords, daughters ill wed, brides of death.
Join me in my wailing.   145
Troy smolders.
I, a mother,
will lead the piercing keening,
sorrowful as the lament of a feathered bird,
but not as I once did when I had the support of Priam's scepter   150
and led the dance in a stately rhythm
to honor the gods of Phrygia.

Parodos[18]

> *The two half choruses exchange lyric laments (a kommos) with Hecuba.*

First Half-Chorus   *Enters from a hut on one side of the stage*

Strophe A

Hecuba, why do you cry out? What makes you utter these words?
Where has your tale taken us?
We heard the wail of lamentation that pierced our chambers   155
piercing our breasts with fear,
darting dread for the women of Troy.
In these dwellings
> *pointing to the tents before the walls*
they grieve over their enslavement.

Hecuba

My children, let me answer. Sailors with oars gripped in their hands
are setting off for the ships of the Achaeans.   160

First Half Chorus

Oi 'go! What do they mean to do?
Will they really carry me from my country over the sea?

---

18   Despite her conception of her threnody for Troy as unsuitable for choral dancing, in line 146 Hecuba has begun a choral song (*molpe*) of lamentation. She is dressed for the part, in the black garb of woman in mourning and with her hair cropped. She is probably wearing what is known as a "mourning mask." The women in the two half-choruses that form before her in the orchestra are in conspicuous public mourning too.

Hecuba

I do not know. I guess that some disaster is at hand.

First Half Chorus

io, io!

Poor women of Troy, hear now your hard fate.   165

You will be taken from your homes by ship.

The Argives are preparing to return home.

Hecuba   *Responding to a commotion within the tent of Agamemnon*

No! No!

Do not let her come out

wild, frenzied Cassandra, dervish, maenad,   170

shame to the Argives.[19] Do not inflict more pain upon me!

io! io!

Troy, o unhappy Troy. You are no more.

Unhappy are those who leave you,

the living and the dead.   175

Antistrophe A

Second Half Chorus   *Enters from a hut on the other side of the stage*

Oimoi.   My Queen, trembling, in fear, I left this tent

of Agamemnon[20] to hear what you have to say.

Have the Argives then decided

to put us to death, though we are already wretched?

Or are the sailors standing at the ships' sterns   180

ready to ply their oars?

Hecuba

Children, I have come in fright, my soul

awakened by the gray dawn of terror.

Second Half Chorus

Has a herald from the camp of the Danaans already come?

To whom have I been allotted as a miserable slave?   185

Hecuba

Your lot, I think, is soon to fall.

Second Half Chorus

io! io!

---

19   Because of the fact that Ajax, son of Oileus, had attempted to rape her and because of the indifference
      of the Greeks to the sacrilege done to Apollo and his priestess at his altar; see the note to line 70.

20   The second choral group has now emerged from the tent of Agamemnon in the orchestra, literally the
      skene or tent stretched before the walls of Troy. Their song is antiphonal to that of Hecuba and reiter-
      ates the movement and meter of the strophe. With line 197 the chorus becomes lyrical (in meter and in
      language).

Which Argive, which Thessalian
will take me away? Or will I be taken to some island far from Troy?

Hecuba

Pheu! Pheu!   190
Who will be my master? Where on earth shall I end up
as a slave in my suffering and old age?
A drudge, a crone, the counterfeit of a corpse,
the cold statue of a dead woman.
   Aiai! Aiai!
Shall I, who was once honored as Queen of Troy,   195
serve as a door keeper or nurse to another's children?

Choral Ode

Chorus

Strophe B

   The two half-choruses now join into a single group

Aiai Aiai   What inarticulate sounds
could you summon to grieve over this black day?
Never again will I push the shuttle
along the frame of looms cut from the trees of Mt. Ida.   200
Now for a last time will I look at the home of my parents.
Still greater hardships than this await me.[21]
I will be forced to share a bed with a Greek—
keep that night and spirit of evil far from me!—
or will I carry water as a pitiable servant
from the sacred stream of Peirene.[22]   205
Could I have my wish, I would go
to the renowned, blessed,
and prosperous land of Theseus.[23]
But never would I go to the eddies of the Eurotas,
hateful river that nurtured Helen,[24]   210

---

21   The chorus now envisage their life in Greece. It is a life Hector had already predicted for Andromache
      in his last meeting with his wife (*Iliad* 6.448-61). The illusion of this choral ode is abruptly shattered
      by the appearance of Talthybios at 235, as the chorus conclude that they will be slaves in a Dorian land
      (234).

22   An abundant spring in Corinth.

23   Attica, a land barely recognized in the Homeric poems. Athens is mentioned in the Catalogue of Ships
      (*Iliad* 2.547), but Athenians play no significant role in either of the Homeric epics.

24   In Greek the Spartan river is qualified as *therapna*. The place where a cult of Helen was located is also
      called Therapne, the place of nurture.

where I would encounter, now a slave,
Menelaos, the sacker of Troy.

Antistrophe B

I have heard rumors of the stately land of Thessaly
watered by the River Peneios,
the fairest approach to high Olympos;   215
I have heard of its fertility, richness, and nodding crops.
After the sacred land of Theseus inhabited by gods
this is the land I would choose.
I have heard of the land
of Mt. Aetna[25] sacred to Hephaistos,   220
a land that faces the country of the Phoenicians,
the mother to the hills of Sicily;
I have heard of a land proclaimed by the wreathes of victory,
the land that lies closest
to the sailor crossing the Ionian sea,   225
the land watered by the fairest of all rivers,
the Krathis,[26]
that flows in streams that turn hair to a ruddy hue,
as its divine springs foster
and make prosper this powerful, populous land.

> *As the chorus has been singing their epinician hymn in praise of Sicily, the herald*
> *of the Greek army has entered the stage. He is accompanied by armed soldiers.*

Now here comes a herald from the army of the Danaans   230
to dispense from his store still new tales.
He comes in a great hurry.
What news is he bringing? What will he tell us?
I know. We are already slaves of a Dorian land.

---

25 Sicily was of particular interest to Euripides and his Athenian audience in the spring of 415, when the
    Athenians were planning their expedition against Syracuse. The language the chorus employ to praise the
    island (not mentioned in the Homeric poems) deliberately recalls the language of the vic-tory odes of Pindar,
    especially those for the Sicilian victors in the Olympic games.

26 A river near the city of Sybaris on the instep of Italy flowing into the Ionian sea. In 444/3 the site of
    Sybaris was recolonized by a group led by Athenians. The new name of the site was Thurii.

First Episode[27]

Talthybios

Hecuba. You know who I am. Woman, I am familiar to you   235
from the many times in the past that I have come to Troy
from the Achaean army.
I am Talthybios. I come with something new to tell.

Hecuba

This, this, dear women, is what I have long feared.

Talthybios

You have already been allotted to your masters, if this is what you feared.   240

Hecuba

Aiai. To what city did you say I am to be taken?
A city of the land of Phthiotis in Thessaly? A city of Kadmos' land?[28]

Talthybios

Each of you has been allotted to her master; you have not been given as a group.

Hecuba

Tell me: Who were the winners in this lottery?
What happy lot awaits the women of Troy?   245

Talthybios

I can tell you, but ask one question at a time, not all at once.

Hecuba

Then tell me:
who was awarded my child, suffering Cassandra?

Talthybios

Lord Agamemnon[29] chose her from the rest, reserving her for himself.

Hecuba

So, to serve as a slave for his Spartan bride.[30]   250
omoi moi.

---

27 Hecuba will remain on stage for the duration of *The Trojan Women*; Cassandra's appearance is the first
    of three scenes in which Hecuba and Talthybios confront one of the captive women assigned to the
    leaders of the Greek army. Like her language, the torch she is carrying is ambiguous. It is a sign either
    of her decision to immolate herself or her impending "marriage" to Agamemnon. In fact, it is a sign of
    her impending "marriage" to Hades, the bridegroom of young women who die before marriage. As is
    the case of all of the women's parts of this play, her language veers from the ecstatic and visionary to the
    sophistically rational.

28 The city of Thebes in Boeotia.

29 In Aeschylus' *Agamemnon*, Agamemnon presents Cassandra to Clytemnestra with these words: "This
    woman before you was my companion, the flower picked from many possessions, the gift of my army"
    (954-5).

30 Clytemnestra, Helen's half-sister and the daughter of Tyndareos and Leda of Sparta.

Talthybios

No, not a slave, but a "bride" to share his bed in secret.

Hecuba

So, he took the virgin of Phoibos,[31] the girl the god
of the golden locks granted a life that would never know a man's bed?

Talthybios

Eros struck him with a barb of passion for the god-frenzied girl.   255

Hecuba   *To Cassandra*

My daughter, throw down those sacred branches![32]
Strip from your body this sacred woven dress!

Talthybios

Is it not a great honor for her to attain a king's bed?

Hecuba   *Who pays no attention*

Why have you taken my youngest child[33] from me?
Where is she?   260

Talthybios

Do you mean Polyxena? or another girl?

Hecuba

Polyxena. To what man was she yoked by her lot?

Talthybios

She has been assigned to serve at Achilles' tomb.

Hecuba

omoi ego.
Did I give birth to a grave attendant?   265
Tell me, my good man:
What Greek custom or ritual is this?

---

31   Apollo granted to Cassandra a life of virginity and the gift of prophecy. She is termed virgin twice in *The Trojan Women* (41 and 252; cf. 453). But, because she deceived the god of prophecy, he made her prophecies fall on deaf—or baffled—ears. This part of her story is briefly told by Cassandra in her exchange with the chorus of Aeschylus, *Agamemnon* 1202-13. But, more immediately, her gift of prophecy and the disbelief it provoked in Troy was a feature of the first play of the "trilogy" of which *The Trojan Women* is the third play; in the *Alexandros* she prophesied the coming of the Greeks to Trojans who would not believe her.

32   Cassandra is wearing on her head a crown of woolen fillets, emblems that put her into contact with divinity, and carrying a branch of laurel, another symbol of her dedication to Apollo. Both are referred to in Aeschylus, *Agamemnon* 1265; in *Trojan Women* 330 Cassandra invokes the shrine of Apollo among the laurels; cf. Euripides, *Andromache* 296.

33   Polyxena, Hecuba's youngest daughter, has already been sacrificed at the grave of Achilles. In the Prologue, Poseidon had announced the death of Polyxena to Euripides' audience (39-40), but it is only later in the play that Hecuba registers the force of Talthybios' ambiguous language (622-9). The same gap in communication occurs in the exchange between Talthybios and Andromache in 715.

Talthybios

Count your daughter blessed. She is happy.

Hecuba

What is the meaning of these words? Tell me:

Does she look upon the light of the sun?   270

Talthybios   *Addressing a woman who does not hear*

She has found her lot in life. She is free of trouble.

Hecuba

And… What of the wife of Hector, the husband who courted her with bronze,

poor suffering Andromache? What is her fate?

Talthybios

She too has been reserved. Achilles' son got her.

Hecuba

And I, whom shall I serve,   275

I who must walk with a cane in my shriveled hand?

Talthybios

You were part of the general lottery. You are awarded to Odysseus,[34]

Lord of Ithaka. You are his slave.

Hecuba

e! e!   This is too much to bear. Strike now your head in mourning.

Draw your nails over your cheeks.   280

io moi moi.   Is it then my lot to be the chattel

of an abominable trickster,

an enemy of right, a rabid, lawless beast,

who with his forked tongue

bends everything to its opposite   285

and back again

making what was once hated loved

and what was once loved hated.

   Turning to the chorus

Women of Troy, begin your lament for me.

I have gone to my evil destiny. I am no more.   290

In my misery I have fallen out as the most unfortunate lot of all.

---

34   There seems to be no earlier tradition that Hecuba was awarded to Odysseus, although in Euripides'
     Hecuba of 424 Hecuba emerges from the tent of Odysseus. In the immediate context of the plays presented
     at the dramatic festivals of 415, Odysseus is the detestable sophist of the *Palamedes*, who, in his spite
     against Palamedes, falsely accused him of treasonable correspondence with Priam. The late fifth-century
     transformation of the Homeric Odysseus into the guileful contemporary sophist explains the vehemence
     of Hecuba's reaction to her fate: the Queen of Troy had become the household slave to the archetype of
     the Athenian demagogue.

Chorus

My queen, your lot I know.
But as for our fate, what Achaean, what Greek has power over it?

Talthybios   *To the chorus*

You, serving women, go! It is time to fetch Cassandra.
Be quick! I must entrust her into the general's hands.   295
Then I must bring the women allotted to the others.

Suddenly turning to the tent of Agamemnon

What is this? Why is a torch blazing inside the tent?
What are the women of Troy doing?
Are they setting their tents afire
because they are about to be taken from Troy   300
to Argos? Do they want to commit suicide by immolating themselves?

To the audience

In a crisis like theirs, the spirit of freedom bends a stiff neck to evils.

To one of his armed attendants

Open the tent.
I won't have what is good for these women
but hateful to the Achaeans get *me* in trouble.   305

Hecuba

You are wrong. They are not lighting fires. In her divine frenzy
my daughter, Cassandra, is rushing out to us.

Cassandra's lyric monody

Strophe A

Cassandra has emerged from Agamemnon's tent and holds a pine torch out to Hecuba.

Hold this torch![35] Take it! Carry the fire! I worship. I burn.

---

35   Cassandra rushes out from the tent holding up a torch and sings a monody in trochees. The power of this
scene derives from her prophecy of her coming death and the murder of Agamemnon in Argos, which
she will describe in grisly detail (448-50). Her true "marriage" is not to Agamemnon, but to Hades, in
the Greek tradition the bridegroom of young women who died unmarried.

Cassandra deliberately evokes the events of the Greek marriage ceremony, with its torches to light
the way of the bridal procession to the house of the groom, its invocations to Hymen, the god of marriage,
its songs in praise of the bride and groom (*makarismoi*), and festive dancing. It is only when Cassandra
calls upon the infernal Hekate (323) that the chill of the reality behind her song and dance invades
Euripides' stage. For the Greek audience of this play Cassandra's invitation to her mother to join her
in the wedding dance would have been a scandal, and the chorus react to it as such (406). Hecuba is in
mourning and is not permitted to join in any festivities. True to her fate, Cassandra is not understood
by the Trojan captives: "Your majesty, will you not stop your daughter?" (342; cf. 407).

Look! Look here!
Lord Hymenaeus, this fire is sacred!   310
Blessed is the bridegroom
And blessed I who will be wed to a royal bed
in the land of Argos.
Hymen, Lord Hymenaeus!

> *turning again to Hecuba*

Since you, mother, are lamenting for my dead father   315
and beloved fatherland with ceaseless tears and cries of grief,
I myself will light the flame
to spring to a brilliant shaft of light
at my marriage,
offering it to you, Hymenaeus.   320
offering the torch to you, Hekate,[36]
to illuminate the marriage bed
of virgins
as custom bids.

Antistrophe A

Let your feet spring into the air,   325
Lead the line of dancers,
euan! euoi! Dionysos, I call on you!
You, mother, are celebrating my father's great blessed fortune!
This is a sacred dance. You, Phoibos,[37] lead it. I offer sacrifice
in your palace among the laurels.   330
Hymen, O Hymenaeus, Hymen!
Dance, mother, lead the chorus line!
Come join me. Wind your step here with mine.
Dear mother, stop here.
Shout out the marriage hymn, Hymenaion, O!   335
with songs of praise
and cries celebrating the bride!

> *To the chorus*

Come now daughters of Phrygians
dressed in your festival gowns, dance, sing the marriage hymn,
sing the groom   340

---

36   A goddess of the underworld, often shown in Greek art as holding a torch.

37   Cassandra calls upon both Phoibos Apollo and Dionysos (328). The two gods, who shared the sacred site of Delphi but who were often viewed as opposite in character, combine to inspire Cassandra with the exultation of a Maenad (see 342) and the clairvoyance of a prophet.

destined for my bridal bed.

Chorus   *Turning from Cassandra to Hecuba*
Your majesty, will you not stop your daughter? She is possessed by a god.
Keep her from whirling in a dance to the camp of the Argives.

Hecuba   *Looking at the torch Cassandra is waving*
Hephaistos, you hold the torch in the weddings of mortal men.
But this flame you ignite gives off a grim light,
something no one would have expected. O, my child, my child,   345
I never thought that you would one day marry like this,
driven at the point of an Argive spear.
Give me the torch. You are not holding it straight,
but dart about like a maenad possessed. Child, your misfortunes
have not taught you any restraint. You have not changed.   350

    To the chorus

Women of Troy. Bring the torches on. Let your weeping
be responsive to the wedding songs of this girl.

Cassandra
Mother,[38] crown my head with the victor's wreath.
Rejoice in my marriage to a king.
Be my escort, and, if my enthusiasm does not match yours,   355
force me to move. If Apollo Loxias[39] is true to his name,
glorious Agamemnon, great Lord of the Achaeans,
will marry in me a bride more disastrous than Helen.
I will kill him and make him pay for the destruction
of my brothers and father. I shall destroy his house.   360
I say no more. We will not sing of the ax[40]
that will fall upon my neck and the necks of others;
I will not sing of the struggle of matricides,
a struggle my marriage will bring about; nor of the house of Atreus toppled.

    Pointing to the walls of Troy

---

38   Cassandra now reverts to the rhythm of ordinary Greek speech, the iamb (or iambic trimeter).

39   One of Apollo's epithets is Loxias. It is often associated with Apollo as a prophet. It means crooked or
      oblique and describes the ambiguous character of his prophecies.

40   As Cassandra did in the prophetic scene in which she throws open the doors of the palace of Agamemnon
      to her own death in Aeschylus' *Agamemnon* (1256-80); at this moment she also prophesies the revenge of
      Orestes and Electra (1280-85). In *The Trojan Women*, unlike the *Oresteia* of Aeschylus, Cassandra claims
      that her marriage to Agamemnon, and not Agamemnon's sacrifice of his daughter, Iphigeneia, will lead
      inexorably to Agamemnon's murder by Clytemnestra and reciprocally Clytemnestra's murder by her son.

I shall demonstrate[41] that this city   365
is more fortunate than are the Achaeans. A god might possess me,
but I shall stand this far distant from his bacchant's dance:
The men who hunted down a single woman and, in Helen, a single Kypris
destroyed countless thousands.
That commander, that sage man, lost all that is dearest to him[42]
for the sake of what is most hateful,   370
surrendering for the sake of his brother the pleasures of children at home,
and for the sake of a woman,
a woman who was carried off not by force of violence, but a willing partner.
Yet, once they arrived at the banks of the Scamander,
the Achaeans began to die, not for land that had been taken from them
or a home or a city with its lofty towers.   375
Those that Ares destroyed never saw their children again;
the hands of their wives did not wrap them in their funeral garments.
They lie buried in a foreign land.
Life in Greece mirrors life in Troy.
Wives died off as widows and fathers died after their sons,   380
having raised children who would never care for them.
There is no one who can bestow at the graves of these men
the gift of a blood-offering to the earth.
The Greek army merits this much praise.
About what is shameful in Greece it is better to keep silent.
I would not have my Muse sing hymns of evil things.[43]   385
I turn to the Trojans. First, their greatest claim to glory:
they gave their lives for their country.
Those who fell in battle were carried to their homes by their family.
They were covered by the embrace of their native land
and decorously laid out in death by those whose duty it is to bury them.   390
Those Phrygians who did not die in battle
lived day by day in the company of their wives and children,
pleasures the Achaeans could not enjoy.

   To Hecuba

---

41   Cassandra's "demonstration" is not inspired by her bacchic and visionary ecstasy, but by the cool calcu-
     lation of the balance of gains and losses on both sides of the Trojan War, both of the victors and of the
     vanquished.

42   That is, his daughter, Iphigeneia, whom he sacrificed to obtain favorable winds for his expedition to Troy
     from Aulis (the subject of Euripides' *Iphigeneia at Aulis*). Euripides deflects attention from Agamemnon's
     crime of murdering his daughter by using the "apotropaic plural" ("all that is dearest to him").

43   Cassandra's silence powerfully evokes the thought of the wives who have been unfaithful to their husbands
     away in Troy and particularly Agamemnon's wife, Clytemnestra, who was seduced by Aigisthos.

Mother, hear the truth about the bitter fate of Hector.
He enjoyed the reputation of being the bravest of men;
    he is now dead and gone.   395
The coming of the Achaeans is responsible for his renown;
had they remained at home, none would have known his worth.
And Paris, he married the daughter of Zeus. Had he not married,
there would have been no word in Troy about this tie of kinship with a god.
Anyone with any sense should avoid war.   400
But, if war comes, there is no shame in dying nobly for one's city.
To die as a coward is the crown of infamy.
For these reasons, mother, you should not mourn for our country
or my coming marriage. By this my marriage
I shall destroy those most loathed by you and me.   405

Chorus   *To Cassandra*

What pleasure you take in the disasters of your home!
The burden of this prophetic song will not be as compelling as you would have it.

Talthybios   *To Cassandra*

If Apollo had not driven you mad[44] in Dionysos' frenzy,
you would not be sending my commanders off from this land
with such sinister prophecies.   410
So it is: What is exalted and wise in people's esteem
collapses into ashes.
The greatest Lord of the assembled Greek forces,
Atreus' beloved son, has been stricken with a passion for this dervish
in preference to all others. I am a poor man,   415
but I would not have chosen this woman for my bed.
You, Cassandra. You are not in your right mind.
I hurl all of your abuse of the Achaeans
and all your praise of the Phrygians to the raging winds.
Follow me now to the ships, a lovely bride for the general.   420

    To Hecuba

And you: whenever the son of Laertes wants to take you, follow him.
You will serve a good, prudent woman;[45]
so say those who come to Ilion.

Cassandra

This man is a clever lackey. How do these men get their titles,

---

44   Again (as in 327 and 329), both Apollo and Dionysos are joined as inspiring Cassandra's prophecy.

45   Penelope, the wife of Odysseus whose prudence is exemplified in her treatment of her suitors and Odysseus in the *Odyssey*, where she has the epithet *echephron*, "restrained."

"heralds"?[46] They are the object of universal detestation among mankind.   425
They are mere minions, creatures attached to tyrants and to cities.

To Talthybios

You, do you bring the message that my mother will go
to the halls of Odysseus?

Looking away

What has become, then, of the god Apollo's words?[47]
They declare that she will die here. I will not utter the shameful part   430
of his prophecy. Unhappy man, Odysseus does not know what sufferings await him.
The day will come[48] when he will look back on my sufferings
and the sufferings of the Phrygians as a golden age.
When he has added ten years to the ten years he has spent here,
      he will arrive at home alone.
He will come first to the narrow passage between cliffs   435
where dread Charybdis dwells. I see the Cyclops,
a mountain cannibal. I see Ligurian[49] Circe, who transforms men into pigs.
I see shipwrecks on the salt sea, the craving for the lotus,
the sacred cattle of the Sun God, whose bleeding flesh
will one day sing a bitter song that will make Odysseus' flesh crawl.   440
I will cut my story short. Still living, he will enter Hades,
and, once he has survived shipwreck at sea,
he will discover countless troubles on his return home.
But, ... why should I harp on the hardships of Odysseus?

---

46   *kerykes* in Greek. The word is clearly meaningful to Cassandra. One explanation of its latent meaning
      is that Euripides connected it with *ker*, a Greek word for the Spirit of Death. It has also been suggested
      that Talthybios played a vile part in the *Palamedes*.

47   In effect, Cassandra is asking: "Will the legend of Hecuba and the plot of any *Hecuba* be altered?" Hecuba
      would in fact die in (or near) Troy, but only once she had been transformed into a rabid bitch. This trans-
      formation occurred after she had avenged the murder of her son, Polydoros, by blinding Polymnestor,
      king of Thrace, and his sons. What is too grotesque for Cassandra to utter is the metamorphosis foretold
      by her blinded but seeing victim, Polymnestor: "You will be turned into a rabid bitch with a sulphurous
      mouth, and your tomb will be called Kynosema [Dog's Mound] by passing sailors" (Euripides, *Hecuba*
      1265-73).

48   A prophecy inspired and confirmed by Odysseus' words (in *Odyssey* 5.306-7), as he recalls the prophecy
      of Kalypso, as a storm overtakes his raft within sight of the island of Skeria (5.206-7):
            Happy, thrice happy, and four times happy are the Danaans
            who died then in the broad plains of Troy, as they sought to please
            the sons of Atreus.
      In her prophecy of the sufferings of Odysseus, Cassandra abbreviates Homer's account of Odysseus'
      return to Ithaka after twenty years; she completely neglects his stay in Phaeacia and the Phaeacians'
      recognition of the valor of Odysseus, and she ignores his final reunion with his family and his triumph
      in Ithaka.

49   On the northwest coast of Italy.

Turning to Talthybios again

Get on your way. Join our bridegroom in the Halls of Hades.   445
That coward will be given a coward's burial, at night, not in the light of day.
You, commander of Danaids not Danaans, of women not men,
you fancy that you are accomplishing some magnificent feat.
And I— my corpse— cast down naked, the deep ravines,
as they run in winter torrent, will yield up to beasts to share,
near the tomb of my groom, I, Apollo's priestess.   450

Cassandra takes the strands of wool that have bound her hair and throws them to the ground.

Wool fillets sacred to the god who is dearest to me,
lovely proud emblems of my bacchanals,
I leave you. I am done with the festivals in which I once exulted.
Leave me, I tear you from my body, while my body is still undefiled.
Let the winds, Apollo, god of prophecy, carry them back to you.

To Talthybios

Where is the general's ship? Which ship must I board?   455
You need not wait for a breeze to fill the sails.
In me you are transporting from this land a Fury, a single avenger of three crimes.[50]

To Hecuba

Mother, do not say good-bye. Beloved country,
brothers beneath its soil, father who sired us,
in a short time you will greet me. I shall arrive among the dead,   460
a victor, when I have destroyed the Atreidai, who have destroyed us.

Exit Cassandra, led off by Tolthybios and his soldiers

Leader of the Chorus   *To some of the chorus*
You who watch over old Hecuba, can't you see
how your mistress has collapsed without uttering a sound?
Will you not help her up? Cowardly women,
will you leave the old woman on the ground? Lift her up.   465

Hecuba
Leave me, girls. Leave me where I have fallen.
There is no love in help when I don't want it.
For what I am suffering, have suffered, and have still to suffer,
I have the right to fall.

---

50   Euripides is not being learnedly precise here and making Cassandra one of the three Furies (Erinyes). Cassandra sees herself rather as avenging three deaths: those of her father, her brothers, and Troy; cf. 359-60 and 461.

Looking up

Gods![51] I call upon craven allies. Even so, there is a kind
   of propriety   470
in calling on you, when one of us mortals meets misfortune.

She gets to her feet

First, now: It is my pleasure to sing of our blessings,
for by their contrast I will impart a more tragic strain to our disasters.
Yes, I was born to royalty and destined to it.
As Queen, I gave birth to children who excelled all others,   475
and not in their mere number did they stand above all other Phrygians.
No mother, Trojan, Greek, or barbarian
could ever boast as do I over my sons.
These sons I saw fall under the arms of the Greeks.
Over their graves I cropped this head in mourning.   480
I wept for Priam, who sired them. No one had to tell me of his death;
I witnessed it with these eyes,

Touching her lacerated cheeks

butchered a suppliant at the altar of our hearth.
And I saw Troy captured. The daughters I brought up
to be the choice brides of the most eligible suitors   485
were raised for other husbands, snatched from my hands.
There is no hope they will ever see me again
or that I will ever again set eyes upon them.
As for the rest of my life's story, the miserable conclusion is this:
I shall arrive in Greece in old age as a slave.   490
My masters will assign me tasks that are not at all fitting
to a woman of my age: to hold keys
as a door-keeper, I, the mother of Hector!
to grind meal and sleep with my back on a hard floor
and ache. I am an old woman, used to the bed of a king.   495
My body will be covered with rags that were once fine robes,
a disgrace for people who were once well to do.
oi 'go talaina   I am so miserable.
The wedding of one woman has caused all this and will continue to cause
   more grief.
Child, maenad dancing wildly with the gods,   500

---

51   Hecuba's appeal to the gods has its parallel in Thucydides' history of the Peloponnesian war in the vain
      appeal to the gods by the desperate people of Melos (5.104) and Nikias' exhortation to the commanders
      of his fleet to pray to the gods just before the final Athenian defeat in Sicily (7.69.2). The gods responded
      to the appeals of neither the Melians nor the Athenians.

what catastrophes have loosened the belt of your purity?
And you, my poor girl, Polyxena, where are you?
Of all the children of this fruitful womb
what son or daughter is here now to help me?

> *Hecuba slumps to the ground and is helped up again by members of the*
> *chorus.*

Why are you helping me up?   505
What can move you to do so?
Lead me in the dance, lead my foot once so delicate in Troy,
now that I am a slave lead me to a straw bed on a dirt floor
with a stone pillow for my queen's tiara. I am fallen.
Women, count no mortal– man or woman– happy[52] before death arrives.   510

Chorus

Stasimon A[53]
Strophe

Muse, sing for me the song of Ilion.
Sing a tearful hymn
of lamentation for the dead;
sing in a new strain.
Now I will sing out to echoing Troy   515
and tell how I was destroyed
and endured capture at spear point
and from the four-wheeled
carriage of the Argives,
when the Achaeans left the horse whose rumble reached high heaven   520
as it rolled with its rattling cargo of arms,
and its golden cheek-piece glittered.
The people of Troy shouted to heaven:
"Go out now, you men who are now at the end of your suffering,
draw this sacred wooden image   525

---

52 The word in Greek is *eudaimon*. This warning, familiar as it is in tragedy, is most familiar as Solon
articulates it in his interview with King Croesus of Lydia (in Herodotus, *Histories* 1.32). It is fitting that
Euripides should give these words to an oriental queen, who speaks of herself and Priam as "tyrants"
(474) and recalls her past prosperity by recalling the Herodotean word *olbios* ("blessed," or "prosperous,"
497). *Eudaimon*, by contrast, involves the favor of the gods.

53 Stasimon A ("The Fall of Troy"). This is the first full choral song of *The Trojan Women*. The chorus has
joined as a whole to perform it. In their entry song (*parodos*) the chorus had divided into two groups and
their singing was antiphonal to Hecuba's lamentation. This lamentation (*kommos*) carries over into this
song, which they begin by asking the Muse to sing in a "new strain" (514). The invocation is epic and recalls
the opening invocations of both the *Iliad* and *Odyssey* (and in the dactylic meter of the epic) and it commemorates a moment in the Trojan War beyond the narrow range of the *Iliad* (but not the *Odyssey*)—the
moment that seemed to mark the triumph of the Trojans in their defensive war of ten years.

up to the virgin goddess of Ilion,[54] daughter of Zeus."
Was there a young woman who did not go out into the streets?
Was there an old man who did not leave his home?
They all felt joy in their festive songs,
and in their delusion they bent under slavery's yoke.   530

Antistrophe

The entire nation of Phrygia
rushed to the gates
to the horse of mountain pine,
to the wood-crafted ambush of the Argives,
in their eagerness to offer this bane to the goddess of Dardanos' land,   535
a thanks offering to the unyoked goddess of the immortal foals.[55]
With ropes of plaited flax they drew it,
like some black ship,[56] soon to stain their country with blood,
to the stone seat
and foundation of Pallas Athena,   540
The dark of night settled
on their labor and joy;
the lotus wood pipes of Libya throbbed out
tremulous Phrygian airs,
and the young women responded to   545
their rhythm with the beat of their feet.
and lifted their festal song.
But in their homes
fierce tongues of fire
gave a black glint to sleep.   550

---

54   Athena. The blindness of the seemingly triumphant and truly pious Trojans is well exhibited in their
      response to this gift of a wooden horse. In Euripides' play there is no Laokoon to question or Helen to
      test this "gift" to Athena.

55   In Greek cult, the virgin goddess (thus "unyoked") Athena, bore the epithets *Hippia* and *Chalinitis*,
      "Goddess of the Horse," "Goddess of the Bridle." It is clear from the *Iliad* and the scene in which the
      women of Troy, led by Hecuba, supplicate Athena in her temple on the acropolis of Troy that she has
      turned her face against Troy (*Iliad* 6.286-312).

56   The comparison is not idle, but it could not belong to the actual experience of Euripides' chorus of Trojan
      women. It belongs rather to the experience of Euripides' Athenian audience seated in the theater of
      Dionysos. Every four years, during the Panathenaia, a cloak woven for the statue of Athena was hoisted
      on the mast of a ship that was drawn up to the acropolis.

Epode

I for my part danced in a chorus[57] within my chambers
and was singing the mountain-ranging daughter of Zeus,
when a blood-curdling shout
crested over
the high battlements of Troy.   555
Babes in arms
clutched with hands
trembling with terror
the robes of their mothers,
and Ares began to emerge from ambush   560
in the horse that was the work of virgin Pallas.[58]
There was slaughter about the altars of the sanctuary.
The cropped hair,[59]
the desolation of young widows,
carried a wreath of fertility   565
to Greece and her young,
but black mourning for the country of the Phrygians.

Second Episode[60]

*A wagon has entered the orchestra. It carries Andromache, her young son,
Astyanax, and spoils taken from Troy. Andromache is dressed in black, her
hair cropped as a sign of public mourning for her husband, Hector.*

The chorus to Hecuba

---

57   It is significant that the women singing this choral ode speak of others as dragging the offering of the
      wooden horse up to the temple of Athena and of still other unmarried women as performing nocturnal
      choral dances in her honor to the accompaniment of a flute (543). The chorus honor another daughter
      of Zeus, Artemis ("the mountain-ranging daughter of Zeus," 551), a goddess who in the *Iliad* favored
      the Trojans and, unlike Athena, did not turn against her votaries. In this way, the chorus appear to
      disassociate themselves from Athena.

58   The author of the strategy of building the Trojan horse was Odysseus; the builder Epeios of Phokis (cf.
      9-10). But clearly Odysseus' cunning owes something to Athena, who is here held responsible for his
      stratagem and the destruction of Troy.

59   Euripides' conceit is difficult because it violently combines two points of view. From one point of view,
      that of the Trojans, the emptiness of the beds of the Trojan widows is paired with the cutting of their
      hair as a sign of mourning (as in Sophocles, *Electra* 52). But, from another point of view, the desolation
      of captive women forever separated from their husbands bears the victor's crown to the Greeks. This
      "crown," symbolized by the close cropped hair of the captive women, can be described as "a wreath of
      fertility," because these slaves will bear new sons to their masters, as did Andromache to Neoptolemos
      (Euripides, *Andromache* 24-5).

60   Second Epode ("Andromache"). This is the middle episode of this episodic play. It is the scene that focuses
      most sharply on the fate of the women taken captive by the victorious Greek army. Hector had foreseen
      the life Andromache would lead once he had fallen and she had been taken away from Troy as a slave
      (*Iliad* 6.448-63), but he could not have foreseen the "hostage syndrome" by which Andromache would
      become reconciled to her new husband, Achilles' son, Neoptolemos. Nor could he foresee Andromache's
      fate as a slave to a woman like Menelaos' daughter, Hermione, the subject of Euripides' *Andromache*,
      written perhaps a decade before the production of the *Trojan Women*.

Hecuba, can you see Andromache[61] being transported in this foreign cart?
Little Astyanax,
Hector's son,   570
rocks to the heaving motion of his mother's breasts.

  To Andromache

Unlucky woman, where are they taking you away from Troy,
mounted on this carriage with Hector's armor
and the spoils of Phrygia
that are the prizes of the hunt in war.
These trophies the son of Achilles   575
will hang on the temples of Phthia.

  Andromache and Hecuba begin an antiphonal song of lamentation kommos).

Stophe A

Andromache
My masters, the Achaeans, are taking me away.

Hecuba
  Oimoi.

Andromache
      Why do you groan this hymn of my triumph?[62]

Hecuba
  Aiai

Andromache
      You groan for our pain.

Hecuba
  O Zeus!

Andromache
      You groan for our ruin.   580

---

61   Andromache has entered the stage platform from the *parodos* (to the right of the audience, indicating that she has come from the city) carried on a cart on which she and her son, Astyanax, are being transported with other loot taken from Troy. Euripides has staged this scene to recall the entry of Cassandra in Aeschylus' *Agamemnon* (906 and 1039) and he has deliberately substituted Cassandra's carriage (*apene*) for a cart (*okhos*). Andromache's entry into the theater conveys in simple visual terms the meaning of the Greek expression for plundering—"carrying and leading." The victorious army would carry its plunder away and lead off domestic animals, women, and children.

62   Euripides' language is difficult once again because of the sudden and violent shift in the point of view (see the note to 564). To the ears of the Greek conquerors, Hecuba's anguished *oimoi* is the sound of a paean of triumph; to the ears of the Trojans the sound of the flutes that accompanied the landing of the Greeks on the coast of the Troad is a "hateful paean" (126). The ambiguity of perspective goes back to Aeschylus, *Agamemnon* 715, where the chorus describe the groans of captured Troy as a "dirge-filled paean" (as I would emend the text).

Hecuba
My children!

Andromache
We were once your children.

Antistrophe A

Hecuba
Gone is our good fortune, gone is Troy.

Andromache
Poor, poor woman.

Hecuba
Gone the noble ancestry of our children.

Andromache
Pheu Pheu

Hecuba
Pheu   Lament then my

Andromache
evils.

Hecuba
Our heart-breaking fate.   585

Andromache
Grieve for our city.

Hecuba
A city now smoldering.

Strophe B

Andromache
My husband, come to me.

Hecuba
You call out to my son, poor woman.
He is in Hades.

Andromache
Come, protect your wife.   590

Antistrophe B

Andromache
I call on you, once the curse of the Achaeans

Hecuba
I call on you, ancient Priam,
Lord of our children.

Andromache

Take me into the halls of Hades.

Strophe C

Andromache

Mine is a deep longing.

Hecuba

                    You are adamant. *We* feel these pains.   595

Andromache

Pain for a city that is no more.

Hecuba

                    Pain heaped on pain.

Andromache

Pain caused by the hostility of the gods from the time when your son escaped
    Hades[63]

the son who, for an abominable marriage, destroyed the citadel of Troy.

Now bodies of the dead lie exposed at the temple of divine Pallas.

Vultures will pick their bones. Athena has put Troy under slavery's yoke.   600

Antistrophe C

Hecuba

Troy, my desolate land!

Andromache

                    You are abandoned. I weep for you.

Hecuba   *Pointing to the walls of Troy*

Now you can see its tragic end.

Andromache

                            You can see the house where I gave birth.

Hecuba

My children. Your mother, who has lost her city, is now abandoned by you.

Tears drip down in an unending stream,   605

shrill is the mourning for our houses destroyed! The dead are dead to our pain.

Chorus

Yes, tears are sweet to those in trouble

and the heart-rending strain of lamentation and the Muse of suffering.

---

63   When she was pregnant with Paris, Hecuba had a dream that she had given birth to a firebrand. Priam's
    decision to expose Paris, rather than incurring the pollution of killing him, and his rescue from death explain
    his "escape from Hades." This matter was taken up in the Prologue of the *Alexandros*.

Andromache   *Calling attention to herself and her son in the wagon*
Mother of the hero Hector, who killed more Argives than any other Trojan,   610
do you see these spoils of war?

Hecuba
What I see is the work of the gods. They raise up to towering heights
what was once nothing. What seems to tower above us do they destroy.

Andromache
I and my son are being carried off as plunder;
Subject to these laws of change, nobility has been reduced
    to slavery,   615

Hecuba
Force is the most terrible thing about necessity. Cassandra has just gone from me,
dragged away by brute force.

Andromache
Pheu Pheu
So it seems that another was Ajax to your daughter.[64]
But your sickness spreads still farther.

Hecuba
There is no end to my sickness, no term.   620
One disaster comes to vie with another.

Andromache
Your daughter Polyxena is dead. She was slaughtered,
a victim at the grave of Achilles, an offering to a lifeless corpse.

Hecuba
Oi 'go   So this is the clear meaning of those riddling words
Talthybios spoke so darkly.   625

Andromache
I saw her body myself. I got down from the wagon,
covered her with a robe, and mourned over her body.

Hecuba
Ai Ai   Child, child! You were the first victim of their abominable rites!
Ai Ai   I cry out in pain for your terrible death.

Andromache
She died as she died. Even so, her fate   630
was kinder than mine. I must go on living.

Hecuba
To see the light of day is not the same as death.
Death is nothing. In life hope still lives.

---

64   Agamemnon, that is, who will follow Ajax, son of Oileus, in his violation of Cassandra. See the note to
    line 70.

Andromache

    [Mother, you who gave birth to Polyxena, Listen to me.
    I have an excellent argument. I want to give your heart
        some joy.]   635
    I say that never to have been born is the same as being dead.
    It is better to be dead than to live a life of distress.
    The dead are done with suffering and feel absolutely no pain;
    but the person who has experienced good fortune
    and falls into ill fortune is distraught at the thought of lost happiness.   640
    Polyxena is now dead. It is as if she had never seen the light of day.
    She knows nothing of the evils that have befallen her.
    But I, I who set my sights on the target of a good reputation,
    who had my share of the goods of Fortune, I missed my mark.
    For all those qualities that are found admirable in a woman[65]   645
    were the object of my constant striving when I lived under Hector's roof.
    First and foremost: I kept inside the house.
    Whether or not there exists real cause for gossip,
    the woman who does not stay indoors attracts a bad reputation
    simply by going out. I gave up all longing for the world outdoors   650
    and did not admit into my chambers the sophisticated talk of women.
    My native good sense tutored me; I did not need the company of other women.
    Rumor of these excellent qualities reached the Achaean camp and destroyed me.
    When it came to the distribution of the women set apart,
    the son of Achilles chose me as his wife.
    I will live as a slave in the house of murderers.   660
    If I thrust from me the beloved head of Hector[66]
    and open my heart to my present husband,
    people will think that I am a traitor to my husband.
    But, if I loathe my new husband, my masters will hate me.
    And yet... they say that a single night   665
    melts a woman's resistance to a man's bed.
    I scorn the woman who rejects her former husband
    for the bed and love of another.

---

65   The Greek word for these admirable qualities is *sophrosyne* ("prudent restraint"). This is an expression of the male ideal of a virtuous wife and, like many other gnomic passages scattered throughout Euripidean tragedy, it helps establish Euripides' reputation as a misogynist. The "ideal" Andromache is holding up for her mother-in-law articulates a system of contrasts. Women are kept indoors and are expected to maintain a modest silence and exercise complaisance before their husbands. Their husbands, by contrast, enter their houses fresh from a world of speech and action outdoors, both in the assembly and on the battlefield.

66   It was the custom for the wife to cradle the head of her dead husband in the rituals of public mourning, a scene often shown in Greek vase painting.

There is no filly who will easily pull the yoke
when separated from the filly she has been reared with.   670
Yet a brute beast is born with no language.
Having no intelligence a beast is inferior to human beings.

Turning away from Hecuba

In you, Hector, I had the husband I wanted.
You were great in intelligence, nobility, wealth, and courage.
When you took me from my father's house[67] I knew no man.   675
You were the first to yoke me as a bride to your bed.
Now, Hector, you are gone. But I will be carried as a captive of war
on a ship to Greece and the yoke of slavery.

Addressing Hecuba

Does not, then, Polyxena's death, which you lament so grievously,
hold fewer evils than my life?   680
I do not even have hope as my companion,
hope, the companion of all other mortals.
I am not deluded. I am set on no noble course. But it is sweet to think so.

Chorus

You have reached the same depth of misfortune as have I.
In your lamentation you have taught me the extent of my own pain.   685

Hecuba

I have never set foot on a ship, but I know ships:
I have seen paintings of them and I have heard about them.
If sailors enjoy moderate weather
they are confident that they will escape difficulties.
One is stationed at the rudder; another at the mast;   690
and another mans the bilge pump. But if a heavy sea
should rage and break over the ship, the crew
surrenders itself to Fortune and commits itself to the running of the waves.
Such a sailor am I. Many are my troubles.
I cannot utter a word. I surrender my power of speech.   695
The disastrous surge of a god-sent storm overwhelms me.

Turning to Andromache

Enough of that. My dear child,
do not dwell overmuch on Hector's fate. Your tears cannot save him now.
Rather, show respect to your present master and owner.

---

67 In her last meeting with Hector, Andromache recalls how Hector took her from the house of Eetion and
    speaks in dread of her desolation if Hector should die. Achilles had killed her father and sacked her city.
    All she has left is her husband, Hector (*Iliad* 6.410-30).

Dangle before him the lure and charm of your good behavior.   700
If you do as I say, you will bring comfort to all your loved ones
and you will, perhaps, one day raise this boy,

>   *Pointing to Astyanax*

son of my son,
to be the salvation of Troy. Sons of your sons
will found Ilion once again,
and once again Troy will become a city.   705

>   *Talthybios and his attendants approach.*

One thought begets another.
What do I see here? Is the Achaeans' lackey
coming to proclaim still new decisions?

Talthybios   *Keeping at a safe distance from Andromache*
Andromache. You are the wife of the man who was once the most heroic
   of the Phrygians.
Do not hate me for what I have to say. It is not my choice   710
   to bring messages from the Danaans and the family of Pelops.

Andromache
What is the message? This is a prelude to some evil tale.

Talthybios
The army has voted that this boy…How can I say it?

Andromache
No! He won't be the slave of another master than mine?

Talthybios
No Achaean will ever be his master.[68]   715

Andromache
Then will they leave him in Troy as the last remnant of the Phrygians?

Talthybios
I know of no good way to tell you evil.

Andromache
I respect your decent hesitation– unless what you have to say is evil.

Talthybios
To tell you the evil truth: they mean to kill your son.

Andromache
Oimoi
These words are an evil greater than what you said about my marriage. 720

---

68   Again, Talthybios' words are ambiguous and misunderstood, as was the case when he spoke to Hecuba
     of the fate of Polyxena in 260-71.

Talthybios
Odysseus prevailed in a speech before the Greek assembly. He said…

Andromache
Ai Ai mal' There is no end to the evil we suffer.

Talthybios
… he said that we should not let the son of a heroic father grow to manhood.

Andromache
I wish he would prevail on the army to sentence his own son to the same fate!

Talthybios   *Still not responding to Andromache*
The decision was that he must be thrown from Troy's towers.   725
Andromache, let this be. Be wise and accept it.

> *Andromache reaches to Astyanax and holds him tight*

Do not cling to the boy. Bear the pain of your adversity with nobility.
Do not think that you have any power when you have no strength.
You have no one to protect you. Consider, as you must:
you have lost your city and your husband.   730
You are now under our control.
For these reasons do not be eager for combat.
Do nothing that would bring disgrace or resentment upon you.
And I will not have you hurl curses upon the Achaeans.
If you utter a word to enrage the army,   735
your son will receive no burial, none of the rites of mourning for the dead.
But, if you keep quiet and manage your misfortunes as best you can,
it is just possible that you will not leave this boy unburied
and that you yourself might find the Achaeans better disposed to you.

Andromache   *Turning to Astyanax*
O, my dearest child, my greatest treasure,   740
you will die at the hands of enemies, leaving your mother to her sorrows.
The noble birth of your father has been the cause of your undoing;
for others this nobility proved their salvation.[69]
Your father's nobility came too early for you.
My nuptials and my marriage were doomed,   745
doomed the house of Hector, which I entered as a bride,
with no thought that the son I bore would become a victim of the Danaans.
I thought he would be monarch over all of fertile Asia.
My child, you are weeping. Do you sense your misfortunes?
Why are you clinging to me, holding onto my robe.   750

---

69 These two lines are bracketed in Diggle's Oxford edition. Possibly, they are an actor's interpolation. But the thought is worth considering: Astyanax was feared by the Achaeans because they believed that he would inherit his father's valor (cf. Euripides, *The Sons of Herakles* 468-70).

like a baby bird quivering under its mother's wings?
Hector will not rise up from beneath the earth
and come, gripping his spear, to save you.
You have no protection in your father's family or the might of the Phrygians.
You will hurtle pitiably from the heights in a dead plunge   755
and break your neck. Your soul will break out from your body.
Let me embrace your dear, young body, and smell your skin's sweet breath.
So, … all my hopes were vain.
This breast nursed you when you were a babe in swaddling clothes.
All my care, all the labor that wore me out were for nothing.   760
Now put your arms around your mother, give me a last hug.
Come to the mother who gave you life.
Wrap your arms around me. Kiss me, child.
You civilized Greeks! With your evil, barbaric inventions!
Why kill this boy? He did nothing to you!   765
And you, daughter of Tyndareos, you were never the daughter of Zeus![70]
I say that you are the spawn of many fathers:
Avenger first, then Spite,
Gore, and Blood, and Death. All the crop of evil Earth yields begot you!
I will never take pride in claiming that Zeus was your father.   770
For many a Greek and many a barbarian you are the black Death Spirit!
I wish you dead! The gleaming light of your lovely eyes
has destroyed in ugly fashion the famous plains of Troy.

    To Talthybios

Now, go: drive off your plunder! Carry it away with you! Throw it down!
If this is your decision.
Feast on this child's flesh. The gods, I know, will our utter destruction,   775
and we Trojans could never shelter him from death.
Cover this tormented body and throw it into the ship.
I am headed for a splendid wedding celebration,
now that I have lost my child.

Chorus

Poor, suffering Troy! Because of a single woman and a loathsome marriage   780

---

70 Andromache regards Helen rather as the daughter of the mortal Tyndareos. Helen resembles the hero
Herakles in that she can be regarded as the child of either a divine or mortal father. Herakles was the
son either of Zeus and Alkmene or of Amphitryon and Alkmene; Helen the daughter either of Zeus and
Leda or of Tyndareos and Leda. Andromache addresses Helen by the name of her mortal father and then
the abstractions she embodies. These abstractions reveal the tradition that Helen had another immortal
mother, Nemesis, the goddess of resentment and retribution ("Avenger first"). But she can also be called
"daughter of Zeus" (*Dios kore*), just as her brothers are known as the sons of Zeus (*Dioskouroi*; cf. 398
and 1109).

you have lost countless thousands.

Talthybios and his men approach Astyanax.

Talthybios

Come, son. Leave the arms of your sorrowful mother
and mount to the towers of your ancestors,
the crown of your city.
There it is decreed that you shall breathe your last.   785

To his attendants

Take him away. It is the duty
of a better friend than am I
to our shameful decision
to make proclamations such as this.

Hecuba

Child, son of my sad son,   790
your life is being snatched from us
unjustly, robbed from your mother and myself.
What will become of me? What can I do for you, doomed child?

Hecuba settles into a mourning position.

We can give you these gestures of mourning as we beat our head and breasts.
Of mourning and lamentation we are masters. *oi 'go.*   795
I cry out for our city; I cry out for you.
What do we now lack? What more do we need
to drive us into utter destruction?

*Talthybios and his attendants lead Astyanax off stage right. Andromache
returns to her wagon.*

Chorus

Second Stasimon[71]
Strophe A

O, Telamon, king of Salamis, land flowering with bees,
you established your home and seat   800
on an island washed by beating waves
facing the sacred slope

---

71   Second Stasimon ("Ganymede"): The chorus look back. In the generation before the Trojan War, Telamon
     (brother of Peleus and father of Ajax, king of the island of Salamis) joined Herakles and Philoctetes in
     the first Greek assault on the Troy of King Laomedon, father of Priam. As a reward for his efforts, he
     received Hesione, daughter of Laomedon, as a slave. The chorus also move back to a time when the gods
     were joined to Troy: Zeus in his passion for the Trojan Ganymede and the goddess of the dawn (Eos) in
     her passion for the Trojan Tithonos. But Troy holds no more charms for the gods (858-9).

where Athena first revealed the sprig of the olive,[72] green and gray,
a celestial crown and jewel for bright, prosperous Athens.
Salamis, you left, you left, with the archer son of Alkmene   805
to share in noble exploits
for Ilion, for Ilion, to destroy our city, what was once our city,
when you came from Greece,

Antistrophe A

When Herakles first led the flower of Greece,
dishonored as he was over the broken promise of the horses,[73]
he brought ships that cleave the sea   810
to rest at the gliding current of the Simois,[74]
and tied them prow up to the shore.
He took from his ships
a cargo of arrows sure of their mark
to carry death to Laomedon.
Then he razed the walls built straight to Apollo's plumb and rule   815
with a crimson blast of fire,
and destroyed the land of Troy.[75]
Twice, in twin strokes
around Troy's walls, did a lance stained with blood
overthrow the walls of Dardanos.

Strophe B

So it is. Ganymede,[76] Laomedon's son, you step daintily now   820
among the golden cups, pouring wine,
filling the cup of Zeus, a noble service,

---

72   Euripides sets Athena's revelation of the olive to mankind in the tradition of another gift of a goddess to
      mankind. In neighboring Eleusis, Demeter "revealed" the crops of grain to mortals and initiated them
      into her rites (in the language of the Homeric *Hymn to Demeter* 474; cf. Euripides, *Ion* 1434). The olive
      tree that was thought to have been planted by Athena was burned in the Persian sack of the acropolis in
      480, but the next day it miraculously sprouted a new shoot (Herodotus, *Histories* 8.55).

73   Laomedon promised Herakles divine horses if he would rescue his daughter Hesione from a sea-serpent.
      Herakles kept his engagement, but Laomedon did not. Thus, the first Trojan War.

74   With the Scamander, one of the two rivers of the Troad. In the tradition of the Argonauts, it was conceived
      of as the port of Troy.

75   The text is disputed. Diggle's emendation of "the descendants of Dardanus" (*Dardanidas*) for "the land
      of Dardanos"(*Dardanias*) is tempting; it makes the descendants of Zeus the victims of two wars and
      prepares the way for the reflections of the chorus on the gods' utter lack of concern for the humans whom
      their passions and rancor involve them with. But the context calls attention to the walls and therefore
      the land of Troy.

76   In Euripides' genealogy, Ganymede was the son of Laomedon; in another genealogy, he was the son of Tros
      (*Iliad* 5.265-6). He stirred the passion of Zeus. To possess him Zeus transformed himself into an eagle
      and carried him up to heaven, where he served as the cup-bearer of Zeus and the other immortals.

but for nothing.
The city of your birth is ablaze. 825
The cliffs
at the sea's edge
cry out the shrill cry
of a sea bird
that has lost her young, 830
their echo eddies along the shore,
the lament for a marriage lost
for children, for old mothers.
Gone now are the fresh pools where once you bathed
and the running courses of the gymnasia. 835
But you, Ganymede, now thrive beside
the throne of Zeus.
Peace, and light and the calm of the sea
radiate from your young face.
But below Greek spears have destroyed the land of Priam. 840

Antistrophe B

Eros, god of passion, once you came
to the halls of King Dardanos.
The eyes of the goddesses of heaven were upon you.
How high did you then make Troy tower,
as you joined Troy in kinship[77] with the gods? 845
But I will say nothing in dispraise of Zeus.[78]

Looking up at the mounting sun

This light of the goddess of the dawn,[79]
carried on pale wings,
light dear to men,
gazed upon the land as a destructive flame, 850
saw the destruction of its citadel.
The goddess of the dawn, Eos,

---

77 The putative bond created between immortal and mortal is termed a *kedos*, a bond that for humans is created by marriage. It establishes a mutual concern between two groups that are not related by blood. Thus, the word can also mean mourning, just as the Greek word for a mother-in-law comes from *penthos*, mourning. The *penthera* is a woman for whom one must mourn.

78 The chorus recognize that they cannot speak frankly of the erotic bond between Zeus and the young Trojan Ganymede as a *kedos* (see note to line 845). The thought they suppress is suggested by the fact that Ganymede's name is transformed into our "catamite" via Latin *catamitus*, which derives from the name Ganymedes.

79 Eos, who became enamored of the Trojan Tithonos and carried him up to heaven in her chariot. In the Homeric *Hymn to Aphrodite*, the narrative of Eos and Tithonos follows directly on the narrative of Ganymede and Zeus, as here (218-38).

kept to her chambers as she saw this.
A husband from this land,
the father of her sons,   855
was carried away in a chariot of stars,
the source of high hope for his native land.
But, for the gods, Troy
holds no more charms.

Third Episode[80]

*Menelaos has entered the stage from stage left. He is accompanied by soldiers
from the Greek army. The group stands before the tent on stage.*

Menelaos   *Looking up*

This light of the sun is a fair blaze!   860
This is the day I will lay hands on my wife,
[Helen. I am Menelaos, the man who suffered so much hardship.
This is the Greek army.][81]
I came to Troy not, as people think, because of a woman,
but to confront the man, who, as a guest in my house,   865
deceived me and stole my wife from my house.
Now, that man has, with the god's help, paid the penalty for his crime,
yes, he and his country, which has fallen to Greek arms.
I have come to take away the *Spartan* woman.[82]
It gives me no pleasure to pronounce   870
the name of the woman who was once my wife.[83]
I know that she is in these captive quarters
tallied out along with the other women of Troy.
The fighting men, who suffered such hardship to take her at spear point,
have given her to me … to kill, or, if I do not kill her,
and it is my wish, to take her back with me to Argos.   875
It is my decision not to kill Helen here at Troy;
rather, I will take her by ship to Greek soil
and give her over for execution there

---

80   The third episode ("Helen"). Euripides gives the director guidance on Helen's costume and demeanor
     in 1022-8.

81   These lines seem so obvious and unnecessary that they are deleted or bracketed by most editors.

82   *Lakaina* (a woman from Lakonia) in Greek. The word is meant to be abusive and its edge was especially
     sharp in Athens in the period of the Peloponnesian War.

83   A sign of Menelaos' ambivalence is his inability to name his wife at first (if lines 863-4 are to be excluded,
     as I think they should be). He calls Helen his "wife" (*damar*), but "the *Spartan* woman" is the description
     he is more comfortable with (869). By contrast, Helen's first word is the imperious "Menelaos" (895).
     The word *Lakaina* is pronounced by the Spartan Menelaos, but in Athens.

in requital for all my friends who died in Troy.

Addressing his men

Now, men, go to her quarters   880
and bring her to me; drag her by her bloody henna hair.
When the breezes freshen from the East,
we will take her to Greece.

Hecuba   *Looking up*

You, you who bear the weight of the earth and have your seat upon the earth,
whoever you are, hard to know and hard to place,   885
Zeus, whether you are the Necessity of Nature or Human Intelligence,
you do I call upon. As you travel your silent course,
you lead all things human on the path of Justice.

Menelaos

What is this?[84] This is a strange new manner of praying to the gods!

Hecuba

Menelaos, you have earned my praise, if you mean to kill your wife.   890
But be careful not to look at this woman. Helen is Hell.[85]
She will make you captive with desire. She turns men's eyes; she overturns cities;
she burns men's homes. So powerful are Helen's charms.
I know her, as do you and her other victims.

*Helen is escorted from her tent on stage. She is flanked by two Greek soldiers
who escort her with great deference. Unlike Hecuba, Andromache, and the
Trojan women, Helen is elegantly dressed and her hair carefully plaited.*

Helen

Menelaos! This rude treatment announces some dreadful thing!   895
Your men have laid hands on me
and have dragged me out here in front of the tent.
I, … I am nearly certain that you hate me.
But I do want to say something. I want to ask:
what have you and the Greeks decided? Will I live, or die?   900

Menelaos

It was no close decision. The army voted unanimously

---

84   Menelaos' reaction to Hecuba's prayer, which stands in stark contrast to his own address to the Sun (Helios),
      is understandably one of amazement. Hecuba's precedent for her strange invocation to Zeus as the hidden
      guarantor of justice in human affairs is the invocation to Zeus of the chorus of Aeschylus' *Agamemnon*
      (160-83), a play produced in 458; but the alternative descriptions of the true nature of Zeus belong to the
      last half of the fifth century.

85   Hecuba is bringing into meaningful association the name Helen (*Helene*) and the aorist stem (*hel-*) of
      the verb *haireo*, "to take, destroy," as had Aeschylus in *Agamemnon* 688-90, a pun Robert Browning
      translated by "Hell on men, hell on ships, hell on cities." The same pun on Helen's name is evident in
      line 1214.

to surrender you to me to put to death. I am the man you wronged.

Helen

Am I permitted to respond to this sentence
and say that, if I die, *we* die unjustly?

Menelaos

I have not come to argue with you. I have come to kill you.   905

Hecuba

Menelaos, let her speak so that she will not die without a hearing.
And give us the chance to refute her.
You know nothing of the troubles inside Troy.
Put the sum of these together and the argument will mean her death.
She will never be acquitted.   910

Menelaos

We have time, and the time is yours. If she wants to speak,
she can. But, understand, it is only to hear what you have to say
that I allow her to speak; not for her sake.

Helen

Perhaps, because you believe that I am your enemy,
you will refuse to reply to me, whether you think I speak well or badly.   915
But I will reply to you by anticipating the charges[86]
that you will lodge against me in your speech
[my charges answering yours and yours mine].
First then: I say that when that woman
gave birth to Paris[87] she produced the beginning of troubles.   920
Second: old Priam[88] destroyed both Troy and me, when he failed to kill the infant,
that bitter dream image of a torch then called Alexander.[89]
Attend now to how the story unfolds.
This Alexander had to judge a triad of three goddesses.
The bribe of Pallas Athena to Alexander   925
was to grant him the destruction of Greece as commander of the Phrygians.

---

86   The debate between Helen and Hecuba is an *agon* (or contest) typical of Euripidean dramaturgy. In this
      pair of set speeches (*rheseis*), the level of language has risen from Hecuba's inarticulate groans in the
      Prologue and *Parodos* to the cold heights of Athenian judicial rhetoric. Similar debates took place in
      the *Alexandros* and *Palamedes*. Helen breaks with judicial procedure in that she speaks first, before the
      accusation against her has been delivered.

87   A reference to Hecuba's dream when she was pregnant with Paris that she gave birth to a firebrand from
      which snakes flared out. This and Priam's exposure of Paris were set out in the Prologue to the first play
      of this "tetralogy," the *Alexandros*.

88   In Greek, the old man. This can, of course, refer to the old herdsman who spared the life of Alexander.
      But an attack on dead Priam is more the likely because it is more outrageous.

89   *Alexandros*, in Greek, means "he who defends," an inappropriate name for the son of Priam who was
      responsible for the Trojan War (see the note to 942).

If Paris should choose her over the other goddesses,
Hera promised him Asia and absolute rule over all of Europe.
And Kypris,° who was astounded by my beauty, promised me as a reward,
if she outstripped the other goddesses in beauty.   930
Consider how the tale now turns:
Kypris was victorious over the other goddesses,
and this victory is the great good my marriage did for Greece.
You are not subject to barbarians; you were not defeated in battle; nor did
    you fall under a tyranny.
All this was Greece's great good fortune. But this was the cause   935
of my undoing. I was destroyed by my beauty, and I am blamed
for acts for which I deserve a victor's crown placed upon my head.
You will say that I have not yet stated the obvious:
I stole away from your house in secret.
Paris came to your house accompanied by no mean goddess,[90]   940
as my avenging demon, call him Alexander, the defender,
if you like, or Paris, the destroyer.[91]
You craven coward! This is the man you left at home in Sparta,
when you sailed off to Crete. I have made my point.
I will speak next– not of you– but of myself.   945
Tell me: How could I have run away from your house with a strange man
and betrayed home and country, were I in my right mind?
Chastise the goddess, not me, and become stronger than Zeus.[92]
Zeus wields power over all the other gods,
but is the slave of this goddess. There is no reason to blame me.   950
As the tale continues, you might have a plausible charge against me.
You could claim, that once Alexander had died and entered the hollows of the earth,
I should have left his house and gone down to the ships of the Argives.
At that time my marriage was not compassed by a god.
This is exactly what I tried to do. I have as my witnesses   955

---

90 A clear version of Gorgias' speech *In Praise of Helen* § 6 (Appendix 4): "If, therefore, responsibility is to
    be fixed on Tyche and divinity, Helen should be acquitted of her infamy."

91 Paris is the name given Priam's son by the shepherds who found him exposed on Mt. Ida, perhaps from
    the fact that he was discovered in a pack (*pera*). Of the two names, Alexandros and Paris, Paris is the more
    sinister. It can be connected with the root *pra* of the verb *pertho*, "to sack a city," as apparently here. In
    the *Iliad*, Hector rebukes Paris as *dyspari*, "evil Paris, loveliest to look at, deceiver" (3.39; cf. Euripides,
    Hecuba 944). The chorus of Aeschylus' *Agamemnon* call him Paris, "the dreadfully bedded" (713) and
    add *pamporthe*, "sacking all" (714).

92 Euripides has Helen repeat the term *kreisson*, "stronger, superior," from Gorgias, *In Praise of Helen* § 6
    (Appendix 4). The Greek attitude to the strength of the gods is revealed in the symposiastic riddle: "
    What is the strongest thing in the world?" The answer "iron" is obvious, but wrong, since the blacksmith
    Hephaistos bends iron; but then Hephaistos' wife, Aphrodite, can subdue her husband.

the guards[93] at the city gates and the watchmen on the ramparts.
Time after time they discovered me trying to steal away,
lowering my body from the battlements to the ground with twisted sheets.
[As for my new husband, Deiphobos,[94] the Phrygians were against the marriage,
but he took me by force.]   960
Tell me, my husband, why do I deserve to be put to death for this?
You would commit an injustice if you did. My last husband forced me to
    marry him,[95]
and my life within Troy was a life of bitter servitude,
not the life of a victor. If you wish to be stronger than the gods,
you are living in a fool's paradise.   965

Chorus

Your majesty, come defend your children and your country.
Demolish this woman's specious arguments. She is a bad woman
who speaks well, and this alarms me.

Hecuba

I will first come to the defense of the three goddesses as their ally.
I will demonstrate that there is no justice in what Helen says.   970
I do not believe that Hera and the virgin Pallas could have ever
    been so ignorant.
Why would Hera want to barter her Argos to barbarians?
Why would Athena want to enslave her Athenians to the Phrygians?
These goddesses did not come to Mount Ida for a childish contest
in peacock pride over their rival beauties. What motive could Hera,   975
a goddess, have to be so enamored of her beauty?
Did she want to get a husband better than Zeus?
Was Athena hunting for a marriage to one of the gods?
It was Athena, who, in her aversion to marriage,
begged her father for the gift of virginity.   980
Do not make fools of the gods[96] to beautify your ugly vice.
Do not think that you will persuade the wise.
You said that "Kypris"—and this is laughable—

---

93 They cannot corroborate Helen's assertion. They are all dead.
94 Son of Priam and Hecuba, who married Helen after Paris was killed by Philoctetes. In the *Odyssey* (4.274) it is said that he accompanied Helen to view the Trojan horse and that, once the Greeks had emerged from the horse, his was the first house they attacked (8.517). In the *Alexandros*, Deiphobos entered into conflict with Paris, after Paris, still thought to be a herdsman and slave, was victorious in an athletic contest.
95 Again, Gorgias comes to Helen's defense: "If she was seized by force and was the victim of violence and criminal outrage, it is clear that the man who seized her is the guilty party, since he is the guilty party, and the party who was carried off as the victim of rape was the unlucky," *In Praise of Helen* § 7 (Appendix 4).
96 Hecuba's theology equates divinity with wisdom, self-sufficiency, and self-restraint. In her refutation of Helen, she relies on the common Greek description of erotic passion (*eros*) as a form of folly (*moria*).

accompanied your son to the house of Menelaos.

As if she could not have remained content in heaven[97]   985

and dragged you to Ilion along with the settlement of Amyklai.[98]

My son was a very, very handsome boy,

but it was your own mind that turned into "Kypris" at the sight of him.

For mortals all the forms folly takes are "Aphrodite."

The second syllable of her name denotes frenzy and folly.[99]   990

When you set eyes on my son and were dazzled by his Asiatic dress

and gold, you became frenzied with lust.

And, once you were away from Sparta,

you fancied that the Phrygian capital

flowed with gold and would shower you with luxuries.   995

The halls of Menelaos were not big enough to hold you

and your pampered style of life.

Enough on that point. Now, you claim that my son brought you here by violence.

What Spartan ever knew of this act of "violence"?

When did you ever let out a shriek? Young Kastor[100] and his twin brother   1000

were still alive and had not yet ascended to the stars.

But, when you reached Troy with the Argives at your heels,

the struggle and agony began, and men fell to the spear.

Whenever you heard a report that Menelaos here was prevailing,

you were all praise for Menelaos to pain my son   1005

with the thought that he had a serious rival for your love.

But, if the Trojans were fortunate in battle, this fellow here was nothing to you.

Your practice was to keep your eye on Fortune

and follow her. Virtue you were never willing to follow.

---

97   That is, could she not act like omnipotent Zeus of the *Iliad* (7.17-27), who boasts that, if all the gods joined to take hold of a golden rope let down from heaven to earth, they could never dislodge him from heaven, but he could hoist them all up to heaven along with the earth and sea?

98   A settlement and cult site southeast of Sparta on the Eurotas. It is associated with Menelaos in the Catalogue of Ships (*Iliad* 2.584), and in the Archaic period was a site of cults for both Menelaos and Helen.

99   Euripides is forcibly connecting the name Aphrodite with the word *aphrosyne*, "ignorance," frenzy," "folly." Our word "frenzy" derives from the Greek root *phren*, meaning the diaphragm or the seat of intelligence. The alpha in *a-phrosyne* (the "alpha privative") negates this. More commonly, Aphrodite's name is connected with the foam (*aphros*) from the severed genitals of Ouranos in which she was nurtured; see Hesiod *Theogony* 195-7.

100   Kastor is the only one of the Dioskouroi (like Helen, the offspring of Zeus) named in the *Trojan Women* (in 132 where Helen is called a disgrace to Kastor). This is the first reference to the metamorphosis into stars (or *asterismos*) of Kastor and his immortal twin, Pollux (Polydeuxes), as the constellation Gemini. Their elevation as stars is a foil to the degradation of their sister, Helen. In the *Iliad* (3.236-44), Helen cannot make her brothers out in the army standing before the walls of Troy, but the narrator is aware that they were buried in Lakedaimon. Their heroization and return to life on alternate days is recognized in *Odyssey* 11.300-4.

Your next point: you claim that you stole away   1010
by lowering yourself from the towers with plaited sheets,
that you would not remain in Troy against your will.
Tell me: When were you ever discovered hanging from a rope
or sharpening the blade of a sword?
Any decent woman would have killed herself in her longing for her former husband.
Many was the time I said to you: "Daughter, leave Troy.   1015
My sons can find other women to marry.
I will help smuggle you out and I will take you down to the Achaean ships.
Put an end to this war between the Greeks and us Trojans."
But you found my good advice a bitter pill.
You lived proud and peevish in Alexander's house.   1020
You wanted the Orientals to prostrate themselves before you.
This was all important to you. And afterwards, you appeared in public like this,
beautifully dressed and carefully made up. And you look upon the same sky
as your husband. I could spit upon you!
You ought to have come out humble, your eyes to the ground   1025
in the torn garments of a widow, with your hair shorn in the Scythian fashion,[101]
with a becoming modesty to outweigh your past shamelessness,
contrite for all your past errors.
Menelaos, now know how my speech will conclude:
Crown Greece with a wreath of victory!   1030
Be worthy of yourself. Kill this woman! And lay this down as a law for
    other women:
The wife who betrays her husband dies!

Chorus Leader

Yes, Menelaos, prove yourself worthy of your ancestors and of your house.
Punish your wife. Do not let Greece call you a uxorious coward.
Even to your enemies you will appear noble.   1035

Menelaos

Hecuba, your argument coincides with my own.
That woman willingly left my house for an adulterer's bed.
And she brought "Kypris" into her speech out of sheer vanity.

To Helen

You, go face the men who will stone you to death.
By a quick death you will repay the long sufferings of the Achaeans.   1040
This will teach you not to shame me!

---

101   The reference is to the habit of Scythian men having their heads completely shaven, not close cropped.

Helen   *Moving closer but remaining standing*

Menelaos, don't, I beseech you. I fall to your knees.

Do not blame me for a sickness that is sent by the gods. Forgive me.

Hecuba

Do not betray the comrades that woman killed.

I implore you by their deaths and the deaths of my children.   1045

Menelaos

Old woman, enough said. I care nothing for her.

I am ordering my attendants to take her down to the ships ready to depart.

She will board ship.

Hecuba

Wait! Do not let her board your ship!

Menelaos   *Derisively*

Why not? Has she put on weight?   1050

Hecuba

Once in love, always a lover, as the proverb has it.

Menelaos

Do you want to give my mind some distance from the object of its love?

I will do as you say. It makes sense.

She will not board the same ship as we.

But, when she reaches Argos, this shameless woman   1055

will die a shameful death and teach all of womankind a lesson in restraint.

This is no easy lesson. Even so, the fate of this woman will instill fear

into their love-crazed hearts,

even if they are more shameless than she.

Exit Helen, led out by Menelaos and attendants

Chorus

Third Stasimon[102]
Strophe A

Zeus, is this how you have betrayed to the Achaeans,   1060

---

102 Third Stasimon ("Sacred Ilion"): This final choral ode of the play continues and develops the theology first announced in Poseidon's speech in the Prologue and brilliantly revealed in the "Ganymede Ode" of the second stasimon. In this choral song, the captive women of Troy divide the world into three levels: the shimmering and remote heights occupied by the gods; the underworld; and the middle earth, which is the site of the living humans who attempt to reach the indifferent gods on high and their unresponsive dead below. In the first strophe and antistrophe, the chorus call upon Zeus and invoke the religion of the city and the pious attempts of their city to join heaven and earth and assure the safety and prosperity of Troy. In the *Iliad*, Troy is called "sacred" (5.648); on its citadel (Pergamos) stood the temples of Athena and Apollo. In the *Odyssey*, Odysseus is identified as a man of many wiles and the sacker of "the sacred city of Troy" (1.1-2).

your temple in Ilion and its smoking altars?
Zeus, you have betrayed
the flame of offerings
and the smoke of frankincense
that lifts up into the clear blue sky.   1065
You have betrayed the sacred citadel of Troy
and Ida and its meadows of ivy cut by snow-fed streams
and the high limit of the earth[103]
first struck by the rising sun
and this generous land filled with light and sacred to the gods.   1070

Antistrophe A

Gone are the god-delighting songs of dancers
ringing throughout the night, gone the night-long festivals,
the golden images of the gods
and the sacred crescent cakes[104] of the Phrygians,
twelve cakes for the twelve months.   1075
I must ask, Lord, I must know
if, mounted on your high throne in the bright blue of heaven,
you are mindful of this worship.
Have you any thought for this city now destroyed
consumed in a fierce rush of fire.   1080

Strophe B

Husband, my dear husband,
your fate is to wander
unburied, unwashed,
a wraith.
My fate is a sea-borne ship   1085
that, gliding over the sea with darting wings, will carry me
to Argos of the horse pastures,[105] the land where the great stone walls
piled up by the Cyclopes reach the sky.

---

103 It is possible that the chorus are recalling once again the relation between the goddess of the dawn, Eos, and Troy (see the note to 847). It is possible too that the chorus are alluding to the tradition that the light of the sun first gathered into the globe of the sun along the ridges of Mt. Ida (as we know the tradition from Lucretius, *On the Nature of the Universe* 5.663-5 and other sources). What is particularly striking is the contrast between the last line of the strophe ("this generous land filled with light", 1070) and the last line of the antistrophe ("a fierce rush of fire," 1080).

104 (*selanai*): These are crescent-shaped cakes (*popana*) offered monthly as the Moon (*Selene*) waxes. They have brought no increase to the Trojans.

105 This epithet is Homeric, but the "Cyclopean walls" of Tiryns and Mycene (both unnamed in this ode) are not. The "walls piled up by the Cyclopes [that] reach the sky" (1087-8) are heavenly, just as the citadel of Troy was once "sacred" (1065).

Here a crowd of children stand at the gates clinging to their mothers
weep and moan incessantly.   1090
Mother, mother, *oimoi*
the Achaeans are taking me
away from you, out of your sight
down to a sea-blue ship,
with oars that graze the sea.   1095
I am destined for Greece:
either for sacred Salamis[106]
or the high acropolis on the isthmus[107] that separates two seas,
where stand the gates to the Land of Pelops.

Antistrophe B

My impossible dream is that a lightning-bolt   1100
from heaven should strike Menelaos' ship
dead center as it moves out
into the open sea of the Aegean,
as he sends me into exile from Ilion,
my eyes full of tears, a slave to Greece.   1105
As I am taken away, Helen departs.
Helen is the daughter of Zeus.
In her hands she holds a golden mirror,
the delight and charm of young women.
Menelaos,—may he never return to the land of Lakedaimon,   1110
to the home and hearth of his fathers,
to the city of Pitana,[108]
to the goddess of the bronze temple.[109]
He has captured that ill-wed source of shame
for great Greece,   1115
of bitter suffering eddying
along the currents of the Simois.

---

106   The island already mentioned in the "Salamis Ode" of the second stasimon (799-808), where it is closely
      associated with Athens and the "sacred slopes" of the acropolis. It has acquired the epithet that once
      described Troy.

107   Corinth, with its mountain acropolis (Acrocorinth) and its two ports on each side of the isthmus. It is
      mentioned as Ephyre in the *Iliad* (6.152), but the Corinthians were not important in the Homeric epics.
      It is an important city in Euripides' world and a power hostile to Athens during the Peloponnesian War.
      Possibly the reference to Acrocorinth, known for its temple prostitutes, is a reminder of the fate of some
      women taken as slaves in battle.

108   Pitana is a district associated with Sparta but quite unknown to Homer.

109   Athena. The temple to Athena occupied the small hill that served as the "acropolis" of Sparta. The statue
      of Athena is described as bronze, and Athena had the cult epithet *chalkoikos*, "Lady of the Bronze House"
      (Pausanias, *Description of Greece* 3.17.2)

The chorus has caught sight of Talthybios and his men who have returned.
They carry the body of Astyanax on the great shield of his father.

io io
The disasters of this land come in a strange procession.
One disaster follows another. Pitiful wives of Trojans,
look on the body of Astyanax brought here before us.   1120
The Danaans have thrown him down from the towers
a grim missile. They have killed him. They now hold him.

Talthybios[110]
Hecuba, one ship is left to sweep the sea with its oars,
ready to freight the spoils and equipment of the son of Achilles
to the coast of Phthia.   1125
Neoptolemos himself has already set sail.
He received word of some trouble involving Peleus.[111]
It seems that Akastos, Pelias' son, has driven him from his land.
This is why he left so soon. He could not delay.
He is gone, and Andromache went with him.   1130
She was a tragic sight. I wept as I saw her
setting off from her land, lamenting her country and calling out to Hector's tomb.
She asked Neoptolemos to bury this child.
The son of your Hector fell from the walls, and his soul broke out
    from his body.   1135

Pointing to the shield holding the body of Astyanax

She asked him not to take this shield,
the shield that made the Achaeans turn in flight,
this bronze-backed shield, that this boy's father kept about his sides,
to the hearth of Peleus or to the chambers she would enter as a bride.

---

110 Exodos ("Astyanax"): Formally the conclusion of the play begins with the words of the chorus at 1118.
     The play ends as the chorus exit to board the Achaean ships (1132). The short episode from the entry
     of Talthybios to the last choral ode of the play might be entitled "Astyanax." It involves Hecuba, who
     remains on stage throughout the play and is the burden of its grief, and the body of Astyanax, which is
     brought on stage on a shield. The small body on the shield seems the visual perversion of the injunction
     of Spartan mothers to their sons as they went out to war: "With this [shield], or on it," that is, return
     with this shield or be carried home on it.

111 Peleus was the father of Achilles. His home was Phthia in Thessaly. He played a role in the saga of Meleager
     a generation before the Trojan War (recounted briefly by Phoinix in *Iliad* 9.524-99). Pelias was king of
     Iolkos in southern Thessaly. The connection between the two men of similar names and neighboring
     kingdoms arises from Peleus' killing of Eurytion during the boar hunt in Calydon. Eurytion had previ-
     ously purified Peleus in Phthia for the murder of Peleus' half-brother, Phokos. To escape revenge for the
     murder of the man who had purified him, Peleus went to Iolkos, where he was purified by Akastos, the
     son of Pelias. That Peleus was driven away from Iolkos rather than purified seems to be Euripides' own
     contribution to the myth. Once again, Euripides is intimating the violence that awaits the victorious
     Achaeans on their return to Greece.

[This woman, who is a sorrowful spectacle,][112]   1140
wanted him to have her son buried
in this shield and no cedar chest and ring of stones.
She asked us to bring him to you.
She has gone now. The haste of her master
prevented her from burying the child herself.   1145
Once you have dressed this corpse in death's finery,
and we have wrapped him in a fold of earth, we will sail.
Do what you have been ordered to do as quickly as you can.
I have spared you one labor.
As I crossed the Scamander,   1150
I washed the body in its waters and cleansed its bloody wounds.
I am going now. I will dig a grave for the boy.
When we have completed our tasks
—we must be quick—
we will launch our ship and sail home.   1155

    Talthybios exits audience left. Hecuba addresses Talthybios' men.

Hecuba
Place this round-rimmed shield of Hector upon the ground.

    Hecuba lowers herself to the ground.

It is a grievous sight that gives me no pleasure.
O Achaeans! Your spears have more heft than your light minds.
Why did you fear this child?
Why did you devise this new form of death?   1160
Were you afraid that one day he would raise up fallen Troy?
When Hector was fortunate in battle, we women were perishing.
Now that Troy has been captured
and the people of Phrygia have been destroyed,
do you actually fear this small babe?   1165
I cannot admire anyone who feels fear, but does not reflect on the grounds
    of his fear.

    Turning to the body of Astyanax

Dearest child, I grieve for the terrible way Death came upon you.
Had you died for your city, having grown to young manhood,
to marriage, to kingship, which makes men equal to the gods,
you would have had a blessed life–

    Looking about her

---

112 A line deleted by many editors, including Diggle, since it merely repeats what had been said by Talthybios
    at 1130-1.

if any of these things here is blessed.   1170
As it is, you have only seen these blessings.
You have formed an image of them in your mind,
but you never actually experienced any of them in your home.
Poor, unfortunate child! What terrible gashes the walls of your ancestors
have inflicted upon your head, those towers built by Loxias.
Your mother would often comb this hair and press it to her lips.   1175
Now your head is shattered and gore grins out from it.
I will not conceal the brutality!
Little hands,[113] you bear the sweet likeness of your father's hands.
Now you lie before me limp and disjointed.
Sweet lips! Once you had brave words for me.   1180
Your voice is gone. You deceived me. You would embrace me and say:
"Mother," you would say, "I will cut a thick lock of hair for you.
I will bring a band of my age-mates to your grave
and address kind words to you."
It is not you who are burying me, but I you, who are younger than I,   1185
you a battered corpse. I am an old woman, with no city and no children.
oimoi   I remember those greetings and your sweet embrace.
I remember all my care for you, your deep slumber. All is gone.
What epitaph could a poet compose for your grave-stone?[114]

The Argives once killed this child   1190
in fear of him.

The epitaph inscribes Greece's shame.
You were heir to none of your father's possessions.
Nonetheless, you will receive this bronze-backed shield as your coffin.

Turning to the shield

You guarded well Hector's stout left arm,
but you have lost your own best and bravest protector.   1195
Hector, your own sweet impression remains on the grip of your shield.
Your sweat stained its well-wrought rim,
when, in the thick of battle,
you would lift it to wipe your beard.

---

113   In death, Astyanax is monumentalized, as is his father Hector. His lifeless hands are the "icons" or images
      of the hands of his father. Just so, the leather strap of Hector's shield bears the impression of the living
      grip of Hector: "Your own sweet impression remains on the grip of your shield" (1195). Even the stains
      of sweat from Hector's brow are seen as his memorials (1196).

114   In the *Iliad*, Helen is well aware that her life will become the subject of song in future generations (3.357;
      cf. *Odyssey* 8.579). This is true of Astyanax and the fate of the Trojan women. This epitaph (and its sequel
      in 1242-3) is one of the few signatures of an author in Greek tragedy. Euripides is referring to himself; the
      epitaph for Astyanax (in iambic trimeters not elegiac verse) is Euripides' own. It is brutal and short.

Handing an embroidered robe to a group of Trojan women on the stage platform

Take this to adorn the broken body of the boy.   1200
Our lesser god gives us nothing of beauty in our misfortunes.
Take this. It is all we have.
That mortal is a fool who takes joy in his prosperity,[115]
thinking that it will last forever. The highs and lows of our life
are a lunatic, who lurches from place to place.   1205
No man can control his own fortune.

Chorus

Here now are the women carrying a robe
from the plunder of Troy to place upon his body.

Hecuba   *Placing the robe over the body of Astyanax*

Child, the mother of your father places this robe over you and this crown,
part of treasures once yours. You were never victorious   1210
over your peers in horse racing or contests of archery,
competitions the Phrygians prize, but not in excess.[116]
No, Helen, that hellion loathed by the gods,
has murdered you, taken your life from you,
and destroyed your hearth and home.   1215

Chorus

e   e   These words touch my heart.
Astyanax, for me you were once the Great Lord of this city.[117]

Hecuba

I dress you in the fine robe you should have worn at your wedding,
when you married the noblest of the daughters of the East.
I fit to your body the rich embroidered robe woven by Phrygian women.   1220

Addressing Hector's shield

And you, once triumphant mother of many victories,

---

115 These lines are sententious, but they express the mature wisdom of Euripides' *Trojan Women*. At the very moment of Greek triumph and conquest, at the moment when the Greeks are carrying and leading away the spoils of war, the wheel of all human affairs has begun to turn, or—to use Euripides' metaphor— lurch like a lunatic.

116 Anachronistically, Hecuba is making a sharp contrast with Greek athletics. The *Iliad* gives us an example of such competitions in the funeral games held for Patroklos (*Iliad* 23). The funeral games for the infant Alexander (presumed dead) in the *Alexandros* might help motivate Hecuba's qualification. The Greek audience of Euripides' *Trojan Women* was familiar with the international competitions at Olympia, Delphi, the Isthmus of Corinth, and Nemea. There is also a suggestion of the alternative to the excessive devotion to the competition of athletics, a city at peace. The garments that wrap Astyanax's body were embroidered for his wedding.

117 A rendering of the name Astyanax, a compound of *asty* (city) and *anax* (lord).

the shield that was once a part of Hector, receive your victor's crown.
You are not immortal, but you will not die with this body.
You are more precious by far than the arms won by that clever
    cower, Odysseus.[118]   1225

Antiphonal Lament (Kommos) of Chorus and Hecuba
aiai   aiai   Child, the earth will receive you.
You are the bitter well of our grief and lamentation.
Mother, join us in our bitter song.

Hecuba
                                        aiai

Chorus
You cry for the dead.   1230

Hecuba
                          oimoi

Chorus
Yours is my cry for evil never to be forgotten.

Hecuba   *Bending again over the body of Astyanax and wrapping him in winding cloth*
I now heal your wounds with these wrappings– I, a healer who suffers,
who am called a healer, but can heal nothing.
Your other needs your father will care for in the Nether World.

Chorus
Strike, strike our temples   1235
blow after blow
io moi   moi

Hecuba
Women, you are most dear to me …

Chorus
Hecuba, speak. What do you want to say to us?

Hecuba   *After a silence*
So, so … the gods never really cared, or, if they cared, they cared
    for my sufferings
and for Troy, a city they picked out for their special hate.   1241

---

118   After the death of Achilles, Ajax and Odysseus made their claims on the divine arms of Achilles before
the Greek army. The army awarded the arms and, by implication, the title "best of the Achaeans" to the
eloquence of Odysseus. In chagrin and a fit of madness Ajax attacked the livestock of the Greek camp,
taking them for his enemies, and, when he realized what he had done, he committed suicide. The *Decision
over the Arms* was the subject of a lost play of Aeschylus; the suicide of Ajax, the subject of Sophocles'
Ajax.

So, we offered them lavish sacrifices of oxen for nothing.[119]
Yet, had not some god turned our world upside down[120]
and buried our towers in the earth, we would have been ciphers.
We would never have been the subject of song;
we would never have provided an argument
for the Muse of mortal poets yet to be born.   1245

To Talthybios' attendants

Go now.
Bury this body in this poor trench.
He has all the finery the dead require.
I think the dead pay little heed to lavish grave goods.
These are the hollow ostentation of the living.   1250

Astyanax's corpse carried off by Talthybios' soldiers

Chorus

io io
I lament your mother, whose high hopes for your life
were dashed to pieces.
The high station of your ancestors lifted you
to great prosperity,
only to plunge to a dreadful death.   1255

ea ea

Looking up to the walls of Troy on the stage building

What is this I see?[121] I see men carrying
blazing torches[122] cresting over the walls of Troy.

---

119 Hecuba's final articulation of the theology of the play is followed by the collapse of the god-built citadel of "sacred Ilion" in smoke and flames. Hecuba's conclusion about the value of Trojan piety is supported, and inspired, by a scene from the *Iliad* now familiar. There (6.286-312) Hecuba had brought a finely embroidered cloak (*peplos*) to the temple of Athena on the citadel of Troy as an offering. Athena lifted her head in a gesture of rejection before the suppliant Trojan women.

120 Hecuba reproduces the thought of Cassandra, who had earlier attempted to console her mother for the destruction of Troy by reflecting that, if the Greeks had never invaded the Troad, Hector's fame would have never spread through the world (394-7). The slaughter of Astyanax has also become the subject of tragedy (see note to line 1188). Now the gods are seen as responsible not only for the destruction of Troy but its survival and celebration in Athenian song.

121 At this point in a Euripidean drama, the audience could expect the appearance of a god to resolve the intractable human conflict (as in the *Antiope*) or to tidy up the ugly human situation by reference to a happier future (as in the *Hippolytus* and *Bacchae*). But, in this case, there is no *deus ex machina*, divine resolution or consoling future. No god appears on the walls of Troy or the *theologeion* of Euripides' theater.

122 The speaker of the Prologue of the *Alexandros*, the first play of Euripides' "Trojan Trilogy," must have referred to Hecuba's dream that she had given birth to a torch. The prophecy of her dream is now fulfilled.

Now some new catastrophe will be added to the tale of Troy.

Talthybios   *To the men who have accompanied him on stage*

Captains, you who have been ordered to set fire to Priam's city,   1260
do not stand here with fire flickering in your hands.
Torch the city!
Once we have reduced the city of Ilion to ashes,
we can rejoice as we set sail home from Troy.

> *To the Trojan women*

As for you, daughters of Trojans, start moving out.   1265
When the generals give the shrill blast of the trumpet,[123]
go down to the ships of the Achaeans to be taken from this land.

> *To Hecuba*

And you, old woman, the most unfortunate of all these women,
come along.
These men have been sent by Odysseus.   1270
You are his prize of war and you will be his slave in Ithaka.

Hecuba

Oi' go talaina
This comes as the crown of all my sufferings.
I leave the land of my birth. Troy is now in flames.
Body, legs slow with age, make this effort now.   1275

> *Turning to the walls of Troy*

I want to say a last farewell to my suffering city.
Troy, Troy, once you held your head so high
among the peoples of the East. Soon you will be stripped of your name and fame.
They are putting you to the torch.
They are taking us women from this land as slaves.
io   Gods! Gods!   But why should I call upon the gods?   1280
In the past they have not listened when we called upon them.
Now, let us race to the funeral pyre of Troy. It would be a noble death
to perish in the flames of my burning land.

Talthybios

Unhappy woman, you are possessed by the demon of your suffering.

> *To his attendants*

Take her away. Do not delay. This woman must be taken   1285
as Odysseus' prize and delivered into his hand.

---

123 The sound of a trumpet was the signal for the departure of the Athenian fleet in summer of 415; Thucydides,
     The Peloponnesian War 6.32.1.7

Hecuba   *In a dirge of lamentation*

Strophe A

otototototoi
Son of Kronos, councilor, begetter, father,
do you witness our sufferings?
The race of Dardanos did not deserve them.   1290

Chorus
Yes, he did witness our sufferings and the great city,
a city no more, has perished,
has perished.

Antistrophe A

Hecuba
otototototoi
Ilion glitters and its high citadel is ablaze.   1295
Flames lick its walls.

Chorus
Our land has fallen to the spear
and is consumed, as fire lifts up on a freshening wing.
Fire rages through hungry halls.
The enemies' spears are now torches.   1300

Strophe B

Hecuba   *Kneeling on the ground*
   io   Earth that nourished my children.

Chorus
   e   e

Hecuba   *Beating the earth*
   Children! Listen to me! Recognize the voice of your mother!

Chorus
   Do you invoke the dead with this shrill cry?

Hecuba
   I do. I will settle this worn old body down upon the ground   1305
   and strike the earth with both hands.

Chorus
   We follow you
   and kneel upon the ground
   and call upon our tormented husbands beneath the earth.

Hecuba

We are taken away as plunder.   1310

Chorus

Your voice is the voice of our pain.

Hecuba

We bend our heads to enter a slave's quarters.

Chorus

Taken from the land of our birth.

Hecuba

io io   Priam, Priam.

You lie in death unburied, with no kin or friend.

You know nothing of the disaster that has befallen me.

Chorus

He can know nothing. Black Death has closed his eyes,   1315

sacred Death, in unholy butchery.

Antistrophe B

Hecuba

io   Look at the palaces of the gods. Look at our beloved city.

Chorus

e   e   Look! Look!

Hecuba

Your lot is blood-red flame and the point of a spear.

Chorus

Soon, you will collapse to the ground, to our native land. Your name will be no
    more.

Hecuba

A cloud of dust and ash lifting up   1320

to the blue of heaven on wings of smoke

will take from me the sight of my home.

Chorus

The very name of our country vanishes into the dark.

Our city slowly crumbles into nothing. Enduring Troy exists no more.

Hecuba   *A trumpet sounds*

Did you hear it? Did you hear that sound?   1325

Chorus

I heard the crash of the citadel.

Hecuba

A quake, a wave of destruction

Chorus

overwhelming the city.

Hecuba   *Talthybios' attendants now lift her to her feet*

io io

Now, my trembling limbs,

tremble, take me away

Take me away to my life as a slave.   1330

Chorus   *Looking back as they too are led away*

O long suffering city. Suffering, we must move now

to the Achaean ships.

   Exit Hecuba, Talthybios, and the Chorus of captive women

An Essay on Sophocles' *Ajax*
by Stephen Esposito

I. Introduction to Sophocles

Sophocles' fame derives from being one of the world's greatest playwrights; it is less well known that he was the only Athenian in fifth century to serve as imperial treasurer (443/2 B.C.E.), military general (441/40), and special state commissioner (*proboulos*) during a time of civic crisis (413). He entered 31 tetralogies (three tragedies and a satyr play) at the Theater of Dionysus and won an astonishing 18 times (58%); he never finished in last (third) place. He averaged one tetralogy every other year for some 62 years. Unfortunately only seven of his 124 plays survive. Euripides, in contrast, won with five of his 18 tetralogies (28%); he never defeated Sophocles. Unlike Aeschylus, who appears to have written some ten connected trilogies, of which only the *Oresteia* survives (458), Sophocles wrote no trilogies. His first victory came when, at the age of 28, he defeated Aeschylus in 468; no plays from his first 20 years survive. His last play, *Oedipus at Colonus*, was written when he was 90 years old.

Sophocles' heroes are outsiders, loners, men and women of extraordinary achievement whose deviating paths simultaneously compel admiration and demand interrogation. The Athenian philosopher Polemon got it right when he dubbed Sophocles 'the tragic Homer.'[1] This is so for one major reason, namely the dramatist's intense love of the *agôn*, the contest. A gallery of audacious, over-reaching protagonists fill the landscape of his fiery imagination: Ajax, Antigone, Oedipus, Heracles, Philoctetes, to name a few of the more famous who have survived the ravages of time. It has been calculated that 43 of Sophocles' 124 plays focused on Trojan themes, a proportion (35%) far higher than in Aeschylus or Euripides.[2]

The legacy of these fictional women and men with their unyielding 'heroic tempers' abides and inspires because of their deep-rooted conviction that individual freedom is the most demanding and defining of human responsibilities. The words of Pericles' Funeral Oration (431 B.C.E.), celebrating the courage of the first Athenians to die in the war against Sparta, might well be applied to Sophocles' heroes: "All the earth is the grave of (these) distinguished men... So now, you too, strive with them, judging happiness to be the fruit of freedom and freedom the fruit of courage. Don't look from the sidelines at

---

1   Polemon, head of Plato's Academy from 313-270 B.C.E., also called Homer 'the epic Sophocles': see Diogenes Laertius (third century C.E.) in *The Lives of Famous Philosophers* 4.20. On Sophocles' use of Homer in *Ajax*, especially the allusions to *Iliad* VI in Tecmessa's speech at 485-524, see P. E. Easterling, "The Tragic Homer" in *Bulletin of the Institute of Classical Studies* 31 (1984) 1-8.

2   Gordon Kirkwood "Homer and Sophocles' *Ajax*" in *Classical Drama and Its Influence* ed. M. J. Anderson (London, 1965) 55 [53-70].

the dangers of war." (Thucydides 2.43.3-4) Sophocles' protagonists have a fierce antipathy to watching from the sidelines. The battles they fight are not in the killing fields of the Peloponnesian War (Athens vs. Sparta, 431-404 B.C.E.) but they are bloody battles nonetheless. For them, as for the Periclean dead, the cost of freedom is courage and that courage often comes in the form of suicide (Ajax, Antigone, Haemon, Eurydice, Jocasta, Deianeira).

No other Athenian bears witness so enduringly and passionately to the drive for freedom in the face of fear. The daring acts of Sophocles' heroes testify eloquently to a deep trust in man's capacity to stake out some degree of independence and freedom in a world circumscribed by the often ruthless and relentless forces of necessity, chance, and divinity. Indeed it is precisely when the yoke of 'necessity' (*anankê*) tightens its grip that we find the likes of Ajax and Oedipus asserting most firmly their own responsibility for their legacies, preferring to die like lions rather than live like dogs (cf. *Ajax* 479). There is little that they fear except being publicly shamed. Their pursuit of the extraordinary life means that they refuse to compromise or waffle. Like the blazing midday sun that watches over Antigone's defiant burial of her brother, Sophocles' heroes at once scorch and revitalize the community of the *polis*; their energies are blinding and luminous, violent and uplifting, polluted and sacred, all-too-human and daimonic. Accordingly the Sophoclean over-reacher is at once heroic and tragic; and we would wish it no other way. Who of us, as we read *Ajax*, does not want him to commit suicide? Over the course of the first 865 lines we come to understand, as he does, that in his world suicide is his *only* option because it is the only *noble* option; and he is, for all his shortcomings, a man of nobility, both in birth and in character. Not only does the play make that clear, but so, too, does his former arch-enemy Odysseus (1336-45).

II. Introduction to *Ajax*

This section presents background information for contextualizing the play and is divided into the following sub-sections: the prologue's three characters, Ajax's family, Ajax's weapons , and the contest for Achilles' armor.

The Prologue's Three Characters: Athena, Odysseus, Ajax

Athena

The virgin goddess of war and victory sprang fully armed with weapons from the head of her Olympian father Zeus. She is also the goddess of wisdom and wiliness, naturally so since her mother was Metis ('Wisdom'). In the *Iliad* she ardently defends the Greek attackers; in the *Odyssey*, whose plot she steers from beginning to end, and in *Ajax* she is the "guardian" (36) of Odysseus who, as her human protégé, personifies cunning intelligence and adaptability. She is the only god to appear on stage in extant Sophocles. Athena probably, and unusually, takes her name from the city of Athens, where she had a spectacular temple, the Parthenon (temple of "the virgin"), built on the Acropolis between 447-432 B.C.E. Within the Parthenon stood a colossal forty-foot-high gold and ivory statue of Athena sculpted by the renowned Pheidias and dedicated in 438; Athena's shield was decorated with the head of Medusa, the Gorgon monster whose face turned to stone anyone who looked at her (cf. *Ajax* 451).

Odysseus

The greatest trickster and probably the most famous hero of the ancient world was the only son of Laertes and Anti-cleia ('Against Glory'), whom he visits in the underworld (*Ody.* 11.152-224). His maternal grandfather was the trickster Auto-lycus ('Lone-Wolf'); his wife was the faithful and prudent Penelope; his son was Telemachus ('Fighter-from-afar', i. e. Bowman). By his enemies Odysseus was often called 'son of Sisyphus', the sinister king of Corinth (*Ajax* 189, *Philoctetes* 417, 625). He is about 40 years old in *Ajax*. Appendix Two shows his full genealogy.

Besides *Ajax* Sophocles wrote several other plays about Odysseus that treated various aspects of his life. The only one that survives is the late *Philoctetes* (409 B.C.E.) which represents Odysseus as a conniving sophist who enlists Achilles' upstanding young son (Neoptolemus) in a scheme to steal the magical bow of the shipwrecked and crippled Philoctetes so that he, Odysseus, can sack Troy. *Odysseus Struck by a Fish Bone* told of the death of Odysseus; *Odysseus the Madman* dramatized how he feigned insanity to avoid going off to the Trojan War. *The Washing* dealt with numerous events of hero's homecoming, especially the story of how Odysseus' old nurse Eurycleia, when she was bathing him, recognized his boar-inflicted thigh wound him and unwittingly almost revealed the hero's identity (cf. *Ody.* 19.386-94, 467-507).

Etymologically Odysseus' name carries two main connotations: 'The man of pain' (*odynê*) and 'The man of odium' (*odyssomai*), i.e. he who is hated by men (e.g. Ajax) and gods (e.g. Poseidon). Several passages in Homer's *Odyssey* deal with the origins of his name (1.60; 5.340, 19.406-9). In a lost play of Sophocles the hero himself puns on his name: "Correctly I am called Odysseus, a name pregnant with harm: for many enemies have odium for me." (fragment 965). The English *Ulysses* derives from Latin *Ulixes* which derives from Greek *Olisseus*.

Ajax

The 'second best of the Greeks' was the son of Telamon (a hero of the first Trojan War) and Eriboea; Zeus was his great grand-father (cf. *Ajax* 387, 824; for a full genealogy see Appendix Two). Odysseus said that Ajax surpassed all the Greek warriors, except Achilles, in beauty and achievement (*Odyssey* 11. 550; cf. *Iliad* 2.768-69; 17.279-80; *Ajax* 1340-1). He towered above his comrades by head and broad shoulders (*Iliad* 3.227). Ajax sailed from his home, the island of Salamis near Athens, with twelve ships, the same small number as Odysseus (Agamemnon had 100 ships!). At Troy he 'anchored' the eastern end of the Greek fleet next to the Athenian ships (*Iliad* 2.558); Achilles 'anchored' the western end, and Odysseus held the middle. Ajax is the only Homeric hero never to receive direct aid from a god, the only one not to be given an 'aristeia' (a scene that describes a warrior's prowess in battle; but cf. *Iliad* 11.543-73), the only one to be described as 'carrying his shield like a wall' (three times), and the only one to commit suicide. He was much more of a defender than an attacker; he nearly kills the attacking Hector (*Iliad* 14.409-20) and he protected the bodies of the fallen Patroclus (*Iliad* 17.747-52) and Achilles (whose corpse he carried to safety). He is never wounded in the *Iliad*, no doubt because his massive shield made him practically invulnerable. Homer describes him, more than any other Greek warrior, as a lion (cf. *Ajax* 987), but he also *speaks* effectively in the embassy to Achilles (*Iliad* 9. 622-42) and to his comrades during Hector's furious attack on the Greek ships

(*Iliad* 15.501-14, 561-4, 726-46). In the funeral games of Patroclus he enters three contests and loses all three; most surprisingly, he is thrown down by Odysseus in a wrestling match (*Iliad* 23. 725-8). He shows no trace of impiety in Homer, although he certainly does in *Ajax*. At the end of Plato's *Republic*, in the myth of Er when each soul gets to choose a life in the afterlife, Ajax chose to be a lion rather than a human being because of his abiding anger at Odysseus over losing the judgment about Achilles' arms (Book X, 620 b 1). For a translation of Ajax's famous meeting with Odysseus in the underworld (*Odyssey* 11.538-67) see the end of this essay.

The name 'Ajax' is the Latinized version of the Greek *Aias* and carries two different connotations. The first was made famous by the Theban poet Pindar, who deeply admired Ajax. Pindar derives the name *Aias* from 'eagle' (*aietos*) since that majestic 'king of birds' appeared to Heracles as an omen at Ajax's birth (*Isthmian* 6. 49-50; written circa 480). Obviously this etymology stresses the hero's grandeur. It is possible that Sophocles alludes obliquely to Pindar's derivation when the chorus, in the most elaborate simile in *Ajax*, compares the insolent Greek leaders, escaping from Ajax's sight, to cackling birds fleeing before the mighty 'eagle' (*aiguptos*, 169). But that 'heroic' etymology, if it is such in that passage, is soon replaced by one much more befitting Sophocles' tragic hero. When he comes back to his senses after his mad rampage, Ajax says to Tecmessa, in the first words of his first major speech (430-33): "*Ai! Ai!* Who ever would have dreamt that this name of mine—*Aias*—would echo and express so exactly these <u>agonies</u> of mine? Twice now I have cause to cry out *ai ai*—even thrice—with such calamity have I collided!" Ajax is punning on a folk derivation of his name that means 'he who is destined to cry *aiai*, woe, woe' (cf. 370, 904, 914). This is the first appearance of this etymology in extant Greek literature. As in the case of Odysseus' name this kind of word-play (Ajax = 'Mr. Agony') reflects the Greek proverb *onoma ornis*, 'a name is a bird (of omen).' The Roman equivalent, *nomen omen*, means that a 'name' carries the 'sign' of a person's destiny. Otherwise put, a name is a visible picture of an invisible reality. Perhaps the most famous Greek example of this belief in the magical power of names is found in the Gospel of Matthew (16.18): "You are Peter (<u>*Petros*</u>) and upon this rock (<u>*petra*</u>) I shall build my church."

Sophocles follows the legend that Ajax's body was *buried* (577, 1141) not cremated (as was customary for Homeric heroes). His legendary and venerated tomb was located on the northeast coast of Troy near Cape Rhoeteum. Alexander the Great is said to have offered sacrifices there and at the tomb of Achilles at Cape Sigeion, northwest of Troy (Pausanias I.35.5). In *Ajax* a 'dummy' is used for Ajax's corpse from about line 1000 onwards.

Ajax's Family: father, mother, war-captive bride, half-brother, son

Father

Telamon, the king of Salamis, was a brother of Peleus, the father of Achilles; hence Ajax was a first cousin of Achilles. Telamon's exploits included the voyage of the Argonauts to fetch the Golden Fleece, the Calydonian boar hunt with Meleager (*Iliad* 9. 529-99), and, most relevantly, the first Greek assault of Troy, led by Heracles (Pindar *Nemean* 4.25; *Isthmian* 6.40; Euripides, *Trojan Women* 799-807). In honor of Telamon's battle-prowess (*aristeia*) Heracles gave to him "the first prize of all the army, and the most beautiful one," the Trojan princess Hesione, daughter of the slain king Laomedon (*Ajax* 434-6). Hesione, as Telamon's concubine / slave, gave birth to Teucer, a boy whom Telamon "nurtured and cherished" (*Iliad* 8. 283). Telamon's name means 'a leather support-strap or belt'; at *Iliad* 7.304-5 Hector gives Ajax as a gift 'a well-cut *telamôn*' (sword-belt). In *Ajax* Telamon is an old man (507) whose sorrow the chorus poignantly imagines at the news of his son's death (641-5); for a less flattering picture of his personality see *Ajax* 1008-21.

Mother

Eriboea was the daughter of Alcathoüs, king of Megara, and a granddaughter of Pelops. She is an old woman who is referred to twice and named once (569; cf. 508) whereas Telamon is named seven times and referred to often. The chorus also poignantly imagines her sorrow when Eriboea hears of her son's fate (622-34).

War-captive bride / concubine

Tecmessa, at the time of the play, has lived with Ajax for several years as his war-captive 'slave' (*doulê*, 489) and 'young bride' (*nymphê*, 894) who bore his only offspring and legitimate heir, Eurysaces. She is at once a foreigner, slave, war captive, young bride and, as Ajax calls her before the fact, a widow (*chêra*, 653). Hence her status is not easy to pin down. Tecmessa was the daughter of Teleutas, a Phrygian (= Trojan) prince whose land Ajax destroyed; both her parents were killed by some unknown stroke of doom (516-18). She does not appear earlier in Greek literature but a vase dated c. 470 B.C.E. by the Brygos painter shows her covering Ajax's corpse; perhaps this vase inspired *Ajax* 915-16. Since she is named in *Ajax* only three times and not until line 331 it may well be that she was already familiar to Sophocles' audience from earlier literary sources.

Half-brother

Ajax's half-brother, Teucer, was a bastard son of Telamon by Hesione, the beautiful war-captive princess and daughter of the slain king of Troy, Laomedon (*Ajax* 434-6, 1301-3; cf. 1229). Homer describes him as the Greeks' best archer (*Iliad* 13.313-14; cf. 23.859-69). His skill with the bow is highlighted when he kills ten Trojans, including Hector's charioteer, before Hector smashes him with a rock. Ajax comes to Teucer's rescue, covering him with his shield (8.266-334; cf. 23.859-69). He is one of the few Greek leaders who returned home safely from the Trojan War. Unfortunately he returned without Ajax, being unable to prevent his brother's suicide because he was off on a predatory raid at the time (*Ajax* 342-3, 564, 720). Irate at Teucer's failure (cf. *Ajax* 1013-15), Telamon banished his bastard son to Cyprus, where Teucer founded another city named Salamis (cf. Euripides, *Helen* 87- 106). Like his half-brother Ajax, Teucer was worshipped as a hero on Salamis.

Son

Eurysaces appears as a young child in *Ajax* at the end of which Teucer, his uncle, has been charged (by Ajax) to take the boy to his grandfather, Telamon, in Salamis. As was often the case with Greek boys, he takes his name Eury-saces, 'Broad-shield,' from his father's most outstanding feature, i.e. Ajax's enormous and impenetrable shield (574-6); likewise Odysseus' son Tele-machus ('Fighter from afar') took his name from his father's skill at archery, and Hector's son Asty-anax ('Lord of the city') from his father's role as Troy's leader and greatest warrior. Eurysaces is perhaps around five years old in the play; a servant leads the boy on stage by holding his hand (542) and then lifts him up into

Ajax's arms (545), like Hector lifting Astyanax in *Iliad* 6. 466-85 (cf. also *Ajax* 1171-81). At 1409-11 Teucer asks him to help lift his father. Although he is onstage for some 300 lines, Eurysaces does not speak.

Ajax's Weapons: shield, sword, whip

Shield

Homer's Ajax was famed for an enormous body shield that symbolized his role as 'the Protector.' In the *Iliad* he carried it 'like a wall' with its seven layers of ox-hide and top layer of hammered bronze (7.219-23; 11.257). In contrast, Teucer's shield had only four layers of ox-hide (15.479). The Greek noun *sakos* means 'shield'; hence the name of his young son, Eury-*sakes*, 'Broad-shield.' Since Ajax bequeaths his sword to his son, it is the only part of his armor that will not be buried with him. There is no solid textual evidence that the shield was ever brought on stage in *Ajax* (cf. 574-6).

Sword

In the *Iliad* Ajax and Hector (greatest Trojan warrior) had a duel that was called off because of nightfall, at which time they exchanged gifts. Hector gave Ajax his sword (7.303-5) and this 'gift' (*Ajax* 662, 817) is the play's most important stage prop, a physical and psychological symbol of the mighty warrior's fame and subsequent infamy. It is probable that the audience first saw the sword when Ajax gave his 'deception' speech (646-92). The sword motif recurs often but becomes much less important in the second half of the play (see 10, 30, 231, 730, 815, 828, 1034, 1408).[3]

Whip

In his night-raid on the Greek commanders Ajax uses a massive whip (*mastix*: 110, 242, 1254) as his weapon. It was this whip which later gave *Ajax* its subtitle 'the Whip-carrier' (*Mastigo-phoros*) to distinguish it from *Ajax the Locrian* (on which, see section IV below).

Thematic Backdrop: The Contest for Achilles' Armor

After Achilles was killed under the gates of Troy by Paris and Apollo (*Iliad* 22.359-60, *Philoctetes* 334-5), his mother Thetis held a contest to determine who was 'the best of the Greeks.' To the victor went the spoils, i. e. her son's panoply made by Hephaistos, the blacksmith god (*Iliad* 18. 468-617). In his meeting with Ajax in the underworld (*Odyssey* 11. 538-67) Odysseus says that the judgment and award of Achilles' armor to him was made by *Trojan captives and Athena*. (For a translation of that passage see the last section of this essay.) According to the version of Ajax and Teucer in Sophocles' play the award was the result of *a rigged vote by the Greek commanders* (442-6, 1135; similarly Pindar *Nemean* 8.26; 7.20-30). It is unclear which is the truer version. It would appear that Sophocles intentionally leaves the issue of the justice or injustice of the award of the

---

3   On the symbolism of the sword and shield see Charles Segal, *Tragedy and Interpretation: An Interpretation of Sophocles* (Cambridge and London, 1981) 116-118.

arms quite vague.[4] In any case, having been judged inferior to Odysseus, Ajax tried to get revenge by attacking the Greek commanders. He failed and then committed suicide. But between the award to Odysseus and Ajax's suicide there was an interval of several days during which time Ajax withdrew from battle and brooded over his options; it is on this time period that Sophocles' play focuses (*Ajax* 192-5, 925-36, 1336-7).

The first play of Aeschylus' (now-lost) Ajax trilogy was called *The Award of the Arms*. One of its fragments refers to Ajax's honesty as opposed to Odysseus' trickery and reads as follows: "For simple are the words of truth." Another fragment, perhaps spoken by Ajax in reaction to his defeat, reads: "For what honor is there in living a life that brings only pain?" The 'arms of Achilles' theme appears several times in *Ajax* (441-46, 935, 1239-40, 1337; cf. *Philoctetes* 364-76).

III. Interpretive Essay

Themes of the prologue

The prologue (1-133) is divided into three parts: **1-90** = Athena and Odysseus (she is audible to him although *initially* invisible); **91-117** = Athena (visible to Odysseus and Ajax), Ajax (visible to Athena and Odysseus), and Odysseus (invisible to Ajax); **118-33** = Athena and Odysseus (both visible to one another). As is evident from this brief summary (with its complex mixture of 'visible / invisible' actors), *the issue of what can be seen and when* is quite problematic and immediately raises the complex issue of how one sees and knows the world. Athena tells Odysseus that she cast "hard-to-bear imaginings" (51) over Ajax's eyes as he was about to kill the Greek leaders, including Odysseus himself. What is the meaning of this ailment that the goddess thrusts upon Ajax? Philip Holt persuasively suggests the following: "Ajax's sickness is not egomania, or lust for revenge, or murderous frenzy, or suicidal despair. It is nothing more, and nothing less, than *a failure to see things correctly—a delusion* that he was killing and torturing Greek warriors when in fact he was only venting his wrath upon sheep and cattle." Holt further argues that "Ajax's *delusion* that cattle were Greek leaders corresponds to a more general *delusion* about the nature of the world; and that his recovery from the former *delusion* early in the play anticipates his recovery from the latter one, which is shown in the much-discussed third monologue (646-692)", i.e. Ajax's famous 'deception' speech.[5] (my emphasis)

The most important immediate function of the prologue is to establish the setting, introduce the characters, and begin the process of exploring the nature of their relationships (e.g. friend / foe, powerful / powerless). The prologue also introduces numerous thematic contrasts that will become ever more textured as the play proceeds: e.g., blindness vs. sight, intelligence *vs.* physical strength; divine power / omniscience *vs.* human

---

4   Cf. Philip Holt's assessment of this important theme: "For Sophocles, the judgment of arms shows the conflict between the assertive and cooperative virtues. Ajax is above all an individualistic hero, bold and self-assertive, proud and independent...He does little to fit in with the community, to accommodate his rugged nature to its demands...In contrast to Ajax, Odysseus is very much the man of the community, endowed with the cooperative spirit, reasonableness, and readiness to try persuasion that Ajax lacks—all qualities necessary for the smooth functioning of society." See "Sophocles' *Ajax* and the Ajax Myth" in *The St. John's Review* 33.3 (1983) 57 [51-61]

5   Holt, "Ajax's Ailment" in *Ramus* 9 (1980) 22 [22-33]. This is a superb article.

impotence / misunderstanding; and harshness *vs.* compassion. Appendix 1 presents a two-page diagram that gives a succinct overview of the entire play and allows particular scenes to be seen in their larger context.

The roles of Athena and Odysseus in *Ajax*

Athena is the only god to appear in the surviving plays of Sophocles. She serves several roles in the *Ajax* prologue. First and most simply she is a useful dramatic device to explain why Ajax has gone mad and killed cattle and sheep rather than the intended Greek commanders. Second she is what we might call an externalization or personification of societal norms that sets limits on outrageous human behavior; that is, she serves as something like 'a law of nature' or 'the reality principle.' As Charles Segal explains, "As a principle of the inexorable realities of the world that the gods often signify, the laws built into the structure of reality, Athena exemplifies the hard fact that there is a price to pay for violence, egotistical self-centeredness, rejection of the conditions of mortal existence. This is the justice of the gods."[6] Third, as an Olympian god, she makes painfully clear the tremendous gap between divine power and human impotence. Fourth, in her cruel toying with Ajax she reminds us that the Greek gods were not known for their beneficence; they were custodians of power, not kindness. Athena does 'love' Odysseus at *Odyssey* 3.218-22 where the word *phil-ein* (as in *phil*-anthropy) appears three times in five lines but that is the exception to the rule. It is as rare in Greek literature to find gods loving mortals as it is mortals loving gods. As Aristotle writes, "It would be absurd if someone were to say that he loves Zeus."[7] Fifth, she acts as a negative foil to Odysseus, the unobserved observer; she encourages her protégé to mock Ajax but, quite to our surprise, he refuses. And what a huge refusal it is (121-6): "I *pity* the poor wretch, even though he is my enemy, because he's been yoked harshly to the harness of a dreadful delusion. Yes, I ponder that man's lot no less than my own. For I see that we are nothing more than ghosts—all we that live—or vacuous insubstantial shadows." Odysseus' compassion for the fragility of 'man' is a sentiment that permeates Greek literature and is one of its distinctive markers. A fragment of Sophocles' lost *Ajax the Locrian* reads: "A man is only breath and *shadow*." This image that we are, in the end, just 'hollow men' is captured beautifully, too, by the great Theban poet Pindar, in a verse written at about the same time that Sophocles produced *Ajax*: "Creatures of a day! What is anyone? What is he not? Man, the *shadow* of a dream."[8] As Odysseus beholds 'the poor wretch' Ajax (121) it dawns on him that he, too, might be 'the poor wretch' (109, 111) except for Athena's intervention. He understands, as he watches this dumb show play out, that Macbeth was right—"life's but a walking shadow, a poor player that struts and frets his hour upon the stage, and then is heard no more."[9]

---

6   Charles Segal "Sophocles" in *Ancient Writers: Greece and Rome*, vol. 1 (ed.) T. James Luce (New York, 1982) 189 [179-207]. Cf. Bernard Knox in "The Ajax of Sophocles" in *Word and Action: Essays on the Ancient Theater* (Baltimore and London, 1979) 8 [3-24]: "Athena is the traditional morality personified, in all its fierce simplicity."

7   Aristotle *Magna Moralia* 1208 b30.

8   Pindar *Pythian Ode* 8. 95-97, written in 446 B.C.E. For Homeric images of man as smoke, shadow, and dream, see *Odyssey* 11.206-7; 10. 495; 11.222.

9   *Macbeth* v.v. 24-27; cf. *Hamlet*: "What a piece of work is a man. How noble in reason!…And yet, to me, what is this quintessence of dust?" (ii.ii. 312)

It is probably fair to say that nothing in Greek literature matches Odysseus' compassion here and nothing so up-ends the Greek moral code of 'helping friends, harming foes.' It is not, of course, a compassion that Athena shares. It is man that makes morality in this play, not the gods.

Athena concludes the prologue thus (132-3): "It is moderate and sound-minded men whom the gods love, while they hate the wicked." This couplet of proverbial wisdom seems simple enough. Yet it raises troubling questions and we should resist the temptation to take such apparent 'words of wisdom' as the moral of the whole story. If, as Athena seems to imply, Ajax is so wicked, why does Sophocles work so fervently to augment his moral stature over course of the play and why does he redeem Ajax's honor in the second half by means of the very man, Odysseus, who refuses to play Athena's parlor game of mockery in the prologue? And if the goddess is so representative of abiding wisdom, why is it that the human character she most resembles is the contemptible king of Sparta, Menelaus, who similarly sings the praises of the 'sound-minded man' but in a way that is patently self-serving (1069-83).[10] It is (probably) not accidental that the actor who 'played' Athena also (probably) 'played' the brutish roles of Menelaus and Agamemnon.

The role of Ajax in *Ajax*

Whereas Achilles' ranks as the Greeks' fiercest attacker at Troy, Ajax ranks as their most stalwart defender. Of Ajax it is generally the case that "the more hopeless the situation becomes the firmer his constancy grows."[11] But despite his enormous size and strength, he was not easily tricked; furthermore he possessed good common sense (*Iliad* 7. 198, 288). Although Hector calls him 'an inarticulate ox' (*Iliad* 13. 824)—a sentiment echoed by Agamemnon in Sophocles' play (1253)—Ajax is hardly a dumb ox; his moving words in the famous embassy to the irate Achilles in the *Iliad* show otherwise (9. 624-42). But it remains the case that in Sophocles he gains a depth and nobility of character absent in Homer.[12] His four monologues in *Ajax*, totaling some 187 lines, are the most arresting ensemble of speeches of any one character in Athenian tragedy. And his third monologue, the famous 'deception speech' (646-92), is arguably the most uncanny and complex speech in extant Greek literature.

Near the end of the *Ajax* prologue Athena, as a way of praising her own invincible strength, praises the unrivalled degree of *forethought* (119) of the man she is cruelly mocking. The fact that the goddess highlights this particular trait of Ajax, which Odysseus also acknowledges, makes the madman's delusion all the more frightening; it also prepares us for the Achilles-like *clarity of vision* which Ajax attains after the madness has dissipated; once he recognizes the hopelessness of his quandary, he proceeds immediately to deal with it by prudently weighing his options and then acting decisively.

Much of the hero's depth and nobility in *Ajax* comes from his almost total isolation. His failure to win the contest for Achilles' armor has caused the collapse of his world. The Homeric code of earning honor, respect, and glory by excellence in battle disappears before his eyes. The degree to which this world vanishes is expressed in one of Sophocles'

---

10   A.F. Garvie (ed. and trans.) *Sophocles: Ajax* (Warminster, 1998) 15 and 223-4.

11   Karl Schefold *Myth and Legend in Early Greek Art* (London 1966) 26.

12   Lewis Campbell (ed.) *Sophocles* vol. II (London, 1881) 3.

saddest ironies, namely that Homer's second bravest warrior unwittingly adopts the chief characteristic of his hated arch-enemy Odysseus, 'the man of many moves' (*poly-tropos*). Not only does Ajax become *deceitful* in action but in word as well: in action, by his solo *night* attack on the headquarters of the Greek commanders; in word, he becomes *the unexpected master of ambiguity* when, with his complex 'deception' speech (646-92), he induces Tecmessa and the chorus into thinking that he has changed his mind and will not commit suicide. And this reversal is accompanied by another surprise almost equally as stunning, namely that Odysseus shows himself to be a man of profound and unexpected empathy, so much so that he alone ends up saving Ajax's reputation (121-26, 1332-45, 1376-80).

Sophocles presents Ajax as deeply ashamed not primarily because he sought, by killing the hated Greek leaders, to avenge his failure. After a fashion, albeit an extreme fashion, he was following the traditional moral code: 'help your friends and hurt your enemies.' One sees a similarly ferocious revenge when Odysseus, Telemachus and a few loyalists, with the help of Athena, slay all 108 of the suitors near the end of the *Odyssey*. Odysseus decapitates one suitor (22.329-30), Telemachus hangs twelve of the disloyal maids (22.470), and then several servants, along with Odysseus' son, in a fit of fury, cut off another suitor's ears, nose, hands, feet, and even his private parts which they fed to the dogs raw (22. 473-6). Such is the harsh world of Greek vengeance. In *Ajax* Athena never condemns Ajax's attempted murder; indeed she invites Odysseus to partake in a version of the same moral behavior (79): "Isn't it the sweetest pleasure to laugh in the face of one's foes?" Nor is Ajax's shame that of an ungodly man. As Jon Mikalson observes, "The impiety of the hero is not central to the play but is necessary to motivate Athena's hostility to him. The impious side of Ajax is not developed, though that tendency does occasionally come to the surface..."[13]

Ajax must kill himself not because he attempted to murder his enemies nor because he was impious but because he failed to succeed in the murder. That failure brings unbearable shame (323-5, 398-400, 457-9, 462-5) which Tecmessa tries to mitigate but cannot. Part of Ajax's tragedy lies in the discrepancy between what he comes to know (head) and what he feels (heart). He *knows* that he should 'give way' to Tecmessa (668-83) but his *feelings* of shame overpower him (382, 440). He comes to understand that "Time, in his long and immeasurable march, begets all things from darkness into light and then once again hides them" (646-7). He comes to understand, too, that friends become enemies and enemies friends. He comes to understand, in his third monologue (646-92), the nature of being *and* time, of being *in* time—that in human affairs everything is constantly changing. This cosmological principle that 'all is flux' was made famous by the pre-Socratic philosopher Heraclitus (c. 500 B.C.E) who may well have been Sophocles' thematic source.[14]

So one might well suggest, as Philip Holt does, that the deception speech at 646-92 represents "the philosophical (if not the dramatic) climax of the play. It marks the end of

---

13   Jon Mikalson *Honor Thy Gods: Popular Religion in Greek Tragedy* (Chapel Hill and London, 1991) 279, n. 41. On the theme of hybris in *Ajax* see N. Fisher, *Hybris: A Study in the Values of Honour and Shame in Ancient Greece* (Warminster, 1992) 314-29.

14   Cf. T.B.L. Webster, *An Introduction to Sophocles* (2nd edn. Oxford, 1969) 31-32.

Ajax's great delusion, a delusion of far more consequence than his earlier confusion about men and cattle. His 'recovery' does not free him from suffering…It does not bring him (as the Chorus thinks) reasons to go on living, but only different and more profound reasons for dying—knowledge of his inability to live in a changing world, and (paradoxically) knowledge of his need to obey the law of change by passing out of existence, like winter before spring or night at the coming of day…Through all his suffering and disgrace, he has won his way through to a correct understanding of the nature of the world."[15]

And yet for all his new understanding of the human condition, Ajax cannot change, especially with regard to friends who have become enemies. Why? I would suggest that the machismo bravery that made him so ferocious in battle trained him *too well*. Ajax's suicide is part of a larger tragedy which implicates the very heroic code by which he lived: the gory glory of Troy's killing fields makes soldiers, but somehow it does not make men, at least not the kind whose heroism reaches beyond the blood and guts of the battlefield.

Why does Ajax commit suicide?

Ajax has rightly been called the most *Iliadic* of Greek tragedies.[16] What does that mean? It means that the play harkens back to a world-view where prowess in battle, and the honor and glory gained therein, symbolize the singular mark and defining quality of the man. Ajax, with his enormous seven-layered ox-hide shield, is the unyielding bulwark of the Greeks, especially in the absence of Achilles. He is fierce, raw, and mighty (205). So when he finds himself stripped of honor by the Greeks and then shamed by his own failed attempt at revenge, he resolves on suicide because that is the only 'test' by means of which he will prove to his father, the epic hero Telamon, that he is no gutless coward (472). It is left to intrepid Tecmessa, his war-captive concubine of several years and mother of his only child, to attempt to pierce her man's seemingly invulnerable armor and convince him to change his mind. In one of the play's most poignant speeches, harkening back to Andromache's heart-wrenching appeal to Hector in the *Iliad* (6.407-39), Tecmessa calls upon Ajax's potent sense of shame (505-7) and begs him not to desert his family—to keep dear the memory of his father and mother and not to abandon his son and lady to a life of slavery. She reminds Ajax that the man of true nobility cherishes the memory of those who have tendered deeds of kindness.

In the midst of his post-rage depression, covered with blood and sitting in humiliation beside the beasts of burden that he has so infamously slain, Ajax responds to Tecmessa's petition for compassion (485-524) with speech that shows no pity whatsoever (545-82). Her very last words to him are these (594): "In the name of the gods, be softened." To which he replies (594-5): "You seem to me to think like a fool if you suppose that even now you can school my character." And that would seem to be the end of the matter except that in his third monologue Ajax says: "My speech has become womanish

---

15   Holt, "Ajax's Ailment" in *Ramus* 9 (1980) 29. For an interpretation that sees the meaning of the deception speech as less stable than the one presented here, wherein Ajax's "rhetoric seems to set up the terms of explanation but blocks the closure of secure interpretation", see Simon Goldhill, *Reading Greek Tragedy* (Cambridge, 1986) 189-92.

16   Oliver Taplin "Yielding to Forethought: Sophocles' *Ajax*" in *Arktouros: Hellenic Studies presented to Bernard M. Knox* (Berlin and New York, 1979) 129 [122-29].

and weak and my sharp edge smoothed by this lady here. *I feel pity* at leaving—leaving behind, among my enemies, a widow and her orphaned son" (651-4). There are complex ambiguities here that are designed to deceive (as is explained in the notes to the text) but "I feel pity" is not one of those ambiguities.

In the face of the harsh stubbornness of Ajax's warrior mentality Tecmessa's pleas do, over time, make belated inroads. Ajax does come to feel pity and that is one primary reason for the 'deception' speech in the first place. Odysseus had earlier said that he "felt pity" for Ajax (121) but his words had no impact on Athena. Ajax is much more like Odysseus than Athena in this respect; he *is* moved. And, I suggest, this should not surprise us. After all it was Ajax who begged Achilles in the famous 'embassy' not to be so savage and hard-hearted, to remember his friends' affection, and to feel a sense of shame and respect before his own house (*Iliad* 9. 624-42). Unfortunately Achilles, though clearly moved by Ajax's words, refused to yield or return to battle. His anger and shame burned so intensely that he could remember only the public disgrace and dishonor of Agamemnon unjustly taking his girlfriend, Briseis.

So it is now with Ajax and Tecmessa. Even if this old-world warrior cannot, because of who he is, activate *in his life* the lesson that he has so painfully learned about the inevitable mutability of the human condition, that does not mean that he does not understand. Indeed he does understand (678) and that understanding has an impact: he wants to spare Tecmessa the pain of his suicide. Sadly the pity that Tecmessa has induced him to feel is not powerful enough to pierce, in any serious way, his massive psychological shield. Indeed this is one of the play's deep sadnesses; the world of the family and of *marital* values cannot work their way into the world of war and its *martial* values. It is the same story that Homer told when Hector, determined to fight Achilles before the walls of Troy, was begged by his mother (Hecuba), his sister by marriage (Helen), and his wife (Andromache) respectively *to stay within the city walls* (*Iliad* 6: 258, 354, 431). Hector, because of his profound sense of shame before the Trojans, refused all of their petitions (6.442 = 22.105). He was slain by Achilles, Troy soon fell, and the innocent women and children were taken as slaves.

The Staging of Ajax's Suicide

It has been a long-standing and contentious debate, going all the way back to antiquity, as to whether Ajax commits suicide *in full view* of the audience? Many argue that because Greek tragedy shows very little on-stage violence Sophocles would not have dared to show *in full view* something as extreme as suicide. But given the paucity of our evidence—we have only some 32 tragedies out of a total of over 1000[17]—this is probably not a very reliable barometer.[18] I suggest three new reasons—one textual, one thematic,

---

17   On the number of Greek tragedies produced in the fifth century as over 1000 see Bernard Knox "Myth and Attic Tragedy" in *Word and Action: Essays on the Ancient Theater* (Baltimore and London, 1979) 8 [3-24].

18   That the convention banning violence from the Greek stage was not absolute is argued by S.P. Mills "The Death of Ajax" *Classical Journal* 76.2 (1980-81) 134-35 [129-35]. For a counter-argument see Scott Scullion, *Three Studies in Athenian Dramaturgy* (Stuttgart and Leipzig, 1994), ch. III "The Staging of Sophokles' *Aias*" 96-97 [89-128]

and one cultural—for agreeing with those who believe that in the original performance Ajax's suicide was performed *in full view* of the spectators.

First the textual evidence. From the outset Sophocles repeatedly emphasizes the *public* revelation of Ajax in every regard. In the prologue Athena says to Odysseus: "Here —to you as well I'll show his sheer lunacy <u>in full view</u> (*periphanê*, 66)." After Odysseus expresses his reservations the goddess asks him, "Do you shrink from seeing a madman <u>in full view</u> (*peri-phanôs*, 81)." Later, after Tecmessa reveals to the chorus their master's abject state, the alarmed sailors exclaim "Oimoi, I fear what is approaching! The man will die <u>in full view</u> (*periphantos*, 228) because with his sword he has slaughtered willy-nilly..." This unique sequence—in all of extant Greek tragedy the word *periphanês* ("in full view") occurs only in *Ajax*—raises a clear expectation of *public* display. Why would Sophocles continually raise the expectation of a suicide <u>in full view</u> only to disappoint at the climatic moment? The strong implication of this textual evidence seems confirmed when later the enraged Teucer challenges Agamemnon: "Yes, since it is honorable for me <u>to die conspicuously</u> (i.e. in public), toiling for this man (Ajax), rather than to die in battle in behalf of your wife (Helen)..." (1311, which echoes 228, "The man will <u>die in full view</u>.")

Secondly, the courage, nobility, and deliberateness of packing his sword in the earth (which action almost certainly did take place in full view, as verse 828 implies), of delivering a long soliloquy, and of leaping on the sword—all this would produce a stunning contrast to the earlier tableau of a blood-drenched and disgraced Ajax sitting for some 250 lines among the beasts of burden that he had ignominiously slaughtered (348-595).[19] It would also produce a stunning contrast with the treatment of his predecessor and arch-rival Aeschylus who had Ajax commit suicide *offstage*. We are told this by a messenger in the only fragment to survive from Aeschylus' (now lost) *Thracian Women*, the second play of his *Ajax* trilogy: "And, since his skin would not yield anywhere to the fatal blow, he kept bending his sword, like a man drawing a bow, until some goddess appeared and showed him the place" (i. e. the armpit).[20] It would be very much in keeping with Sophocles' innovative tendencies to deviate from his predecessor and rival by showing the suicide *onstage*. This renowned scene was represented by painters and sculptors with some frequency before Sophocles; the metope on the Temple of Hera (570-550 B.C.E.) near Paestum (southern Italy) is one such conspicuous example.[21] These various artistic representations may have encouraged the dramatist to set aside any dramatic conventions about the staging of such violence. In this context it has been reasonably suggested that a beautiful cup by the great Brygos Painter (c. 470), showing Tecmessa covering Ajax's corpse, inspired verses 915-16 of Sophocles' tragedy.[22]

Thirdly, and more speculatively, I suggest that in staging Ajax's suicide Sophocles was staging the death of a world-view, the death of a heroic perspective on the human con-

---

19   Lewis Campbell (ed.) *Sophocles* vol. II (London, 1881).

20   Translated by A. Sommerstein (ed.) *Aeschylus: Fragments* vol. 3 (Loeb, 2008) frag. 83, pp. 100-1.

21   For a collection of pre-Sophoclean images of Ajax's suicide see Ron M. Brown *The Art of Suicide* (London, 2001) 25-30; Jennifer March "Sophocles' Ajax: the Death and Burial of a Hero" *Bulletin of the Institute of Classical Studies* 38 (1991-3) 1-36; *Lexicon Iconographicum Mythologiae Classicae* 1.1.314-36; 1.2.232-52 (Zürich, 1981-).

22   A.F. Garvie *Sophocles: Ajax* (1998) 3.

dition that was rooted in the Homeric past. By the mid-fifth century, as radical Athenian democracy and its cooperative value system gained momentum and put more power in the hands of the people, the aristocratic world of the hoplite warrior (heavily armed infantryman) was fading fast. The staging of Ajax's suicide symbolizes the death of this archaic world, which for all its nobility and grandeur, was being replaced, for better or worse, by the brave new world of Athenian radical democracy, a world symbolized simultaneously by the deft, compassionate Odysseus and by the petty sophistries and small-mindedness of leaders like Menelaus and Agamemnon.

The Second 'Half' of *Ajax*

What happens after Ajax's suicide? What is the purpose of the final 555 lines (866-1420)? In essence Ajax's angry Greek enemies—first Menelaus, then his doublet Agamemnon—try to desecrate Ajax's corpse by preventing his burial on the grounds that he did not respect their political authority. Otherwise put, the bitter and partisan past returns and tries to impose its ugly and self-righteous will on the present. But Sophocles is interested in moving on. Ajax's epic legacy, however troubled, is simply too big, too important, too courageous to fall victim to the unheroic likes of Atreus' sons. Or, as Nietzsche put it, "The errors of great men are venerable because they are more fruitful than the truths of little men."[23] Not that either Menelaus or Agamemnon speak many truths.[24]

After Menelaus exits (1162) Tecmessa enters and at this point Sophocles stages one of the most emotionally charged scenes in Greek drama. Teucer, Tecmessa, and Eurysaces huddle around Ajax's corpse as if it were an altar, a sanctuary, an asylum for the beloved. Around this corpse at center stage, which gradually gathers a certain mysterious power as time passes, the trio of brother, widow, and son conduct a brief put powerful ritual of remembrance and burial (1168-84). After this 'ceremony' Tecmessa, with her young son, remains on stage but does not speak for the final 250 lines; W. B. Stanford imaginatively suggests that this is so because Sophocles wants her to serve "as a symbol of passive grief and as a dumb [silent] protest against the men's self-important language."[25]

When, after the long and acrimonious Teucer vs. Agamemnon debate (1223-1315), Odysseus enters unexpectedly at 1317 the chorus-leader addresses him thus: "Lord Odysseus, know that you have arrived just in time if you're here not to share in the *binding* but rather in the *loosening* of the quarrel." Both Menelaus and Agamemnon have been interested in binding the play and its players to the angry past and for 270 lines Teucer, Ajax's half-brother and guardian, has done his best to ward off their hybris, almost as if he were Ajax warding off the Trojans from destroying the Greek ships. It is a necessary exercise for these men to get into the ring and keep throwing their political punches. The only way to work through the past, especially the angry past, is, as Freud suggested, by calling it up, remembering it, repeating it. But sometimes, in the case of such a contentious past, even after that working-out process, impasse is reached. So it is here. The play needs new energy

---

23   Walter Kaufmann (ed. and trans.), *The Portable Nietzsche* (New York, 1954) p. 30. Nietzsche wrote these words in 1867 at the age of 24.

24   The best discussion I have seen on the play's second 'half' is Philip Holt's "The Debate-Scenes in the *Ajax*" in *American Journal of Philology* 102 (1981) 275-87.

25   W. B. Stanford, *Sophocles: Ajax* (London and Toronto, 1963) p. 205.

and fresh perspective to explode out of its labyrinth of hate and rhetorical gamesmanship. Odysseus brings that new energy by shifting the focus of debate from the political to the ethical. As Ruth Scodel has pointed out, "Odysseus arguments to Agamemnon rest on familiar Greek ethics: justice towards the dead and the gods, recognizing the merit even of an enemy, listening to the wise advice of friends."[26]

By arguing for and obtaining the burial that the small-minded Agamemnon tries to forbid, Odysseus finally frees Ajax from the shame to which he had been inextricably bound and from which he could never liberate himself. I conclude this section by suggesting that after his final exit the perspicacious Odysseus has left behind, as his particular contribution to Ajax's burial rites and to any possible future hero cult, a challenging parable which is as relevant to the man he has saved as it is to each of us. We might set down that Odyssean parable in the following way: Imagine, Ajax, that you visited Apollo's oracle at Delphi and asked not, as Oedipus did, "Who are my parents?" but rather "Why did the gods allow Achilles' armor to go to Odysseus rather than to me?" And imagine, Ajax, that the great god of riddles answered you thus: "Who would you be without your shame?"

The Chorus in *Ajax*

The chorus is the most foreign and perhaps most difficult element of a Greek tragedy for the student to understand. That the chorus, which usually accounts for about 20 to 25% of the text of a Sophoclean tragedy, plays a crucial role is beyond question: just as we are the external audience, they are the internal audience who provide us with an alternative perspective by which to view the events of the plot. In order to survey the role of Ajax's sailors, it will be useful to have the structure of the play before us. A fuller analysis can be found in the two-page synopsis in Appendix 1 but the brief outline below will suffice for our present purpose. Ajax, which has been called the story of 'the destruction of the indestructible man,'[27] can usefully be schematized as follows:

1. Exposition: Ajax's madness, precipitated by Athena's intervention
   (Prologue = 1-133 and Act 1, scene 2 = 201-347)
2. Confrontation #1: friends vs. friends (husband vs. wife)
   (Act 1, scene 2 = 348-595 and Act 2 = 646-92)
3. Climax #1: Ajax's suicide
   (Act 3 = 719-865)
4. Confrontation #2: friends vs. enemies (Teucer vs. Menelaus / Agamemnon)
   (Act 4 = 974-1184 and Epilogue, scene 1 = 1226-1315)
5. Climax #2: Ajax's burial, precipitated by Odysseus' intervention
   (Epilogue, scene 2 = 1316-1420).

This division can be broken into two at the moment when the protagonist, who is on stage only one-fourth of the play (338 lines), leaps on his sword at 865: lines 1-865 prepare for the suicide and lines 866-1420 prepare for the burial. This diptych design follows and may even be the result of the play's double plot of divine and human revenge.[28]

---

26   Scodel, "The Politics of Sophocles' *Ajax*" in *Scripta Classica Israelica* 22 (2003) 42 [31-42].

27   Richmond Lattimore, *Story Patterns in Greek Tragedy* (London, 1964) 53-54.

28   James Tyler "Sophocles' *Ajax* and Sophoclean Plot Construction" *American Journal of Philology* 95 (1974) 36; cf. A. Hinds "Binary Action in Sophocles" *Hermathena* 129 (1980) 51-57.

The first three-fifths of *Ajax* enacts the consequences of Athena's anger which was itself provoked by Ajax's arrogant affronts to her. Indeed the wrath of the vengeful goddess frames the first half of the diptych, appearing prominently in the prologue and in Act Three (Calchas' prophecy, 758-79). The second two-fifths enacts the wrath of Menelaus and Agamemnon who want to desecrate Ajax's corpse in order to avenge his attempted murder of them, an action itself undertaken by Ajax to avenge the awarding of Achilles' armor to Odysseus.

The plot, then, revolves around the suicide and burial of the mighty Homeric warrior. How will Sophocles transform into a tragic hero the pathetic man whom we hear roaring like a bull in his hut (322) even before we see him rolled out on the *eccyclêma* (trolley) at 346-47, blood-stained and prostrate among the cattle he has slaughtered? Certainly Ajax's four memorable monologues and the poignancy of his solitary suicide are one instrument of this transformation. Another is the voice of the chorus, the sailors from his hometown of Salamis and his only remaining friends (349-50, 360) to whom Teucer will entrust the corpse while he goes off to prepare his half-brother's grave (1182-84). Ajax's shipmates present a first-hand account of their leader's prowess, thereby functioning as a consistent foil to the mockery of Athena and the slander of the Atreus' two sons. It is from the chorus that we come to appreciate Ajax as a hero who deserves praise.[29] Just as the loving Tecmessa opens up a private and female perspective on her husband, so the loyal sailors reveal a public and male perspective. They fear dishonor (143, 174), loss of homecoming (900-1) and even, along with their leader, stoning to death by the angry Greek army (227-9, 254; cf. 728).

From the outset Sophocles reveals a deep bond of friendship between the sailors and their captain. The entry song (*parodos*), moving from marching anapests (134-170) to more emotional lyrics (171-200), pleads with the absent hero to refute the rumors of his madness. The chorus' petition is followed immediately and unusually by a lyric dialogue (201-62) where Tecmessa's anapests respond to the chorus-leader's lyrics. This, in turn, is succeeded by still more dialogue, now in calmer iambic trimeters (263-347). Then a second lyric dialogue (348-429) follows, commencing with the long-postponed entry of Ajax. Here the chorus-leader speaks (in iambic trimeters) while the actor sings (in lyrics), a striking reversal of the normal modes of delivery which serves to evoke the tragic pathos of the scene.[30]

The degree of choral participation at the beginning of the tragedy is extraordinary.[31] In one form or another the sailors are involved in the first 296 lines following the prologue. Throughout the first half of Act One (201-429), up until the Ajax-Tecmessa debate (430-595, which is the first of four debate scenes), the chorus becomes virtually a second actor, speaking some 56 lines (compared to 71 for Ajax and 101 for Tecmessa).[32] Indeed besides Tecmessa they are the only other participant in Act One until Ajax's entrance at 338. Nowhere else in extant Sophocles are there two formal lyric dialogues in one act. This strategy of involving the chorus so intensely in the narrative has several important

---

29   Hugh Parry, *The Lyric Poems of Greek Tragedy* (Toronto and Sarasota, 1978) 117.

30   R. W. B. Burton, *The Chorus in Sophocles' Tragedies* (Oxford, 1981) 17.

31   Cynthia Gardiner, *The Sophoclean Chorus* (Iowa City, 1987) 52.

32   *Ibid.*, 52.

effects. Dramatically it maintains the tense atmosphere created by the mystery of what has happened to Ajax. Secondly it makes immediately apparent the degree to which the chorus' well-being depends upon their captain. For although Ajax's shipmates are shield-bearing warriors (565) who fought at Troy with him (201-2), they are more dependent on the protagonist's fate than any other surviving Sophoclean chorus.[33]

The revelation of Ajax's full character comes progressively through his four main speeches (187 lines in total) between verses 430 and 865. The third and fourth of these speeches are at the heart of the tragedy and Sophocles uses his chorus brilliantly to emphasize their centrality. The second choral song (= the first stasimon, 596-645) laments the hero's reversal of fortune and his 'god-sent madness' (611). Ajax unexpectedly returns to stage and delivers his 'deception' speech (646-92); these 47 lines constitute the entirety of Act Two; this is the only instance in extant tragedy of one speech comprising the whole of an act.[34] The surprised chorus immediately sings a song of joy (693-718) celebrating their hero's apparent yielding and his change of mind. This is the first of four "joy-before-catastrophe" odes in surviving Sophocles. Aelius Donatus, the most famous grammarian of the fourth century A.D., referred to this type of song as a method for dramatic 'stretching out' or 'intensification.'[35] To judge from the fact that there are no such odes in the six (or seven) surviving plays of Aeschylus and only one in the eighteen of Euripides it may well be a technique invented by Sophocles.[36] Besides intensifying suspense and highlighting the contrast between elation and subsequent sorrow, this 'stretching out' device conveys, in a very short space, two of Sophocles' favorite themes, namely the fallibility of human reasoning and its thematic soul-mate, the mutability of human fortune.

From a structural point of view, then, Ajax's 'deception' speech is preceded by a choral lamentation and succeeded by a choral celebration. Sophocles' unique method of framing this controversial monologue underscores its importance. His framing of the protagonist's next speech is even more striking. Just prior to Ajax's suicide soliloquy the chorus leaves the orchestra (814). Dividing up into two search parties, the sailors hurry off by opposite ramps. Then the scene changes from the hero's hut to some desolate place near the Trojan seashore during which time both orchestra and stage are vacant—a rare scenario in Athenian tragedy. This is an extraordinary moment of silence and stillness after all the noise and commotion. Nowhere else in extant Sophocles is there a choral exit in mid-play; and nowhere else is there a scene change.[37] The evacuation of orchestra and stage allows for the isolation of Ajax so that he can commit suicide. The dramatist's framing of the hero's final soliloquy (815-65) by a divided choral exit (814) and a divided choral entry (866) so decisively secludes the soliloquy that it becomes, like the 'deception' speech, practically an act in itself.

---

33   David Seale, *Vision and Stagecraft in Sophocles* (London, 1982) 161.

34   Taplin, *Greek Tragedy in Action* (London, 1978) 128.

35   Albin Lesky *Greek Tragic Poetry*, trans. M. Dillon (New Haven and London,1983) 127 and *A History of Greek Literature*, trans. James Willis and Cornelis de Heer (New York, 1966) 277-78.

36   Burton, *The Chorus in Sophocles' Tragedies* (Oxford, 1981) 31; the Euripidean example is *Heracles* 763-814.

37   Taplin, *The Stagecraft of Aeschylus* (Oxford, 1977) 375 reviews the five examples of a chorus departing during a tragedy.

Ajax leaps on his sword at 865 in full view of the audience, or at least so I have argued for the reasons set forth above; this is only *onstage* suicide in surviving tragedy.[38] Two half-choruses immediately re-enter the orchestra in disorder and from opposite sides of the theater, still searching for their leader. This unique choral re-entry begins with a rare a-strophic dialogue between the two leaders of the semi-choruses (866-78). Their exchange serves as a second choral entry song (*epi-parodos*), a phenomenon unparalleled in extant Sophocles.[39] The play now virtually starts over and it does so, appropriately, with a second search scene that mirrors the play's beginning when Odysseus was searching for Ajax.[40] After the chorus has reunited (879) they continue to search the orchestra before being suddenly interrupted by Tecmessa's cries and her discovery of the corpse (891). This begins a long and complex third lyric dialogue (891-960). Just as the first choral entry song (*parodos*) was followed by a lyric dialogue between the chorus and Tecmessa, so too is the second choral entry song (*epi-parodos*).

As the second half begins, then, and the descent of the hero is beginning to shift into ascent, Sophocles has pulled out all the dramatic stops. David Seale observes that one of the ironies of Ajax's suicide is that at the very moment when the chorus returns to save him, he has found his own salvation and by his death will save them.[41] Indeed we see this enacted on stage. Just as the salvation of Ajax's honor is epitomized by the final funeral procession (1409-20), so, too, the chorus' honor is saved by their inclusion in his last rites. Oliver Taplin, speaking of the two exits of the sailors in Ajax, puts it well: "Earlier the chorus had dispersed in disarray on a lost cause: now they march together on a mission which leads to a secure success, even as it marks the final fate of the tragic hero."[42]

In each half of the play, then, Sophocles has used his chorus provocatively to capture the pathos of Ajax's descent into shame and subsequent ascent into honor. It is noteworthy, too, that the 362 lines of the chorus are evenly divided between the three lyric dialogues and four lyric songs. This equal apportionment reflects Sophocles' artful integration of his chorus into the action of the drama.[43]

IV. Ajax Elsewhere in Sophocles

Sophocles' three other (now-lost) plays on the Ajax story

Teucer

Sophocles' now-lost *Teucer* presented a sequel to the events of *Ajax* and dealt with the return of Teucer to Salamis from Troy, his banishment by his father for failing to protect Ajax (cf. *Ajax* 1007-19), and his departure to Cyprus where he was commanded to found another Salamis. Its characters included Oileus (father of the 'Lesser' or Locrian

---

38   Evadne leaps onto an *offstage* funeral pyre in Euripides' *Suppliant Women*, 1071.

39   Taplin, *Greek Tragedy in Action*, 148-50 and *The Stagecraft of Aeschylus*, 379-80, 384-85.

40   J.C. Kamerbeek, *Sophocles' Ajax* (Leiden, 1953) 178; R. P. Winnington-Ingram, *Sophocles: An Interpretation* (Cambridge, 1980) 57.

41   Seale, *Vision and Stagecraft in Sophocles*, 166.

42   Taplin, *Greek Tragedy in Action*, 42.

43   The material in this section on the chorus has been adapted from Stephen Esposito "The Changing Roles of the Sophoclean Chorus" *Arion* 3rd series, 4. 1 (Spring 1996) 86-89 [85-114].

Ajax) and Odysseus (who perhaps, if *Ajax* itself is any indication, pleaded to Telamon on Teucer's behalf). There is a lovely fragment (#577) that records Telamon's sorrow on hearing of Ajax's death: "Oh my son, what an empty pleasure I took delight in when I heard you praised as though you were alive. For the Fury, escaping my notice in darkness, fawned on me, deceived in my joys." The play was produced sometime before 423 B.C.E. and perhaps even before *Ajax*. Aeschylus (525-456) wrote a now-lost tragedy, *Women of Salamis*, the third play of his *Ajax* trilogy, which dealt with the same story.

Eurysaces

From Sophocles' *Eurysaces* there survives only one word ('unexpected'). It would have been good to learn what kind of son Eurysaces became after his father's suicide and after the banishment of his uncle Teucer by his grandfather Telamon.

Ajax the Locrian

Sophocles' now-lost *Ajax the Locrian* told the story of the 'Lesser' Ajax, son of Oileus, a brutal man who once "in his anger at Amphimachus cut off his head from his soft neck and threw it spinning like a ball through the throng of fighters. And it fell in the dust at the feet of Hector." (*Iliad* 13.202-5). Athena's wrath against the 'Lesser Ajax' was fierce because from her shrine in Troy he dragged away both the sacred prophetess Cassandra (to rape her) and the goddess's own wooden image. Ironically the 'Lesser' Ajax was temporarily spared when he took refuge at Athena's shrine. But for his outrageous misdeeds the indignant Greeks themselves wanted to stone him to death. In the event Poseidon drowned him in a terrible storm because Ajax boasted that he did not need the help of the gods to survive the shipwreck (*Ody.* 3.135, 4. 499-511, Euripides, *Trojan Women* 69-71, 171). In *Ajax the Locrian* Athena appeared on stage (in the place of the Greek seer Calchas, who appears in *Ajax*) and announced to the Greeks her wrath at the 'Lesser' Ajax.

V. Ajax in Athenian History

Ajax and his family played an important role in the history of sixth and fifth century Athens. Ajax was known to the Athenians as a great hero in three ways. First, of course, because of his prowess as a warrior in Homer's *Iliad*. (c. 750 B.C.E.) That fame is reflected in several Athenian drinking songs: "Son of Telamon, Ajax, spearman, they say that after Achilles you were the best of the Greeks to come to Troy." And another: "Telamon, they say, was the first among the Greeks to come to Troy; and Ajax second, after Achilles." Odysseus expresses a similar sentiment at *Ajax* 1340-41.

Second, Ajax was known from Athenian tribal cult. In 508/7 the founder of Athenian democracy, Cleisthenes, reorganized the city into ten tribes which were named after mythical heroes. Who were these 'heroes'? As Philip Holt explains, "A *hêrôs*…is a person who has died but who continues to exercise unusual power over human life and who demands worship at his (or sometimes her) grave. Heroes are not honored because they are good; they are appeased and conciliated because they are powerful and dangerous…The debate on Ajax's burial at the end of Sophocles' play is important partly because a proper funeral and a recognizable tomb are generally prerequisites for a hero-cult."[44]

---

44   Holt in "Sophocles' *Ajax* and the Ajax Myth" in *The St. John's Review* 33.3 (1983) 59 [51-61].

The 'heroes' of Athenian democracy were chosen by the oracle of Apollo at Delphi from a large list of names submitted by the Athenians. The ninth of the ten tribes was called the *Aiantis* after *Aias* (Ajax). Each tribe had its own officials, sanctuaries, and religious calendars. A bronze statue of each of the ten heroes stood in the city's famous Monument of the Eponymous Heroes which was built (probably) c. 430-25 in the Athenian agora (market-place). One of the reasons the Greeks had hero cults was to invoke their renowned ancestors for aid in battle; an obvious offshoot of such hero worship is the Christian cult of saints, although Greek heroes were hardly saints. Despite being one of the famed ten eponymous heroes of Athens, Ajax did not originally have a hero shrine on the mainland of Attica (the district in which Athens was located); this is because he was born and raised in Salamis which stood outside the local tribal divisions and was not part of Attica.

Eurysaces, Ajax's son, did have a hero shrine in Attica and it was here that Ajax's cult was introduced, perhaps as a result of Cleisthenes' reforms in the late sixth century. Eurysaces' sanctuary, called the *Eurysakeion*, was established c. 560 in the *deme* (village) of Melite just west of the Athenian agora; decrees of the 'Ajax' tribe were displayed there (Pausanias I.35.3). The reason that Eurysaces had a hero shrine in Attica and his father originally did not is as follows. Eurysaces and his brother Philaeus (not mentioned in Sophocles' *Ajax*) are said to have adopted Athenian citizenship in exchange for handing over Salamis to the Athenians (Plutarch, *Solon* 10). Eurysaces moved to Athens; his brother Philaeus moved to Brauron (on the east coast of Attica) where the *deme* of Philiadai was named after him. Also named after him was the distinguished and powerful aristocratic family of the Philaids who were opponents of the Peisistratid tyrants in the 540s and later. Among the most famous progeny of this family were two great fifth-century Athenian generals of the Persian Wars, Miltiades (hero of the Battle of Marathon, 490, where the *Aiantis* tribe held the right wing) and his son Cimon (Battle of Eurymedon, 469). And the most important Athenian religious festival, the Great Panathenaea in honor of Athena, was said to be founded in the 566/5 by Hippocleides, the chief magistrate (*archôn*) of Athens and member of the Philaid clan.

Thirdly, Ajax's family was known through military history. Telamon and Ajax were invoked as allies by the Greeks before the famous naval battle at Salamis in 480 (against the Persians of King Xerxes). After their victory, which made the island of Salamis instantly famous, the Athenians dedicated a captured Phoenician warship to Ajax (Herodotus 8.64; 121). Sometime later a commemorative festival, the *Aianteia*, was established on Salamis in which teenage boys (*ephebes*) had an important role, thus linking the upcoming generation to the traditions of their deceased ancestors. This *Aianteia* remained a major cultic festival until at least the 2nd century. The close bond between Athens and Salamis, which can be seen in numerous passages in Sophocles' *Ajax*, is reflected by the fact that one of the two special state *triremes* (swift 200-man warships) used by Athens on sacred embassies and official business was named the 'Salaminia' (cf. Thucydides 3.33).

VI. Ajax's Afterlife

In one of the most poignant scenes in Greek literature, the homeward-bound Odysseus tells of his attempted reconciliation with Ajax during his descent to the Underworld (*Odyssey* 11.538-67):

So I (Odysseus) spoke, and the soul of the swift-footed Achilles
roamed off, huge-striding through the fields of asphodel,
540   rejoicing because I had spoken of his son's renown.
And the other souls of the dead corpses stood grieving,
and each asked after his cares in the upper world.
Only the soul of Ajax, son of Telamon,
had stood apart, **angered** because of the <u>victory</u>
545   which I had won over him alongside the ships, defending my right
to Achilles' armor. His august mother, Thetis, set forth those weapons
as a prize and the sons of the Trojans and Pallas Athena passed judgment.
Would that I had never won <u>victory</u> in a contest like this!
Such a head did the earth cover in a grave because of Achilles' armor,
550   Ajax, who surpassed in beauty and in deeds of war
all the other Greeks except the peerless son of Peleus.
So I addressed him with soothing words:
   "Ajax, son of stately Telamon, could you never, even in death,
   forget your **anger** against me because of these accursed arms?
555   The gods made them a cause of grief for the Greeks,
   such a towering rampart did they lose when you died. And for you
   we Greeks grieved incessantly just as for the head of Achilles,
   son of Peleus, when he died. And no other
   is responsible but Zeus, who hated terribly
560   the army of Greek spearmen, and set this fate for you.
   But come here, king, that you may hear this spoken word and story
   of ours. Restrain your **vehemence** and stubborn spirit."
So I spoke but he did not answer me; no, he went off into the dark under world
among the other souls of the perished dead.
565   And there, despite his **anger**, he might have spoken to me or I to him;
but the soul in my breast yearned to see the souls of the other dead.

Scholars have noted the studied chiastic structure of Odysseus' speech:[45]
   A = forget your anger (553-5)
   B = the gods are to blame (555)
   C = the Greeks grieved for you just as they did for Achilles (557)
   B = Zeus is to blame (558-60)
   A = repress your anger (561-2)

---

45   See esp. Irene de Jong, *A Narratological Commentary on the Odyssey* (Cambridge, 2001) 292-3.

With his soothing speech Homer's master of words tries, but fails, to make his peace by concentrating on Ajax's anger and glossing over his suicide. Odysseus focuses on the cause (his victory in the rivalry over Achilles' armor) and the effect (extravagant Greek lamentation) of Ajax's tragedy and simultaneously shifts the onus of responsibility squarely on the gods. But, as his arresting silence so eloquently testifies, that is not how Ajax saw it then nor sees it now.

Virgil must have had this sublime passage in mind when the spurned Dido, Queen of Carthage, met Aeneas in the Fields of Mourning (*Aeneid* 6.467-74):

> "With such words Aeneas tried to soothe Dido's blazing heart
> as it glared at him with fierce regard, provoking tears.
> *That lady, turned away, kept her eyes fixed on the ground,*
> *her face unmoved by the speech he had begun,*
> *her body staunch as stubborn flint or cragged mountain marble.*
> At length she sped off, still his foe, fleeing
> into a forest of shadows, where her former husband,
> Sychaeus, comforts her cares, lavishing love for love."

About my translation of *Ajax*

I wish to acknowledge the scholarship of many before me from whom I have learned a great deal in working on *Ajax*. In an anthology like this it is not possible to give adequate recognition. In terms of traditional philological commentaries on the ancient Greek text I have found most helpful the work of F. W. Schneidewin (1851), Lewis Campbell (1879), F. A. Paley (1880), R. C. Jebb (1896), J. C. Kamerbeek (1963), W. B. Stanford (1963), Sir Hugh Lloyd-Jones and Nigel Wilson (1990 and 1997), and A. F. Garvie (1998). For various kinds of word searches Georges Rigo's *Sophocle: Opera et fragmenta omnia: Index verborum, Listes de fréquence* (Liège, 1996) has proven invaluable. About stagecraft I have learned much from the work of Oliver Taplin (1978) and David Seale (1982). The translations which I have found most illuminating are those of Robert Whitelaw (1883), George Young (1888), E. P. Coleridge (1893), R. C. Jebb (1896), Sir Hugh Lloyd-Jones (1994), A. F. Garvie (1998), and the collaborative endeavor of Herb Golder and Richard Pevear (1999).

An Essay on Euripides' *Hecuba*
by Robin Mitchell-Boyask

Part I. Introduction

Euripides made his debut at the tragic competitions, one year after the death of Aeschylus, in the Athenian City Dionysia of 455 B.C.E., with a career that lasted roughly a half-century until his death, possibly in Macedon, in 406.[1] During the fifth century the Athenian drama "industry" produced over nine hundred tragedies, and the scholars of Alexandria in the third to second centuries B.C.E. attributed 92 of these to Euripides. Four of these were regarded then as spurious and of the remainder 78 survived intact to Alexandria to be gathered as the Collected Works. Eighteen plays (nineteen if we reject scholarly consensus that the *Rhesus* belongs to a now anonymous fourth-century playwright) have outlasted the dangers of existence on papyrus, parchment and paper. In antiquity scribes preserved poetry on rolls of papyrus which each could contain a single drama, collected alphabetically. It thus received priority during the Byzantine era, when it became, along with the *Phoenissae* and the *Orestes*, part of the "Byzantine Triad", the three most popular dramas of Euripides which were read by students at school. Such rankings were extended in time when manuscripts, preserved through the Middle Ages, began to be read during the Renaissance, which had already acquired a taste for bloody tragedies such as the *Hecuba* due to the influence of Senecan drama.

The *Hecuba* was composed by Euripides during the middle of his career, with the likely time of first production the mid to late 420s.[2] For the non-specialist reader, the difference between a production date of 425 and 423 is fairly insignificant, since the drama's psychological and moral world is not shaped by the events of any particular year, but by the more general crisis in the Athenian *polis* brought on by the Peloponnesian War (431-404) and by cultural forces such as the Sophists who had unleashed the power of rhetoric and questioned traditional conceptions of morality and religion. With its depiction of violent revenge by a female against her male oppressors, the *Hecuba* stands firmly in the model of Euripides' *Medea* roughly six to eight years before, and its characters and themes point forward to Euripides' (currently) more famous *Trojan Women* a decade later. It shares with both those dramas a concern with the power of persuasion. Its focus on the status of women, those out of power and at the margins of society, and it innovative use

---

1   See Scullion (2003) on the new doubts about this part of the biography of Euripides.

2   We cannot be sure of the exact year of the first production. The drama's metrical usage and content suggest a later date of roughly 423; see Collard (1991) 34-35, though Mossman (1999) 10-11 argues for an earlier date.

of myth characterize Euripides from his earliest extant drama, the *Alcestis* of 438, to his final tragedies, the *Bacchae* and the *Iphigenia at Aulis*, produced posthumously in 405.

The Characters and Myth

Readers of this Greek tragedy, and of others, should always keep in mind that dramatists had a fair amount of freedom in their handling of myth; for example, Iphigenia might be hoisted on a sacrificial altar by her father, as Aeschylus's *Agamemnon* depicts, but she does not necessarily die, as seen in Euripides' *Iphigenia among the Taurians*, wherein she serves as a priestess to Artemis after the goddess had substituted a deer for her at the moment of death. Euripides is generally thought to have treated myth with much more freedom and self-consciousness than Aeschylus or Sophocles had.

In Euripides' *Hecuba*, three named characters should be familiar to a reader with a passing knowledge of Greek mythology and literature: Hecuba, Odysseus and Agamemnon. The concern here should thus be with how Euripides' presentation of them resembles and differs from other texts. Three other characters, Polydorus, Polyxena and Talthybius, are mentioned elsewhere, but are typically not prominent, which leaves Polymestor, who is a creation, it appears, of Euripides. Let us briefly examine the characters in order of their appearance.

Polydorus

In the *Hecuba*, Polydorus is the last surviving son of Hecuba and Priam, while Homer makes him Priam's son by Laothoe and has him killed by Achilles near the start of his rampage following the death of Patroclus (*Iliad* 20.407). In both texts he is a young man, not a boy. Despite the differences in maternity and death, Euripides does remain true to the character's Homeric role in Priam's reported refusal to allow Polydorus to fight, and this tradition likely motivates Euripides' shift of Polydorus to safe-keeping in Thrace. Ghosts seldom appear in the surviving Greek tragedies, and thus likely made a great impact in the theater; Darius, an earlier king of Persia, features in *The Persians* (681) of Aeschylus, who also staged the appearance of the ghost of Clytemnestra (94) in *The Eumenides*. Apparently, Sophocles, in his lost *Polyxena,* brought on the ghost of Achilles as a speaking character.

Hecuba

The old widow of Priam, king of Troy, now a slave to Agamemnon, features most prominently in Books 6, 22 and 24 of Homer's *Iliad*. Her fierce maternal loyalties and protectiveness of her sons characterize her in Homer as in Euripides, though Euripides changes her lineage to make her the daughter of Cisseus, not Dymas (*Iliad* 6.299), with a Thracian lineage. Most poignant in Book 22 of the *Iliad* is her exposure of her maternal breasts, while utterly distraught at Hector's impending death, in the effort to convince Hector to come inside the Trojan walls to escape Achilles. Euripides does not veer far from Homer's depiction of Hecuba's ferocious hatred of her great son's destroyer (*Iliad* 24.212-14): "I wish I could bite into the middle of his liver and consume it." In both texts she is a suffering old woman, but not a completely passive figure, since she would defend her children at any cost to others and to herself. Polymestor's prophecy of her transformation into a dog is likely a Euripidean innovation; see the discussion in the notes below. In the

Hecuba, she serves as Agamemnon's slave, while in *The Trojan Women,* produced roughly a decade later, she is assigned, much to her horror, to Odysseus.

Polyxena

The last virgin daughter of Hecuba and Priam; her sole surviving sister, Cassandra, has become Agamemnon's concubine. The tradition of her sacrifice by Neoptolemus at his father Achilles' tomb goes back at least as far as the lost epic *The Sack of Troy,* and another lost epic, *The Returns Home,* showed Achilles' ghost stopping the Greek fleet from departure. A poem by the lyric poet Simonides and a lost tragedy by Sophocles, *Polyxena,* also depicted Achilles' ghost demanding the sacrifice of Polyxena, a specific demand which is especially significant because the Euripidean drama does not name his desired victim. The shape of the larger Troy myth clearly creates a doublet for the sacrifice of Iphigenia in *Polyxena;* the repetition of virgin sacrifice provides closure to the Trojan War. Euripides returned to this subject at the end of his life in the *Iphigenia at Aulis,* with an Iphigenia who suddenly chooses death in sacrifice; indeed, Polyxena's speech at her sacrifice seems almost a dry run for Iphigenia's testimony (albeit more ironic) roughly twenty years later.

Odysseus

Achilles and Odysseus were the two greatest Greek warriors who fought at Troy. In the Homeric tradition he is renowned for his intelligence and his skill as an orator, though the *Odyssey* depicts him often as a trickster. While other sections of the larger Epic Cycle likely darkened the essentially ethical hero in Homer, his reliance on stratagems and his persuasiveness made him, on the Athenian stage, a ready representative of the ideas of the Sophists or their students, the demagogic politicians of post-Periclean Athens. Odysseus' reported manipulation of the debate over the sacrifice of Polyxena, and his self-serving justification of the act to Hecuba, would have seemed all too familiar to the original Athenian audience.

Chorus of captive Trojan women

One of the striking paradoxes of Greek tragedy is that the communal voice of the Greek chorus often comes from characters who are not central members of the theater's community. While the male elders of the *Antigone* or *Oedipus Tyrannus* seem natural vehicles for communal sentiments to the all or overwhelmingly male audience, it might come as a surprise, given the context of performance, that the chorus is made up of slave women, prisoners of war before an audience whose members are grappling with what to do with prisoners in their own war.

Talthybius

Talthybius is known in the *Iliad* as the herald of Agamemnon whose "voice was like a god" (19.250). In this drama he delivers the first "messenger speech," a substantial narrative that occurs in almost every extant Greek drama, that allows the playwright to represent significant actions without a substantial change of scenery or to represent deaths that were not (or could not be) shown in the theater itself. This messenger speech is unusual in that it occurs very early in the dialogue (Polymestor's account of his punishment is another surrogate messenger speech) and in that its speaker is not anonymous. Since he, a common soldier, is the only Greek who displays both genuine pity for Hecuba and admiration for Polyxena, we might surmise that he is serving as a foil to show further the moral inadequacies of the Greek leaders.

Agamemnon

King of Argos and leader of the Greek army at Troy, Agamemnon here, as in virtually every other work of Greek literature in which he appears, is shown to be a weak, vacillating leader whose capabilities and character clearly are not suited to the demands of his responsibilities. Just as his selfish mistakes in Book 1 of Homer's *Iliad* unleash the wrath of Achilles, so too in Euripides' *Hecuba* he seems more determined to preserve his own position and keep his hands clean than to do the right thing.

Polymestor, king of Thracian Chersonese

There is no surviving evidence from antiquity of a Polymestor before Euripides' *Hecuba,* and Euripides does not given any ancestry to Polymestor, which further suggests Polymestor was his invention and characteristic of the plot's "Thracianized" content; Achilles' tomb is located in Homer (*Odyssey* 24.82) on the coast of Troy, across the Hellespont from where Euripides places it, and Euripides innovates Hecuba's ancestry to make it Thracian (perhaps to foreshadow her violent reaction to her son's murder). Euripides makes the setting of this drama integral with its events. Polymestor seems as harsh morally as the climate of the land that he rules, a climate that affects the Greek army when it votes for human sacrifice.

Plot and Unity

A summary: the ghost of Polydorus, son of King Priam and Queen Hecuba of Troy, forecasts the discovery of his corpse and the sacrifice of his sister Polyxena, serving alongside her mother as slaves, at the tomb of Achilles. When news reaches them of the decision to sacrifice Polyxena, Hecuba and her daughter lament her imminent death. Odysseus resists Hecuba's pleas to spare Polyxena or kill Hecuba herself instead. Polyxena surprises all by welcoming death as a liberation from slavery. The Greek herald Talthybius narrates the scene of Polyxena's death, where she shows great nobility and courage. Hecuba's grief is partially ameliorated by this report, and she prepares to see to Polyxena's burial, but when a corpse is brought in she discovers it is not her daughter but her last son, Polydorus, whom Priam had lodged with Polymestor, a king in Thrace, during the Trojan War. Polymestor, upon learning of Troy's fall, immediately murdered his guest in order to get his hands on the gold that had accompanied him for safekeeping. With the tacit complicity of Agamemnon, Hecuba plots her revenge against Polymestor by drawing him into her tent with the promise of news of more gold. Once inside, she and her fellow slaves murder Polymestor's children and blind him. The final scene is a trial in which Agamemnon rules in favor of Hecuba, but the drama dissolves into a furiously bitter exchange of denunciations until Polymestor prophesies both Hecuba's metamorphosis into a dog and Clytemnestra's murder of Agamemnon.

The plot thus falls into two parts and concerns have thus been raised about its unity. As Collard notes (21), "the plot is a revenge action developed from apparent helplessness," a type Euripides uses in *The Children of Heracles* and the *Orestes.* Yet other tragedies, such as the *Heracles,* show a similar essentially bifold division. Conditioned by the simpler, unified teleology of *Oedipus Tyrannus,* scholars have, until fairly recently, condemned such structures. Hecuba's seemingly sudden shift from helpless embodiment of despair to a figure of violent vengeance has contributed to these concerns; is the change in her credible, does she thus become as morally bankrupt as Polymestor, or is there even really a change?

Concerns about unity can be allayed by a greater attention to detail which reveals that the characters themselves see the deaths of Polyxena and Polydorus as linked, that Hecuba's words in the first half do not show a figure devoid of a desire to respond to suffering, and that the drama as a whole is a study in whether morality is conditioned by circumstances. Euripidean dramas typically open with a character who otherwise does not appear in the drama's action giving the background to the plot and an indication of what will occur over the next roughly 75-90 minutes, and the *Hecuba* is no exception, for Polydorus, after initially explaining his murder and the demands of Achilles' ghost, explicitly tells the audience that Hecuba will on this day see both Polyxena's corpse and his own. Euripides, however, does not indicate how, if at all, Hecuba will respond to this discovery. Agamemnon closes the drama with instructions to Hecuba to see to the burial of her children, thus bringing to fruition that early prophecy of Polydorus. The return of Polydorus as a dead body, visible to the audience for much of the second half, provides further signs of dramatic unity, as does the living body of Hecuba, out of sight only for two brief moments during the entire production; first (629-57) in reaction to the report of her daughter's death (and immediately before the arrival of Polydorus' corpse) and the second (1023-43) in order to prepare and perform her punishment of Polymestor. Moreover, Hecuba herself, as she begins to supplicate Agamemnon after the discovery of the murder, worries that (749-50), "Without this man I would not be able avenge my children." Hecuba clearly sees her subsequent actions as a single response to the two deaths.

The text also binds together the deaths of the children through parallel images and verbal echoes. Polydorus' position above the tent of his mother and his demands for a tomb foreshadows in the text's language (and recalls in the sequence of events) Achilles' appearance above his own tomb and demands for honor at that tomb (30-50). Hecuba's portentious dream of a wolf destroying a deer "slaughtered, rent from my knees without pity" (90-91) suggests both the death of Polyxena in its imagery of a victimized animal and the savage murder of Polydorus. The needs of the dead and the burial of children thus join the two actions together into a single movement.

Odysseus, both directly and indirectly, links the two halves of the drama. Directly, he plays a part in the sequence of two debate scenes that show Hecuba's progression from victim to avenger, from failed to successful persuader. A Greek audience would have recognized the structural parallels between the futile attempt to win Odysseus over to her side and her two-fold victory over Polymestor, first in persuading him to enter her tents and second in verbally conquering him in the trial scene at the end. These parallels become stronger, and richer in meaning, when we consider allusions to the *Odyssey* in the blinding of Polymestor and the very meaning of Polymestor's name. Let us consider his name first, by way of discussing two other related names. The prefix "poly-" is attached to the names of three characters here, Polyxena, Polydorus, and Polymestor, creating names that resonate in the themes and language of the drama as a whole. The Greek adjective *poludôros* in Homer means "bringing her family a great dowry,"[3] a meaning which, of course, would not apply to Polydorus but to his sister, and, in fact, Polyxena's future as a slave and not a bride who fetches a great price for her parents (350-66) figures prominently in her acceptance of her death, and, moreover, her death insures that she will only ever be the proverbial Bride of Hades, the girl who, like Persephone, marries Death. So his name is somewhat ironic, and this irony is furthered when we consider his name as also meaning "many gifts," and the text signals this meaning by the parallels between Polydorus, the man of many gifts who actually has none, and the Achilles who believes he is *adôrêtos*, "lacking gifts," when he is the most honored of all warriors. The name of his sister, Polyxena, functions similarly, as it means "the host of many." Walter Burkert has speculated that her name points to a possible ancient practice where, before a maiden was sacrificed, she had to offer herself to all participants in a hero's funeral.[4] While we cannot verify the relevance of this practice to the *Hecuba*, still her name points to the theme so important to this tragedy, the *xenia*, or guest-host relationship. While the *xenia* will be discussed fully below, for now it should be noted that an adjective cognate with Polyxena's name (*poluxenos*) is used elsewhere in Euripides as a description for the perfect host, Admetus (*Alcestis* 569), and her brother has been murdered by his own host. The names of Polydorus and Polyxena thus point to each other in a shared experience of the drama's themes.

The name Polymestor further unifies the action as it evokes Hecuba's opponent in her first debate, Odysseus, with her second, Polymestor himself. *Mêstôr* means counselor, adviser, or deviser; so *polumêstor* suggests "he who counsels much," or "the man with many devices." Both in sound and sense this strongly resembles *polumêtis* ("of many counsels or devices"), one of the epithets that most strongly characterizes Odysseus in Homeric epic.[5] As Justina Gregory has observed, one of the *Hecuba*'s primary concerns is with the separation of morality from power, and this schism figures most prominently in the actions of Polymestor and Odysseus; the latter manipulates the debate of the response to the vague demands of Achilles' ghost so that the sacrifice of Polyxena, who has already suffered greatly, suddenly becomes the only possible solution to their problems. Yet Euripides presents an Odysseus so utterly inhuman that he does not even argue that Polyxena must die in order for the fleet to depart; he simply argues for the need to honor an army's warriors as much as possible.[6] Odysseus' specious appeal to the need to preserve the viability of the warrior code is matched by Polymestor's justification of the murder by appeal to a future invasion of the region in order to find the last surviving son of Hecuba and Priam. Hecuba, however, is able to defeat the second man of many devices, because she has already shown his lust for gold and trapped him in an obvious show of duplicity.

A further link between Polymestor and Odysseus, though a more tangled one, is that Hecuba's blinding of Polymestor is modeled on Odysseus' of the Cyclops Polyphemus in

---

3   *Iliad* 6.394, *Odyssey* 24.294

4   Burkert (1983) 67.

5   E.g. *Iliad* 1.311, 3.200, 4.329; *Odyssey* 2.173, 4.763, 5.214. Note, though, that *mêtis* and *mêstôr* derive from different verbs.

6   Mossman is succinct here, (1999) 117: "Euripides ruthlessly undercuts his moral standing by clever manipulation of the standard rhetorical ploys he gives him to speak." Mossman's book is valuable in many ways, not least for its examination of rhetoric.

Book 9 of Homer's *Odyssey*.[7] One needs to be careful about too exact a comparison here as otherwise one winds up with a pat formula like "Polyphemus=Polymestor, therefore Odysseus=Hecuba," which creates obvious problems in itself. It does, however, seem likely that Euripides wants us to see Hecuba adopting Odyssean guile here to mutilate a monstrous figure whose murderous behavior evokes the Cyclops, the eater of Odysseus' men and violator of the guest code. As Polymestor is made more inhuman as a result of the comparison, so is Hecuba elevated in stature. But I think the connection between the name of Polymestor and the epithet of Odysseus, combined with Hecuba's stated concern with avenging both of her children, shifts the impact of the allusion to the *Odyssey* to make her vengeance actual on Polymestor and symbolic on Odysseus. Moreover, the linkage of Polymestor and the Odyssean Polyphemus would be even more compelling and appropriate if, as some believe, Euripides' *Cyclops* was the satyr play that followed the *Hecuba* and the two other Euripidean tragedies that year.[8]

The trial scene, then, brings back the assembly and the world of Athens and re-inforces the larger arc of the action as a set of scenes mirrored in each half of the drama. Political debates and trial scenes, while anachronistic, are characteristic of Athenian drama. Athens had a fully developed court system and its language and concerns frequently appear in Athenian drama, starting with the trial of Orestes in the final part of Aeschylus' *Oresteia*, the *Eumenides*. Indeed, from the virgin sacrifice to female vengeance to the court scene itself, the *Hecuba* alludes to many aspects of the *Oresteia*.[9] Yet, just as the political assembly depicted in the first half of the *Hecuba* shows an ailing body politic easily manipulated by demagogues, so too does its end depict a trial that, unlike its Aeschylean prototype, does not prevent violence, but merely punishes it, and points to its continuation after the stage action has ended.

Part II. Interpretive Essay

Euripides' *Hecuba* is, to my mind, the single most disturbing of the surviving Greek tragic dramas. It opens, uniquely, with the ghost of an adolescent male describing the mutilation of his body at the hands of a family friend, and it ends with a blazingly dissonant *fortissimo* of angry emotions, as first two and then three characters violently denounce each other. No other Greek tragedy, not even the *Medea*, goes out of its way to make its audience so uncomfortable from the first line to the last. At the very least it belongs to that rarified category that George Steiner has termed "absolute tragedy," in which "the absolute despair, the nihilism in respect of hope" has been obliterated by the drama's events.[10] Steiner includes in this group the *Hecuba, Bacchae, Trojan Women* and *Antigone*. I believe that *Hecuba* goes even further than these other three in its portrayal of the wreckage of human character and in its utter denial of any form of redemptive suffering. These aspects appeal universally to the emotions of modern audiences, yet they must have

---

7   See the essays on the *Hecuba* in Segal (1993) and Zeitlin (1996). Mossman's warnings (1999) 191-92 against oversimplifying the allusion are well heeded.

8   Thus argues William Arrowsmith in the introduction to his translation of the *Cyclops*, in *The Complete Greek Tragedies, Euripides*, volume 2, eds. D. Grene and R. Lattimore (Chicago 1956).

9   On the relationship between Euripides' *Hecuba* and Aeschylus's *Oresteia* see Thalmann (1993).

10   Steiner, "Tragedy Pure and Simple", 538 in Silk (1996).

been equally shattering to ancient ones, and in no small part because *Hecuba* enacts the violation and perversion of several central codes of Greek ethics. Following my exploration of these terms, I shall discuss the themes of slavery and necessity as they are embodied by the Chorus, as well as exploring the role of the Chorus in Euripides' *Hecuba*.

Euripides' *Hecuba* and the Crisis of Values

Reciprocity was the driving force in much of the Greek value system governing relations between human beings and between humans and gods.[11] Several Greek ethical terms, which are all related and lack simple English equivalents, are key to the moral crisis of the *Hecuba*. The reader meeting these terms for the first time should not feel immediately at sea or panicked at the potential conceptual baggage, since, I submit at the risk of a gross exaggeration, this world of reciprocal relations is not completely alien to certain monuments of American culture, such as the *Godfather* films, which represent a world where "favors" are given and expected in return, as is violence. My own students have seen such similarities. So these Greek ethical terms might not be so completely alien after all. The first is *xenia*, the institution of the guest-host relationship that established alliances across generations between families, after initially guaranteeing the security of both guests and hosts from the first contact among strangers.[12] The second is *aidôs* the sense of recognition, reverence, respect, even shame, towards someone of a particular status or with whom one has a special relationship.[13] Then there is *kharis*, the idea of reciprocal gratitude. Next, suppliancy, *hiketeia*, requires that the person supplicated answer and protect the supplicant.[14] Last, blood sacrifice is an institution of reciprocity between gods and men. Each of these five concepts suffers violation, inversion or perversion during the course of the *Hecuba* and their violation leads directly the most unsettling of all Greek reciprocal actions: vengeance. Let us now examine how each works in the drama.

Xenia

The debasement of the guest-host relationship lies at the heart of the *Hecuba's* plot and in some respects is the easiest Greek concept to understand here. The violation of the *xenia* is prevalent throughout the myths of the Trojan War and Homeric epic. Paris absconds with Helen and much of Menelaus' property while acting as Menelaus' innocent guest in Sparta; Zeus, in his cult guise as protector of the *xenia* authorizes the Trojan War to avenge this criminal act. In Book 6 of the *Iliad* the Trojan ally Glaucus and the Achaean warrior Diomedes decide not to fight when they discover their ancestors were guest-friends, and they renew their alliance with an exchange of armor. From its first book, the *Odyssey* is replete with scenes of guests being entertained by their hosts, or not. The suitors of Penelope, refusing to leave her house until she chooses one of them, are certainly bad guests, but they also manage to be simultaneously bad hosts when they do not welcome the disguised Athena and later abuse Odysseus when he masquerades as an old beggar; the suitors, like the Trojans, die for such crimes. And the cannibalistic

---

11   On reciprocity in Greek culture see Seaford (1994), and Gill, Postlethwaite and Seaford (1998).

12   M. I. Finley (1979).

13   Cairns (1993).

14   Gould (2001).

Cyclops Polyphemus certainly asks for his blinding when he scorns the Zeus who protects guests; on the other hand, Odysseus and his men certainly are not model guests either! "All strangers (*xenoi*) are protected by Zeus," exclaims Nausicaa (6.207-8), the daughter of Odysseus' final hosts before his return to Ithaca. One thus harms the guest at considerable peril to one's own life.

The Thracian king Polymestor virtually guarantees his own destruction when he kills the young Polydorus, sent by his father Priam to Polymestor because of the latter's status as a guest-friend, a *xenos*. The greed of Polymestor for Priam's gold overwhelmed his morality. The text is quite insistent on this point, introducing it early and reminding us of it continually. Polymestor is introduced as the guest-friend (*xenos*) of Priam (7). When Polydorus describes his murderer, it is not by name, but by status: "my father's guest-friend slays me." Hecuba similarly, at her horrid realization of her son's death, immediately identifies the killer not as Polymestor but as (710) "my guest-friend," and immediately then asks (715) "Where is the justice of guest-friends?" When Agamemnon asks Hecuba who killed her son, she again says (774), " The Thracian guest-friend killed him." Begging for Agamemnon's help, Hecuba stresses the particular nature of Polymestor not as a simple murder, but a murder of a guest-friend (789-96). She hammers away at this identification of Polymestor as an impious *xenos* (853, 890, 1096, 1216, 1234) until Agamemnon pronounces his judgment of Polymestor in the same language (1243-5):

> To my mind, so that you know, you seem to have done a favor neither to me
> nor to the Achaeans by killing a man who was a guest-friend,
> but merely so that you could have the gold in your own home.

Polymestor, during the trial scene, attempts to justify the murder as an act of *kharis* to the Greek army. Here at least, one reciprocal relationship holds more moral weight than another. One final irony with this concept is that the name of her other dead child, Polyxena, evokes this very relationship: "she who is the guest-friend of many."

Aidôs

Such a complex set of ideas and emotions involving inhibition are bound up with *aidôs*: respect, fear, shame, reverence. Euripides, so seemingly preoccupied with human psychology and motivation, is particularly interested in its elusiveness. In the *Hippolytus*, produced only a few years before the *Hecuba*, Phaedra, struggling with her unexpressed passion for her stepson Hippolytus, speculates, enigmatically, that the are two types of *aidôs*, one good, the other bad, as each motivates a different behavior. *Aidôs*, despite its seemingly inwardly-directed nature, is in fact bound up with these other forms of social obligations. Indeed, *aidôs* could be described as the emotion that drives the adherence to the *xenia* and suppliancy codes.

Polymestor's failure to respect his duties to Polydorus could be described as a failure of *aidôs*. Polymestor is literally shameless, completely lacking in a concern for how others might view him and his actions in violating some of his society's most basic norms. Blindness is thus an apt punishment both practically and thematically. Gregory notes that a Greek proverb holds that *aidôs* resides in the eyes, and *aidôs* is the very quality Polymestor has shown himself to lack.[15] Moreover, there is a connection between *aidôs* and its specific incarnation in Polymestor, his violation of the *xenia,* which resonates in one of the models for the blinding scene, the Cyclops episode in Homer's *Odyssey.*[16] For her part, Hecuba first begs Odysseus to have *aidôs* for her after recounting his suppliancy of her in Troy, and then, when Polymestor arrives, she claims that *aidôs* prevents her from looking him in the eye. She thus subtly points out the sense of shame that he lacks.

Kharis

Kharis is almost reciprocity itself, meaning something like favor or gratitude that is felt to be owed to someone. It too is exploited in both parts of the play by those who have no real sense of it. First, Odysseus, summing up his argument that warriors should receive as much visible honor as possible so that they will continue to desire to fight, asserts,"gratitude (*kharis*) lasts a long time." Odysseus seems to suggest that only warriors are worthy of *kharis*, since he has just rejected Hecuba's reminder that he owes her his life. Hecuba, desperate to respond to the death of her children, manipulates this value as she did *aidôs*. In one episode which some critics have seen as marking Hecuba's rapid moral decline, she uses Agamemnon's sexual relationship with her daughter Cassandra to suggest he owes her a "favor" (830). She then tries to win Agamemnon's passive assistance that he not interfere with her actions, closing her argument with the promise that he will not appear to be acting on the basis of *kharis* (874). Polymestor then, in the trial scene, appeals to Agamemnon that he killed Polymestor as a favor (*kharis*) to Agamemnon (1174), and Hecuba throws his language right back at him (1201). It might be significant that Hecuba's oppressor in the drama's first half and her enemy in its second both sophistically use words central to Greek ethics in order to win arguments against her.

Hiketeia

Supplication is a ritualized act in which the suppliant abases himself before a more powerful being and requests assistance or protection. It is part of the same structure of reciprocity as *kharis, aidôs* and *xenia*. Supplication occurs with an expectation of reciprocity, it requires as sense of *aidôs* in order to be effective, and supplication typically takes place between individuals who are not part of the same group; that is, *xenoi*. Physical contact between the players is fundamentally important, since it guarantees the suppliant's status; once the Nurse lays hold Phaedra in the *Hippolytus*, Phaedra cannot deny her requests. As already observed, there are two central scenes of supplication in the *Hecuba* but important also are a refusal to supplicate and the narration of a past act of supplication.

Hecuba figures in all of these acts of supplication. First, she recalls for Odysseus his supplication of her when he was caught by Helen, while he was spying on Troy. He adopted the full suppliant position, on the ground with his hands on Hecuba's knees (245). Foreshadowing his refusal to honor reciprocally Hecuba's request to spare her daughter, he lied to her about his activities. Hecuba now, with the tables turned, drops to her knees

---

15   Gregory (1999) 170.
16   See *Odyssey* 9.269-71 and Cairns (1993) 105-13 on *aidôs* and the concern for guests and guest-friends.

in self-abasement and reaches out to Odysseus (273-75).[17] If Hecuba is in fact touching Odysseus, he must break away either at the beginning or end of his own speech, given Hecuba's subsequent lament about her inefficacy. Polyxena must then present a more formidable suppliant than her mother, or the combined pleas of the mother and daughter would move even the hardened Odysseus, since Polyxena's first words to him describe his attempts to avoid her supplication (342-45). She, however, rejects the very idea of self-abasement, but prefers to reclaim the nobility she had lost when the Greeks enslaved her, which she cannot achieve otherwise. Hecuba last supplicates Agamemnon (750) in order to acquire his assistance in obtaining vengeance against Polymestor. She sinks to her knees and remains there for an extended conversation with Agamemnon; she mentions being on her knees still at 787 and remains there at least until Agamemnon seems to break contact with her at 812. Agamemnon, however, unlike Odysseus, at least acknowledges her suppliancy, yet vacillates between the conflicting imperatives of Polymestor's crimes and Polymestor's relationship with Agamemnon's own army. While Hecuba's suppliancy does not win an active assistance from Agamemnon, it does achieve a passive one, since he leaves her with the knowledge that she is inviting Polymestor to her tents with the intention of doing something to him.

Blood Sacrifice

Just are humans are bound to one another with acts of reciprocity, so too are humans to the gods through the exchange of sacrificial victims. Humans make offerings to the gods, usually in the form of domestic animals, and the gods grant blessings to humans in return.[18] The sacrificers burn part of the animal and cook most of the rest for their own consumption. The sacrifice honors the gods, yet provides its participants with a renewed sense of community and a meal. In Book 1 of Homer's *Iliad*, when Chryses, the Trojan priest of Apollo whose daughter has been taken as a prize for Agamemnon, asks for Apollo's help, he reminds the god of the nice temple he has built for him and the numerous animals he has sacrificed in his honor. Apollo, of course, punishes the Greek army with plague. Later in Book 1, once the Greeks restore Chryses' daughter to him, they perform propitiatory sacrifices to Apollo and consume the results. Sacrifice in the *Hecuba* certainly does not function so cleanly, even beyond the human nature of the victim.

Absent from Homer (save for Sarpedon in *Iliad* Book 16), yet prevalent in Greek tragedy, is another sacrificial institution: hero cult. Greek cities that claimed affiliation with the great heroes of the mythic past worshipped them as semi-divine powers whose local graves could grants blessings and curses, the fertility of the earth and victory in war. We see this most clearly in Sophocles' final tragic drama, *Oedipus at Colonus,* where the grave of Oedipus will grant the city that has welcomed it power in battle over its enemies. Greeks would worship heroes in cult similar to gods, with libations of wine and sacrificial killing of animals, though wine and blood would be poured into the ground

---

17   Gould (2001) 41 says Hecuba's supplication is "figurative" and not enacted. I take her words literally and see an actual supplication which Euripides intended to contrast with Polyxena's refusal to engage in any form of supplication, whether real or figurative. Hecuba does spend much time on the ground in this drama.

18   Burkert (1985) 53-60 provides a brief and clear overview of Greek sacrificial ritual.

over the grave, essentially to give sustenance to the hero's spirit. The emotional power of the apparition of Achilles' ghost and the need to appease it arise from hero cult. Achilles demands honor just like divinities in other Euripidean tragic dramas, such as Dionysus in the *Bacchae* and Aphrodite in the *Hippolytus*. Otherwise, divinity is almost completely absent from Euripides' *Hecuba*, in a sense very reminiscent of its cousin, another tragedy of female vengeance, the *Medea*.

Sacrifice in the *Hecuba* is problematic because it involves a human victim, but also because of the nature of the being demanding it and the distinct lack of clarity in the reasoning for the sacrifice. The sacrifice of Polyxena at the end of the Trojan War is symmetrical with that of Iphigenia before the war and the earlier sacrifice is clearly evoked in Euripides' drama. The comparison is instructive. In Aeschylus' *Agamemnon* the prophet Calchas interprets the inability of the Greek fleet to depart Aulis, combined with the destruction of a pregnant hare by two eagles, as signaling the displeasure of Artemis, an anger that can only be appeased by the sacrifice of Agamemnon's daughter Iphigenia to the goddess. This event, while effective for enabling the departure of the fleet, causes an immense crisis and precipitates the entire action of the *Oresteia*. In the *Hecuba*, however, it is unclear what, exactly, Achilles demands; there is a public debate over its fulfillment, and the sacrifice does not seem to achieve the desired outcome, as the winds refuse to turn favorable after the sacrifice.

The ghost of Achilles, like his living predecessor in Homer's *Iliad*, makes a demand of a prize gift of honor that has a discordant effect on the Achaean army. His demand is not represented directly, but reported through three different sources, leaving the motivation for the sacrifice questionable. First, the ghost of Polydorus announces to the theater audience Achilles' demands for a prize, and specifies Polyxena as the victim (40-41). Yet Polydorus does not state that Achilles is preventing the ships from leaving Thrace, leaving open the possibility that Achilles has so confused the army that it finds itself unable to leave. Odysseus repeats that Achilles requests Polyxena in particular (305, 389) and also does not connect causally the apparition of Achilles with any restraining winds. Hecuba's version of the apparition is that the prize should be "some one of the many-troubled Trojan women", yet not necessarily Polyxena. But the Chorus, which narrates at the greatest length the apparition of Achilles, merely quotes a demand for a prize, with no clear idea of its nature (114-15), and then depicts the debate over how best to honor Achilles, whether with blood sacrifice or not. The Chorus seems to imply that the desire to kill Polyxena in sacrifice comes not from Achilles, but from the assembly of the army and Odysseus. Polyxena, as the only available pure virgin typically chosen in Greek myth to appease divine anger, is, to some members of the assembly, the obvious offering. That Achilles' demands are not causing the inability of the fleet to depart is then suggested by Agamemnon's observation that the continuing ill winds after the sacrifice allow Hecuba the time to act against Polymestor. Agamemnon's comment that "god releases no fair breezes" (901) suggests some other force is at work, since "god" (*theos*) cannot denote Achilles and in prior Greek literature heroes lack the power to control weather. Then, his last lines in the drama note that the winds have arrived to take the Greeks home (1290). How has this happened? Why did the sacrifice fail and Hecuba's revenge seemingly work?

The answer, I believe, lies with the crimes committed against Polydorus and his request to the gods for a proper burial. The laws of guest-friendship, sanctified by the gods, are broken, and a human is offered to a hero in sacrifice, against all cultural norms, and, presumably, divine sanction. Polydorus tells that he has been hovering about his mother's tents for as long as she and her captors have been camped in Thrace, a stay prolonged by the appearance of Achilles (30-35). He has asked the gods for burial by his mother, but this cannot happen if the Greeks leave before his body is discovered. The demands of Achilles and the winds are related only in so far as they have some connection with the gods' desire that Polydorus be buried and the crimes of Polymestor be punished. The gods are, in Segal's words, remote and obscure,[19] but they are, in the end, effective. They accept the vengeful punishment of Polymestor almost as an offering to them, a form of sacrifice.[20] Hecuba thus restores the codes of reciprocity among men and between men and gods.

Yet there is little comforting about this restoration, as it comes with a terrible cost to all concerned with the action. Polyxena's beautiful, noble death provides her with escape from the hated life of slavery, yet it need not have happened at all. Hecuba has now matched her antagonist's brutality. The stylized trial debate over her revenge takes place with the bodies of three murdered children in full view of the audience, with a fourth never out of anyone's mind for long. The drama's ending itself disintegrates into a barrage of angry yelling, prophecies of murder and metamorphosis, and an order to abandon the bloody, blinded murderer on an island. Hecuba, depicted as miserable especially in terms of her lost innocent children, has killed two more, and now she will change into a dog with fiery eyes, a transformation that either suggests her fierce maternal loyalties, or, as I believe, externalizes her inner savagery. No commands to establish new rituals are made, as they so often are at the end of Euripidean tragedies, and so there is no hope of order emerging from this chaos. The final words from an actor are spoken by a character the audience knows will die soon himself once the winds he sees rising carry him home. Indeed the winds themselves are of little comfort, since they are, as the audience likely realized, the harbingers of the god-sent storm that will almost completely destroy the Greek fleet as it attempts to leave the area. The Chorus exits with the concluding observations that they must accept their position as servants in their masters' tents and ships because of harsh necessity, *anankê*. So many Greek tragedies end with what often sounds to us like pithy, trite observations about the many shapes of the gods, or how the gods provide unexpected outcomes to events. Here we find only bleak necessity as the driving force of human existence. Humans have enacted this sequence of events, but with little help or prompting by the gods, who are very remote indeed, and who remain, literally, outside of human consideration at the tragedy's close. Euripides *Hecuba* simply projects nothing positive or constructive into the future.

But what has been projected into the future for the characters has been prophesied by Dionysus, whose theater the original audience of the drama is occupying while they hear Polymestor reply to the astonished, furious Hecuba when she asks him how he knows her future (1287): "The prophet to the Thracians, Dionysus, said these things." The god of theater is the prophet of violence and the metamorphosis of humans into beasts. Earlier (1076), the enraged, blinded Polymestor had similarly linked to Dionysus the murderous female slaves who had helped Hecuba, calling them "the Bacchants of Hades," whom,

---

19   Segal (1993) 219.
20   Mitchell-Boyask (1993).

he believes, would "carve up" his sons, presumably for some kind of horrific feast. This association of Dionysus with metamorphosis, with pedicidal fury and the violation of the most sacred human customs, all in the name of justice, points forward to Euripides' culminating vision roughly fifteen years later in the *Bacchae*. The gods are remote, but they have names. They act mysteriously, and the relation of their power to justice in the lives of the humans in this story is as questioned and contested as is that same relationship in the lives of the humans in Athens who watched this drama in the Theater of Dionysus sometime during the 420s, as the moral chaos of the Peloponnesian War grew in intensity.

The Chorus and the Themes of Euripides' *Hecuba*

The Chorus of Trojan slave women exits the orchestra evoking the power of Necessity, a moment which by itself sums up many of the major themes of Euripides' *Hecuba*. The Chorus throughout this drama serves as a sounding board and focal point for the meaning of the actions articulated by the main characters. This group consists of women of a mix of ages and backgrounds, as typified by the speaking characters of the former Queen Hecuba and the loyal serving woman who presumably had been with her before the sack of Troy. They share their vivid memories of Troy's destruction and their new status as slaves. The protagonist of the drama, unusually, shares the status of the chorus members: a slave, neither higher nor lower, she is like them. Let us now examine the chorus first and then its integration with the drama's main themes.

While the chorus is the one absolutely indispensable part of Greek drama (despite the neglect of it in Aristotle's *Poetics*), it has also been the most difficult to assess properly and thus numerous, and persistent, misunderstandings have arisen over the years.[21] A playwright's participation in the festival of the City Dionysia was completely predicated on his being "granted a chorus" by Athens. The City Dionysia itself can be seen as a choral festival, since, in addition to the dramatic productions, there were choral competitions of dithyrambs (songs in honor of Dionysus), involving dozens of "teams", some of men and others of boys, organized according to deme affiliations which reached across the entire city of Athens. Virtually everybody in the theater audience would have participated in these competitions themselves or had a relative who had done so; the theatrical chorus thus played to an audience of experts. In the theater the chorus dominated each play visually, for it almost never left the orchestra once it entered and their costumes and dancing must have been spectacular, and aurally, for its lyric songs contrasted strongly with the spoken meters of the actors and provided emotional contexts for the experiences of the characters. The chorus, however, was *not* necessarily the vehicle for the poet to express "what he really thought," since the chorus' words were so often driven by the exigencies of the situation. Nor was the chorus, while it frequently served as a communal foil against the heroic egoism of the characters embodied by the actors, necessarily representative of the civic collective of the city of Athens, simply because its identity could be foreign, slave, female, and sometimes all three combined. While the chorus can be the vehicle for more extended

---

21   Three particularly valuable recent essays that focus on the chorus and its role are "A Show for Dionysus" and "Form and Performance," both by P.E. Easterling (36-53 in Easterling 1997) and John Gould, "Tragedy and the Collective Experience" (217-43 in Silk 1996). For a general treatment of the chorus and the ancient evidence for it, see Csapo and Slater (1995) 349-68.

meditations on the meaning of the drama's events, it must be considered a character in the drama. Chorus members express fears, hopes, joy and sadness. A chorus can be confused; indeed, to some a chorus can seem stupid at these moments of confusion (and one might productively compare here the frequent bewilderment of Jesus' disciples in the Gospels). In other words, a dramatist's use of a chorus will shift as the needs of a situation require, so it is better to restrict discussion of the function of the chorus to broad parameters. I thus offer two. First the chorus serves as a sounding board for the events that have occurred in the scene before an ode, offering some initial guidance for the audience to think about those events, even if the initial focus is confusion or terror. The thoughts of the chorus can also prepare the audience for the next scene by considering the possible sequence of events that might ensue; such preparation can involve misdirection by the poet, wherein the chorus establishes an expectation that is frustrated. The chorus thus helps shape the action into the broader parameters of human experience and understanding. Second, the chorus can be agents in that action. Such function ranges from a chorus that conspires with the protagonist but has no physical part, as in the case of the Corinthian Women in Euripides' *Medea* or the Sailors in Sophocles' *Philoctetes*, to a chorus that not only participates, but hounds the protagonist across the stage, as with the Furies in the *Eumenides* of Aeschylus. In some sense, the best ways for us to view the chorus is, first, that the dramatist used it according the particular needs of the individual drama and that this function could shift inside the drama depending on the given situation. Second, the choral voice contrasts with the named heroes on stage and, in the words of John Gould (222), "articulates a collective 'anonymous' experience and response to events. The central, heroic characters of the tragic action struggle to maintain and enforce an individual identity and authority and to impose meaning on the flux events in terms of that identity, the individual 'I'." These comments are broad, yet effectively describe a very diverse range of tragic dramas, from the *Oedipus Tyrannus* to the *Hecuba*.

The Chorus of Euripides' *Hecuba* is typically Euripidean in its identity, since Euripides frequently makes his chorus female, barbarian or slaves (here all three!) but slightly less typical in its organic relationship to the action. Over the centuries, critics, beginning with Aristotle in the *Poetics*, have faulted Euripides' handling of the chorus for being insufficiently connected to its drama's action, but, while such charges are, I believe, overblown and based on unsympathetic readings, the *Hecuba* is certainly one drama that directly refutes them. Its protagonist is "one of them", and they not only commiserate with her, but also conspire with her and assist in her vengeance against Polymestor. Their songs clearly are meditations, often quite moving ones, on their experiences and they are deeply engaged with the events of the drama; like Hecuba, they were once free and now are slaves. They shared the nightmare of Troy's destruction. Gould further comments on the particularly Euripidean nature of choruses that are so frequently women, foreign and captives of war in dramas that are dominated by female protagonists:

> …Euripides simultaneously creates a further perspective, in those plays which place a woman at the centre of the tragic action (and they are a majority of his plays), by setting up a single axis of dramatic tension which aligns, rather than confronts, female protagonist with female chorus and thus enforces a point of view from which the 'heroic' world of men is thus seen as wholly alien: sometimes

frighteningly and violently destructive, sometimes distant and incomprehensible, sometimes despicable and without honour.

Gould's general assessment of Euripidean choruses and their place in the larger dramas fits the *Hecuba* to a tee, for it thus captures the ability of the women to "stay on message" in the face of different heroic male worlds of first Achilles (violently destructive and terrifying) and then Odysseus (without honor) and Polymestor (despicable).

These demands of this male world are so totalizing that they receive the title of Necessity in Euripides' *Hecuba*, and this concept becomes one of the major themes of this drama.[22] In my translation, forms of "necessary" and "necessity" occur fifteen times (and "compel" or "compulsion" another seven), covering a wide range of situations, and almost invariably at crucial moments in the action. Hecuba asks, in response to the news of Polyxena's impending death, "Was it that necessity compelled them to human sacrifice"(260); the question itself implies its own answer. Polyxena's resignation to the act, "Thus shall I submit both for the sake of necessity, and because I desire death." (346-47)," suggests a more contingent form of necessity, an attitude Hecuba then picks up in her plea to Odysseus to kill her alongside Polyxena: "There is great necessity for me to die with my daughter" (396). Later (1237) the Chorus laments how "the laws of necessity" radically alters friendships and enmities among men, and the raging blinded Polymestor prophecies to Hecuba "necessity is that your daughter Cassandra die" (1275). The Chorus then closes the drama with the observation (1295) "necessity does not bend." Those last two instances point towards a more traditional Greek conception of Necessity as part of Moira, the Greek word that most closely approximates our notion of fate, but, for the most part, necessity in the Hecuba seems frequently more a projection of the inner desires of a character, or a pretext used to cover more undesirable actions– political, not moral or cosmic necessity. It seems also to be used to connote the recognition of the harsher realities of human suffering in a world increasingly dominated by power politics or the acknowledgement of an almost Aristotelean inevitability of events once certain actions occur, given human nature. In both of these senses, what is necessary is really what one must accept out of the weakness of one's position. Thus, the Chorus, remembering the events of a decade previously, realizes that pain and disaster became "necessary" as soon as Paris began cutting the wood to make the ship to sail after Helen (629-33). Yet, Necessity, as an impersonal structure of the universe, is closely allied with *Tuchê*, best translated as "Fortune" or "Luck," and Hecuba herself articulates the belief that nobody's *Tuchê* lasts forever, and the rulers will eventually become the ruled, the killers the killed.

Hecuba and her comrades have lived that recognition, having endured slavery, and slavery is our next subject. The primal scene of Greek myth is the destruction of a city, Troy, which functions like the loss of the Garden of Eden in the Greek mythic consciousness, and perhaps the most overwhelming horror, I would suggest, in the literary incarnations of the fall of Troy is what happens to its victims; not to the dead, but to the living. This fear is especially true during the years of the Peloponnesian War, when Greece saw cities annihilated, their men killed and their women taken away into slavery. Sitting in the Theater of Dionysus, watching Euripides' *Hecuba*, would have been men who had

---

22   See Arrowsmith's brief but powerful discussion of this theme, (1959) 490-92.

several years before debated the destruction of the entire population of Mytilene on the island of Lesbos, voting first to condemn all and the next day a reversal, with only those guilty of active rebellion sentenced to death. Roughly a decade later, these men would decide to kill all of the grown men of Melos, enslaving the women and children, because the Melians refused to become part of the Athenian empire. The experience of watching other men act the part of female slaves after their city is ruined in war was not simply an aesthetic one for this audience, since the treatment of prisoners of war surely was an issue being debated with regularity in Athens.

The reality of the loss of freedom is depicted with great regularity in Greek drama, from Aeschylus' *Suppliant Women* through the late dramas of Euripides. It is thus important for a modern American reader to keep in mind that slavery in classical Greece differed from American slavery before the Civil War in being based on the success (or lack thereof) in war and not on skin color. Defeat in battle meant death or slavery, and, thus for the Greeks there was a fate worse than death: slavery. While some slaves served as tutors for children in prosperous families, many others suffered terribly laboring in the silver mines which Athens owned and which helped finance the wars in which these human beings might became slaves. The slaves in Euripides' *Hecuba* and Hecuba herself lament that they did not die at the sack of Troy. Polyxena sees her own death as a form of liberation from her slavery. The sociologist Orlando Patterson has seen in the slave choruses of Greek tragedy, especially in those of Euripides, an expression of "a powerful drive for personal freedom"[23] that represented the deep preoccupation in Athenian thought with liberty. In the funeral oration of Pericles which Thucydides preserves in his *History of the Peloponnesian War*, Pericles regularly circles back to the fundamental concept and reality of freedom that drive the conduct of their struggle against Sparta. In Pericles' speech, Patterson observes, "personal freedom is here defined in terms of an antithesis to slavery."[24] Thus, to an Athenian watching Euripides' *Hecuba*, the experiences of Hecuba, Polyxena and the Chorus of Trojan women represent his deepest fears. Slavery, and the fear of it, drives the drama's themes and imagery; the constant references to light and dark, to eyes and blindness, are metaphors for freedom and slavery. We see this expressed with particular power in Polyxena and Polymestor. As Polyxena expresses her desire to die she proclaims, "From free eyes I release this light" (366-67)" and then, further preparing for death, "now I shall behold the sun's final ray and circle," and even her final lines evoke her departure from the sun of the living (435). The metaphorical complement to Polyxena's free eyes is the blinding of Polymestor, since, set in such a context, "the gouging out of eyes, then, must mean the destruction of a person's freedom."[25] Euripides underscores Hecuba's approximation of Polymestor to her condition by presenting him, after the blinding, moving like her in her first appearance, singing like her in some of the same disconnected, frantic speech patterns. Once he loses the trial to her, his horror is that he has been beaten by and is thus now lower than a slave woman.

---

23   Patterson (1991) 110. See in general Chapter 7, "A Woman's Song", for a discussion of slavery in Greek tragedy.
24   Patterson (1991) 101.
25   Patterson (1991) 118.

And yet, this tragedy forces its audience to ask who are the real slaves? Polyxena dies in utter freedom, in control of the circumstances of her own death. The king Polymestor, as we have already seen, becomes like a slave in the control greed has over his actions, a condition his blindness then makes physically manifest. Odysseus and Agamemnon seem slaves to the opinion of others. Indeed, it is the latter's reluctance to help Hecuba out of concerns over appearance to assert openly (864): " There is nobody among mortals who is free." Euripides seems to be suggesting that inner freedom is the more meaningful form of liberty.

With the nature of the chorus in general and these two themes of necessity and slavery established, let us see how the choral songs in Euripides' *Hecuba* reflect on and interact with the drama as a whole. The songs are all outlined in the structural synopsis located earlier in this volume, just before the translation. In general one might say that the primary impetus of these songs, as in so many Greek tragedies, is for the Chorus to make sense, both for itself and the audience, of what is happening. For answers, the Chorus looks first to the future, then to the past, and finally to the distant past.

444-83 First Choral Song: Polyxena has thus expressed her desire to escape slavery through a noble, willing death on the sacrificial altar, which prompts the Chorus to wonder about its own future. They know they will be slaves, but, despite that generally unwelcome reality, they know that a slave's life can vary widely in its level of hardship, so they hope for the best, and they thus speculate at their possible destinations, first speculating about Greece in general, then Delos and then Athens itself. The insertion of Athens here, as with the language of the Athenian Assembly and the mention of the sons of the Athenian hero Theseus in the debate over the sacrifice of Polyxena, moves the world of the Trojan War closer to the world of the theater audience than anything even implied in Homer. Even Delos, one of the two main shrines to Apollo, has contemporary significance, because the Chorus wonders whether it might participate in the Dance of the Maidens at the Delian Festival of Apollo, which may have just recently been restored by the Athenians (Thucydides 3.104). But such festival dances were more the venue for free women, not slaves, a cold reality that is set against their similarly false hopes for life in Athens in the succeeding *strophe*, where the Chorus entertains the fantasy that it might help embroider the robe to be presented to the goddess Athena at the Panathenaic Festival, another anachronism designed to bridge the mythical world of the action and the contemporary world of the audience. Again, these hopes are delusion. Polyxena's fine words have inspired the Chorus to dream, yet such dreams last only a moment, and the chorus members seem to awaken suddenly, in the closing *antistrophe*, from their reverie to face anew that their home is gone and they are now slaves. Their lament, "I in a foreign land am called slave," echoes Polyxena from the previous scene where first in her list of reasons to prefer a noble death over a wretched life is the very title of "slave:" "But now I am a slave. First, the very name, unaccustomed, makes me love death" (357-58). They then see Talthybius enter with his report of the death of Polyxena.

629-57 Second Choral Song: That sacrificial narrative, followed by Hecuba's lamentful recognition that human achievements and happiness are only ephemeral, unstable vanities, prompts the Chorus to surrender its earlier concerns for the future and instead to probe the past for an understanding of their suffering, with the first of two songs specifically on the fall of Troy; this is the briefest of the three songs, a relatively quick interlude between the impact of the two separate deaths of her children on Hecuba. Their remembrance of Paris' departure to win Helen is filled with the language of necessity, compulsion, labor, as if the Chorus, faced with the renewal of suffering in the form of Hecuba's grief over Polyxena, has surrendered itself to the acceptance of their lot as "necessary" and inevitable. The squalor of their new life and the destruction of their marriage beds in the epode contrasts poignantly with Paris' pursuit of "the bed of Helen, whom gold-gleaming Helios illuminates as most beautiful" (635-37). Yet, like the first choral song, the second closes with an even more extraordinary bridge between suffering ancient and modern, with its evocation of two grieving women in Sparta: one, a young bride weeping, presumably at the news of her husband's death, and the other an old woman shredding her face with her fingernails in agony over her lost children. There were many cities cooperating in the mythical war at Troy, so the poet's choice of Sparta here surely has contemporary urgency for the real Peloponnesian War, especially with the anachronistic references in the first choral song. Euripides sets before his audience a Hecuba-like figure in the city of the audience's enemy, grieving like the figure in whom the audience has just invested a tremendous amount of highly emotional sympathy. This is the detritus of war, which here lacks a noble purpose and heroic vision. Again, there is no redemptive suffering here. Yet this sense of the humanity of one's enemy is not new in Greek literature, for Homer's epic takes great pains to depict the Trojans as full human beings with the same dreams and nightmares as the Greeks, most notably in the engagement of Priam and Achilles in the last book of the *Iliad*.

905-51 Third Choral Song: The Chorus moves back to the past again here, but with a more individualized reminiscence of Troy's fall. Instead of linking the mythical past with the present as in the previous two songs, Euripides dwells on a transient moment of domestic happiness, and its loss, that are recognizable by any human being. The women of the Chorus present a distinctly feminine version of that night, dwelling on their last evening with their husbands in false joy over the departure of the Greek armada. Marriage, after emerging in the previous song as a theme, becomes the prominent theme in this ode, contrasting the lost marriages of the Trojans with the happiness of Paris and Helen for the past decade. The husband and wife here further suggest the denial of adult life to Polydorus and Polyxena, dead before they even have a chance to lose their married happiness. In the epode the Chorus expresses their sorrow over losing their identities first as wives and then as Trojans, all because of Helen and Paris, whom they close the song by cursing. The verbal violence of this curse signals their transformation, mirroring Hecuba, from passive sufferer to active avenger.

Here the songs cease, the Chorus stops dancing, and it becomes an accomplice to the deception of Polymestor, taunting him after he exits into Hecuba's tents in pursuit of gold and exulting in the screams of pain they hear from him within. The Chorus produces a few couplets to provide transitions between the speeches of the main characters, but it seems to lose its capacity to frame and to contextualize the action as it becomes part of it. Polymestor takes over the normal laments that we see late in tragedies, but nobody joins in with him in his solo songs, because nobody can sympathize with him and thus participate in his grief. His is the most solo of monodies imaginable. The slaves have won. They are triumphant. After Agamemnon decides the trial in favor of Hecuba, Polymestor's raging grief turns immediately to disgust that he was beaten by "a slave woman" (1252-

53). Yet the triumph is short-lived, as Agamemnon sees it is now possible to depart and orders the ships ready. The Chorus now must face the permanence of their new lives as slaves. Thus they finally concede to that great principle (god?) Necessity, for "Necessity does not bend."[26]

About this Translation

My goal here has been to produce a translation that has as little to do with me as possible; this means I do not introduce any new metaphors through the process of translation, I try to keep the English lines as close to their Greek counterparts in number and placement as I can without making the English excessively awkward, and I try to translate the Greek into English using the same English words consistently. This translation will thus not be the most poetic available (though I do sometimes strive to render Euripides' use of alliteration) and sometimes English idiom will be sacrificed to the goal of preserving the flow of ideas from the original Greek lines, though without, I hope, falling into the trap of "translationese." What is gained is a more accurate approximation of Euripides' Greek than has sometimes been the case in translations of the *Hecuba* so that readers can follow shifts in word use and language more coherently. Another result of a more literal translation is that English words will now show Euripides' insistence on certain key themes as embodied in the drama's language. For example, the Greek idiom *didômi dikên* is normally translated as "I pay the penalty (for transgression)", and rightly so, since it connotes punishment. But it literally means "I give justice." Justice (*dikê*) is, arguably, the most important theme in the play, and this idiom thus allows the audience to hear "justice" repeatedly. I believe that English readers need to see (and hear) this insistence preserved, so I have compromised with the translation "to pay justice." Similarly, Euripides uses two words to denote Hecuba's children, *teknon*, which I have translated as "child," and *pais*, which I have translated as "boy" for Polydorus and "daughter" for Polyxena; "boy" in English, coming from a mother, has a much greater emotional range, I think, than just "son." It connotes Polydorus' child-like helplessness against the machinations of his host, and a mother's despair over losing the one son, her "baby," she believed was safe.

One of the difficulties of translating Greek tragedy for a modern audience is that modern American English has an impoverished vocabulary for lamentation. "Alas" is, at best, extremely stilted, and, at worst, inducing of giggles. Thus, when I do chose to translate *pheu* as "alas", that is when I feel a character's stated grief is insincere. Other terms of grief, such as *aiai* or *oimoi*, I leave untranslated, since the inarticulate interjections seem, in some ways, more powerful than any actual English equivalent.

The first readers of this translation were the students in my introductory Greek Drama and Culture course in the spring of 2002 at Temple University. I inflicted an extremely awkward first draft on them, and asked them to help me write the notes and commentary by telling me what they needed to know. As complete novices, they were the best judges of what other students would need in the final edition. I am extremely grateful to them for their help.

---

26   The adjective *sterros* here, meaning "inflexible, rigid," echoes line 296 here it is applied to human nature (*sterros anthrôpou phusis*).

These students also helped me with the stage directions, and about stage directions I must also say a few words. The manuscripts that led to modern editions lacked any stage directions, and, indeed, even changes in speaker were indicated by simple marks. Any stage direction in a modern translation comes from the translator's imaginative interaction with the contents of the play itself. Some directions, such as indications of a speaker's tone, are more imaginative than others. Readers who consult multiple translations will find wide differences in matters such as when exits occur and in what direction. Some of my stage directions will raise eyebrows, but I have tried to indicate which directions are more imaginative than others; in general, they are based on information in the text and from my working on possible dramatic reconstructions with my students. One last note about directions: directions are given according to the audience's perspective, and so, for example, "right" is the audience's right.

Readers will notice that some passages are placed inside brackets. These are used to represent where modern editors have reached a conclusion that a part of the received manuscript is not genuine; those lines were added subsequently, usually by actors. These additions are called interpolations.

I am here indebted to many people, both through their scholarship and through their direct assistance to me. My Greek text, unless otherwise noted, has been Justina Gregory's splendid edition from 1999. In preparing this translation and commentary I have learned not just from Professor Gregory's wisdom in her Greek edition, but also from the earlier commentary of Christopher Collard. I stand firmly and gratefully on their shoulders. Revisions to my first manuscript were made during a happy period as Visiting Fellow at Wolfson College, Cambridge and Visiting Scholar in the Faculty of Classics at the University of Cambridge; I am thus especially full of thanks to Robin Osborne and Pat Easterling for facilitating my Fellowship, and to Temple University for a Study Leave to fund my Cambridge sojourn. Last, I am grateful to Peter Meineck for helping me think about the important of performance in general a decade ago, and to Stephen Esposito for his initial encouragement and his comments on an earlier draft.

An Essay on Euripides' *Trojan Women*
by Diskin Clay

He grew old among the flames of Troy
and the quarries of Sicily.
    —George Seferis, *Euripides The Athenian*

I. The Flames of Troy: Euripides and the Aftermath of the Iliad

The Trojan Women is a play on the consequences of war and the fate of those defeated in war and the fate of their victors. Like Aeschylus' *Persians*, it is presented from the point of view of the conquered. It was written in the middle of the Peloponnesian War (431-405) and produced in the competitions of the festival of Dionysos in spring of 415, just months before the Athenians launched their great armada against Syracuse and Sicily. If *The Trojan Women* is a war play, it is not about a specific war; it is about all wars.

The title of the play is *Troades*, *The Trojan Women*. It centers on the Trojan women taken captive during the sack of Troy in the tenth year of the Trojan War. One of the captive Trojan women, Polyxena, was murdered before the opening of Euripides' play. The rest are about to be dispersed as slaves throughout the Greek world, and the son of Hector will be murdered by the victorious Greek army. Yet Euripides' *Trojan Women* survives in the dramatic literature and opera of Europe and even in the musical setting for soprano voice of Hecuba's lament by Gustav Holtz. We are reminded by Gilbert Murray's version of the play at the beginning of World War I (1915) and the version Jean-Paul Sartre produced during the Algerian War (*Les Troyennes*, 1965) that Euripides' *Trojan Women* revives in the crisis of war and is endlessly adaptable.

Euripides might have been born in 480, the year of the defeat of the Persian fleet off the island of Salamis, an island that he seems to have been peculiarly attached to. (There are two references to it in *The Trojan Women*.) There is a tradition that he composed his tragedies in the isolation of a cave on the island. But Seferis was right in his *Euripides the Athenian*: Euripides grew old in the light of the flames of Troy and the darkness of the quarries of Syracuse, where the remnants of the Athenian expeditionary force were imprisoned in 413. A tradition has it that some Athenian prisoners awaiting death were freed because they could sing for the Syracusans arias from the plays of Euripides. It has been suggested that the lyrics of *The Trojan Women* were much appreciated in Syracuse and saved some Athenian lives.[1]

The immediate setting of Euripides' *Trojan Women* was the major dramatic festival of the spring of 415, when Euripides was 65. In late March and the Attic month of Elaphebolion, the sea became, as the proverb went, navigable. Visitors from the subject states of the Delian league could cross the Aegean to witness this festival held to honor Dionysos and to magnify the state of Athens. As a part of this long seven-day festival, Athenians (women included) and visitors to Athens gathered in the theater of Dionysos where they could admire the tribute of the "allied" city-states, as this was carried into the orchestra of the theater and displayed, even before the actors and chorus of the first tragedy had made their entry. The audience could also view the procession of the orphaned children of Athenians who had fallen in battle.[2]

There are more remote settings to *The Trojan Women*. They frame the *Iliad*. These are the traditions on the periphery of the *Iliad* that provide the history of Troy in the generation before Priam. Euripides knew these traditions and expected that his audience would recognize them in the background of his play. Before the first Greek assault on Troy, there was an earlier assault by Herakles, Philoctetes, and Telamon. In Trojan history there was the legend of Hecuba's dream that she had given birth to a torch; alarmed by the portent, she and Priam exposed the infant Alexandros. He was saved from exposure by a herdsman and, as a young herdsman, Paris made a fateful choice of one of three goddesses who presented themselves to him in a contest of beauty. These traditions are barely recognized in Homer's *Iliad* (cf. 24.23-30), but the traditions concerning what happened in Troy before the wrath of Achilles were set out in the first play of what is sometimes called Euripides' "Trojan Trilogy," the *Alexandros*. The second play of this "trilogy" is the *Palamedes* (a hero not mentioned by Homer). It too takes place before the opening of the *Iliad*. The last play of this unique Euripidean "trilogy" is *The Trojan Women*. It takes place after the fall of Troy and the burial of Hector, "the tamer of horses" (as he is described in the last line of the *Iliad*). The satyr play performed last and making a tetralogy of a trilogy was the *Sisyphos*.

The story Homer did not tell is supplied by the short post-Homeric epics known in antiquity as The Epic Cycle. Three of these epics concern us most directly, as they concerned Euripides: the so-called *Cypria*, where the Judgment of Paris is described, the *Little Iliad*, and *The Sack of Troy* (*Iliupersis*). These events were also depicted in vase painting. Euripides dramatized the subjects of these minor epics to provide a history both of the causes of the Trojan War and the fall of Troy that follows on the death of Hector. It is not a continuous history, as is, for example the one surviving trilogy, Aeschylus' *Oresteia*.

The final episode in *The Trojan Women* is one that justifies Euripides' title as the "most tragic" of tragedians: this is the last scene in which Hecuba bends over the body of

---

1   The tradition that Athenians who could sing lyric passages from Euripides were spared by the victorious Syracusans is attested in Plutarch, Nicias 29.2-3. That they chose to sing arias from The Trojan Women is the congenial conjecture of Léon Parmentier, Euripide, Les Troyennes (Paris 1959) 25.

2   Simon Goldhill has written an important study of the ceremonies surrounding the production of Athenian tragedy and the "ideology" of the major festival of Dionysos in Athens, "The Great Dionysia and Civic Ideology," in John J. Winkler and Froma I. Zeitlin, eds., Nothing to Do with Dionysos? (Princeton 1990) 97-129.

her grandson, Astyanax, and laments his death. In *The Little Iliad*, the murder of Hector and Andromache's son Astyanax is described. In this version, it is Achilles' son, Pyrrhos, who takes the infant from his nurse and throws him down from the one of the towers of Troy. This report helps us appreciate Euripides' choice of Odysseus as the Greek responsible for the murder of Astyanax.[3] As we shall see, Odysseus plays a villain's role in the *Palamedes* as well as in *The Trojan Women*. Another source for the incidents immediately following the death of Hector is *The Fall of Troy* by Arktinos of Miletos. The theme is often depicted on Attic vases.

There is a unique scene from the *Iliad* that looks grimly forward to the fate of the Trojan women. It clearly impressed Euripides. This is the narrative in *Iliad* 6 of Hector's return to Troy for a last time. Here Homer describes his meeting with his mother Hecuba and the supplication of the cult statue of Athena on the Trojan acropolis by Hecuba and the women of Troy. Then follows the scene of Hector's last meeting with his wife Andromache and his last moments with his infant son Astyanax, who is frightened by the nodding plume on his father's helmet (236-501). The indifference of the gods of "sacred Ilion" (in this play Zeus, Poseidon, and Athena) to their votaries and the rejection of the rich gift of a cloak draped on the knees of the goddess Athena (addressed by her priestess as "Savior of the City," *Iliad* 6.305) is evoked in the last choral ode of the play. Hector's last words to his wife are recalled in the Prologue as the chorus contemplate their fate as slaves in Greece. Hector's words were prophetic, and Euripides listened closely to his prophecy (*Iliad* 6.448-63 in my translation):

> The day will come when the sacred city of Troy will fall
> and Priam and the people of Priam of the strong ash spear.
> But in this future I am not as pained for the Trojans
> or for Hecuba herself or for Lord Priam
> or for my brothers who will fall bravely in great numbers in the dust
> under the spear and sword of enemy warriors as I am pained for you.
> Some Achaean in a bronze tunic
> will lead you away with him, and you will weep as he takes from you
>   your day of freedom.
> In Argos you will weave at a loom for a new mistress;
> you will carry water from the springs of Messeis and Hyperie
> and suffer still other disgraces. Strong Necessity will lie upon you.
> And the man who sees you in tears will say of you:
> "This is the wife of Hector, who was once the greatest warrior
> of the Trojans who break horses when they fought around Ilion."

Euripides' appreciation of this scene from the *Iliad* is manifest not only in the *Parodos* of the *Trojan Women*, where the captive women wonder to what part of Greece they will be taken and from which springs they will be forced to draw water as slaves,

---

3   This is T 20 Malcolm Davies' *Epicorum Graecorum Fragmenta*, Göttingen 1988. The Epic Cycle is conveniently presented by Davies in *The Greek Epic Cycle*, second edition, London 2001. The evidence for the poems of the Cycle is set out here in pp. 1-12.

but in the scene that introduces Andromache in the *Andromache* carrying a golden vessel from a spring (166-67).

II. The Quarries of Sicily: Athens 415-413

In the *Iliad*, Hector named two springs, Messeis and Hyperie; there is now no certainty as to where they are to be located. By contrast, the geography of *The Trojan Women* is both precise and significantly anachronistic. Anachronism in Euripides is not a symptom of ineptitude. It is the poet's way of making the events of Troy contemporary and relevant to his audience in the theater of Dionysos. In the *Parodos*, the chorus of Trojan women mention a spring, Peirene (205-6). Peirene is a spring in Corinth (mentioned in *Medea* 69 and Pindar, *Olympian* 13.61), but unnoticed in Homer. They mention Athens. Athens is a place that barely stood on the far horizon of the *Iliad*. Yet for Euripides' Trojan women it is the "renowned" and "blessed" land of Theseus (208-9). As for the "land of Theseus", Theseus was so marginal to Homer that attempts to associate him and Athens with the Trojan War provoked the proverb "nothing without Theseus" (Plutarch, *Theseus* 28.3). Thessaly (214), the second wishful choice of the chorus, is a natural choice, for Achilles' home, Phthia, was a part of Thessaly. But Sicily, a land the chorus mention after Athens (220), is unnamed in the Homeric poems. It is the object of the Athenian expedition that was to leave Athens three months after the production of *The Trojan Women*. Last named is the River Krathis on the Ionian Sea (224-39); it flows by a colony founded under Athenian leadership in 444/443 after the destruction of Sybaris, as the Athenians moved a long step closer to Sicily.

The most striking symptom that in Euripides' *Trojan Women* Troy stands as an emblem for the vanity of victory and conquest is the anachronism that transforms Homeric Greece into Euripides' Greece. The past of Troy is the present of Greece. Euripides represents on stage and in the orchestra the action of a single day after the taking of Troy. But his play wears the face of Janus: it turns us back to the past and forward to the future.

The lyrics of the *Trojan Women* look back (in the first *stasimon*) to the night Troy fell to the stratagem of the Wooden Horse (511-67); in the second *stasimon* the chorus look back on the more distant past of their city and the first expedition launched from Greece against Troy (799-818). The chorus in its lyrics and Cassandra in her trochaic tetrameters also look forward: Cassandra to her fate, the fate of her captor, Agamemnon, and the fate of Odysseus (427-61); the chorus to their fate as slaves to Greeks (in lines 197-229 of the *Parodos*).

But the language of the chorus, and occasionally the language of Euripides' actors, looks deeper into the future. An odd, but significant, anachronism occurs in the Prologue. Here Poseidon speaks of the Athenians as having taken their share of captive Trojan women in the Greek lottery that disposed of them (30-31). In the *Iliad*, the Athenians —"the pride of Athens, Theseus' sons"—play a role that rivals that of the Arcadians in its insignificance. Athens was a minor state in the Homeric epic; but in Euripides' *Trojan Women* it is a power to be reckoned with. It figures in the imagination of the Trojan women as the place they would choose, if they could have their choice, for their captivity and slavery: "the renowned, blessed, and prosperous land of Theseus" (208). Significantly, the more distant horizons of the island of Sicily now enter their far reaching thoughts (220-29). Athens remains on their mind. In their evocation of the memory of Ganymede in the second stasimon (820-39), the history of Telamon and the first Greek expedition against Troy evokes the thought of Telamon's island kingdom, Salamis, and Athens on the mainland of Attica opposite. The association is meaningful only in the context of the fifth century.

Athens is described by the chorus in language that is so unmistakably epinician and Pindaric that it now deserves more generous quotation. Pindar wrote victory odes in which both the victor at the panhellenic games and his city were praised. Euripides, who wrote a victory ode for Alcibiades, composed these lines in praise of Athens (799-804):

> O Telamon, King of Salamis, land flowering with bees,
> you established your home and seat
> on an island washed by beating waves
> facing the sacred slope
> where Athena first revealed the sprig of olive, green and gray,
> a celestial crown and jewel for bright, prosperous Athens.

Athens, the brilliant, holy, god-graced city that glimmers on the horizon of the Trojan women's imagination, is not introduced into the scene of the destruction of Troy as an attempt to please the crowd in the theater of Dionysos. As Socrates remarked in Plato's *Menexenus*, it is easy to praise Athens in Athens (236A). In the lyrics of the *The Trojan Women*, Athens seems a privileged place, chosen and protected by divinity, like the Trojan Ganymede of the Salamis ode. But Athena, who displayed her sacred olive on Attic soil in a hierophantic gesture, is, like the other gods, a fickle god, the god who is, as Poseidon describes her, capable of leaping from friendship to hostility (67-68).

Another setting for Euripides' *Trojan Women* is larger than the theater of Dionysos and the Greater Dionysia of 415. It is the theater of the Peloponnesian War, which had entered into its second stage after the "Peace of Nicias" (of 421) was dissolved by Athenian intrigue in the Peloponnesus. In this larger context two events loom large. The first is the brutal treatment of the independent state of Melos in the Cyclades, an island that had attempted to remain outside the bipolarity of power that divided the Greek world into Athenian and Spartan leagues. This came in the summer of 416. The issues involved in Athens' easy conquest of Melos are articulated in the "dialogue" Thucydides composed to illustrate the rhetoric of Athenian power. The power of this rhetoric was grounded on a force of thirty-three ships carrying some 3,000 troops. When the power of words failed, the Athenians turned to force and put to death all Melians of military age and enslaved the women and children (*The Peloponnesian War* 5.84-116). The second event in the theater of the Peloponnesian war lay in the future: the Athenian invasion of the island of Sicily.

Thucydides' narrative continues with the winter of 416 and the Athenian decision to send an expedition against the Dorian states of Sicily. In the syntax of his narrative of the events of the war he gives an indication of his silent judgment of the arrogant confidence of the Athenians. This expedition, launched on a wave of popular enthusiasm, looms in the immediate future of the Greater Dionysia of 415. In a way, it comes as the fulfillment of Cassandra's prophecy in *The Trojan Women* as she speaks of Odysseus' fate after he leaves Troy in ashes (431-40):

Unhappy man, Odysseus does not know what sufferings await him.
The day will come when he will look back on my sufferings
and the sufferings of the Phrygians as a golden age.
When he has added ten years to the ten years he has spent here, he will
    arrive at home alone.
He will come first to the narrow passage between cliffs
where dread Charybdis dwells. I see the Cyclops,
a mountain cannibal. I see Ligurian Circe, who transforms men into pigs.
I see shipwrecks on the salt sea, the craving for the lotus,
the sacred cattle of the Sun God whose bleeding flesh
will one day sing a bitter song that will make Odysseus' flesh crawl.

Euripides could not know the outcome of the Sicilian expedition which was being planned as he entered the tragic competitions in the spring of 415. But Sicily to the west was very much on the horizon of Athenian ambitions. By the time of Thucydides, the Island of the Sun of the *Odyssey* was commonly identified as Sicily. Because of the folly of his hungry men roasting cattle sacred to the Sun (Helios), Odysseus lost those of his companions who had survived that far on their way home to Ithaka (*Odyssey* 12.260-419).[4] Talthybios had warned Cassandra against using the threatening language of prophecy as the Greek army prepared to sail from Troy (408-10), but his warning fell on deaf ears.

There were few voices like that of Cassandra raised in the spring of 415 when the sea—both the Aegean and the Ionian—opened for travel. One motive for travel was *theoria*, the desire to observe the festival of Dionysos in Athens; another was military. In mid-summer, the major part of the expedition to Sicily set out from Athens. The mood in Athens is recorded by Thucydides (*The Peloponnesian War* 6.30-32.2 in my translation):

The Athenians and any allies who were in Athens at the time went down to Piraeus at dawn on the day appointed and manned the ships to put out to sea. The rest of the people, in fact, almost the entire population of Athens, citizens and foreigners alike, went down to the Piraeus with them. The natives had people to see off on their way, friends, or relatives, or sons. They came full of hope and full of lamentation at the same time, thinking of the conquests that might be made and thinking, too, of those whom they might never see again, considering the long voyage they were undertaking from their own country. At this moment, when they were on the point of parting from each other to face all the risks ahead, the danger of the situation came home to them more than it had at the time when they voted for the expedition. Nevertheless, they were heartened by the strength they had and the kinds and the quantity of equipment displayed before their eyes. As for the foreigners and the rest of the crowd, they came merely to see the show and to admire the incredible ambition of the thing.

---

4   An island called Thrinakie is mentioned in *Odyssey* 11.107. One of the names for Sicily (once called Sikania) was Trinakria, the island with three capes. (Coins of Syracuse show the emblem of three legs in recognition of this.) The association between the island of the Sun, Thrinakie, and Sicily is made by Thucydides in *The Peloponnesian War* 6.2.2.

A blast of a trumpet signaled the beginning of the expedition as ships cast off from the Piraeus. In his translation of *The Trojan Women*, Gilbert Murray had a trumpet sound at the end of the play as a signal that the captive women are to be taken to the waiting Greek ships. Clearly, Murray wanted to connect the trumpet blast that signaled the forced departure of the Trojan women from Troy (1266-7) and the trumpet blast of the summer of 415.[5]

Euripides knew that the sub-epic narrative of the destruction of Troy, the *Iliupersis*, was only a half a tale. Beyond this tale lay the *Nostoi* or the returns home, many of which involved the sufferings of the Greek victors, commemorated not only in the *Odyssey* but in dramatic form in Aeschylus' *Oresteia* and Euripides' own *Palamedes*. Beyond the brutal treatment of Melos in the winter of 416/415, which was still a vivid memory when Athens fell to the Spartan admiral, Lysander in 404,[6] lay the great embarkation of the Athenian fleet, the final defeat of the armada and Athenian land forces in 413, and the imprisonment of the survivors in the quarries of Syracuse. Euripides could not have foretold the precise details of the two years of Athenian history that followed the production of his *Trojan Women*. The play won only second place, but, if Euripides was not popular in Athens (a city he left forever in 408), his lyrics were popular in Syracuse.

The thought that humans are not powerful enough to secure their successes from reversal is simply expressed in Euripides' epigram for the Athenians who were lost during the Sicilian expedition:[7]

> These brave men here defeated the men of Syracuse
> in eight battles, when divinity stood equally on each side.

The gods did not stand equally by the Athenians to the end, no more than they stood by the Trojans. If Euripides' *Trojan Women* was produced in times of war and in the middle of the grueling Peloponnesian War, it is not about any particular war. It is about war, in which conquerors and conquered are all victims.

III. The "Trojan Trilogy" of 415: *Alexandros, Palamedes, Trojan Women*

All tragedies entered into competition at the festivals of Dionysos in Athens count as "tetralogies." Three tragedies and one satyr play were entered by each of the three competing tragedians. In the case of Aeschylus' *Oresteia*, our only surviving "trilogy," the connection among the three tragedies entered in 458 (*Agamemnon, Choephoroi, Eumenides*) is so deliberate that, if only the *Eumenides* survived, we would not be in a position to interpret it as the final play of the trilogy. The satyr play of the "tetralogy" was the *Proteus*, a divine figure from the *Odyssey* connected with Menelaos' return home and, therefore, with Aeschylus' trilogic history of the House of Atreus. In the case of Euripides' *Trojan Women* we have the last play of a tragic "trilogy" preceded by *Alexandros, Palamedes*, and followed by the satyr play, *Sisyphos*. It has been convincingly argued from the consider-

---

5   Euripides, *Trojan Women*, London 1915; also *Euripides and his Age* (second edition, Oxford 1946) 87.

6   The scene is powerfully described by Xenophon in his *Hellenika* 2.2.3.

7   Euripides, no. II in Denys Page, *Epigrammata Graeca* (Oxford 1975) p. 44.

able evidence for the first two tragedies of the group that this "Trojan trilogy" constitutes Euripides' only coherent attempt to produce three plays with close thematic and dramatic connections.[8] What this means is that the last play of the trilogy relied for its full effect on the audience's immediate knowledge of the two plays that preceded it.

We have more materials for reconstructing the *Alexandros* than for either *Palamedes* or *Sisyphos*. Because of the sententiousness of his speakers, memorable lines from Euripides are often excerpted by anthologists. Language from his choruses usually survives, if it survives at all, in papyrus fragments. There are also papyri giving the arguments of some of the plays of Euripides (known as "Tales from Euripides") and accounts of the legends he worked with (and might have influenced) by mythographers such as Hyginus and Apollodorus. In the case of the *Alexandros* we have a papyrus argument, lyric fragments in papyrus, quotation, and a mythographic summary.[9] The background of the play is set out by the speaker of the Prologue (perhaps Aphrodite): to avert the portent of an ominous dream Hecuba had during her pregnancy, King Priam gives the infant Alexander (as he is called) to a herder to expose on Mount Ida. The herder pities the infant and brings him up as Paris. Hecuba is disconsolate over the loss of her baby, and she and Priam establish annual funeral games in his honor.

When he has grown into a young man, Paris, unrecognized as Alexander, competes in these games and is victorious over Hector and other sons of Priam. Because he is a slave and because of his innate arrogance towards his fellow herders, he is brought before Priam and denounced by Deiphobos, a son of Priam and the husband of Helen after the death of Paris (cf. *Trojan Women* 959-60). It seems that Paris is acquitted. But he is not out of danger. Out of concern for the position of their family, Deiphobos and Hecuba plot to murder Paris. His death is prevented by the confession of the herder who brought him up.

We do not know how the judgment of Paris was treated in the *Alexandros*. Paris' choice of Aphrodite over her rivals, Athena and Hera, is referred to in *The Trojan Women* (by Helen in 923-37 and by Hecuba in 969-90); it was probably described in the Prologue to the *Alexandros*. The chorus of this play consisted of Trojan women close to Hecuba and the palace; there is evidence for a subsidiary chorus (*parachoregema*) of Paris' fellow herdsmen. A papyrus fragment in Strasbourg has a scene in which a speaker attempts to console Hecuba for the loss of her new-born son, and the anthologist, Stobaeus, cites commonplaces of consolation from Euripides' *Alexandros*. Both *Alexandros* and *Trojan Women* have choruses of Trojan women, but only in the first play of the "trilogy" is consolation possible.

Next comes the *Palamedes*. It is set sometime before the action of the *Iliad*. It begins with the quarrel between Achilles and Agamemnon in the tenth year of the war. The point of view of both the *Alexandros* and *Trojan Women* is Trojan; the action takes place at Troy. The point of view of *Palamedes* is Greek; the action takes place in the Greek camp outside the walls of Troy. We know nothing about the lyrics of the chorus, but the

---

8   By Ruth Scodel, *The Trojan Trilogy of Euripides* (Hypomnemata 60), Göttingen 1980. She pursued the argument made by Gilbert Murray first in 1932 and then in a fuller and more satisfactory form in "Euripides' Tragedies of 415 B. C.: The Deceitfulness of Life," in *Greek Studies* (Oxford 1946) 127-48.

9   See Scodel 1980: 20-42.

chorus must consist of Greek soldiers. Of the characters, we know of Odysseus (who must speak the Prologue to reveal his plot against Palamedes); a soldier of Odysseus who reports Palamedes' treasonable correspondence to Agamemnon; Palamedes; Agamemnon, who acts as judge of the charges Odysseus brings against Palamedes; a messenger who probably reports on the execution of Palamedes; and his brother Oiax, who comes to Troy after Palamedes has been executed.

In *Palamedes*, Odysseus is well worth watching. He will reappear. Although he does not appear in a speaking role in *The Trojan Women*, he is the engineer of the strategem of the Trojan horse and he persuades the Greek army to murder Astyanax. Hecuba is allotted to him as a slave. His role in *Palamedes* and his off-stage machinations in *The Trojan Women* prepare for the appearance of Sisyphos in the satyr play that closes this tetralogy. According to tragic traditions hostile to Odysseus (including Sophocles' *Philoctetes* of 409), Sisyphos and not Laertes was the father of Odysseus.[10] As in the case of Sophocles' *Philoctetes*, where Odysseus frames the plot to bring Philoctetes to Troy, Odysseus is the contriver of the plot of the *Palamedes*. This is to turn Palamedes' invention of writing against him by composing a forged letter to Priam to convict a dangerous rival of treason. To corroborate his frame-up of Palamedes, Odysseus has Trojan gold buried in his tent in his absence. There are, as one would expect, additional complexities in a plot devised by Odysseus (and Euripides), but *Palamedes* seems to add something to the "Trojan trilogy" that prepares the audience for the action of *The Trojan Women*: sophistry. Odysseus is actuated by two motives: resentment and rivalry. He resents Palamedes because it was Palamedes who exposed Odysseus' feigned madness on Ithaka to avoid having to join the expedition against Troy; he is jealous of Palamedes because, as the inventor of the arts of civilization (including writing), he threatens to outshine Odysseus as an intellectual (*sophistes*).[11]

Two illustrations will serve to demonstrate how the plays of the "trilogy" connect. First: in the Prologue of the *Alexandros* (whoever delivers it), Hecuba's dream is described as an essential part of the background of the play. She dreamt that she gave birth to a torch from which snakes flared out, an evil omen for Troy that Priam attempts to abort. He gives the infant to a herdsman to do away with, but Alexander is saved by the herdsman and grows up to be the cause of Troy's destruction (cf. *Trojan Women* 922). The torch Hecuba saw in her dream was an omen. It appears as a reality when it is sighted by the Trojan women at the end of the "trilogy," as Greek soldiers put torches to the walls of Troy (1256-8 and 1318). Second: In the first lines of the *Alexandros*, Troy is described as "famous" (*kleinon*). As the god-built walls of this "famous" city collapse in flame and ashes, Troy survives only in tragedy, even as the chorus lament that its "famous name" has perished (*The Trojan Women* 1278).

Torches and fame are thematic connections. There are also connections that are intellectual and dramatic. Each of the three plays of Euripides' "Trojan trilogy" features

---

10   See *Philoctetes* 417; this genealogy can be taken back to Aeschylus' *Decision over the Arms*, fr. 175 Radt (texts and translation in the appendix of Hugh Lloyd-Jones to Herbert Weir Smith's *Aeschylus II* [London . Cambridge, Massachusetts 1971] 438-41). In Plato's *The Apology of Socrates*, Socrates is eager to interview both Odysseus and Sisyphos in the Underworld (41C).

11   The importance of intelligence and the title *sophos* (wise, or, in its debased sense, clever) in the Palamedes plays of Aeschylus, Sophocles, Euripides, and the *Prometheus* of Aeschylus is properly stressed by Dana Ferrin Sutton in *Two Lost Plays of Euripides* (New York 1987) 126-29.

an *agon* or contest.[12] In *Alexandros*, the *agon* pits Paris, who is taken to be a slave and, thus, in Greek terms, ineligible to compete in athletic contests, against his brother Deiphobos, soon to succeed him as Helen's husband. An angry and defeated Deiphobos denounces Paris before Priam. Paris, who will soon be revealed as free born and a prince, makes the case for the nobility of the slave in terms that so impressed the anthologist John of Stobi (Stobaeus) that some of his speech survives. The *agon* of *Palamedes* is judicial and involves Odysseus as prosecutor and Palamedes as defendant. The appeal of this trial of two clever men before Agamemnon and the Greek army was irresistible to two of Euripides' contemporaries. One of them wrote a *Defense of Palamedes*; the other a speech *Against Palamedes*. Gorgias, the author of the *In Praise of Helen* (translated in Appendix 8), defended Palamedes, and his pupil, Alkidamas, who responded by acting as plaintiff and composing Odysseus' brief against Palamedes.[13] The last of these tragic contests (*agones*) comes in *The Trojan Women* when Helen and Hecuba square off in a debate over who is responsible for the destruction of Troy. Now Menelaos, and not Agamemnon, sits as judge and the conclusion of the debate is foregone, once Menelaos has become reacquainted with the beauty of a wife he has not seen for ten years. Helen breaks with judicial procedure and speaks first, anticipating the charges that will be leveled against her (914-65). After the chorus remark that Helen speaks well but acts badly,[14] Hecuba responds to all of her arguments, except her charge that Hecuba herself was responsible for the destruction of Troy, since she gave birth to the firebrand that has destroyed Troy (919-22). Hecuba's long speech (969-1032) lifts her far above the inarticulate sounds of grief with which she begins to speak. Helen's defense relies conspicuously on Gorgias' praise of her. Menelaos sentences his offending wife to death. But any reader of the *Odyssey* is familiar with the scene of Menelaos and Helen rejoined in Sparta in their autumnal middle age. The debate scene in *The Trojan Women* might seem incongruously sophistic and out of place in a play that dramatizes bereavement. But it might be another indication of Euripides' appreciation of the only power the powerless possess: language and poetry.[15]

IV. Dramaturgy

In staging *The Trojan Women* Euripides was granted the same resources as his rivals: three actors, an oboe player (*auletes*), and a chorus of fifteen. He also employed a number of actors who did not speak. Astyanax is one of these. All actors in Athenian tragedy were men. Now we remember Katherine Hepburn as Hecuba and Irene Pappas as Helen in Michael Cacoyannis' *The Trojan Women* (1971). It comes as a shock to realize that the actors who played the part of Hecuba and Helen were the male protagonist

---

12   This crucial *agones* of the three plays are well assessed by Scodel, 1980: 80-104.

13   A translation of Gorgias' speech can be found in Rosamond Kent Sprague, *The Older Sophists* (Indianapolis . Cambridge, Massachusetts 2001) 54-63; Alkidamas' speech is translated by J. V. Muir in *Alkidamas: The Works & Fragments* (London 2001) 20-33. Aeschylus had staged a very similar *agon* between Odysseus and Ajax over their competing claims for the arms of Achilles and the title "best of the Achaeans" in *The Decision over the Arms*. Only fragments of this play survive.

14   Repeating the words of Palamedes after Odysseus had spoken, fr. 883 in August Nauck, *Tragicorum Graecorum Fragmenta* (second edition 1887).

15   "Speech," Gorgias claims in his *In Praise of Helen* §8, "is a mighty Master" (the full text can be found in Appendix 4). Speech is a master even for those who in Euripides' *Trojan Women* are enslaved.

and deuteragonist (the first and second actors—or, in Greek, competitors). Hecuba is on stage from the beginning of the play to its end. In the Prologue, the second actor plays the part of Poseidon and the third actor the part of Athena. Then, the assignment of roles is straightforward: in the first episode the deuteragonist plays the challenging part of Cassandra; the tritagonist (or third actor) the part of Talthybios. In the next two episodes, the second actor plays the part of Andromache and Helen, and the tritagonist the parts of Talthybios and Menelaos. The human actors move on stage. The gods stand on a platform above the stage, the *theologeion*. This platform represents the walls of Troy. The chorus files into the orchestra in two groups (*hemichoroi*) during the entrance song (*Parodos*). They have joined and taken their place in the orchestra during the three *stasima* (or choral passages) that follow. Actors and chorus all wear masks.

Formally, *The Trojan Women* has the articulations of every Greek tragedy. It is constructed out of familiar building blocks: a Prologue spoken by a god which gives, as is Euripides' manner, the background of the action of the play and an intimation of its outcome. This is followed by the *Parodos*, or the entrance song of the chorus as they occupy their place in the orchestra of the Theater of Dionysos after they have entered through the *parodos* (or lateral entranceway). The Prologue is spoken in iambic trimeters, the formalized rhythm of speech used throughout the play. The *Parodos* involves a lyric exchange between the chorus of fifteen (young men dressed as) women and Hecuba. They speak in the first person singular, and sing in the Doric dialect in a variety of meters employed only for the song and dance of lyric poetry accompanied by the *aulos* (in range, the oboe). From their entrance song, speech alternates with song and *epeisodia* with *stasima* until the final scene of the play, or *Exodos* (exit). If tragedy originated out of the dithyramb,[16] a circular dance which, in Athens, was performed by a leader and a chorus of forty-nine young men or adults, the original meaning of the term *epeisodion* becomes clearer: these are the "interludes" of speech between two or among three actors "interrupting" song and dance. Literally, a *stasimon* is a song performed by the chorus when they have taken their position or "stand" in the orchestra.

The Trojan Women is structurally unusual (if any of our nineteen surviving tragedies can be said to be unusual) in its use of the half choruses of the *Parodos* and the lyric and antiphonal exchanges between Hecuba and Andromache in the second episode. And, as the chorus look for a god to appear on the walls of Troy to release them from their fate as slaves to their Greek conquerors, no god appears on the platform known as the *theologeion*.

Prologue and Exodos   The scene that opens *The Trojan Women* has the Prologue familiar from the tragedies of Euripides. The stage of the action of the play is set by Poseidon, a god who, with the help of Apollo, built the walls of Troy for King Laomedon. He addresses the audience directly and pays no attention to the woman in black writhing on stage below. It is only at line 36 that he looks down to "this poor creature." Poseidon is leaving "famous" (*kleinon*) Troy. His reasons are simple and expedient (28-9):

> When a terrible desolation takes a city,
> the world of the gods sickens and will not receive its honors.

---

16   Aristotle, *Poetics* 4.1449a10-11.

These words are the beginning of the theology of *The Trojan Women*, a theology most fully expressed by the chorus who have come to realize that all their tendance of the gods has not protected their city from utter destruction. At the end of the play they look up to the walls on which Poseidon stood as the play opened, as if hoping for salvation from some Euripidean *deus ex machina*. Prologue and Exodos mark the beginning and end of Euripides' treatment of the gods who protect cities, but who are fundamentally indifferent to their human votaries.

Hecuba   Hecuba is on stage, either prostrate or standing, throughout the play. Her language can be plotted on a scale: silence; inarticulate sounds of grief (*aiai aiai, omoi, oimoi, io, pheu, pheu*); the agonized, antiphonal lyrics of the *Parodos* accompanied by her rocking body; her sober dealings with an ecstatic daughter (Cassandra); her cold advice to the wife of her son Hector (Andromache); and her calculating response to Helen's speech in her own defense. The final scene of the play ("Astyanax") is the moment of her greatest dramatic power, as she bends down over the small broken body of her grandson and recalls his childhood, his father, and laments the life he will not have.

Formally, her first lyric monologue is part of the Prologue. It bears some resemblance to the monologue of Hecuba in the Prologue to the *Hecuba* (59-97) in its meter (it is heavily anapestic), situation, and context. In the *Hecuba* (of the 420s), Hecuba has just been visited by the ghost of her murdered son, Polydoros, and is surrounded by a group of captive Trojan women. In *The Trojan Women* the barely articulate grief of Hecuba contrasts with the calm, calculating, and literally elevated language of the two gods who stand on the walls of Troy. The anapestic rhythm of her speech is a vigorous marching measure that contrasts violently with her status as a prisoner and the pain that racks her body.

Hecuba bears the burden of grief and loss in the play. As the play opens, she has lost Priam, who was slaughtered at the altar of Zeus in their palace enclosure (481-83); and she has lost her sons (480-82). When she asks the herald from the Greek army about the fate of her youngest daughter, she does not understand that Polyxena had been slaughtered too, at Achilles' tomb (260-68; cf. 622-29) (See Fig. 2). She goes on to face her own fate as the drudge of Odysseus on Ithaka (277); the loss of Cassandra, who had already been dragged from the altar of Athena by Ajax, son of Oileus (70, 171); of Hector's wife, Andromache, who will be taken away by Achilles' son; and her grandson, Astyanax, whose body is brought to her for burial on the shield of his father.

Another theme announced in Hecuba's monody is that of the power of poetry, a poetry that rises from the inarticulate but meaningful sounds of lamentation to the lyrics that are the monuments commemorating human loss. This is the "Muse of misery" (120). This poetry, which begins as threnody, is the only thing over which the victims of war have any control. Even the argument Hecuba urges against Helen is an expression of the power of the powerless. The chorus recognize the pleasure and power of lament in two passages: first as they join in the antiphonal lament and respond to Hecuba's lament (608-9):

> Yes, tears are sweet to those in trouble
> and the heart-rending strain of lamentation and the Muse of suffering.

This is the pleasure and consolation of the present. There is also the consoling thought that in the future they will be the theme of song (1242-45):[17]

> Yet, had not some god turned our world upside down
> and buried our towers in the earth, we would have been ciphers.
> We would never have been the subject of song;
> we would never have provided an argument
> for the Muse of mortal poets yet to be born.

Cassandra   Cassandra is the first of three women who will enter the stage as deuteragonist to Hecuba. She acts on center stage in the first episode of *The Trojan Women*, a play that is open to Aristotle's criticism of the "episodic" plot, in which one action follows another without a plausible or necessary connection.[18] But the episodic character of *The Trojan Women* should not be counted a fault. Andromache follows Cassandra on stage in the second episode and Helen, Cassandra in the third; finally the small body of Astyanax is brought in stage in the final "episode" of the Exodos. All these episodes have an intimate and necessary connection, as the fate and character of the women who have been reserved for the commanders of the army are brought out from their tents to take leave of Hecuba and prepare for their forced departure from Troy. These scenes are "tragic" in Aristotle's conception of tragedy, for they reveal and provoke the tragic emotions of pity and fear. Aristotle was accurate to his own conception of tragedy when he called Euripides "the most tragic" of tragedians.[19]

Cassandra had played a prophetic role in the *Alexandros*. She plays a prophetic role here as well. Her situation is ambiguous. The torch she waves over her head in ecstasy is not the instrument of her self-immolation and it is not a marriage torch, except as the symbol that her "marriage" will be to Hades, the bridegroom of young women who die unmarried.[20] Her mother is no more capable of understanding her gestures and language than are the other Trojans. Cassandra is driven and divided by two divine forces: Apollo, the god of prophecy, and Dionysos, the god of ecstasy.[21] More immediately, she had been dragged from the altar and cult statue of Athena by Ajax, son of Oileus (69-71).[22] This scene is depicted in the interior of a large cup now in the Villa Giulia Museum, Rome, showing in its interior the rape of Cassandra and the murder of Priam, at the altar of Zeus of the Enclosure. What is particularly grim about this last scene on the inner tondo (or

---

17   These passages are well treated by Charles Segal in a larger context, *Euripides and the Poetics of Sorrow: Art, Gender, and Commemoration in Alcestis, Hippolytus, and Hecuba*, Durham . London 1993.

18   *Poetics* 9.1451b33-33.

19   *Poetics* 13.1453a30, where he concedes that Euripides is not a master of plot construction; see Segal, 1993: 25-29.

20   For the prevalent connection of marriage and death in Greek culture, see Rush Rehm, *Marriage to Death: The Conflation of Wedding and Funeral Rituals in Greek Tragedy*, Princeton 1994, especially Chapter 9.

21   See the notes to lines 329 and 408. Clearly she is presented as a Maenad, or ecstatic female votary of Dionysos. The only scene in Homer where Maenads are mentioned is that describing the overpowering grief of Hecuba at the death of Hector, as she is compared to a Maenad, *Iliad* 22.460.

22   This scene from the post-Homeric Sack of Troy (*Iliupersis*) has its lyric treatment in a poem preserved in two papyrus fragments of Alcaeus, David A. Campbell, *Greek Lyric Poetry I: Sappho and Alcaeus* (Loeb Classical Library), (Cambridge, Massachusetts and London 1984), no. 298 (pp. 338-41).

rim) is the instrument by which Neoptolemos kills Priam: the dead body of Astyanax. The outer surface of the cup shows two scenes of the warfare outside the walls of Troy: Briseis being led away from Achilles and the duel of Hector and Ajax.

Cassandra is capable of stepping out of her bacchant's dance (366) and placing before her grieving mother the paradox that the Trojans are more fortunate than the Achaeans (364-77). Her "demonstration" borders on (and was meant to suggest) sophistry. It is not on the level of Andromache's proof that Polyxena is happier dead than alive (635-42) or Helen's outrageous speech of exculpation in which she provokes the jury in Euripides' theater by claiming that Hecuba and Priam were actually responsible for the Trojan War (914-22). Cassandra's reckoning involves first the cost of the war to the Greeks (365-405) and then the countervailing advantages of the Trojans. In her powerful statement of the cost of war to the Greeks, Cassandra is not wrong. The serious lesson invested in her "demonstration" is that in war there are no victors: only suffering. Cassandra then turns to the hidden present to predict the future sufferings of Odysseus on his way home from Troy and at home in Ithaka (431-42); she finally reverts to her earlier mode of prophetic frenzy, as she foresees her own death in Argos (445-61).

Andromache   The second episode might be entitled "Andro-mache." Andromache now takes center stage. She and her son are carried onto the stage on a cart laden with other spoils of war. Andromache and Astyanax have been reduced to chattel. This scene resembles the "Cassandra" episode in one respect. Just as Cassandra moves from bacchic frenzy to a balanced calculation of the fortune of Troy set against the fortune of the Greeks, Andromache moves from the long antiphonal and lyric lament with Hecuba (577-633) to the paradoxical argument that Polyxena is more fortunate than she (634-83). Her careful articulation of "those qualities that are found admirable in a woman" to prove that she was the perfect wife (645-79) concludes her long and seemingly incongruous speech to her mother-in-law.

A little more than a decade before Euripides staged *The Trojan Women*, Andromache's "ideal" had been voiced by Pericles in his speech at the state funeral for those who had fallen during the first year of the Peloponnesian War. He has virtually nothing to say to the women in his audience. His parting words—which come almost as an afterthought—are not to mothers who had lost sons to war or the daughters who had been orphaned by it, but to the new widows of Athens: "If I am obliged to say something about the virtue of a woman [or: of even a woman] to those who are now widows, let me compress my remarks into a single piece of advice. Your greatest claim to a good reputation is not to be inferior to your nature. Your greatest glory is to be spoken of least among men—either for your virtue or your vices" (*The Peloponnesian War*, 2.45). It is precisely and ironically the talk of Andromache's "virtue" in the Greek army that destroyed her (657). In Euripides' *Andromache* this ideal had been voiced by Andromache herself, who would not only prevent women from leaving the house and being seen in public; she would not even allow other women within her house, "for they are the tutors of mischief" (943).

More than misogyny, justly or unjustly imputed, is involved in these lines. In this play Euripides is concerned with exploring just what power the weak and helpless possess. Unlike Cassandra, Andromache does not face death; nor can she look forward to Helen's autumnal and golden years of amnesty and amnesia. Her fate is that of a widow and slave. She will be forced to live under the same roof as the son of the man whose father killed both her husband (Hector) and her father (Eetion). And she will live the "hostage syndrome" of forming an attachment to and dependence on her new master. Her third and last marriage to her countryman, Helenos, only glimmers on the far horizon of her life and is not glimpsed in *The Trojan Women*.[23]

Helen   The third episode (860-1059) centers on Helen. In staging and in costume Euripides offers a characterization of Helen and Menelaos which is as effective and dramatic as anything said on stage. *Opsis*, or spectacle, is one of the crucial elements of this episode. We first see Menelaos and his men from the Achaean army enter the stage. Menelaos delivers a brave address to the sun and the audience, but he speaks to no one in particular until he gives orders to his men to go into the tent and drag Helen out by the hair (880-2). When Helen emerges from the tent, she is elegantly dressed and her hair is carefully arranged. The contrast with Hecuba and the other mourning women in black is stark and offensive. Hecuba gives the director of *The Trojan Women* directions when she expresses her outrage at Helen's conduct after the death of her "husband" Paris (1023-7):

> And afterwards, you appeared in public like this,
> beautifully dressed and carefully made up; and you look upon the same sky
> as your husband. I could spit upon you!
> You ought to have come out humble, your eyes to the ground,
> in the torn garments of a widow, with your hair shorn in the Scythian fashion.

Even as she crosses the Aegean, presumably on her way to her death in Sparta, the chorus imagine Helen as seated contemplating her image in a golden mirror (1107-8).

It is true that Helen indignantly protests her rough treatment: "Menelaos, this rude treatment announces some dreadful thing!" (895). But a director would know better than to treat her with violence. Vase painters were well aware of the dramatic potential of the scene when, after ten years of absence, Menelaos confronts his wayward wife. They show him dropping his sword at the sight of her. Perhaps the most striking representation of this scene is on a gladiator's parade helmet from Pompeii. In Euripides' play, Menelaos and his men stand at a respectful and admiring distance from her.

There are no sounds of mourning in the Helen episode, but, as in the Cassandra and Andromache episodes, there is a set speech urging a paradox: that Helen is innocent of leaving Menelaos for Paris and that Priam and Hecuba are the guilty causes of Troy's destruction. The great judicial *agon* with Menelaos as judge has been introduced in our treatment of Euripides' "Trojan trilogy." Helen speaks first; then Hecuba attempts to refute her. Helen breaks with judicial conventions in that she speaks first, before the accusation against her has been heard. Neither Menelaos or Hecuba object. In anticipating the speech of the prosecution, Helen formulates the charges against her in her own terms. Not only does she shift blame for her flight from Sparta and the Trojan War on others—Hecuba, Priam, Aphrodite, and even Menelaos himself ("you craven coward!" 943); she praises herself for having saved Greece from barbarian hegemony (932-37). She makes Menelaos

---

23   This marriage is glanced at in Euripides, *Andromache* 1264 and Aeneas meets her with Helenos at Buthrotum on the coast of north-west Greece, Virgil, *Aeneid* 2.294-6.

agree to her claim that a god compelled her to follow Paris when she deals with the charge that she should have left Troy after the death of Paris: "At that time my marriage was not compassed by a god" (943). She even calls upon the watchmen at the gates and sentinels on the ramparts as witnesses that she then attempted to escape (955). These witnesses, of course, cannot testify on her behalf; they are all dead.

Astyanax   In Greek tragedy, there were characters on stage who did not speak. In Aristophanes' *Frogs* (911-13) the comic character Euripides complains of Aeschylus' use of silent characters (known as *koupha prosopa*). But no silent character in Greek tragedy has a more powerful role than does Astyanax, whose broken body is brought on stage by Greek soldiers, who themselves do not speak. His death prompts the thought of what his life would have been and the memory of what his father's life had been. Talthybios' report of the fear of the Greek army that son would grow up to be like his father (724) resembles the fear of the tyrant Eurystheus that Herakles' sons would grow up to be like their father (Euripides, *The Sons of Herakles* 468-70). In this final scene, we are left not only with grief: we are meant to recall the contests over nobility already staged in the *Alexandros* and *Palamedes*. Finally, we are left in the world of Odysseus.

***The Chorus: The Power of Lamentation* (Kommos):**   The for-mality of the antiphonal song exchanged between Hecuba and the chorus in this movement of the *Parodos* is alien to European poetic traditions, but it was very much a part of the long Greek tradition of ritual lament, a family duty and prerogative that belonged entirely to women in the world of ancient (and modern) Greece.[24]

The *Parodos* of *The Trojan Women* is already familiar. *Parodos* in Greek has two meanings: the entrance into the orchestra of the theater and the entrance song of the chorus. The chorus enter in two groups and respond to Hecuba's laments (all in lyric meter). Hecuba's position on the ground is that of a mourning woman. What can be added to the formal analysis of the *Parodos* is the shift in the strophe (197-213) from the Greece of Corinth, Athens, and Sparta as destinations to the Vale of Tempe, Olympos, Sicily, and south Italy in the antistrophe (214-29). In the *Hecuba* the chorus move from thoughts of Lacedaemon and Phthia in the strophe—both hostile nations (444-53), to thoughts of Delos in the antistrophe—the sacred site of the cult of Apollo (454-65). In the final strophe they end with the choice of Athens where they could serve as *ergastinai*, the cult title of the Athenian women of important families who contributed to the quadrennial festival of Athena by weaving a *peplos*, as the Trojan captives had done in Troy (466-74).[25] The concentration on Athens in both plays creates a Greek world that is both anachronistic and Athenocentric.

---

24   An illustration of this tradition comes from an Attic black-figure vase [*loutrophoros*] of the Sappho painter and ca. 500 B. C. This shows the corpse of a warrior laid out in state; his widow or mother holding his head; and a line of women in black and lamentation. This vase should be studied with other figures in Margaret Alexiou's *The Ritual Lament in the Greek Tradition*, Cambridge: Cambridge University Press 1974 (Figure 1). A similar scene, from another black-figure vase now in the Louvre is the appropriate illustration on the cover of Shirley A. Barlow's *Euripides: The Trojan Women*: Warminster, Wiltshire 1986.

25   The Trojan women's gift of a *peplos* placed on the cult statue of Athena on the acropolis of Troy is described in *Iliad* 6.271-3 and 287-311.

Stasimon 1: The Fall of Troy   This the first full choral song of *The Trojan Women*; the chorus has joined as a whole to perform it. In their entry song (*parodos*), they had been divided into two groups and their singing was antiphonal to Hecuba's lamentation. This lamentation (*kommos*) carries over into this song, which they begin by an invocation to a Muse, asking her to sing "in a new strain" (514). The invocation is epic (in dactylic meter) and it commemorates a moment in the Trojan War that lies beyond the range of the *Iliad* (but not the *Odyssey*)—the moment that seemed to mark the triumph of the Trojans in their defensive war of ten years. This anthem is new too in its point of view. It does not look back upon the event it commemorates from the vantage of a remote and impersonal memory; it is the expression of a group of captive women's experience of the disaster in which they are still involved. The world within Troy is reflected in the personal inner world of the chorus and its memory.

Another tragic text that contains an ominous prediction of the fate of the Greek victors who did not respect the shrines and temples of "sacred Ilion" (see the note to line 123) is Aeschylus' *Agamemnon* where Clytemnestra says of the victorious army (338-42):

> If they treat with reverence the gods who hold the city,
> the gods of this captured city, and what is sacred to the gods,
> what they have destroyed will not come to life again.
> Let no lust possess the armies,
> Let them not destroy what they must not destroy
> and become captives to their greed.

The messenger from the Greek army in Troy makes the fate of the victorious clear as he reports (527-8):

> The altars of the gods have vanished, and the statues and shrines of the
>   gods,
> and the seed of the whole land has been destroyed.

Poseidon ominously repeats Clytemnestra's explicit warning in *The Trojan Women* (95-7). The warning is as relevant in 458, when Aeschylus staged his *Oresteia* as in 415, when Euripides' staged his *Trojan Women*; as it is on May 17, 2004 when I write these words.

In the *Odyssey*, the Trojan horse is seen from the point of view of the trials of the warriors within and of Odysseus especially (in the war memories of Menelaos, 4. 272-89 and Odysseus, 9. 523-32). In this choral ode, the Trojan horse is seen from without and the sack of Troy, from within. The Trojan horse, the product of the skill of Epeios and the strategy of Odysseus, "the child of Athena's cunning" (560), is an emblem of the deceptiveness of proud appearances. To the Trojans it seems a magnificent gift, with its cheek-piece of gold; but it is pregnant with death within. In an instant the reality within the horse is revealed, and the victory festival of torches, song, and dancing into the night is transformed into the horror of a city sacked. The powerful and latent ambiguities of this scene—with its black and white contrast between appearance and reality—are well expressed by the "dark radiance" of the hearth fires within the houses of the sleeping Trojans.

Stasimon 2: Salamis, Athens, Ganymede, Tithonos (799-859)[26] This choral
ode divides into two sets of strophe and antistrophe. The first strophe and antistrophe look
back to the first Greek expedition against the Troy of Laomedon and, only at the end of
the first antistrophe, is the destruction of the Troy of his son, Priam, alluded to (817-19). In
the second strophe and antistrophe, the chorus suddenly shift from a city twice destroyed
to heaven and the love of Zeus for Trojan Ganymede and the love of the goddess of the
dawn (Eos) for the Trojan Tithonos. But there is a residue of Trojan grief and loss in both
strophe and antistrophe, and it becomes the more bitter as the joy and serenity of life in
heaven is contrasted with life on earth. The order of Ganymede followed by Tithonos is
already established in the Homeric *Hymn to Aphrodite* (202-10; 210-27).

The chorus begin by evoking Salamis and, strangely enough, Athens on the mainland opposite. In the generation before the Trojan War, Telamon (brother of Peleus and
father of Ajax, and king of the island of Salamis) joined Herakles in the first Greek assault
on Troy. For his efforts he received Hesione, daughter of Laomedon, as a slave. In the
first stasimon (511-30), the chorus sang of the fall of Troy in a single night. Now they
move back a generation. They are not, however, acting as historians to Euripides' audience. The first strophe of the Ganymede ode has a single function: that is to display the
all too human physiognomy of the Greek gods that ranges from ardent rapture to cold
indifference. Eros, the god of sexual passion, has joined heaven and earth in the passion
of Zeus for Ganymede and of Eos (the goddess of the dawn) for Tithonos. The putative
"bond" is termed a *kedos* (845). This is the Greek word for the bond created by marriage;
it establishes a mutual concern between two groups that are not related by blood. The
word also means a funeral.

We have already examined the Pindaric and epinician language that attaches Athens
to Salamis and Athens to Troy. But we have not commented on the Pindaric background of
the language the chorus choose to describe Athens. One possible reading of these passages
in which Greek lands are described in the epinician language of praise is that Euripides
is writing what Pindar wrote in only one of his epinician odes (*Pythian* VII for Megalkes
of Athens)—a praise of Athens, whose ennobling epithets, "renowned", "blessed", "sacred
land of Theseus, where divinity dwells", seems to recall the language that once described
the "sacred," "famous" (*kleinon*), and prosperous city of Troy. At some point of his career
as a tragic poet, Euripides wrote an epinician ode to celebrate the victories of Alcibiades.[27]
It is plausible that his praise of Alcibiades involved a praise of Athens. But let us face still
another possibility; that Euripides' epinician praise of Athens is designed to place his native
city on the high pedestal of the victor. Standing on this pedestal is both a privileged and
a precarious position.

Athens of the first strophe belongs to the remote world of Ganymede and Tithonos
and stands in sharp contrast to Troy. Athens is favored by the very divinity that was first
hostile, then friendly, to Troy, Athena. On the acropolis of Athens Athena "revealed" the
branch of olive to mankind (804). In this ode this olive branch is not a symbol of peace

26   There is a revealing study of this ode by Anne Pippin Burnett, "*Trojan Women* and the Ganymede Ode,"
     Yale Classical Studies 25 (1977) 291-316.
27   An ode known to Plutarch (*Alcibiades* 11).

but it is plaited into the crown of the victor. The acropolis is sacred (802) and Athens prosperous (804), as once was Troy.

Ganymede is recalled in the antistrophe. The Euripidean contrast between the undisturbed and serene joy of heaven, where Ganymede is employed as the cup-bearer of Zeus, and the pain of the mortals left in desolation upon the plain of the Troad is already present in the Homeric *Hymn to Aphrodite*. Here the bliss of Ganymede's life in heaven is contrasted with his father's grief over the loss of his son (202-10). Euripides seems intent on contradicting the theology of the Homeric hymn. In this ode there is no hint of Zeus's pity for Ganymede's father or the happy ending in what Aphrodite tells her mortal husband, the Trojan Anchises, of Zeus's recompense for the loss of a son by the gift of a team of horses (210-27).[28] The bliss of Zeus and Ganymede as they lift up towards heaven is beautifully rendered in an Archaic terra cotta group now in the Olympia Museum.

But the gods are not concerned with those to whom they are related as *kedestai* (or the ties not of blood but of "marriage"). The pious service of Ganymede as steward in the halls of the feasting gods (824-5) is worthless to Troy. On Olympos he walks softly in his luxuriant pride while his city burns. And Eos, the heavenly goddess who had conceived a passion for the Trojan Tithonos, carried him off to heaven, and had a son by him (Memnon), looks down from her radiance upon the fires consuming Troy with divine indifference.

Stasimon 3: Sacred Ilion   This final stasimon of the play continues and develops the theology first announced in Poseidon's speech in the Prologue and brilliantly revealed in the "Ganymede Ode" of the second *stasimon*. In this final choral song, the captive women of Troy divide the world into three levels: the shimmering and remote heights occupied by the gods; the underworld; and, in between, the earth which is the site of living humans as they attempt to reach both the indifferent gods on high and their dead below. In the first strophe and antistrophe the chorus call upon Zeus and remind the gods of the pious attempts of their city to join heaven and earth and assure the prosperity and safety of Troy. In the *Iliad*, Troy and its citadel is called "sacred"; its citadel (Pergamos) was the site of the temples of Apollo and Athena.[29]

The Trojan captives begin their song by calling to mind the festivals of their city that once had made it sacred in its contact with Zeus and the gods. The details of their lyrics are all meaningful and informed by a contrast: first of past and present and then, and by implication, of the human and the divine.[30] The altars of Troy are smoking, and the smoke of frankincense "lifts up into the clear blue sky" (1065). The high ridges of Ida are filled with the radiance of the first sacred light of day and this height overlooking Troy on the plain below is seen as "a generous land filled with light and sacred to the gods" (1070). The offerings recalled in the antistrophe—sacrifices, the song and choral

---

28   The theme of immortal horses seems a part of the "trilogy." There is, of course, the Trojan Horse. Athena is called goddess of immortal horses in the first stasimon (536 and note) and the mares of the savage king of Thrace, Diomedes, figured in the *Sisyphos*.

29   Ilion (in the form Ilios) is called sacred (*hiere*) twice in the only book of the *Iliad* that allows us to enter the doomed walls of Troy (6.277 and 403). There is a fine study of the meaning of this epithet for Troy in the *Iliad* by Stephen Scully in *Homer and the Sacred City* (Ithaca, New York 1990), Chapter 2.

30   The closest parallel to the contrast of ruin and prosperity is in Aeschylus' *Persians* 249-52. For the larger parallels, see Alexiou 1974: 83-85.

dancing of the night festivals of young women, the golden statues of the gods, and the moon-shaped cakes offered to the gods—are human gestures designed to conciliate the divine to the human. The chorus do not mention prayer to the gods. Their address to Zeus is not a prayer but an indignant question. This question is answered by silence and then, at the play's end, by the final collapse of "holy Troy" in flames. The last choral song and dance constitutes a gesture of alienation.

V. Theology

The theology of *The Trojan Women* is introduced on the *theologeion*, or the platform on the walls of Troy from which Poseidon speaks the Prologue and encounters Athena. In the Prologue, Hecuba has nothing to say about the gods as she lies prostrate and in agony beneath the two gods above her. She speaks only of a *daimon*, a powerful, unrecognized divine power that compels her (102). But she is capable of a more philosophical view of what constitutes divinity as she looks up at the sun Menelaos greets in triumph as Helen has fallen to him, with Troy (884-88):

> You, who bear the weight of the earth and have your seat upon the earth,
> whoever you are, hard to know and hard to place.
> Zeus, whether you are the Necessity of Nature or Human Intelligence,
> you do I call upon. As you travel your silent course,
> you lead all things human on the path of Justice.

Menelaos' reaction to Hecuba's prayer, a startling innovation to match his own address to the sun (Helios), is one of amazement. Hecuba's precedent for her strange invocation to Zeus as the hidden source of justice in human affairs might be taken back to the invocation to Zeus by the chorus of Aeschylus' *Agamemnon* (160-83). But the alternatives offered by Hecuba as proper descriptions of the true nature of Zeus belong to the last half of the fifth century. Zeus is first seen in Presocratic terms as the fiery element of *aither* (or fiery globe) that surrounds the earth, then as human intelligence or the necessity of nature, terms that have been traced to Anaximenes, Anaxagoras, and Democritus.

The challenge of interpreting these lines is not only that of placing them in their intellectual context in the fifth century; they must also be returned to their context in *The Trojan Women*.[31] What calls for explanation is their apparent incongruity. Immediately, they seem to serve as a foil to Menelaos' complacent dullness. But they also serve to introduce the innovative rhetoric of the age of the sophists —a rhetoric that will become manifest when Helen seeks refuge in Gorgias' *Praise of Helen* to urge her own apology against the charges that will be made against her.

Then there is that moment at the end of the play when Hecuba's conception of Zeus as *aither* and the force that leads all things mortal to justice is belied by the final collapse of Troy, whose smoke ascends like the futile smoke of sacrifice (*knise*) up to a bright and godless *aither* (1298-99 and 1320), a passage now familiar from our analysis of the third *stasimon*. The theology of *The Trojan Women* is articulated by those who know of the

---

31   Two admirable attempts to place them in their context in fifth century thought are those of Scodel, 1980: 93-95 and Charles H. Kahn, "Greek Religion and Philosophy in the Sisyphus Fragment," *Phronesis* 47 (1997) 247-62.

justice of Zeus as captives, and who, before the destruction of their city, had worshipped the gods of "holy Troy."

> When a terrible desolation takes a city,
> The world of the gods sickens and will not receive its honors.

The theology of this play is even grimmer than that announced in Poseidon's farewell to Troy (27-28). For the Trojan women there is no possibility of a theodicy, or a Miltonic justification of the ways of the gods towards man. The gods of this play do not finally desert a city because in its desolation it can no longer offer sacrifice. Despite the protests of Athena (69), the gods of *The Trojan Women* are remote from humans and indifferent to human religion. Zeus seems to possess the only stability present in the world of captured Troy. He sits secure on his high throne in heaven and its shimmering bright air (1079-80); but he seems indifferent to, oblivious to "the fierce rush of fire" that consumes Troy and its temples. In Euripides' Greek the noun *aither* is echoed in the participle describing the rush of fire that destroys Troy (*aithomena...horma*, 1080). This last line of the antistrophe answers "the generous land filled with light and sacred to the gods" (1070).

Does this language imply that the contact between *aither* and the world of divinity and the human and terrestrial is destructive? The language of the final scene of the play (the Exodos) seems to vindicate what is suggested in these words. As for the human world, the husbands who died in war and the sack of Troy must wander in death, unburied, unwashed (1082); their widows and children must make their way as slaves to their various destinations in Greece. The final wish of the chorus in the last antistrophe of this ode is for the destruction of Menelaos' ship on its way home. Their wish is never fulfilled. As for Menelaos, he escapes the fate threatened in the Prologue for the returning army of Greeks (cf. 77-86); his destiny will take him to the Islands of the Blest (*Odyssey* 4.561-70). As for Helen, she faces serene years of dignity and comfort in Sparta (beautifully described in *Odyssey* 4.120-280).

At the conclusion of Euripides' *Electra*, when Orestes and Electra stand over the body of the mother they have murdered and are exposed to the terrible public resentment their matricide will provoke —in Argos and in the Athenian audience—the chorus suddenly look up to the roof of the poor house in which the murder has been committed (1233-37):

> But look, there! On the roof of this house
> I see two figures. Are they lower spirits
> or gods from heaven? This is not the path
> of mortal men. What has brought them
> to this epiphany before mortal eyes?

As Clytemnestra's twin brothers appear, and Kastor addresses Orestes, Euripides has produced still another sensational ending to a play that has no human solution at its end. One thinks of other plays rescued by a god who appears *ex machina* on top of the stage building to tidy up the insoluble mess of human affairs: the *Medea, Andromache, Heracles, Ion, Helen, Orestes, Antiope,* and still others, including possibly the *Alexandros*.

The "path" of the gods in *The Trojan Women* is the walkway on top of the walls of Troy, where Poseidon meets Athena and looks down upon Hecuba on the stage platform below him. This privileged eminence is the *theologeion*, the place from which the gods speak to the human in the audience. It is elevated above the stage and remote from the scene of human suffering below it. In Euripides' *Hippolytus*, the goddess Artemis appears on the roof of the palace of Troezen. The dying Hippolytus can just catch the scent of her divine presence, yet, as a good goddess, she will not approach death (1392).

In the *Andromache*, the epiphany of Thetis is announced by the chorus of enslaved Trojan women in the same language that the chorus of the *Electra* used to greet the coming of the Dioskouroi (1226-30):

> What is happening now? What divinity do I sense?
> Girls, look, strain your eyes:
> Here is a divinity who is making his passage
> through the white brightness of the sky
> to set foot on the plains of Phthia where horses graze.

In *The Trojan Women* there is no such epiphany of a god or *deus ex machina* appearing on the walls of Troy, where Poseidon and Athena stood as the play opened. Silent Greek soldiers appear on top of these walls and they defeat any hope that a god will appear to save Troy from their flames. A blast from a trumpet signals the departure of the Trojan women. The chorus look up from the stage that has absorbed their attention throughout the play and, as they catch sight of the Greek soldiers above them, they too ask a question:

> What do I see? What men are these
> with torches darting here and there
> on Ilion's fiery crest?
> Some grim new catastrophe
> appends Troy's story.[32]

On the Translation   I began this translation in 1975 by producing a "literal" version that was to guide my friend and collaborator, Stephen Berg, in his translation of the play for William Arrowsmith's Greek Tragedy in New Translation series (Oxford University Press). That led to the first collapse of *The Trojan Women*. Our version left Arrowsmith discontented. Two other poets were enlisted to save Troy from the same fate for the same series: Daniel Mark Epstein and Mark Rudman. Both of these versions succumbed to the stern judgment of two editors: Arrowsmith and Herb Golder. In the summer of 2002 I decided to translate the play myself, and take on the roles of both Hellenist and poet. I finish in the summer of 2004.

One of my first challenges was to find a way of conveying the sounds of grief and lamentation. In Greece, the formal and very public drama of lamentation allows the survivors to find an outlet for their grief and, as women (never men) sing and wail in what are now called *moirologia* (songs of fate), they take some control over their fate. The sounds they make—*e e, oi' go, oimoi, omoi, oimoi talaina*, and the strange sigh *pheu*, are untranslatable in English because there is nothing similar in our culture to batten onto.

---

32   This catastrophe is glimpsed in Homer in a striking simile that compares the grief in Troy at the news of Hector's death to the collapse of its walls in flames, *Iliad* 22.410-11, as Adrian Poole once observed, ""Total Disaster: Euripides' *The Trojan Women*," *Arion* New Series 3:3 (1976) 278.

Grief in Anglo-Saxon culture is best expressed by silence, or silent prayer, and in small groups. Or appeals to God! I have attempted to avoid the bathos of "miserable me," "oh, oh," "alack, alas," by leaving a director and audience with the Greek sounds of mourning in italics.

I base my translation on the edition of the Greek text by James Diggle, *Euripidis Fabulae*, volume 2, Oxford 1981. My line numbers closely approximate his, so that a reader who wants to consult the Greek can easily turn to the original. Only rarely do I depart from his text. When I do, or when I have difficulty accepting his text, I usually note my departure and perplexity. Square brackets indicate those passages Diggle and other editors regard as interpolations to the original text. Helpful guides in translating and commenting (if only briefly) on the play are: Léon Parmentier, *Euripide*, vol. 4, Paris 1959 (in the Budé series); Kevin H. Lee, *Euripides: Troades*, London 1976; and Shirley A. Barlow, *Euripides: Trojan Women*, Warminster 1986.

This translation is the product of many years of thinking and meditating on the play in times of war. It is dedicated to my daughters, who I pray will have a better future than the women of Troy. It owes a great debt to the friendship and inspiration of William Arrowsmith, who taught me how, as he described it, to "liquefy the foundations," and make Greek tragedy convincing as dramatic, and, I hope, poetic English, and to visualize the action of *The Trojan Women* as well as that of the earlier plays I have helped translate with two poets (Sophocles' *Oedipus the King* with Stephen Berg and *Philoctetes* with Carl Philipps). Now I am left to translate myself, with the help of Andrea Purvis. And in the last leg of this translation Focus Publishing has provided me with a very helpful reader's report, and my series editor (friend and student) Stephen Esposito has helped me as I entered final revisions. He was a student of William Arrowsmith and it seems fitting that he should have the last word—the result of which he is not finally responsible for.

Finally, I acknowledge two further and now remote debts: to T. V. Buttrey, who, in a memorable lecture on *The Trojan Women* given at The Johns Hopkins University, opened my eyes to the meaning of the last scene of the play, as I looked for gods who did not appear on the walls of Troy to save us; and to George Boas, who, during my first years at The Johns Hopkins University, allowed me to read Euripides with him. He was then still a vigorous man in his 80s. We did not read the full text of any of Euripides' plays; only the excerpts from Stobaeus.

EXPOSITION (1-347)

madness revealed

Athena's wrath → Ajax's madness

CONFRONTATION #1 (348-865)

over suicide

Ajax's encounter with family and friends

Prologue (1-133)	Act I (201-595)	Act II (646-692)	Act III (719-865)
a madman found, a goddess's revenge	a hero's plight and shame: horrific revelation	a purpose concealed with sword in hand	fear, search, and suicide by the enemy's sword
Scene: Ajax's hut on shore of Troy; 10th year of Trojan War *ENTER ATHENA / ODYSSEUS* **Search Scene #1** (1-90): An (initially) invisible Athena tells Odysseus how she drove Ajax mad as he tried to murder the Greek commanders. *ENTER AJAX, carrying his bloody cattle-whip (91)* Athena cruelly toys with the boasting Ajax (91-117) *EXIT AJAX (117)* Odysseus' pity for Ajax; Athena's boasting about the power of the gods and their hatred for evil-doers (118-133) *EXIT ATHENA / ODYSSEUS*	*ENTER TECMESSA (201)* **Lyric Dialogue #1** (201-262): Tecmessa and chorus-leader. She verifies Ajax's madness and his slaughter of cattle 263-83: Tecmessa + chorus-leader 284-332: Tecmessa's 1st speech: explains Ajax's past + present acts 333-47: Tec, chorus-leader + Ajax *ENTER AJAX on trolley (348)* He *sits* for 250 lines among the beasts he has slain in his madness. **Lyric Dialogue #2** (348-429): Ajax, Tecmessa, chorus-leader. Only Ajax has *lyrics*; he reveals his sense of shame, desire to die.	*ENTER AJAX (with sword) and TECMESSA (646)* **Ajax's Deception Speech** (646-92) [forms an entire act in itself] *EXIT AJAX by side ramp and TECMESSA into the hut (692)*	*ENTER MESSENGER (719)* **Messenger Scene** (719-814): Report of Calchas' prophecy: "Confine Ajax to his hut *just for today* and he will live hereafter freed from Athena's wrath!" *ENTER TECMESSA (786)* *EXIT TECMESSA, CHORUS, and MESSENGER (814)* Chorus splits into 2 search parties **Scene changes to seashore** *ENTER AJAX with sword (815)* a. 3 reasons to commit suicide b. 5 invocations to various gods c. farewell to Salamis + Athens *AJAX'S SUICIDE (865)*
	Ajax vs. Tecmessa (430-595) Ajax (430-80): his dilemma Tec. (485-524): asks for pity *ENTER EURYSACES (545)* Father's farewell to son (545-82): "Be like me, only luckier!" Ajax vs. Tecmessa (585-95): tense *EXIT AJAX on trolley (595) and TECMESSA w/ EURYSACES*		
SONG #1 (134-200) Enter Chorus of 15 sailors of Ajax a. What god caused your attack? b. Can the rumor be true? c. Rise up, Ajax, refute the rumor! (3 stanzas)	**SONG #2 (596-645)** a. yearns for pleasures of home b. laments Ajax's *god-sent madness* c. laments his mother's sorrow d. laments his father's sorrow (4 stanzas)	**SONG #3 (693-718)** "Joy-before-catastrophe ode" a. excited invocation of Pan and Apollo to lead their dance b. reason for joy is the unexpected happy change of mind by Ajax (2 stanzas)	

SOPHOCLES' AJAX (1st half = 1-865)

SEARCH #2 | **CONFRONTATION #2 (974-1373)** over burial | **AFTERMATH (1374-1420)**

Where is Ajax?	Ajax's (Teucer's) encounter with enemies		Resolution	Summary of 2 part (= diptych) structure
Epi-parados (866-973)	**Act IV (974-1184)**	**Exodus (1223-1420)**		
a body found, a wife's sadness	a brother's sadness/defiance, a son's farewell		one enemy's resistance, one enemy's assistance	**[1-865]**
Mirror Scene of Search #1 **RE-ENTER CHORUS (866)** in 2 separate groups.	*ENTER TEUCER (974)* *EXIT TECMESSA (989)*	*ENTER TEUCER (1223)* *ENTER AGAMEMNON (1226)*		**Hero's Descent** Preparation for suicide Plot #1→divine retribution: Athena's wrath + its effects
<u>Structure of this complex scene:</u>	a. Teucer's long lament (992-1039): he uncovers the corpse (1003-5) and pulls out the sword (1024-7)	a. Angry quarrel #2 (1226-1315): Agamemnon, forbidding burial (1226-63) vs. Teucer (1266-1315)		**[866-1420]**
Intro: chorus searches (866-90) a. lyrics by chorus (879-90) ***ENTER TECMESSA (891):*** **she discovers Ajax's corpse** b. lyric dialogue (891-914) c. speech by Tecmessa (915-24) she shrouds Ajax's corpse a. lyric by chorus (925-36) b. lyric dialogue (937-60) c. speech by Tecmessa (961-73) = her last words of the play	*ENTER MENELAUS (1047)* b. Angry quarrel #1 (1047-1162): Menelaus, forbidding burial (1052- 1090) vs. Teucer (1093-1117) *EXIT MENELAUS (1162)* *ENTER TECMESSA / SON (1168)* c. Ritual commemoration (1168-84) Eurysaces puts 3 locks of hair on Ajax; Teucer curses Agam. / Men. Tecmessa is silent for duration of her final appearance (1168-1420).	*ENTER ODYSSEUS (1318)* b. Debate about burial (1318-74) Agamemnon yields to Odysseus because of their friendship. *EXIT AGAMEMNON (1374)* c. Teucer praises Ody. and curses Men. / Agam. but forbids Ody. to participate in the burial rites. *EXIT ODYSSEUS (1401)* d. funeral procession with corpse		**Hero's Ascent** Preparation for burial Plot #2 → human quarrel: brothers (Teucer + Ajax) vs. brothers (Menelaus + Agamemnon)
	EXIT TEUCER (1184)	*EXIT TEC., EURY., CHORUS*		
	SONG #4 (1185-1222) a. Let us leave Troy and its miseries b. A curse on the inventor of war! c. For he put an end to life's joys! d. Since impetuous Ajax is no more, let us return home to holy Athens. (4 stanzas)	**Ajax's 4 main speeches** 430-80 to Tecmessa (= 51 lines) 545-82 to Eurysaces (= 38 lines) 646-92 "Deception" (= 47 lines) 815-65 "Suicide" (= 51 lines)		

SOPHOCLES' AJAX (2nd half = 866-1420)

GENEALOGY CHARTS FOR SOPHOCLES' *AJAX*

THE HOUSE OF AJAX

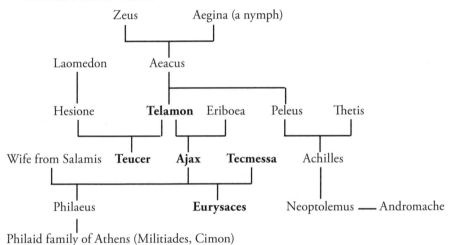

THE HOUSE OF ODYSSEUS

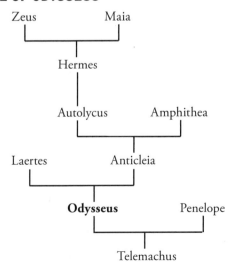

Genealogy Charts for *Hecuba* and *Trojan Women*

THE HOUSE OF TROY

Zeus   (son of Kronos, brother and philandering husband of Hera)

Dardanus   (ancestor of the Trojan kings; *Iliad* 20.215)

Erichthonius (richest of mortal men; owned 3,000 horses; *Iliad* 20.219)

Tros   (ancestor of Trojan kings; *Iliad* 20. 230-40)

Ilos   (founder of <u>Ili</u>on = Troy; hence *The <u>Iliad</u>*)

Laomedon   (deceitful king of Troy whose walls were built for him by Apollo and Poseidon; his city was sacked by Heracles in 1st Trojan War)

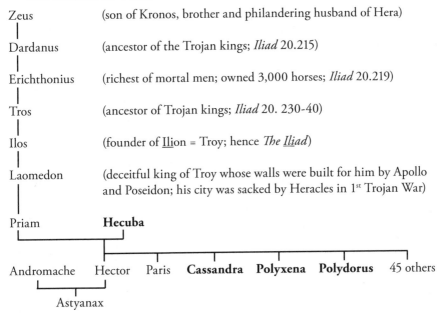

Priam   **Hecuba**

Andromache   Hector   Paris   **Cassandra**   **Polyxena**   **Polydorus**   45 others

Astyanax

THE HOUSE OF ATREUS

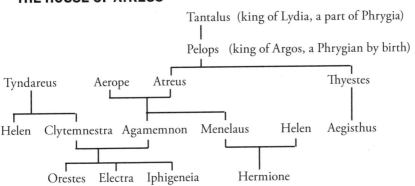

Tantalus (king of Lydia, a part of Phrygia)

Pelops (king of Argos, a Phrygian by birth)

Tyndareus   Aerope   Atreus   Thyestes

Helen   Clytemnestra   Agamemnon   Menelaus   Helen   Aegisthus

Orestes   Electra   Iphigeneia   Hermione

Appendix 4

In Praise of Helen, by Gorgias of Leontini

Translated from Diels-Kranz, *Die Fragmente der Vorsokratiker,* sixth edition, Berlin 1952 (reprint 1960), 82 B 11 (volume 2, pp. 288-94):

(1) The bravery of its men is the crown of a city, beauty, of a body, wisdom, of a soul, of action, virtue and success, and truth, of speech. The opposites of these are disgrace. A man and a woman, a speech and a deed, a city and an action worthy of praise should be honored by praise; but reproach should be applied to what is unworthy [of praise]. For equal are the ignorance and error of blaming what deserves praise and praising what deserves blame.

(2) One and the same speaker [must] both say what is needful and reprove...[1] those who blame Helen, a woman concerning whom the reliability of the poets who have heard of her, the fame of her name, and the memory of her tragedy is homophonous and unanimous. It is my desire to give a demonstration in speech and put an end to her bad reputation and the blame attached to it, to remonstrate before all that those who blame her lie, and to demonstrate the truth and put an end to their ignorance.

(3) That this woman, who is the subject of this speech, was pre-eminent among men and women pre-eminent in birth and lineage is not unclear nor known to [only] a few. For it is clear that her mother was Leda, her father was in truth a god, but was said to be mortal: Tyndareos and Zeus.[2] Of the two, Zeus seemed to be her father, because he actually was; the other was said to be her father, because he seemed to be.

(4) As the daughter of parents such as these, she possessed a beauty equal to that of the gods. Receiving this [beauty], she was not mistaken in possessing it. In the greatest number of men she inspired the most intense desire of passionate love, and with a single body she brought together the bodies of many men who were haughty because of their high achievements. Some of these possessed a great treasure of wealth, others the glory of an ancient lineage, others the glorious ground of their own valor, others, the power of an acquired wisdom. And all of these came

---

1   Something has been lost from our manuscripts here.

2   An allusion to the myth of Leda and Zeus as her lover in the assumed form of a swan. I adopt the reading ἐλέχθη ("was said to be") rather than the ἐλέγχθη ("was disproved") printed in Diels-Kranz.

[to Sparta], impelled by a passion that pitted them as rivals and a sense of pride that knew no rivalry. (5) Now, who it was, and for what reason, and how he took this object of passion—this Helen—and sailed away [with her] I will not say. To speak to those who know what they are knowledgeable of is measure enough; it brings no pleasure. I have now trespassed beyond the time allowed for that speech past; at present, I will go on to the beginning of future speech, and I will set before you the causes that made reasonable the conveyance of Helen to Troy.

(6) We face a choice. Either she did what she did by the will of the goddess Tyche and the willful plans of the gods and the edicts of Necessity, or she was carried off by force, or persuaded by words, or <taken captive by the passion of love>.[3] Now, if [she left] for the reason first given, he who blames her deserves blame. For no human provision can prevent the vision of a god. It is no law of nature that the stronger and superior is prevented by the weaker.[4] The law commands that the weaker be ruled and led by the stronger and that the stronger lead and the weaker follow. A god is something superior to a human being in force and wisdom and in other respects as well. If, therefore, the responsibility is to be attributed to the goddess Tyche and to the divine, Helen must be acquitted of her ill fame.

(7) But if she was carried away by force and criminally compelled and unjustly outraged, it is clear that the man who carried her away is criminal as a rapist, but that the woman who was carried away was the victim of misfortune, since she was the victim of outrage. The stranger who undertook this undertaking, which is barbarian in word, in custom, and in deed is, therefore, worthy of verbal reproach, on the one hand, and, on the other, of suffering the dishonor of law and the penalty of actual deed. How can it be that the woman, who was the victim of violence and the victim deprived of her country and the victim made an orphan to her family, is not more reasonably deserving of pity than words of blame? The man did dreadful things; she suffered dreadful things. Justice calls us to pity her and to despise him.

(8) Now if Speech (*Logos*) was the agent that persuaded her and deceived her soul, it is no difficult matter to defend her against this charge and free her of blame. Speech is a mighty Master; one, who, with the smallest and least apparent body, accomplishes things most divine. For speech has the power to quell fear, remove distress, produce joy, and increase pity. I will show how this is the case. (9) I must show this to my audience by a show of plausibility. All Poetry I opine and define as speech in meter. Those who listen to Poetry are affected by the fright of terror and the pity that brings a flood of tears and a longing that loves grief. And merely because of the fortunes and misfortunes in the affairs and the bodies of others, the soul suffers a private emotion on account of words. Attend now as I move from one argument to another.

---

3   The language missing in our manuscripts can be supplied from the sequel to this argument in § 15.

4   Compare Helen's defense in *Trojan Women* 948-50 and 964-65. The mention of Deiphobos forcing marriage on Helen (948-50) is bracketed by some editors (Wilamowitz and Diggle), but it must figure in her defense.

(10) Inspired and divine incantations bring on pleasure through words and conduct pains away. When joined with the soul's Imagination, the power of the charm [of words] bewitches the soul, persuades it, and transports it by its witchery. Two arts for witchery and magic have been discovered: these are Misleading the Soul and Deceiving the Imagination. (11) All those, who have persuaded and persuade all those they persuade concerning the objects of their persuasion, persuade by fashioning a false argument. If in all matters all men had memory of things past, and <an awareness>[5] of things present, and foresight of things to come, Speech would not be similar in a like manner [to what it is now], for men in their present state find it difficult to recall the past, to inquire into the present, and to divine the future. As a result, most men rely on their Imagination as Councillor to their souls. And this Fancy and Imagination (*doxa*), since it is slippery and unstable, involves those who rely on it in a success that in far from certain. (12) †What reproach, then, prevents Speech from capturing Helen in its toils and coming to her when she was but a young woman and carrying her off by [its] force, as if it were a mighty lord?†[6]... Speech was the agent that persuaded her soul, which it did persuade, and it compels [her] to believe what was spoken and to commend what was done as well. Now, the agent that persuaded is guilty, since it compelled, but the woman who was persuaded should afford no reason for blame, since she was compelled by Speech. (13) Persuasion (*Peitho*) approaches the soul with her speech and can strike whatever impression upon the soul she will. One can understand this from the case of what is said concerning the phenomena of the atmosphere and heavens. These words replace one opinion by impressing another [upon our souls] and they make what is incredible and remote from us appear as visible to the eyes of the Imagination. A second proof are the contests of Necessity, which are conducted by words. In these a single speech (*logos*) charms a great crowd and persuades, if it is written with skill, even if it is not spoken in Truth. Third, the disputes of philosophical arguments. In these the quickness of the mind is shown as something that can shift its ground and create confidence in the Imagination. (14) The power of the Word possesses an analogy to medicine: its power over the composition of the soul is like a prescribed drug in its relation to the constitution of the body. Just so, in the case of drugs, some remove one set of humors from the body and others others; some bring disease to an end, others bring life to an end. Just so, in the case of words, some cause pain, others cause joy; some cause fear, others inspire their audience with confidence; others poison and bewitch the soul with a kind of malign Persuasion.

(15) It has been said that, if she was persuaded by Speech (*logos*), she committed no wrong. Now I will go over the fourth accusation in a fourth argument.

---

5   The necessary supplement of Friedrich Blass.

6   The daggers in the text indicate that this passage is somewhat garbled in the two mss. that preserve this speech. I have given the likely sense and suggest that the poetic word βιάτας ("a mighty force") might have been corrupted into (the unattested) βιατήριον. It would, then, describe *logos* as a mighty (and violent) lord.

If the passion of Love (*Eros*)[7] is the agent responsible for all of this, [Helen] will have no difficulty in being acquitted of the blame for the fault that was said to have been incurred. Now what we see does not have the character we would give it, but it is as each individual thing happens to be. In its character too the soul is impressed through its seeing. (16) Now as soon as Vision beholds hostile bodies and an enemy formation arrayed against enemies fully armed in bronze and iron, the one for protection the other for offense, it is thrown into turmoil and disturbs the soul, so that often soldiers are terrified, taking a future danger as a present and actual danger, and flee from the field. Custom has established a powerful habit on account of the panic fear that comes through the eyes. When it comes, this Vision makes soldiers neglect the sense of honor which is distinguished by custom and the good that comes through victory. (17) As soon as they catch sight of terrible things, some people abandon their present prudence in the present time [in its presence]. So does Fear extinguish and drive out Thought. And many become caught up in sufferings that have no cure and in dreadful diseases and incurable madness. This is how Vision engraves in the mind the images of things seen. Many of the things that cause terror are left behind [in the mind], but what is said is similar to those [images of] things that remain [in the mind]. (18) And, in a like manner, painters delight the eyes, when they finish one body and one attitude to perfection, creating it out of many bodies and colors. The making of statues of men and the production of statues of the gods provide the eyes a pleasing sight. So it is that the nature of some things is to please the eyes; of others, to cause them pain. For many men, many objects produce passion and desire for many things and many bodies. (19) If, now, Helen's eyes were pleased by the sight of Alexander's body and transmitted to her soul a desire and the striving of love, what wonder is there in this? If Eros is a god and possesses the divine power of a god, how could one who was weaker thrust him off and defend oneself against him? But if [Eros] is the creation of human thought and the soul's lack of thought, [a reaction like Helen's] should not be a matter for blame; it should be regarded as a misfortune. [Alexander] came, as he came, as a snare of the goddess Tyche, not as the Counsel of Intelligence, and he came, by the necessities of Eros, not the provisions of Art.

(20) How, therefore, should we deem the blame of Helen to be just? Either she was the victim of Passion; or she was persuaded by Speech; or she was carried off by Force; or she was compelled by divine Necessity to do what she did. In any of these cases, she is acquitted of blame.

(21) I have removed by Speech the evil fame that attaches to the woman. I have kept to the condition I laid down at the beginning of this speech. I have attempted to free [Helen] from the injustice of blame and the ignorance of Imagination. I wanted to write this speech: for Helen a praise, for myself to amaze.

---

7   Compare Helen's argument in *Trojan Women* 940-42 and Hecuba's refutation in 987-90, a refutation that reflects the argument of § 17 below.

Appendix 5

Bibliography

The fifteen sections of the bibliography are divided as follows:

I. GENERAL BOOKS ON GREEK CULTURE

Burkert, W., *Greek Religion* trans. J. Raffan (1985)

Buxton, R. (ed.), *Oxford Readings in Greek Religion* (2000)

Cairns, D., *Aidôs: The Psychology of Honour and Shame in Ancient Greek Literature* (1993)

Dodds, E. R., *The Greeks and the Irrational* (1951)

Finley. M. I., *The World of Odysseus* [2] rev. ed. (1979)

Gill, C., Postlethwaite, N. and Seaford, R. (eds.), *Reciprocity in Ancient Greece* (1998)

Gould, J., *Myth, Ritual Memory and Exchange* (2001)

Mikalson, J., *Athenian Popular Religion* (1983)

Oakley, J. and Sinos, R., *The Wedding in Ancient Athens* (1993)

Parker, R., *Miasma: Pollution and Purification in Early Greek Religion* (1983)

Parker, R., *Athenian Religion: A History* (1996)

Patterson, O., *Freedom in the Making of Western Culture* (1991)

Seaford, R., *Reciprocity and Ritual. Homer and Tragedy in the Developing City-State* (1994)

Williams, B., *Shame and Necessity* (1993)

II. REFERENCE BOOKS ON GREEK TRAGEDY

Ashby, C., *Classical Greek Theatre: New Views of an Old Subject* (1999)

Bushnell, R. (ed.), *A Companion to Tragedy* (2005)

Csapo, E. and Slater, W. J., *The Context of Ancient Drama* (1994)

Easterling, P. E. and Knox, B. (eds.), *The Cambridge History of Classical Literature* vol. 1 (1985)

Easterling, P.E. (ed.), *The Cambridge Companion to Greek Tragedy* (1997)

Easterling, P. E. and Hall, E. (eds.), *Greek and Roman Actors: Aspects of an Ancient Profession* (2002)

Gregory, Justina (ed.), *A Companion to Greek Tragedy* (2005)

Lesky, A., *Greek Tragic Poetry* trans. M. Dillon (1983)

McDonald, M. and Walton, J. M. (eds.), *The Cambridge Companion to Greek and Roman Theatre* (2006)

Pickard-Cambridge, A., *The Dramatic Festivals of Athens* [2] rev. edn., John Gould and David Lewis (1988)

Sommerstein, A., *Greek Drama and Dramatists* (2002)

Storey, I. and Allan, A., *A Guide to Ancient Greek Drama* (2005)

Walton, J. M., *Found in Translation: Greek Drama in English* (2006)

III. REFERENCE BOOKS ON GREEK DRAMA AND THE ARTS

Green, J. R., *Theatre in Ancient Greek Society* (1994)

Green, J. R. and Handley, E., *Images of the Greek Theatre* (1995)

Taplin, Oliver, *Pots and Plays: Interactions between Tragedy and Greek Vase-Painting of the Fourth Century B.C.* (2007)

Webster, T. B. L., *Monuments Illustrating Tragedy and Satyr Play* [2] (*Bulletin of the Institute of Classical Studies*, Supplement 20, 1967)

Webster, T. B. L. and Trendall, A. D., *Illustrations of Greek Drama* (1971)

IV. GENERAL BOOKS ON GREEK TRAGEDY

Barrett, J., *Staged Narrative: Poetics and the Messenger in Greek Tragedy* (2002)

Burnett, A., *Revenge in Attic and Later Tragedy* (1998)

Buxton, R. G. A., *Persuasion in Greek Tragedy: A Study of Peitho* (1982)

Des Bouvrie, S., *Women in Greek Tragedy: an Anthrological Approach* (1990)

Foley, H., *Female Acts in Greek Tragedy* (2001)

Golder, H. and Scully, S. (eds.), *The Chorus in Greek Tragedy and Culture* in *Arion* 3.1 (1994-5) and 4.1 (1996)

Hall, E., *Inventing the Barbarian: Greek Self-Definition through Tragedy* (1989)

Hall, E., *The theatrical cast of Athens: interactions between ancient Greek drama and society* (2006)

Hall, E. *et al.* (eds.), *Dionysus since 69: Greek tragedy at the dawn of the third millennium* (2004)

Loraux, N., *Tragic Ways of Killing a Woman* trans. Anthony Forster (1987)

McClure, L., *Spoken Like a Woman: Speech and Gender in Athenian Drama* (1999)

Pelling, C. (ed.), *Greek Tragedy and the Historian* (1997)

Rehm, R., *Greek Tragic Theatre* (1992)

Segal, C., *Interpreting Greek Tragedy: Myth, Poetry, Text* (1986)

Silk, M. (ed.), *Tragedy and the Tragic: Greek Theatre and Beyond* (1996)

Taplin, O., *Greek Tragedy in Action* (1978)

Vernant, J. P. and Vidal-Naquet, P., *Myth and Tragedy in Ancient Greece*, trans. J. Lloyd Wiles, D., *Tragedy in Athens: Performance Space and Theatrical Meaning* (1997)

Wilson, P., *The Athenian Institution of the Khoregia: The Chorus, the City, and the Stage* (2000)

Wohl, V., *Intimate Commerce: Exchange, Gender, and Subjectivity in Greek Tragedy* (1998)

V. ARTICLES ON ASPECTS OF GREEK TRAGEDY

Arrowsmith, W., "The Criticism of Greek Tragedy" *Tulane Drama Review* 3.3 (1959) 31-57 = *Oedipus Rex: A Mirror for Greek Drama* (ed.) Albert Cook (1963) 155-69

Arrowsmith, W., "A Greek Theater of Ideas" *Arion* 2.3 (1963) 32-56 = *Ideas in the Drama* (ed.) John Gassner (1964) 1-41

Carter, D. M., "Was Attic tragedy democratic?" *Polis* 21 (2004) 1-25

Croally, N., "Tragedy's Teaching" in *A Companion to Greek Tragedy* (ed.) Justina Gregory (2005) 55-70

Esposito, S., "What is Greek Tragedy?" in *Euripides: Medea, Hippolytus, Heracles, Bacchae* (ed.) Stephen Esposito (2004) 1-9

Golden, L., "Toward a definition of tragedy" *Classical Journal* 72 (1976) 21-35

Goldhill, S., "Representing Democracy: women at the Great Dionysia" in Robin Osborne and Simon Hornblower (eds.) *Ritual, Finance, Politics: Athenian democratic accounts presented to David Lewis* (1994) 347-69

Goldhill, S., "The Audience of Athenian Tragedy" *The Cambridge Companion to Greek Tragedy* (1997) 54-68

Griffin, J., "The Social Function of Attic Tragedy" *Classical Quarterly* 48 (1998) 39-61

Hall, E., "The Sociology of Athenian Tragedy" in The Cambridge Companion to Greek Tragedy (ed.) P. E. Easterling (1997) 93-126

Halliwell, S., "Plato's Repudiation of the Tragic" in *Tragedy and the Tragic* (ed.) Michael Silk (1996) 332-50

Heath, M., "The 'Social Function' of Greek Tragedy: Clarifications and Questions" in *Dionysalexandros: Essays on Aeschylus and his fellow tragedians in honour of A. F. Garvie* (eds.) D. L. Cairns and V. Liapis (2006) 253-81

Humphries, W., *The Tragic Vision and the Hebrew Tradition* (1985)

Lee, K. H., "The Dionysia: Instrument of control or platform for critique?" in *Gab es das Griechische Wunder? Griechenland zwishcen dem Ende des 6. und der Mitte des 5. Jahrhunderts v. Chr.* (eds.) D. Papenfuss + V. Strocka (2001) 77-89

Lesky, A., "What is Tragedy?" in *Greek Tragedy* trans. H. Frankfort (1965) 1-26

Mastronarde, D., "Actors on High: The *Skênê* Roof, the Crane, and the Gods in Attic Drama" *Classical Antiquity* 9 (1990) 247-94

McAlindon, T., "What is Shakespearean tragedy?" in *The Cambridge Companion to Shakespearean Tragedy* (ed.) Claire McEachern (2002) 1-22

Most, G., "Generating Genres: The Idea of the Tragic" in *Matrices of Genre: Authors, Canons, and Society* (eds.) Mary Depew and Dirk Obbink (2000) 15-35

Nagy, G., "Transformations of Choral Lyric Traditions in the Context of Athenian State Theater" *Arion* 3 (1995) 41-55

Nuttall, A. D., *Why Does Tragedy Give Pleasure?* (1996)

Raaflaub, K. and Boedeker, D., "Tragedy and City" in *A Companion to Tragedy* (ed.) Rebecca Bushnell (2005) 109-27

Rabinowitz, N., "Embodying Tragedy: The Sex of the Actor" *Intertexts* 2.1 (1998) 3-25

Rhodes, P.J., "Nothing to Do with Democracy: Athenian Drama and the Polis" *Journal of Hellenic Studies* 123 (2003) 104-19

Scodel, R., "The Poet's Career, The Rise of Tragedy, and Athenian Cultural Hegemony" *Gab es das Griechische Wunder? Griechenland zwishcen dem Ende des 6. und der Mitte des 5. Jahrhunderts v. Chr.* (eds.) D. Papenfuss + V. Strocka (2001) 215-27

Scullion, S., " 'Nothing to Do with Dionysus': Tragedy Misconceived as Ritual" *Classical Quarterly* 52 (2002) 102-37

Seaford, R., "The Social Function of Attic Tragedy: A Response to Jasper Griffin" *Classical Quarterly* 50 (2000) 30-44

Segal, C., "Catharsis, Audience, and Closure in Greek Tragedy" in *Tragedy and the Tragic* (ed.) Michael Silk (1996) 149-72

Simon, B., "From Epic to Tragedy: The Birth of Tragedy" in *Tragic Drama and the Family: Psychoanalytic Studies from Aeschylus to Beckett* (1988) 13-27

Simon, B., "Catharsis and Psychotherapy" in *Mind and Madness in Ancient Greece: The Classical Roots of Modern Psychiatry* (1978) 122-54

Wilson, P., "Costing the Dionysia" in *Performance, Iconography, Reception: Studies in Honour of Oliver Taplin* (eds.) M. Revermann and P. Wilson (2008) 88-127

Wohl, V., "Review Essay: The Romance of Tragedy and Psychoanalysis" *Helios* 35 (2008) 89-110

VI. GREEK DRAMA AND POLITICS

Amit, M., "The Melian Dialogue and History" *Athenaeum* 56 (1968) 216-35

Brock, R., "Did the Athenian Empire Promote Democracy?" in *Interpreting the Athenian Empire* (eds.) J. Ma, N. Papazarkadas and R. Parker (2009) 149-66

Carter, D. M., *The Politics of Greek Tragedy* (2007)

Connor, W. R., "City Dionysia and Athenian Democracy" Classica et Mediaevalia 40 (1989) 7-32 = Aspects of Athenian Democracy (ed.) W. R. Connor et al. 1990) 7-32

Connor, W. R., "Civil Society, Dionysiac Festival, and the Athenian Democracy" in *Demokratia: A Conversation on Democracies, Ancient and Modern* (eds.) J. Ober and C. Hedrick (1996) 217-26

Finley, M. I., "Athenian Demagogues" in *Athenian Democracy* (ed.) P. J. Rhodes (2004) 163-84

Goldhill, S., "Greek Drama and Political Theory" in The Cambridge History of Greek and Roman Political Thought (eds.) C. Rowe and M. Schofield (2000) 60-88

Goldhill, S., "The Great Dionysia and civic ideology" *Journal of Hellenic Studies* 107 (1986) 58-76 = *Nothing to Do with Dionysus? Athenian Drama in its Social Context* (eds.) John Winkler and Froma Zeitlin (1990) 97-129

Griffin, J., "Sophocles and the Democratic City" in *Sophocles Revisited: Essays Presented to Sir Hugh Lloyd-Jones* (ed.) Jasper Griffin (1999) 73-94

Meyer, C., *The Political Art of Tragedy* (1993)

Murray, G., "Reactions to the Peloponnesian War in Greek Thought and Practice" *Journal of Hellenic Studies* 64 (1944) 1-9

Murray, G., *Euripides and His Age* ² (1946); a very influential book

Ober, J. and Strauss, B., "Drama, Political Rhetoric and the Discourse of Athenian Democracy" in *Nothing to Do with Dionysus? Athenian Drama in its Social Context* (eds.) John Winkler and Froma Zeitlin (1990) 237-70

Osborne, R., "Competitive Festivals and the polis: a context for dramatic festivals at Athens" in *Tragedy, Comedy and the Polis* (ed.) Alan Sommerstein *et al.* (1993) 21-38 = *Athenian Democracy* (ed.) P. J. Rhodes (2004) 207-24

Rhodes, P. J., "Drama as democratic performance" in *Ancient Democracy and Modern Ideology* (2003) 77-81

Rhodes, P. J., "Nothing to do with democracy: Athenian Drama and the Polis" *Journal of Hellenic Studies* 123 (2003) 104-19

Rhodes, P. J., "Democracy and Empire" in The Cambridge Companion to the Age of Pericles (ed.) Loren J. Samons (2007) 24-45

Saïd, S., "Tragedy and Politics" in *Democracy, Empire and the Arts in Fifth-century Athens* (eds.) Deborah Boedeker and Kurt Raaflaub (1998) 275-96

Salkever, S., "Tragedy and the Education of the Demos: Aristotle's Response to Plato" in *Greek Tragedy and Political Theory* (ed.) J. P. Euben (1986) 274-305

VII. SOURCE BOOKS IN TRANSLATION ON THE ATHENIAN EMPIRE

Osborne, R. (ed.), *The Athenian Empire* [4] (Lactor 1, 2000)

Roberts, J. W. (ed.), *Athenian Radical Democracy: 461-404* (Lactor 5, 1998)

VIII. EURIPIDES: GENERAL ARTICLES

Arrowsmith, W., "Euripides' Theater of Ideas" in Erich Segal (ed.) *Euripides: A Collection of Critical Essays* (1968) 13-33

Arrowsmith, W., "Euripides and the Dramaturgy of Crisis" in *Literary Imagination* 1.2 (1999) 201-26

Collard, C., "Formal Debates in Euripides' Drama" *Greece and Rome* 2nd series, 22.1 (1975) 58-71

Davidson, J., "Euripides, Homer and Sophocles" in *Euripides and Tragic Theatre in the Late Fifth Century* (ed.) Martin Cropp *et al.* (= *Illinois Classical Studies* 24-25, 1999-2000) 117-28

Dodd, E. R., "Euripides the Irrationalist" *Classical Review* 43 (1929) 97-104 = *The Ancient Concept of Progress and other Essays on Greek Literature and Belief* (1973) 78-91

Finley, J., "Euripides and Thucydides" *Harvard Studies in Classical Philology* 49 (1938) 23-66 = *Three Essays on Thucydides* (1967)

Gregory, J., "Euripides as Social Critic" *Greece and Rome* 49.2 (2002) 145-61

Jaeger, W., "Euripides and His Age" in *Paideia: The Ideals of Greek Culture* [2] vol. I, trans. G. Highet (1945) 332-57

Kovacs, D., "Introduction" in *Euripides: Cyclops, Alcestis, Medea* (Loeb, 1994) 1-42

McDonald, M., "Moving Icons: Teaching Euripides in Film" in *Approaches to Teaching the Dramas of Euripides* (ed.) Robin Mitchell-Boyask (2002) 60-69

Mitchell-Boyask, R., "Materials for Studying Euripides" in *Approaches to Teaching the Dramas of Euripides* (ed.) Robin Mitchell-Boyask (2002) 3-34

Michelini, A., "A History of Euripidean Interpretation" in *Euripides and The Tragic Tradition* (1987) 3-51

Michelini, A., "The Unclassical as Classic: The Modern Reception of Euripides" *Poetics Today* 9.4 (1988) 699-710

Michelini, A., "Euripides: Conformist, Deviant, Neo-conservative?" *Arion* 3rd series, 4.3 (1997) 208-22 = a review of 3 important books on Euripides

Reinhardt, K., "The Intellectual Crisis in Euripides" in *Euripides: Oxford Readings in Classical Studies* (ed.) Judith Mossman (2003) 16-46

Scullion, S., "Euripides and Macedon, or the Silence of the Frogs" *Classical Quarterly* 53 (2003) 389-400

Wolff, C., "Euripides" in *Ancient Writers: Greece and Rome* vol. 1 (ed.) T. J. Luce (1982) 233-66

IX. EURIPIDES AND THE PHILOSOPHERS

Allan, W., "Euripides and the Sophists: Society and the Theatre of War" in *Euripides and Tragic Theatre in the Late Fifth Century* (ed.) Martin Cropp *et al.* (= *Illinois Classical Studies* 24-25, 1999-2000) 145-56

Allan, W., "Tragedy and the Early Philosophical Tradition" *ibid.* (2005) 71-82

Conacher, D. J., *Euripides and the Sophists: Some Dramatic Treatments of Philosophical Ideas* (1998)

Eden, K., "Aristotle's *Poetics*: A Defense of Tragic Fiction" in *A Companion to Tragedy* (ed.) Rebecca Bushnell (2005) 41-50

Halliwell, S., "Nietzsche's 'Daimonic Force' of Tragedy and Its Ancient Traces" *Arion* 11 (2003) 103-23

Henrichs, A., "Nietzsche on Greek Tragedy and the Tragic" in *A Companion to Greek Tragedy* (ed.) Justina Gregory (2005) 444-58

Irwin, T. H., "Euripides and Socrates" *Classical Philology* 78 (1983) 183-97

Irwin, T. H., "Socrates and the Tragic Hero" in *Language and the Tragic Hero* (ed.) Pietro Pucci (1988) 55-83.

Moline, J., "Euripides, Socrates and Virtue" *Hermes* 103 (1975) 45-67.

Muir, J. V., "Religion and the new education: the challenge of the Sophists" in *Greek Religion and Society* (eds.) P. E. Easterling and J. V. Muir (1985) 191-218

Porter, J., "Nietzsche and Tragedy" in *A Companion to Tragedy* (ed.) Rebecca Bushnell (2005) 68-87

Sansone, D., "Plato and Euripides" *Illinois Classical Studies* 21 (1996) 35-67

X. EURIPIDES AND THE GODS

Knox, B., "Athenian Religion and Literature" in *The Cambridge Ancient History* 2 vol. V (ed.) David Lewis *et al.* (1992) 268-86

Lefkowitz, M., "Impiety and Atheism in Euripides" *Classical Quarterly* 39 (1989) 70-82 = *Oxford Readings in Classical Studies: Euripides* (ed.) Judith Mossman (2003) 102-21

Ostwald, M., "Atheism and the religiosity of Euripides" in *Literary Imagination, Ancient and Modern: Essays in Honor of David Grene* (ed.) T. Breyfogle (1999) 33-49

Sansone, D., "Language, Meaning and Reality in Euripides" in *Ultimate Reality and Meaning* 8.2 (1985) 92-104

Warrior, V., "The Gods in Sophocles and Euripides" in *Greek Religion: A Sourcebook* (2009) 165-86

XI. SPECIALITY BOOKS ON EURIPIDES

Barlow, S., *The Imagery of Euripides: A Study in the Dramatic Use of Pictorial Language* [2] (1986)

Halleran, M., *The Stagecraft in Euripides* (1985)

Jong, I. J. F. de, *Narrative in Drama: the Art of the Euripidean Messenger-speech* (1991)

Lloyd, M., *The Agon in Euripides* (1992)

XII. EURIPIDES: *HECUBA*

Arrowsmith, W., "Introduction to Euripides' *Hecuba*" in *The Complete Greek Tragedies, III: Euripides* (eds.) David Grene and Richmond Lattimore (1959) 488-93

Burnett, A. P., "Hekabe the Dog" *Arethusa* 27 (1994) 151-64

Collard, C., *Euripides: Hecuba. Introduction, Translation and Commentary* (1991); there is a fine introduction for the general reader.

Daitz, S., "Concepts of Freedom and Slavery in Euripides' *Hecuba*" *Hermes* 99 (1971) 217-26

Dué, C., "The Captive Woman's Lament and Her Revenge in Euripides' *Hecuba*" in *The Captive Woman's Lament in Greek Tragedy* (2006) 117-35

Gregory, J., "Genealogy and Intertextuality in Hecuba" *American Journal of Philology* 116 (1995) 389-97

Gregory, J., *Euripides: Hecuba: Introduction, Text, and Commentary* (1999)

Gregory, J., "*Hecuba* and the Political Dimension of Tragedy" in *Approaches to Teaching the Dramas of Euripides* (ed.) Robin Mitchell-Boyask (2002) 166-77

Heath, M., "*Iure principem locum tenet*: Euripides' *Hecuba*" *Bulletin of the Institute of Classical Studies* 34 (1987) 40-68) = *Oxford Readings in Classical Studies: Euripides* (ed.) Judith Mossman (2003) 218-60

Hogan, J. C., "Thucydides 3.52-68 and Euripides' *Hecuba*" *Phoenix* 26 (1972) 241-57

Kovacs, D., *The Heroic Muse: Studies in the Hippolytus and Hecuba of Euripides* (1987)

Lane, N., "Staging Polydorus' Ghost in the Prologue of *Hecuba*" *Classical Quarterly* 57 (2007) 290-94

Meridor, R., "Hecuba's Revenge" *American Journal of Philology* 99 (1978) 28-35

Meridor, R., "The Function of Polymestor's Crime in *Hecuba*" *Eranos* 81 (1983) 13-21

Mitchell-Boyask, R., "Sacrifice and Revenge in Euripides *Hecuba*" *Ramus* 22 (1993) 116-34

Mossman, J., *Wild Justice: A Study of Euripides' Hecuba* (1999)

Nussbaum, M., "The betrayal of convention: a reading of Euripides' *Hecuba*" in *The Fragility of Goodness: luck and ethics in Greek tragedy and philosophy* (1986; rev. edn. 2001) 397-421

Pantelis, M., "The Dead Hero: Euripides' *Hecuba*" in *Achilles in Greek Tragedy* (2002) 58-83

Rabinowitz, N., "The Terrifying *Mater Dolorosa*: Hekabe" in *Anxiety Veiled: Euripides and the Traffic in Women* (1993) 103-24

Reckford. K., "Concepts of Demoralization in the *Hecuba*" in *Directions in Euripidean Criticism* (ed.) Peter Burian (1985) 112-28

Scodel, R., "*Domôn agalma*: Virgin Sacrifice and Aesthetic Object" *Transactions of the American Philological Association* 126 (1996) 111-128

Scodel, R., "The Captive's Dilemma: Sexual Acquiescence in *Hecuba* and *Trojan Women*" in *Harvard Studies in Classical Philology* 98 (1998) 137-51

Segal, C., *Euripides and the Poetics of Sorrow: Art, Gender, and Commemoration in Alcestis, Hippolytus, and Hecuba* (1993)

Thalmann, W., "Euripides and Aeschylus: The Case of Hekabe" *Classical Antiquity* 12 (1993) 126-59

Zeitlin, F., "The Body's Revenge: Dionysos and Tragic Action in Euripides' *Hekabe*" in *Playing the Other: Gender and Society in Classical Greek Literature* (1996) 172-216

XIII. EURIPIDES: *TROJAN WOMEN*

Alexiou, M., *The Ritual Lament in the Greek Tradition* (1974)

Barlow, S., *Euripides: Trojan Women: Introduction, Translation and Commentary* (1986); there is a fine introduction for the general reader

Burnett, A.P., "*Trojan Women* and the Ganymede Ode" *Yale Classical Studies* 25 (1977) 291-316

Croally, N. T., *Euripidean Polemic: The Trojan Women and the Function of Tragedy* (1994)

Davidson, J., "Homer and Euripides' *Trojan Women*" *Bulletin of the Institute of Classical Studies* 4 (2001) 65-79

Dué, C., "A river shouting with tears: Euripides' *Trojan Women*" in *The Captive Woman's Lament in Greek Tragedy* (2006) 136-50

Dunn, F., "The End Refigured: Reversal: *Trojan Women*" in *Tragedy's End: Closure and Innovation in Euripidean Drama* (1996) 101-14

Erp Taalman Kipp, A. M. van, "Euripides and Melos" *Mnemosyne* 4. 40.3-4 (1987) 414-19

Goff, B., *Euripides: Trojan Women* (Duckworth Companions to Greek and Roman Drama, 2008)

Green, P., "War and Morality in Fifth-Century Athens: The Case of Euripides' *Trojan Women*" *The Ancient History Bulletin* 13.3 (1999) 97-110

Hamilton, E., *Euripides: Trojan Women* (1971)

Havelock, E., "Watching the *Trojan Women*" in *Euripides* (ed.) Erich Segal (1968) 115-27

Johnston, H., "Vergil's Debt to the *Hecuba* and *Trojan Women* of Euripides" *Classical Weekly* 3 (1909) 50-52, 58-60

Kovacs, D., "Gods and Men in Euripides' Trojan Trilogy" *Colby Quarterly* 33 (1997) 162-76

Lloyd, M., "The Helen Scene in Euripides' *Trojan Women*" *Classical Quarterly* 34 (1984) 303-13

Maxwell-Stuart, P., "The Dramatic Poets and the Expedition to Sicily" *Historia* 22 (1973) 398-404

McCallum-Barry, C., "Trojan Women: sex and the city" in *Essays on Trojan Women* (eds.) David Stuttard and Tamsin Shasha (London: Actors of Dionysos, 2001) 74-90 = *Euripides talks* (ed.) Alan Beale (2008) 116-25

Murray, G., *Euripides, Trojan Women* (1915)

Murray, G., "Euripides' Tragedies of 415: The Deceitfulness of Life" in *Greek Studies* (1946) 128-48

O'Neill, E.G., "The Prologue of the *Trojan Women* of Euripides" *Transactions of the American Philological Society* 72 (1941) 288-320

Poole, A., "Total Disaster: Euripides' *Trojan Women*" *Arion* n.s. 3.3 (1976) 257-87

Rehm, R., "War Brides and War Dead: Euripides' *Trojan Women*" in *Marriage to Death: The Conflation of Wedding and Funeral Rituals in Greek Tragedy* (1994) 128-35

Roisman, J., "Contemporary Allusions in Euripides' *Trojan Women*" *Studi Italiani di Filologia Classica* 15 (1997) 38-47

Rosenbloom, D., "Empire and its Discontents: Trojan Women, Birds, and the Symbolic Economy of Athenian Imperialism" in *Greek Drama III. Essays in Honour of Kevin Lee* (eds.) John Davidson, Frances Muecke and Peter Wilson (Bulletin of the Institute of Classical Studies, Supplement 87, 2006) 245-72

Rutherford, R., "The Cassandra scene" in *Essays on Trojan Women* (eds.) David Stuttard and Tamsin Shasha (London: Actors of Dionysos, 2001) 90-103 = *Euripides talks* (ed.) Alan Beale (2008) 126-33

Scodel, R., *The Trojan Trilogy of Euripides* (1980)

Sidwell, K., "Melos and the *Trojan Women*" in *Essays on Trojan Women* (eds.) David Stuttard and Tamsin Shasha (London: Actors of Dionysos, 2001) 30-45

Spatharas, D., "Gorgias' *Encomium of Helen* and Euripides' *Trojan Women*" *Eranos* 100 (2002) 166-74

Winnington-Ingram, R. P., "Euripides: *Poiêtês sophos*" *Arethusa* 2:2 (1960) 127-42 = *Oxford Readings in Classical Studies: Euripides* (ed.) Judith Mossman (2003) 47-63

XIV. SOPHOCLES: AJAX

Belfiore, E., "Killing one's closest *philos*: self-slaughter in Sophocles' *Ajax*" in *Murder Among Friends: Violation of Philia in Greek Tragedy* (2000) 100-116

Blundell, M., *Helping Friends and Harming Enemies: A Study in Sophocles and Greek Ethics* (1989) 60-105 on *Ajax*

Bradshaw, D., "The Ajax myth and the polis: old values and new" in *Myth and the Polis* (eds.) D. Pozzi and J. Wickersham (1991) 99-125

Brown, R., *The Art of Suicide* (2004) 25-30 on *Ajax*

Burian, P., "Supplication and Hero Cult in Sophocles' *Ajax*" *Greek, Roman, and Byzantine Studies* 13 (1972) 151-6

Crane, G., "Ajax, the Unexpected and the Deception Speech" *Classical Philology* 85 (1990) 89-101

Esposito, S., "The Changing Roles of the Sophoclean Chorus" *Arion* 3rd series 4.1 (1996) 85-114

Garrison, E.P., *Groaning Tears: Ethical and Dramatic Aspects of Suicide in Greek Tragedy* (1995); 46-52 on *Ajax*

Garvie, A.F., *Sophocles: Ajax* (1998); there is a fine introduction for the general reader

Garvie, A.F., *The plays of Sophocles* (2005) 11-20 on *Ajax*

Golder, H., "Sophocles' *Ajax*: Beyond the Shadow of Time" *Arion* 3rd series 1.1 (1990) 9-34

Goldhill, S., "Mind and Madness" in *Reading Greek Tragedy* (1986); 181-98 on *Ajax*

Goldhill, S., "The audience on stage : rhetoric, emotion, and judgement in Sophoclean theatre" in *Sophocles and the Greek tragic tradition* (eds.) Simon Goldhill and Edith Hall (2009) 27-47

Guthrie, W. K. C., "Odysseus in the *Ajax*" *Greece and Rome* 16 (1974) 115-119

Heath, M., "Sophocles' *Ajax*" in *The Poetics of Greek Tragedy* (1987) 165-208

Heath, M. and Okell, E., "Sophocles' *Ajax*: Expect the Unexpected" *Classical Quarterly* 57 (2007) 363-80

Henrichs, A., "The Tomb of Aias and the Prospect of Hero Cult in Sophokles" *Classical Antiquity* 12. 2 (1993) 165-80

Hesk, J., *Sophocles: Ajax* (Duckworth Companions to Greek and Roman Tragedy, 2003)

Holt, P., "The Debate-Scenes in the *Ajax*" *American Journal of Philology* 102 (1981) 275-87

Holt, P., "Sophocles' *Ajax* and the Ajax Myth" *The St. John's Review* 33 (1983) 51-61

Hubbard, T., "Pindar and Sophocles: Ajax as Epinician Hero" *Echoes du monde classique / Classical Views* n.s. 19 (2000) 315-32

Hubbard, T., "The Architecture of Sophocles' *Ajax*" *Hermes* 131 (2003) 158-71

Kirkwood, G., "Homer and Sophocles' *Ajax*" in *Classical Drama and Its Influence* (ed.) M. J. Anderson (1963) 53-70

Kiso, A., "Sophocles and Odysseus" in *The Lost Sophocles* (1984) 87-109

Knox, B., "The *Ajax* of Sophocles" *Harvard Studies in Classical Philology* 65 (1961) 1-37 = *Sophocles: A Collection of Essays* (ed.) T. Woodard (1966) 29-61 = *Word and Action: Essays on the Ancient Theater* (1979) 125-60 = *Sophocles: Modern Critical Views* (ed.) Harold Bloom (1990) 5-32

Lawrence, S., "Ancient Ethics, the Heroic Code and the Morality of Sophocles' *Ajax*" *Greece and Rome* 52 (2005) 18-33

Mahaffy, J. P., "The degradation of Odysseus in Greek Literature" *Hermathena* 2 (1973-4) 265-75

March, J., "Sophocles' *Ajax*: The Death and Burial of a Hero" *Bulletin of the Institute for Classical Studies* 38 (1991-3) 1-36 with plates

Ormand, K., "The *Ajax*, or Marriage by Default" in *Marriage in Sophoclean Tragedy: Exchange and the Maiden* (1999) 104-23

Padel, R., "Madness in Fifth-Century Athenian Tragedy" in *Indigenous Psychologies: The Anthropology of the Self* (eds.) Paul Heelas and Andrew Lock (1981) 105-31

Panoussi, V., "Vergil's Ajax: Allusion, Tragedy, and Heroic Identity in the *Aeneid*" *Classical Antiquity* 21 (2002) 95-134

Podlecki, A., "Ajax's Gods and the Gods of Sophocles" *Antiquité classique* 49 (1980) 45-86

Rose, Peter, "Historicizing Sophocles' *Ajax*" in *History, Tragedy, Theory: Dialogues on Athenian Drama* (ed.) Barbara Goff (1995) 59-90

Scodel, R., "The Politics of Sophocles' *Ajax*" *Scripta Classica Israelica* 22 (2003) 31-42

Scullion, S., "The Staging of Sophokles's *Ajax*" in *Three Studies in Athenian Dramaturgy* (1994) 89-128

Seale, David, "The *Ajax*: The Shame of Revelation" in *Vision and Stagecraft in Sophocles* (1985) 145-180

Segal, C, "Ajax" in *Tragedy and Civilization: An Interpretation of Sophocles* (1981) 109-51

Simon, B., "The *Ajax*" in *Mind and Madness in Ancient Greece* (1978) 124-30

Sorum, C., "Sophocles' *Ajax* in Context" *Classical World* 79 (1986) 361-77

Stanford, W.B., "The Degradation of Odysseus" *Hermathena* 73 (1949) 33-51; 74 (1949) 41-56

Stanford, W.B., "The Stage Villain" in *The Ulysses Theme: A Study in the Adaptability of a Traditional Hero* (1963) 102-17

Stanford, W.B., *Sophocles: Ajax* (1963); with an excellent introduction for the general reader

Stanford, W.B., "Light and Darkness in Sophocles' *Ajax*" *Greek, Roman, and Byzantine Studies* 19 (1973) 189-97 = *Sophocles: Modern Critical Views* (ed.) Harold Bloom (1990) 97-103

Sutton, D. F., *The Lost Sophocles* (1984); fine translation of the fragments with commentary

Synodinou, K., "Tecmessa in the *Ajax* of Sophocles" *Antike und Abendland* 33 (1987) 99-107

Taplin, O., *Greek Tragedy in Action* (1978); superb on the stagecraft of *Ajax*

Taplin, O., "Yielding to Forethought: Sophocles' *Ajax*" in *Arktouros: Hellenic Studies presented to Bernard M. Knox* (ed.) Glen Bowersock *et al.* (1979) 122-29

Winnington-Ingram, R.P., "The mind of Ajax" and "The burial of Ajax" in *Sophocles: An Interpretation* (1980) 11-56 and 57-72

Worman, N., "Odysseus *Panourgos*: the Liar's Style in Tragedy and Oratory" *Helios* 26 (1999) 35-68

Zanker, G., "Sophocles' *Ajax* and the Heroic Values of the *Iliad*" *Classical Quarterly* 42 (1992) 20-26

XV. SOPHOCLES' POLITICAL CAREER

Avery, H. C., "Sophocles' Political Career" *Historia* 22 (1973) 509-14

Brown, N. O., "Pindar, Sophocles, and the Thirty Years' Peace" *Transactions of the American Philological Association* 82 (1951) 1-28

Jameson, M., "Sophocles and the Four Hundred" *Historia* 20 (1971) 541-68

Karavites, P., "Tradition, Skepticism, and Sophocles' Political Career" *Klio* 58 (1976) 359-65

Westlake, H. D., "Sophocles and Nicias as colleagues" *Hermes* 84 (1956) 110-16

Woodbury, L., "Sophocles among the Generals" *Phoenix* 24 (1970) 209-24

A Map of Ancient Greece and Asia Minor

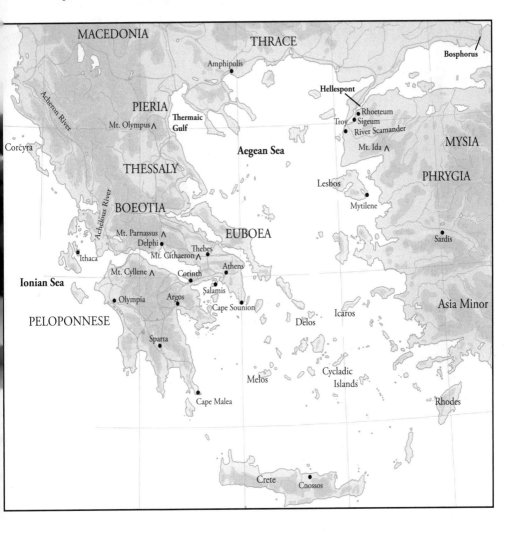